THE NEW GEOPOLITICS OF MINERALS

This is the first book to situate the Canadian mineral trade and Canada's changing status as a resource exporter and importer within the context of the ongoing debate over strategic minerals. As such, it is significant to our understanding of Canadian mineral policymaking in its international as well as its domestic setting and to such broader issues as the contemporary relationship between mineral resources, foreign policy initiatives, and international distribution patterns of power and influence. The contributors analyze and explicate major questions that have interested specialists in international security and political economy for some decades.

The current controversy regarding minerals and national and international security and economic interests is far from the alarmism between 1973 and 1983, yet complacency—at least on the part of importing countries—is not appropriate either. This book explores the current mood among industrialized states and identifies particular Canadian interests that are and can be affected by developments in the geopolitics of minerals. These concerns include the security implications of Canada's role as a supplier of strategic minerals to the United States and its vulnerability as an importer of other crucial minerals.

The New Geopolitics of Minerals will appeal to readers interested in international political economy, international security, Canadian foreign policy, and Canadian-American relations.

DAVID G. HAGLUND is Director of the Centre for International Relations and an associate professor in the Department of Political Studies at Queen's University.

The New Geopolitics of Minerals: Canada and International Resource Trade

Edited by David G. Haglund

University of British Columbia Press
Vancouver 1989

Canadian Cataloguing in Publication Data
   Main entry under title:
   The new geopolitics of minerals

   Includes bibliographical references and
index.
   ISBN 0-7748-0307-X

   1. Strategic materials. 2. Strategic
materials – Government policy – Canada.
3. Mineral industries – Political aspects –
Canada. I. Haglund, David G.
HD9506.C22N49 1989   382'.42   C89-091143-6

This book has been published with the help of a grant from the Institute of International
Relations, University of British Columbia.

Contents

PART FIVE

vi

Preface and Acknowledgments

This book is concerned with the interrelationship between economics and security. As such, it draws on the expertise of contributors whose interests are located in either political economy or strategic studies (or, in a few cases, in both areas). Recently, there have been several scholarly efforts to span the gap between international political economy (IPE) and international security. One thinks especially of some of the major contributions to the current debate in the West over whether the United States is in "decline," and if so what the ultimate implications of broad economic trends must be for the post-Second World War security arrangements created and sustained by the Western industrialized countries. But there is another body of IPE literature, one that predates by decades the current speculation about "hegemonic stability" and "post-hegemonic cooperation," and it is from that older corpus of writings that this book derives its conceptual foundations. The authors of this volume have all sought, in one way or another, to probe the relationship between an important economic factor (raw material endowment) and a set of international and domestic political issues, ranging from differential distribution of international power and influence to conflict over scarce resources, in domestic as well as in foreign policy. As the subtitle indicates, the book's specific focus is Canadian resources, but much of what is contained in the following pages is of relevance to broader inquiry into the role of minerals in world affairs.

This book had its origins in the early 1980s, a time when mineral security questions (in oil and in nonfuel minerals) were attracting a relatively high degree of attention on the part of policymakers in Western industrialized states. The immediate inspiration for the project that would culminate in this volume was a set of grant applications made by Mark Zacher of the Institute of International Relations at the University of British Columbia. One application was to the Donner Canadian Foundation, for a multidisciplinary project on Canada and International Trade. The other was to the Military and Strategic Studies Program of the Department of National Defence (DND), to further the teaching and research efforts of the Institute in strategic studies. Both applications resulted in generous levels of support being accorded the Institute, and it is a pleasant task indeed to acknowledge with gratitude not only the two funding agencies without whose backing this book could never have materialized, but also Mark Zacher, who was and remains its intellectual godfather.

The book is not only a pluridisciplinary initiative, it is also a multi-institutional one. In addition to the critical role played by the UBC Institute of International Relations, two Centres at Queen's University have contributed human and material resources to the project. The Queen's Centre for Resource Studies (CRS) has been an invaluable source of material and intellectual support, and my highest appreciation goes to David Anderson and Margot Wojciechowski, respectively former and current Executive Directors of the Centre. As well, attention should be drawn to the Mining Association of Canada and to Energy, Mines and Resources Canada, both of which have been consistent and generous contributors, through sustaining grants to the CRS, to scholarly research and publication on Canadian mineral policy. Also at Queen's, the Centre for International Relations, which I direct, provided administrative, scholarly, and infrastructural resources to this book. I should like to acknowledge in particular the indispensable contribution made to the Centre over the years by DND's Military and Strategic Studies Program.

Numerous individuals have given freely of their time and ideas. In particular, I should like to thank the following experts on mineral policy, all of whom I had the privilege of interviewing over the past few years in Europe, the United States, and Canada: Robert Andrigo, Lance Antrim, Thomas Atkinson, Charles Bennett, Larry Boggs, Eleaner Busick, Audrey Buyrn, V. Anthony Cammarota, Shirley Coffield, Will Dare, Michael Dauderstädt, John Edwards, Rod Eggert, Herman Enzer, Peter Frank, Paul Gilman, David Glancy, Steve Goldman, Ed Hanrahan, David Humphreys, Joel Johnson, Enid Jones, M. Gordon Jones, Günther Keil, Ullrich Krauss, Martin Kürsten, Paul Lafleur, Hans Landsberg, Jeanne Laux, Tony Maconey, Hanns Maull, John Morgan, John Newman, Peter Nicholls, Jim O'Donnell, Gordon Peeling, Don Phillips, David Price, Bob Reilly, Bob Reinstein, John Richards, Borden Ronald, Josiah Royce, Wolfgang Sames, Hans Schade, Jack Schanz, Hans-Luther Schmidt, Helmut Schmidt, Michael Shafer, Robert Shank, David Scourfield, Walter Sies, David Slater, O.B. Stauffer, Denis Tytgat, Tony Werner, Michael West, Howard Wilson, Glenn Wittur, Prescott Wurlitzer, Jan Zwartendyk, and Klaus Zwilsky.

Earlier versions of parts or all of my three chapters have appeared in print. I am grateful to the publishers of the following journals for permission to use material that originally appeared in these articles: "Strategic Minerals: A Conceptual Analysis," *Resources Policy* 10 (September 1984):146–52; "The New Geopolitics of Minerals: An Inquiry into the Changing International Significance of Strategic Minerals," *Political Geography Quarterly* 5 (July 1986):221–40; "Canadian Strategic Minerals and United States Military Potential," *Journal of Canadian Studies* 19 (Autumn 1984):5–31; and "The Debate over Strategic Mineral Vulnerability: Implications for Canada," *Raw Materials Report* 5, 3 (1987):16–35.

Finally, I happily record my continuing astonishment that no matter how poorly scrawled the original draft they received, Betty Greig (at UBC) and Mary Kerr and Kay Ladouceur (at Queen's) never failed to produce finished pages that gave the impression, however fleetingly, that their author knew what he was talking about. My warm thanks go to them for all that they have done in this regard. Also greatly appreciated is the work done by Marilyn Banting in compiling the index and checking the page proofs.

DAVID G. HAGLUND

Introduction

Those concerned with our future mineral supplies believe that the least tractable problems of the international mining industry are now developing in the field of geopolitics. —Thomas Atkinson, "Future Strategic Mineral Supplies for the EEC," *Mining Engineer* (April 1979):721

Recent bouts of speculation about the effect that political turmoil in South Africa might have upon international raw materials markets come as a reminder that from time to time minerals issues take on heightened political significance. Although it may adopt various aspects, this significance ultimately inheres in a certain "inequitable" mineral distribution pattern. It constitutes what we label in this volume the "geopolitics" of minerals. Images of F-15 fighter aircraft flitting across one's television screen, accompanied by a newscaster's sombre observation that without such South African minerals as manganese, chromium, or vanadium, planes like this would never be able to fly reinforce the impression that the South African crisis, quite apart from its profound and horrifying human rights implications, has important implications for the security and defence of Western countries.[1]

This is far from the first time that international political developments have been considered relevant for mineral exporting and importing countries, or that minerals have been pregnant with "geopolitical" meaning. The sheer economic impact of mineral market fluctuations can take on political importance, as the oil crisis of a decade ago showed. Though their most visible effect was on the erratic (indeed, hyperactive) performance of one *economic* variable, namely the price of a barrel of oil, the two oil shocks of the 1970s are widely and legitimately seen to have been *political* problems with political origins, especially from the point of view of dependent consuming states.[2] More recently, the mineral glut of the first half of the 1980s, though arguably a much clearer instance of an economic sequence of cause and effect, carried with it political connotations, especially for some luckless Third World states dependent upon mineral sales to earn foreign exchange. These examples demonstrate what few would care to deny—that economic well-being can and does make a direct contribution to the security of states.

Minerals take on geopolitical importance in other ways and these too can be seen in the crisis in South Africa. At one extreme, minerals have been implicated in the most fundamental "problematique" of international relations, the causes of war and the conditions of peace.[3] But considerations of "resource war" apart, minerals are politically significant for two principal reasons. First, minerals constitute the "base" of any advanced economy, despite the protestations of some that we live in a post-industrial age. As such, they are vital for the creation of industrial and, ultimately, military capability. They *do* contribute materially to the power of states. Second, minerals figure in the attempts by states to utilize techniques of "economic statecraft."[4] The current debate over the feasibility and desirability of sanctions (and the possibility of counter-sanctions) regarding South Africa illustrates but the most recent instance of the potential application of this form of statecraft.[5]

Minerals, then, can affect both the power and the influence of states. If we accept that minerals possess political significance in international relations, then we must conclude that Canada, an advanced industrialized country that is also an important mineral importer and the world's leading exporter of nonfuel minerals, should have a set of interests extending across a variety of issues involving strategic minerals. Canada surely has what comes close to being an a priori economic interest, flowing logically from the contribution made by mineral production to the Canadian economy and balance of payments: in recent years some 10 per cent of the GNP and more than 25 per cent of the country's exports can be associated with such production.[6] More importantly for the purposes of this book, Canada also has political interests that are linked to the freedom of manoeuvre it possesses vis-à-vis the international political system. For example, Canadian oil policy over the last decade has been affected by turbulence in international oil markets—turbulence occasioned more dramatically by political rather than economic developments. Thus it is appropriate to say that the geopolitics of minerals has visited challenges upon Canadian economic and political fortunes. Nor is oil an exception to the rule that holds both exporters and importers to be hostages of the system and of each other; indeed, any usefulness in the concept of "interdependence" is precisely to be found in the notion of a mutual hostage relationship.[7]

At times Canada has sought actively to use minerals as levers of economic statecraft. This was especially true during the 1970s, when Ottawa attempted to restrain a global tendency toward nuclear proliferation by attaching stringent safeguards to Canadian exports of nuclear technology and nuclear raw materials, especially uranium.[8] Less deliberate, but no less important, have been the politico-strategic contributions that Canadian minerals have made to the military potential of certain allied countries, the United States above all, during the past several decades. It is clear that Canadian minerals have played and will continue to play a political as well as economic role. Our goal in this book will be to introduce and analyse the many important ways in which Canadian mineral interests and mineral policy have both affected and been influenced by the geopolitics of minerals.

In Chapter 1, "The New Geopolitics of Minerals," I examine some of the major concepts and themes that will be developed in subsequent chapters, which explore various aspects of Canadian mineral policy and interests. This chapter will locate our topic within the larger body of literature concerning the geopolitics of minerals that has developed over several decades. It pays particular attention to two of the core concepts of our volume, "geopolitics" and "strategic minerals," showing how each of these often-abused terms can be useful for political analysis. In addition to explaining concepts, Chapter 1 uses diachronic (or comparative-historical) analysis to illustrate the changes that have transpired in the international politics of minerals since the topic first began to attract the attention of large numbers of international relations specialists during the interwar period. Three questions strike me as being particularly significant for our analysis: How are mineral distribution patterns related to the causes of war and the conditions of peace? In what sense can it be said that minerals contribute to military potential? And, what is the likelihood that mineral scarcity will constitute a real challenge to economic growth, with all that this might portend for social and political prospects in developed and developing states alike? Each of these three questions in turn generates a set of subsidiary issues that will constitute a starting point for many of the topics addressed in subsequent chapters.

Andrew Fenton Cooper demonstrates this in Chapter 2, "Canadian Mineral Policy in an International Context," where he provides a sketch of the major international policy questions that have confronted mineral producers and consumers, particularly during the critical 1973–83 decade. Cooper especially seeks to probe the logic and utility of states employing minerals as levers in their "resource diplomacy." His primary goal is to articulate the challenges and opportunities presented to Canadian mineral policy by this form of economic statecraft. He finds that Canadian policy has been schizophrenic: at times it has suggested an affinity with the efforts of mineral-exporting Third World states bent on extracting greater "economic rent" and value-added benefit from their resources; at other times it has reflected the concerns of the industrialized consuming countries, reluctant to endorse the more redistributive features of the proposed "New International Economic Order."

If Cooper supplies the recent international context in which Canadian mineral policy has been formulated, David Yudelman offers a detailed view of the domestic factors that led to the adoption of important policy stances—positions that in some instances were staked out on the basis of faulty, even anachronistic, assessments of *international* minerals developments. In Chapter 3, "Interference or Safety Net: Government and the Canadian Mining Industry," he traces the complicated interrelationship between certain Canadian policy initiatives, particularly those concerning the questions of foreign ownership and further processing of raw materials in Canada, and the external environment. By the mid-1970s, he relates, mineral policy had become more "pro-active" than ever before in Canada, as both federal and provincial bureaucracies generated proposals to redistribute what seemed to be ever-increasing wealth from a thriving mining industry. Ironically, Yudelman notes, the international environment was sending out signals that masked what would soon become apparent: that, far from thriving, the Canadian mineral industry was in most sectors experiencing growing difficulties competing in an increasingly harsh world market. The era of "structural change" had dawned, and, states Yudelman, "the federal and provincial governments and the mining industry drifted into an abyss. . . which might have been avoided had there been a coherent mineral policy to draw on."

Mineral policy seems to have been modified in the past few years, and in an effort to make it more reflective of contemporary reality, policymakers have been putting great emphasis on international marketing, market access, and productivity—an emphasis evident in the mineral policy community's advocacy of the Canada-U.S. free trade agreement.[9] The watchword today, for those charged with formulating policy, is "managing maturity," and as Yudelman concludes, "the clear implication of this. . . is that more so than at any other time, Canadian mineral policy will be constrained and conditioned by the international aspects of mineral production and trade."

Jock Finlayson focuses his attention on the import side of Canadian mineral trade in Chapter 4, "Canada as a Strategic Mineral Importer." Identifying four commodities that are found on many lists of "problematical" minerals (chromium, manganese, bauxite, and tin), he argues that although Canada might be said to face potential supply difficulties with respect to chromium and manganese, the country is "less vulnerable overall than its allies to interruptions in mineral supplies." Nevertheless, if there were a serious disruption of mineral supply, the protection afforded Canada by its greater mineral self-sufficiency could be significantly offset by the indirect effects of economic misfortunes experienced by the country's more dependent trading partners in the Organization for Economic Cooperation and Development (OECD).

Finlayson lists some ways by which both Canada and its industrialized trading partners (many of whom are also its military allies) might reduce their individual and collective vulnerability to supply disruptions. Among these ways are: import diversification; substitution, recycling, and conservation; domestic production; and stockpiling. Canada, he concludes, has several avenues open to it in its bid to reduce vulnerability, assuming, of course, that the risks of inaction are considered sufficiently high to justify the purchase of an insurance policy for mineral supply.

Until perhaps the past year or two, oil has been widely considered as the mineral about which industrialized Western countries had the greatest reason to worry. It is no surprise, therefore, that oil is the only mineral to have occasioned the construction of an ambitious and, on paper at least, effective "collective security" scheme intended to reduce the vulnerability of most OECD members: the International Energy Agency (IEA). In Chapter 5, "Canadian Participation in the International Energy Agency," David Blair explores the rationale and operation of this organization, and its implications for Canada.

Blair traces the origins of the IEA to the first of the two upheavals in world oil markets during the 1970s, and argues that several considerations may have impelled Ottawa to take part in collective measures to enhance the oil-import security of Western industrialized states. Significantly, not all of these considerations stemmed primarily from concern about oil security. Blair finds that overall Canada has derived net benefit from its participation in the IEA, even though Ottawa has shown itself to be less than an eager participant in such collective defence proposals and plans as have been adopted by the organization in its fourteen-year history. Employing collective-goods theory to identify the reasons that have led various Canadian governments to respond to IEA emergency preparations in at best a lukewarm manner, he concludes by urging policymakers to pay more heed to collective means of oil-import security. He concedes, however, that this is unlikely to occur as long as the glut in world oil markets persists.

The United States is one country that for most of the post-Second World War years has tended to put a premium on insuring its mineral supply, though not primarily by such collective measures as discussed by David Blair. In Chapter 6, "Canadian Strategic Minerals and U.S. Military Potential," I try to identify the extent and nature of U.S. dependence upon Canadian minerals, particularly insofar as such dependence can be considered a contributing factor to U.S. military potential. I concentrate my analysis on three minerals, and in doing so I argue that they comprise the most significant of the strategic minerals that the U.S. has been importing from Canada—*nickel, oil,* and *uranium.* Above all, I seek to test the degree to which Canadian minerals have constituted power assets, both for the U.S. and Canada. In this endeavour I rely on the classic distinction developed some decades ago by Albert O. Hirschman, who demonstrated brilliantly that trade takes on both a "supply effect" and an "influence effect," and that each can and does contribute to the power and influence of states.[10]

After examining bilateral trade in the three minerals, I find that recently the U.S. has decreased its reliance on Canadian sources of supply for two of them (nickel and oil), while uranium faces growing protectionist pressure in the U.S. This finding challenges conventional wisdom in at least two noteworthy ways: it contradicts the common view of the United States as a profligate gobbler of Canadian resources—an argument frequently encountered in the literature reflecting a "resource nationalist" perspective; more surprisingly, it casts some doubt on the assumption that considerations of national security dictate an American mineral-sourcing strategy that consciously aims to secure more Canadian raw materials for the U.S. defence industrial base. The section on uranium demonstrates that, at least in some minerals, national security arguments can be and have been invoked to keep Canadian minerals *out* of the U.S. marketplace.

Because of its especially poignant military implications and its emotive symbolism, uranium really does rank in a category by itself among the strategic minerals and gets the most attention in our book. It is the subject of Michael Webb's Chapter 7, "Canada as an Insecure Supplier." Unlike any other mineral exported by Canada, uranium has stimulated intense public debate and has featured prominently in the most ambitious attempts at influence ever made by Canadian governments desirous of practising economic statecraft with raw material assets. Webb identifies the basic dilemma of Canadian uranium export policy: the need to reconcile the often conflicting interests of, on the one hand, strengthening an international nonproliferation regime and, on the other, enhancing the volume and value of Canadian mineral production and exports. He shows that for a brief period during the late 1970s policymakers imagined that it might be possible to square the circle of competing interests by drawing upon an "influence effect" in uranium that (mistakenly, it turned out) they felt resulted from Canada's prominent position as a uranium exporter.

When Canada imposed very stringent safeguards on its exports of nuclear technology and materials in the aftermath of India's "peaceful" nuclear explosion in 1974, it was assumed that in this area at least, it could count on its being a "principal power"[11] and force its customers to accept political conditions as a necessary price of doing business with Canada—or else face the risk of an embargo. "Underlying all of these considerations," writes Webb, "was the critical perception that Canada had the market power to make its embargo effective. Consumers would have little choice but to accept Canada's demands because of Canada's dominant position as a uranium supplier at a time of rapidly rising international demand."

Attempts to practise economic statecraft with raw material assets can be costly and may even prove counterproductive. In the concluding chapter, I draw attention to the instances in which Canada has been singled out as an unreliable source of supply. At the same time, it would be unwise to overstate the costs and potential counterproductive aspects of attempts to gain influence through the use of minerals. In this last chapter my objective is to assess the potential mineral implications, for both Canadian importing and exporting interests (but particularly the latter), of the most recent climate of concern regarding strategic minerals—concern largely triggered by the events that have unfolded in South Africa over the past few years. In framing my assessment, I first consider an aspect of the new geopolitics of minerals that deserves a lofty position on the rubbish heap of inquiry: the alarmist notion that the superpowers sometime in the late 1970s became involved in a "resource war" pitting a predatory Soviet Union against a defensive, import-dependent West. At its most extreme, the resource war advocacy became transformed, not without a few misgivings, it is true, into a hue and cry for the defence of South Africa, possessor of so much that is truly essential in the international supply chain of strategic minerals and thus the supposed bulwark of the West's collective material basis of civilization.

In dismissing the resource war thesis, however, it is far from my intention to minimize the mineral implications of the current South African situation. It is to these implications, especially insofar as they bear on Canada's export interests, that I devote the remainder of the chapter. I conclude with a set of observations that will sound few alarm bells, but one that might yet contribute to the double goal that has animated the writing of this book—the goal of providing both a context for the analysis of Canadian minerals interests and a framework for the contemplation of mineral policy options.

DAVID G. HAGLUND

Introduction

NOTES

1 As, to take one example, was the case of ABC's "Nightline" broadcast of Tuesday, 22 July 1986. For another analysis that stresses the tight link between U.S. security and the question of mineral availability, see David K. Shipler, "U.S. Morals and South Africa's Metals," *New York Times*, 15 Feb. 1987, p. E2.

2 During the 1970s and early 1980s, the problem of dependence upon oil was nearly completely identified as a problem facing importers; today, ironically, it is *exporters* that have been wrestling with ways to reduce *their* dependence upon oil. See "Venezuela Seeks Less Oil Dependency," *Latin American Weekly Report*, 24 July 1986, p. 6. However, that oil shortages might once again, in the next decade, disturb the political and economic equilibrium of the United States and other Western countries is the thesis of Daniel Yergin, "Energy Security in the 1990s," *Foreign Affairs* 67 (Fall 1988):110–32.

3 For a discussion of this "problematique" see K.J. Holsti, *The Dividing Discipline: Hegemony and Diversity in International Theory* (Boston: Allen & Unwin 1985).

4 David A. Baldwin, *Economic Statecraft* (Princeton: Princeton University Press 1985).

5 The impact of sanctions on a range of strategic minerals is discussed in David G. Haglund, "South Africa, Minerals, and Sanctions," *International Perspectives* (May/June 1985):3–5.

6 Energy, Mines and Resources Canada, *Canadian Minerals Yearbook 1985: Review and Outlook* (Ottawa: Minister of Supply and Services 1986), 1.1–1.12.

7 Good discussions of the meaning of "interdependence" may be found in Robert O. Keohane and Joseph S. Nye, *Power and Interdependence: World Politics in Transition* (Boston: Little, Brown 1977), 11–19; Bruce Russett, "Dimensions of Resource Dependence: Some Elements of Rigor in Concept and Policy Analysis," *International Organization* 38 (Summer 1984):481–99; Kenneth N. Waltz, *Theory of International Politics* (Reading, MA: Addison-Wesley 1979), 138–60; and David A. Baldwin, "Interdependence and Power: A Conceptual Analysis," *International Organization* 34 (Autumn 1980):471–506.

8 Although the current glut in world mineral markets has put a damper on the eagerness of states to engage in "resource diplomacy," the impulse to seek influence through actual or threatened manipulation of exports dies hard. See, for example, the recent suggestion by the former energy minister of British Columbia, Stephen Rogers, that the province consider utilizing its exports of hydroelectric power to the United States as a lever with which to apply pressure on U.S. lumber producers seeking to get countervailing duties imposed on Canadian exports of softwood lumber. "Power Exports Seen as Bargaining Chip," *Vancouver Sun*, 24 July 1986, p. A10.

9 See Energy, Mines and Resources Canada, *The Canada-U.S. Free Trade Agreement and Minerals and Metals: An Assessment* (Ottawa: Minister of Supply and Services 1988).

10 Albert O. Hirschman, *National Power and the Structure of Foreign Trade* (Berkeley: University of California Press 1945), 14–15.

11 This imagery, of course, comes from David B. Dewitt and John J. Kirton, *Canada as a Principal Power: A Study in Foreign Policy and International Relations* (Toronto: John Wiley & Sons 1983).

Contributors

DAVID BLAIR is a former Research Associate of the Institute of International Relations, University of British Columbia, who is now completing a doctorate in International Relations at the Institut universitaire de hautes études internationales, in Geneva.

ANDREW FENTON COOPER, an Assistant Professor of Political Science at the University of Waterloo, specializes in Canadian foreign policy.

JOCK FINLAYSON is a public policy consultant in Ottawa and a PH.D. candidate in the Department of Political Studies, Queen's University.

DAVID HAGLUND is the Director of the Centre for International Relations and an Associate Professor in the Department of Political Studies, Queen's University.

MICHAEL WEBB, a PH.D. candidate in Political Science at Stanford University, is a Research Associate of the Institute of International Relations, University of British Columbia.

DAVID YUDELMAN was a Senior Research Fellow of the Centre for Resource Studies, Queen's University, and is currently Senior Strategic Projects Officer for Ontario Hydro.

Part I

I

The New Geopolitics of Minerals: An Inquiry into the Changing International Significance of Strategic Minerals

David G. Haglund

INTRODUCTION

Twice in this century resource questions have emerged as major issues in international politics. The first time was during the period between the two world wars; the second dated from the 1973 OPEC oil price increase to the early 1980s. Although the specific commodities and actors involved in the "politicization"[1] of resources may have been different, in one fundamental respect the eras were similar: in each, industrialized states were concerned about access to what are now called "strategic minerals." Alone among raw materials, strategic minerals have been deemed indispensable building blocks for industrial, military, and political power. More so than with any other class of commodities, the question of *access* has characterized policy planning and policymaking regarding the strategic minerals. This has been and remains so not because minerals are the materials most essential to sustain human existence—for food and water are clearly more important in this regard—but rather because of the inequitable manner in which mineral wealth has been distributed among countries.

Differential distribution militates against self-sufficiency in minerals for all countries in a way that differential distribution of technology and other factors does not militate against agricultural self-sufficiency for most of them. Seeds, know-how, fertilizer, manpower, and, to an extent, even water are all transferable, so in a physical (if not economic) sense agricultural autarky is a policy that all but the very ill-situated can contemplate. Indeed, countries have commonly moved beyond contemplation to the actual implementation, with varying degrees of costliness, of such policies. Self-sufficiency in agriculture is possible but at a price. The same cannot be said for minerals, however, even taking into account the wonder-working properties of modern technology, for *no* country has a sufficiently ample resource base to allow it to produce all the minerals it needs. The words of C.K. Leith, a leading minerals analyst of the interwar period, are as relevant today as they were a half-century ago: "It is a costly and, in the long run, a futile effort to create by enactment something which was not created by nature."[2] Each state lacks some important mineral needed by its industries, and many have lacked and will continue to lack a wide range of such industrial inputs.[3] Without adequate domestic sources of needed minerals, states have sought and will continue to seek foreign supplies.

Thus, for minerals, as for no other commodity, the most salient international political concerns centre on the question of access. It is sometimes assumed, usually by those analysts who find persuasive the idea that a "resource war" has raged between the superpowers, that resource conflict is a recent phenomenon of international politics. To those who think this, Hanns Maull's observation that minerals have been implicated in international political rivalry for thousands of years comes as a needed and timely reminder.[4] In what follows, I will argue, mindful that it might be chronologically fallacious to do so, that the twentieth century has witnessed the most significant developments in the international politics of strategic minerals, for a variety of reasons to be explained in the various chapters of this volume. In developing my argument, I will resort to a comparative-historical, or diachronic, model of inquiry.[5] This method allows for a comparative analysis of the relevant aspects of the access question as it has arisen in two discrete eras, and seems especially well-suited, if not obligatory, for an investigation that presumes to ask whether there is in fact a "new geopolitics" of minerals. Before attempting to answer this question, it would be well to resolve two related conceptual/definitional matters: the relevance to political analysis of the concept of "geopolitics," and the meaning of "strategic minerals."

GEOPOLITICS: A CONCEPTUAL ANALYSIS

Among contemporary political scientists, particularly those who specialize in international relations, geopolitics is only beginning to recover from the fall from grace that it experienced in the aftermath of the Second World War.[6] Before the fall, geopolitics had been as much, if not more, in fashion among students of international politics as integration, interdependence, regimes, or any of the other theoretical problems that attracted scholarly attention in subsequent years. The causes of the fall are varied. The imperative of changing intellectual fashion is one, but not the most important, reason for the abandonment of explicitly geopolitical analysis. The capture of geopolitics (to the extent it still exists in Anglo-American academe) by political geographers is but a symptom, not a cause, of its abandonment by political scientists. Among the explanations for its demise, three stand out as being especially worthy of attention.

The first is that the method of approach we call geopolitics had become tainted by association with the pre-Second World War German "science" of *Geopolitik*—a pseudo-science that in *some* ways was similar to the geopolitics of leading British and American theorists like Mackinder, Mahan, Fairgrieve, and Spykman, but was fundamentally characterized by its normative stress on the necessity of German expansionism.[7] Indeed, the taint-by-association syndrome is still with us, and has dissuaded at least one scholar from situating his work on the assessment of world power plainly within the corpus of geopolitical writing. That scholar, Ray S. Cline, has noted that his decision to label his own approach "politectonics" was in large measure a function of there being no suitable concept now in use that better conveyed the shifting realities of the international power system, the subject of Cline's inquiry. Geopolitics *could* have suited his purposes, but unfortunately it "fell into disrepute some time ago. . . . "[8]

Second, if some have shunned the concept primarily as a matter of etiquette, still more have refrained from employing it out of the conviction that it is simply too imprecise to serve as an effective tool for political analysis. To be sure, political scientists have learned to live with the fact that ultimately theirs is a discipline whose concepts can never be submitted to the test of truth in any objective, certifiable form. We are all reminded, more often than necessary, perhaps, of the definitional problem that confronts us, and we try to come to grips with it by adopting reasonably succinct operational definitions that are at minimum consistent within the arbitrary limits we establish for them. From this perspective, the primary drawback of geopolitics is that it is conceptually so broad that it means all things to all people. That it is prone to manipulation by those who are most comfortable with deterministic theories and models is only an added deficiency, for its basic flaw is its ambitiousness. Once we have been told, as a frequently cited definition of the concept puts it, that geopolitics is "the study of political phenomena (1) in their spatial relationship and (2) in their relationship with, dependence upon, and influence on, earth as well as on all those cultural factors which constitute the subject matter of human geography (anthropogeography) broadly defined," what else is there to say?[9] The past two decades have not been propitious for the cultivation of geopolitical or any other kinds of "grand" theory in the realm of international relations. Is it surprising, then, that geopolitics should have been caught up in what Kal Holsti has labelled the retreat from theoretical utopia?[10]

A third case made against geopolitics as a useful concept for analysis is that it is obsolete. According to this view, whatever merit geopolitical grand theory may have had in former years, it is of much less use in the nuclear age. Spatial considerations (for example, being a maritime power as opposed to being a land-based power) have become less important in the post-Second World War decades, and so have other geographical phenomena, such as the importance of raw materials as a cause of war or a means of carrying on a war.[11] The diminished utility thesis has an obvious affinity with John Herz's well-known argument that the onset of the nuclear age constituted a "Great Divide" between an international politics rooted in the concept of territoriality and one in which that concept has been stripped by technology of most of its meaning.[12] Although proponents of the diminished-utility perspective would not be prepared to argue that political implications of geography are irrelevant, the thrust of their critique leads them to concentrate upon another, non-geographical factors as the primary variables in international politics.

The case against geopolitics seems to have been persuasively made as far as most political scientists are concerned, but the concept is not without its defenders. As noted above, Ray Cline approves of the concept of geopolitics but does not like to call it that. Someone who likes both concept and label is Colin Gray, who urges a revival of explicitly geopolitical analysis, because in a world faced with the threat of an expansionary Soviet Union, "the concepts contained in the classic literature of geopolitics were never so relevant to international political reality as they are today."[13] According to Gray, one could do much worse than construe the current Soviet threat in terms of a struggle between a Mahanian insular empire (composed of the United States and its allies) and a Mackinderesque "Heartland" empire (composed of the Soviet bloc). The stakes of the struggle, at least in the immediate future, are none other than control of the Eurasian-African "Rimlands," the importance of which Nicholas Spykman stressed nearly fifty years ago.[14] They, it is maintained, remain the key to global mastery.

Although I have chosen to title this chapter "The New Geopolitics of Minerals," I do not subscribe to the view that a revival of geopolitics on the grand scale is either imminent or desirable. To a certain extent, geopolitics as a concept of political analysis *is* flawed and does deserve the relative neglect into which it has fallen. That said, however, it is apparent that whatever one's views on the concept, the *word* itself is far from disappearing from common usage. It most typically appears in a context intended to connote some vague relationship between political phenomena and geography. One can scarcely open a newspaper or tune in to a news broadcast without being apprised of the geopolitical implications of whatever subject happens to be at hand.

The price of gold, we are often informed, seems to be constantly responding to "geopolitical" events. Oil remains topical, and whatever the current marketing prospects for crude, there seems to be no slackening in the demand for analysis of "the geopolitics of oil." Other minerals have not been without their perceived geopolitical implications. Soviet and southern African domination of production and reserves of chromium, platinum, manganese, cobalt, and other metals was held not too long ago to be "developing into an ominous geopolitical threat to the industrialized countries of the West."[15] Nor have minerals been the only cause of geopolitical musings. Iran, Afghanistan, Poland, the Falkland Islands, and now even Central America—these and various other parts of the world are all deemed to be fraught with geopolitical implications.[16]

For all the problems associated with it as an analytical tool, I would argue that it still is possible to put geopolitics as a *concept* to scholarly service, provided we avoid falling into the bad habit of asking it to do too much. If we are unable to banish the word, we may as well agree that, in the context of our limited inquiry into strategic minerals, it possesses some helpful conceptual properties— properties that would allow us to speak meaningfully of the "geopolitics of minerals." The Sprouts suggest that geopolitical hypotheses seek to account for international distributions of power and influence by reference to geographical factors. If we accept this, we can perhaps reduce the concept of geopolitics to those factors that clearly have not been significantly affected by the post-1945 changes in the international political environment that have made the bulk of geopolitics obsolete. Again following the Sprouts, let us accept that geopolitical hypotheses in the past have fallen into three general categories, namely, those that sought to account for differences in power and influence primarily as (1) a function of *geographical configuration* (Mahan, Mackinder), (2) a function of *climate* (Ellsworth Huntington), and (3) a function of security of *access* to needed raw materials.[17]

It seems that the case against geopolitical hypotheses has been made most successfully against those that focus on *configuration* (because of technological changes, especially regarding nuclear weapons delivery systems) or *climate* (because of the deterministic tendencies inherent in this kind of hypothesis). It *used* to be thought, fairly early in the post-Second World War era, that raw materials too had lost much of their former significance. As I shall argue below, however, by the early 1970s it was once again apparent that raw materials, particularly minerals, continued to be highly significant variable factors affecting the distribution of international power and influence.

It is my contention that it does make sense to speak of a geopolitics of minerals, if by that we mean the international political significance of the continuing differential distribution of mineral wealth rather than the size and shape of continents or the influence of climate upon history. Because this distribution pattern is a function of geography, the political problem of access becomes by definition a matter of geopolitical importance; it cannot be otherwise. But if it seems clear that there is an operational geopolitics of minerals, it remains to be determined whether such a geopolitics is *new* and, if so, how it differs from the old. Prior to making such a determination, however, we should attend to the second conceptual/definitional matter cited previously.

STRATEGIC MINERALS: WHAT ARE THEY?

In the preceding section, "mineral" and "strategic mineral" were used interchangeably. In reality, not all minerals are strategic, but for the kind of minerals that are commonly involved in international trade—that is, for those that are constituents of the access problem—the distinction between "ordinary" and strategic minerals quickly blurs. Without too much exaggeration, one could paraphrase Shakespeare and state that there is nothing either strategic or nonstrategic but thinking makes it so. Like most concepts, that of strategic minerals possesses inherent expansionary tendencies.

Much has been written, especially in the past decade, about "strategic minerals." Though the concept dates back to the 1930s, strategic minerals have recently become an increasingly familiar part of the vocabulary of scholars interested in international resource questions. The discipline of political science has witnessed a swelling of the ranks of those who analyse the international politics of strategic minerals, and the discipline of economics is similarly paying more attention to the study of these commodities, albeit with a different focus. Nor is it just in the social sciences that one encounters this interest. As governments have become increasingly concerned with commodities issues over the past decade, policymakers have come to rely more and more upon the expertise of such "hard" scientists as geologists and mining engineers.

While few would disagree that strategic minerals have been attracting attention lately, there is disagreement over what they are. Like other political concepts, that of strategic minerals is shaded by nuance and characterized by ambiguity, suggestive of what British philosopher W.B. Gallie calls "essentially contested concepts"—concepts that are at minimum appraisive and complex. A hallmark of such concepts is that "the proper use of [them] inevitably involves

8

endless disputes about their proper uses on the part of the users."[18] Though evidently not one of the more exotic or momentous examples, the concept of strategic minerals has engendered debate as to its proper use. And not only for members of the scholarly community—on occasion it has also become relevant for policymaking.

The first explicit use of strategic minerals as a connotative expression occurred in the United States during the interwar years. The label may have originated in the U.S., but the concept owed its existence primarily to the recognition on the part of the major European combatants during the First World War that modern wars of attrition depended more upon a state's capacity for industrialization and its ability to ensure a continuing flow of vital industrial inputs than upon such qualitative factors as leadership and combat morale.[19] Among the vital industrial inputs, none were held to be as essential for war-fighting capability as minerals. And among the minerals iron ore and coal were accorded pride of place.[20] There were, however, already signs by the end of that war that petroleum was likely to become the most important energy commodity in international trade, and perhaps the most important of what would soon come to be known as the strategic minerals. By the mid-1920s, French statesman Aristide Briand could remark, with only slight exaggeration, that "international politics today are oil politics."[21] During the remainder of the interwar period, oil gained in perceived geopolitical significance. This was reflected not only in the oil diplomacy of the great powers but also in the appearance of a body of literature that sought to establish a causal link between scarcity of oil and other minerals and the increased incidence of international conflict.[22]

It is perhaps ironic that the label strategic materials should have been developed in the United States, for during neither the First World War nor the interwar years was it terribly dependent upon imports for most of the minerals that contributed to military power.[23] Nevertheless, U.S. mobilization efforts in 1917 and 1918 had been affected to an extent by shortages of specific materials. These were enumerated during the immediate postwar period when the War Department drafted a list of the twenty-eight materials (not all of them minerals) that had presented wartime supply difficulties.[24] During the 1920s this list, called the "Harbord List" after its author, was expanded by the commodity committees operating in the War Department's planning branch. In the course of the committees' work, the label strategic materials was introduced. It was followed in the 1930s by a further analytical category, "critical materials."[25]

By 1939 the concepts of strategic and critical materials had been developed by the U.S. Army and Navy Munitions Board. *Strategic* denoted those items deemed essential for defence, the supply of which came wholly or in large part from foreign sources and for which strict conservation and other control measures would be necessary in wartime. *Critical* referred to items also held to be essential for defence but whose wartime supply was not as problematic as that of strategic materials.[26] However, the two concepts were collapsed into the new expression "strategic and critical materials" when, in an attempt to remove some of the ambiguities associated with the 1939 definitions, the Munitions Board decided in 1944 that henceforth "strategic and critical materials [were] those materials required for essential uses in a war emergency, the procurement of which in adequate quantities, quality, and time is sufficiently uncertain for any reason to require prior provision for the supply thereof."[27]

Despite the Munitions Board's desire to clarify the terminology, its omnibus definition of strategic and critical materials has really not been of much analytical use. The words "strategic" and "critical" continue to enjoy U.S. governmental endorsement, but there has been growing dissatisfaction with them, both in the United States and abroad. In Section 12 of the U.S. Strategic and Critical Materials Stockpiling Act of 1979, strategic and critical materials are those "that (A) would be needed to supply the military, industrial, and essential civilian needs of the United States during a national emergency, and (B) are not found or produced in the United States in sufficient quantities to meet such need."[28] Critics of this definition object to it on two grounds, one cosmetic, the other substantive. The cosmetic objection, voiced by the National Strategy Information Center, is that two words are being employed, "like Tweedledee and Tweedledum," where one word would be adequate.[29]

Those who raise the substantive objection do so primarily because they feel the current official definition is too broad to have any analytical precision and focuses on the wrong set of issues. In short, the definition fails to provide guidance either for the purposes of scholarly inquiry or, more importantly, the making of materials policy.[30] Some have called for the outright abolition of the term strategic minerals, while others have urged that its use be severely restricted.

Prominent among those who wish to see usage of the term drastically restricted is the group of minerals experts at the British Geological Survey (BGS) in London, who in 1982 gave evidence to the committee of the House of Lords that was studying the strategic minerals position of the European Community.[31] One of the BGS minerals analysts, Alan Archer, has written that it would be preferable if the term strategic minerals were to fall into disuse, because its inherent ambiguity has led to the concept becoming so broad as to be practically useless. "In short, the term's traditional military or defence meaning has been so abused and its wider meaning is so obscure that, as an adjective applied to minerals, 'strategic' has little or no value."[32]

One who would agree with most of the Archer criticism is Hans Landsberg, an economist with Resources for the Future in Washington. Landsberg does not necessarily advocate the outright abolition of the term, but he would prefer that it be used sparingly. Instead of the scores of items often included, Landsberg would confine the category to a mere handful of commodities, including chromium, manganese, cobalt, the platinum group metals, and (presumably) oil.[33] Not only is the term strategic mineral analytically flawed, but the concept is a potentially costly one, as the proliferation of such minerals reinforces a political perception that minerals access is threatened on a broad front. This, in turn, implies that industrialized countries should adopt materials policies that are more comprehensive (and expensive) than most can reasonably afford, whereas the problem of guaranteeing access to vitally needed materials, preferably at stable prices, can be solved more economically if the number of minerals is minimized. This is justified if we accept the restrictionists' argument that "vulnerability" is a defining characteristic of strategic minerals.[34]

Before we discuss this argument, we should examine the case made by those who would conceive of strategic minerals in the broad sense. For them the category strategic minerals embraces all those minerals held in the U.S. Strategic Stockpile, as well as some of the "essential" and imported items that are not stockpiled, such as iron ore, phosphate, and molybdenum, to name but a few.[35] For broad interpretationists there are really only two major defining characteristics: strategic minerals must be in some way essential to national defence, and they must to some important degree be imported.

Given these two defining characteristics, it is not difficult to account for the enlargement of the strategic mineral category in recent decades. Not only is "essential" vague and therefore easily expandable, but "national defence" has become more elastic over time, along with the broadening of the idea of national security that has occurred in the post-Second World War years. National security has always been an ambiguous symbol,[36] but it is arguable that in the interwar period it was more narrowly focused on the question of a state's *physical* security, while today it includes both physical and *economic* security. It has even been suggested that the latter has been gaining in importance, as a result of the "domestication" of the international political system, which is increasingly concerned with the distributive processes that had been the preserve of the state.[37]

The idea that security depends on a healthy economy as much as, if not more than, it does on anything else has gained widespread international acceptance. According to those holding this point of view, among them former West German Chancellor Helmut Schmidt, "the world economic crisis of today is at least as great a strategic danger to the cohesion of the West as anything we have talked about so far. It is strategic danger because it does spread social and political unrest in our countries, and it entails the danger of national economic protectionism against each other within the West."[38]

The economic dimension of security takes on added significance in the context of the West's acknowledged dependence upon imports for such minerals as oil, which are evidently essential.[39] President Reagan expressed his concern that disruptions in supply of important raw materials, especially minerals, "could have serious consequences for United States and allied security by disrupting capabilities to produce military and essential civilian goods either in a declared national emergency or wartime mobilization."[40]

John D. Morgan, an official of the U.S. Bureau of Mines, has pointed out that the link between economic and physical security can justify a very broad interpretation of strategic minerals. "Viewed in this context adequate supplies of virtually every known material are a strategic necessity."[41] What to the broad interpretationists seems a logical extension appears an absurd one to others. Making practically every material strategic, say the restrictionists, obscures the very significance that the label strategic was originally intended to convey.

What was, or should be, connoted by the term strategic minerals are, to the restrictionists, the properties known as "vulnerability" and "criticality." Their principal objection is that the broad interpretationists equate import dependence with the vulnerability of consuming states to supply disruptions, and thereby miss the original point of the concept of strategic minerals. The conditions that bear on whether or not countries are vulnerable to supply disruptions include: (a) the degree of concentration of production of the mineral in question, (b) the identity of the supplying countries, (c) whether there are alternative supply prospects (including domestic alternatives), (d) the opportunities for substitution, (e) the opportunities for recycling and conservation, and (f) the presence of stockpiles in the consuming countries.[42]

The American experience with nickel is a good example of why import dependence should not be equated with vulnerability. Canada has always been by far the principal source of nickel for the United States, and remains so.[43] Because of contiguity and a general similarity of outlook on most major foreign policy issues, Americans have tended to look upon Canadian supply "as equivalent to a domestic source."[44] As one prominent minerals analyst of an earlier generation put it: "The possibility that Canada would sever diplomatic relations with the United States and cut off our nickel supply seems no more likely than the possibility of a revolt in northern Minnesota and the consequent cessation of the iron supply from that region."[45]

The minerals specialists at the BGS, when they attempt to define strategic minerals also introduce the idea of "criticality."[46] Criticality as employed here is not to be confused with its usage in the abovementioned official United States definition of "strategic and critical" materials (where it is the "Tweedledum" of an adjectival pair). Rather, it corresponds to the more frequently employed term "essential." In other words, criticality to the restrictionists need carry no ascription as to the source of the mineral (whether domestic or foreign), but instead is a function of the importance of the mineral to the military and industrial well-being of a country.

While the restrictionists may indeed have logic on their side in arguing that vulnerability, not import dependence, and criticality should serve as the analytical foci, it is less clear that their strictures against a broad usage of the term strategic minerals merit adherence. Even if we could police the use of concepts, would we be warranted in insisting that strategic minerals be accorded a greatly diminished role? For all its flaws, it may be more difficult to dispense with the concept of strategic minerals than to retain it. The restrictionist case illustrates some of the difficulties associated with the attempt to avoid employing the offending concept. This attempt possesses some problems of its own, the most important of which I shall call the fallacy of ethnocentrism.

Since vulnerability to supply disruption is not associated with all minerals, the restrictionists would have us reduce the vulnerability issue to its proper dimensions by getting rid of most of the strategic minerals and calling strategic only those that everyone would agree are worth worrying about. The objection to this proposition is contained in the proposition itself, for it is not possible to achieve consensus on the list of worrisome minerals of the present, let alone on the list of those that have caused or might cause concern in another era. Adopting the logic of restrictionism would oblige us incessantly to qualify strategic minerals by indicating to whom and at what period they were or are strategic, a process that would be clumsy at best, ridiculous at worst. Indeed, the logical consequence of restrictionism must be abolitionism, for of what use would be a concept so encumbered by qualifications that it possesses no meaning on its own?

The broad interpretationists, who insist that to be strategic a mineral must to a significant degree be imported, are similarly guilty of the ethnocentric fallacy. The problem with requiring that import dependence be a necessary (though not a sufficient) condition determining whether a mineral is strategic to any given country is that it becomes logically absurd to speak of states being *exporters* of strategic minerals, unless of course they are also importers of the same item.[47] Import dependence may be an interesting phenomenon in and of itself, but should not determine whether a mineral is or is not strategic.

What has happened over several decades to the concept of strategic minerals is what usually happens to contested concepts, especially political ones. They grow, both because their controversy (or ambiguity) encourages expansion and because the conditions extant when they first came into use have changed. T.D. Weldon wrote of the effect that changing conditions have on concepts, and though he was a political philosopher and not an expert on minerals, his words are worth pondering. Facts change, he wrote, and this requires that adjustments be made in the way we express them. The adjustments can be of two kinds: we can invent a new technical word or concept to reflect the change, or we can expand a familiar word or concept. "Usually the second method is preferred, partly because it avoids more confusion than it creates, indeed it seldom confuses anybody but political philosophers, and partly because the extended use has often come to be adopted uncritically in the natural course of events."[48]

We have seen that both the broad and the restrictionist interpretations of the term strategic mineral are flawed; each produces a certain amount of analytical confusion, which in turn has potential policy implications. The problem with this term cannot, however, be overcome by restricting its use, not least importantly because it is natural for expanded concepts that have entered into popular usage to resist abandonment. They may be used in ways that we do not prefer, but they *will* be used. One book dedicated to showing policymakers how to avoid shortages in strategic minerals starts out by confronting the definitional problem—and surrendering to it. Pursuing the logic of the restrictionists, Bohdan Szuprowicz arrives willy-nilly at the conclusion of the broad interpretationists when he writes that "the definition of what is truly a strategic and critical material will vary not only from country to country but also among industries and even enterprises within each country."[49] Szuprowicz is not advocating the proliferation of strategic minerals, but if all consumers are free to decide what does or does not deserve the label, it is hard to see how either proliferation or confusion can be avoided.

Since words should clarify, not obscure, meaning, perhaps a truce between the contending definitional camps can be arranged. A case can be made, paradoxically, both for a broad usage of the term strategic minerals *and* for the argument that ultimately what is important about such minerals is the extent to which consumers (or supplies) are vulnerable. This case rests on the assumption that those minerals deserving to be described as strategic should fulfil two admittedly subjective conditions. They must be deemed essential to the national security (either in the narrow military sense or in the wider understanding that equates national security with economic well-being); and they must be traded internationally to a significant degree. This second condition recognizes that in a world where all states are self-sufficient in minerals, no minerals are strategic, but at the same time avoids the ethnocentrism of defining strategic minerals solely from the perspective of the importing countries.

The attractiveness of such a proposal would perhaps be greater for countries like Canada, for whom strategic minerals are more important as export than as import commodities. At the very least, one could then speak and write logically of Canadian *exports* of strategic minerals, and have it understood that what was being referred to were those minerals in international commerce that were essential to at least *one* (and usually more than one) of Canada's trading partners.

A principal drawback, however, would be that in out-broadening the broad interpretationists such a construe would lead to most base metals being listed as strategic. To a degree, this problem already exists, as a glance at the common minerals (such as lead and zinc) contained in the U.S. National Defense Stockpile indicates. More to the point, there really is no a priori reason for excluding common minerals from the strategic category; minerals such as iron ore were widely considered to be highly strategic not so very long ago and, if Brian Skinner and others are to be believed, might again be so considered.[50]

To summarize, the strategic mineral category *is* flawed, and for the most part the restrictionist critique is legitimate. Knowing only that a mineral is strategic really does not tell us whether any particular country might have grounds for considering itself vulnerable to supply disruptions. If it were possible to "uninvent" words, perhaps minerals analysts would all be better off if the concept could be abolished. But such a thing is not possible, and as the passage from Gallie quoted earlier in this chapter indicates, one can expect both that strategic minerals will continue to be a topic of discussion, and that the discussion will involve endless disputes about the term's proper meaning.

From the above discussion, one might conclude that the minerals access problem has assumed greater importance over time as a factor in international politics, that the geopolitics of minerals is now vastly more significant because of the proliferation of strategic minerals in our era. I would caution against such a conclusion. What can be stated unequivocally is that minerals retain their political meaning, that they are a part of geopolitics that has not been rendered obsolete in the decades since the end of the Second World War. But to go beyond that statement requires an analysis that contrasts the various dimensions of the contemporary access problem with those of the interwar years, the only other period in which minerals problems were as relevant. Let us therefore seek to determine what changes have occurred with respect to three issues directly related to the differential distribution of minerals: minerals as a cause of international conflict, minerals as a factor contributing to military potential, and the issue of scarcity. These categories are not meant to be exhaustive; rather, they are meant to illustrate the most important developments in the geopolitics of minerals over the past half-century.

MINERALS AS A CAUSE OF INTERNATIONAL CONFLICT

Because war or the threat of war remains the most serious problem confronting the international political system, any analysis of the geopolitical significance of minerals must begin with their relationship to the larger problem of international conflict. Although the relationship can be traced back through centuries, only in the twentieth century have minerals become a reason *for*, not merely a means *of*, fighting. The First World War was a watershed as far as minerals were concerned. Prior to 1914 states appeared relatively indifferent to the access problem. Either they were self-sufficient in minerals (as in the case of the United States and the British Empire), or they were confident that what they lacked could always be acquired through the channels of untrammeled free trade. To be sure, wars in the nineteenth century had wrought substantial redistributions of minerals by rearranging national boundaries, but even the highly redistributive Franco-Prussian War did not arise because either belligerent wanted to acquire mineral wealth. Although in retrospect it appeared that the war had in fact been an "exchange of blood for iron," archival research has revealed that minerals did not figure in the decision of either side to go to war.[51]

It was really only the experience that all belligerents encountered with materials supply during the First World War that underscored the strategic relevance of minerals in modern wars of attrition. As C.K. Leith observed, "the war brought a rude awakening to the fact that no nation could be sure of a steady supply from abroad. . . . As for the Central Powers, the acute shortage of essential minerals which they experienced was a very considerable factor in their ultimate defeat."[52] More rudely awakened than any of the other participants was Germany, which in the interwar years experienced what a contemporary political scientist termed a "real claustrophobia in . . . national psychology."[53] This predisposition became especially pronounced after Hitler came to power in 1933, for Germany under the Nazis incessantly argued for a more "equitable" distribution of the earth's mineral and other raw material supply, which meant *at minimum* that Germany's lost African colonies be restored to it. The German case for a new international economic order rested, as does the more recent argument for the NIEO (New International Economic Order), on a concept of "equality" that was nothing if not ambiguous.[54] Apart from this similarity, however, the arguments made for changing the international economic status quo in the interwar years were of a radically different nature from contemporary arguments for equality, in that Germany, the leader of the minerals "have nots," was nonetheless one of the wealthier countries on earth.

It was not, of course, a more equitable division of wealth that Hitler sought, but rather territory, for territorial redistribution seemed to offer a way out of

Germany's minerals dilemma.[55] For its leaders, self-sufficiency in minerals and other raw materials offered Germany its only chance of living as an equal with the other powers; but to other countries this could only mean territorial expansionism, or imperialism. Germany had never been particularly well-situated with regard to minerals even when it had an overseas empire, but losing the war in 1918 had meant the loss of Lorraine iron ore as well. From being nearly self-sufficient in this one mineral in 1914 Germany became largely dependent in the interwar years on imported iron ore, mostly Swedish.[56] Nor was iron ore an exception; in fact, Germany was self-sufficient in only two of the thirty-five raw materials that were at that time considered necessary for modern warfare—coal and potash.[57] It lacked (in many cases completely) the following minerals, most of them essential to an industrial economy and *all* of them essential for a society contemplating war: petroleum, copper, nickel, sulphur, tungsten, titanium, tin, manganese, chromium, lead, mica, graphite, industrial diamonds, quartz crystal, and bauxite.[58]

But if Germany showed that losing a Great War could have serious consequences where minerals were concerned, Japan and Italy demonstrated that being on the winning side did not necessarily provide easy solutions to the problem of mineral maldistribution. If anything, Japan's situation was worse than Germany's, for of the new materials essential to modern industry, it possessed only sulphur and artificial nitrates in abundance. Italy was in a better position, but only marginally; it had to import all the essential minerals except bauxite, mercury, and sulphur.[59] Together, these three states constituted what came to be called the "have-not" countries. In contrast to their plight was the comfortable situation of the "haves": the United States, Great Britain and its dominions and colonies, and the Soviet Union. Between them, the United States and Great Britain alone controlled some two-thirds of global mineral reserves, and the United States was far and away the world's leading producer of minerals.[60]

In ascribing significance to various factors implicated in the onset of the Second World War—and in this connection it might be wiser to date the beginning of the war in the Pacific from the Japanese invasion of Manchuria rather than from Pearl Harbor—one must be extremely careful to avoid succumbing to reductionist theories of causation. It is surely impossible to isolate any single cause of the war, but high on the list of predisposing conditions has to be the mineral access problem. It is a matter of record that during the interwar period there was a widespread conviction that differential minerals distribution posed a threat to peace. Hjalmar Schacht, director of the Reichsbank, was only stating the conventional wisdom when he wrote that "a nation which is cut off from the essential necessities of life must be a source of unrest in the world."[61] He wrote this in 1937, when Italy and Japan had already launched wars of territorial conquest that were explicitly justified by reference to each state's need for more "living space." In the case of Italy, conquests in Africa did not do much to redress shortages of minerals (and did even less to relieve so-called "population pressure" at home), but Japan was able to secure some needed minerals, getting coal, low-grade iron ore, and magnesium from Manchuria and North China.[62]

To recapitulate, it is not possible, nor is it my purpose to argue an immediate causal link between the minerals question of the interwar years and the origins of the Second World War. But it does seem that T.S. Lovering's assessment of some forty-five years ago has stood the test of time. According to Lovering, "the immediate causes of the second world war were clearly psychological and political; but the immediate causes grew out of social conditions, and the social conditions in turn were profoundly affected by the distribution and control of raw materials."[63] More recently, Alfred Eckes, jr., has observed that apart from the political and social causes of the war, "there was also an important structural problem—the uneven global distribution of raw materials among industrial states—that contributed directly to the collapse of world peace."[64]

However conceived, the conclusion appears inescapable that the problem of access to minerals was an important factor in the breakdown of world order during the late 1930s. Put into contemporary terminology, we might say that access issues contributed highly to "East-West," or interbloc tension. Would it be possible to make the same kind of statement about the other era with which our analysis is concerned, the period from 1973 to the early 1980s? That is, were questions about minerals access of as much perceived importance in Moscow and Washington at the start of this decade as they were in Berlin, Rome, and Tokyo on the one hand, and London and Washington on the other, during the 1930s?

To answer this requires that we differentiate between conflict on the scale of a world war—that is, the kind of war between superpowers that might start out as an exchange of tactical nuclear weapons but quickly escalate into an all-out strategic exchange—and conflict that is more clearly containable. It may be that the latter type of superpower conflict will ultimately prove to be a conceptual impossibility, but it is at least arguable that we have already had, in the form of several proxy wars of the past decade or so, evidence that armed superpower rivalry need not lead to a war to the finish. The point is important, for if what is meant by "war" is the nuclear equivalent of the Second World War, then minerals access will likely not—barring an epidemic of insanity in Washington and Moscow—constitute an important cause of war ever again. Thus, in the context of East-West tension, one clear distinction between the new and the old geopolitics of minerals is that minerals access problems will probably not be a reason for fighting a major war, and are not likely to result in a serious threat to world peace.

It is still likely, however, that minerals access will remain at least an incidental source of tension between West and East. Because the question of access is of vital interest primarily to the Western industrialized states, given the Soviet Union's relative self-sufficiency in minerals, the question of resorting to arms to preserve access to raw materials is one that has caused much interest in the West, especially in the United States, in the years following 1973.[65] Initially, most of the speculation about the possible use of force focused on the question of Persian Gulf oil.[66] When fears about access first surfaced in the mid-1970s, the Soviet Union was not considered the primary cause of any future supply disruption. Hence use of force, to the extent it was contemplated at all, was considered in the context of strictly regional issues, not in the broader framework of East-West relations.

But with the decline of détente and the growing perception in parts of the West that the Soviet Union was running out of oil—a perception fed by a series of 1977 CIA reports that have subsequently been radically modified—policy planning in Washington began to assume that Soviet expansion into the Gulf area might soon occur as a direct consequence of the Soviet need for foreign oil. It quickly became apparent that the Soviets might continue enjoying self-sufficiency in oil for some time to come,[67] so those who still preferred to regard Soviet meddling as the leading threat to Western access began to concentrate on another presumed motive: Soviet desire to cripple Western economies by interfering with their supply of Persian Gulf oil.[68]

Although there never was any solid evidence upon which to rest the contention that the Soviets were in fact out to menace Western oil supply, analysts in the West did not refrain from extending their assumptions about oil to other strategic minerals. What Soviet power might portend for oil supply it apparently could also portend for other mineral imports. There seemed to be two main concerns. The first was that the Soviets, by building up their navy, might eventually be strong enough to interdict Western sea lanes.[69] The other was that the Soviets would step up their political and military involvement in southern Africa, with a view to making Western access to the region's mineral wealth more problematical. In this regard, it is important to note the high degree of concentration of certain strategic minerals. Twenty-five per cent or more (usually more) of total global production of the following minerals takes place in the southern African region, comprising Angola, Botswana, Congo, Lesotho, Mozambique, Namibia, South Africa, Swaziland, Tanzania, Zaïre, Zambia, and Zimbabwe: diamonds, vanadium, platinum-group metals, chromite, cobalt, and manganese.[70] By contrast, in 1985 Persian Gulf countries accounted for less than a third of total world oil production.[71]

Despite the fears of observers like Frank Barnett, head of the New York-based

National Strategy Information Center, that "the age of détente is shading into the era of the resource war,"[72] it bears repeating that an important—perhaps the most important—implication of the new geopolitics of minerals is that as a potential source of armed conflict between rival world power blocs, minerals simply do not possess the significance that they had in the interwar years. On this most relevant issue, I believe the Arads are correct in writing that "the undeniably growing importance of raw materials and the politics of using or securing them will probably be conducive to a less stable world. . . [in which]. . . there will be more international disputes involving access to resources. But all are likely to fall short of causing major upheavals that may lead to war."[73]

MINERALS AS A FACTOR CONTRIBUTING TO MILITARY POTENTIAL

Military potential, like strategic minerals, is a twentieth-century concept. In fact, the two concepts stemmed from the same period, the interwar years. The evolution of both is in large measure testimony to the impact of the great lesson of the First World War: that modern wars of attrition would be won by those states that had the most secure resource bases and lost by those that did not.

In its early years, the concept of military potential was known by another name, "war potential." But irrespective of which label was employed, the basic idea was of a reserve of "national resources available for producing and maintaining armed forces. Whenever a nation creates or expands military forces in peace and war, it mobilizes military potential."[74] Given the amplitude of such a definition, it is no surprise that military potential should be a difficult concept to measure, for not only are objective constituents of national power such as population, GNP, or energy production factored into the overall equation, but so too are subjective qualities like socio-political structure and patterns of culture. With due regard to the inherent flaws of any attempts to formulate numerical indices of the power potential of various states,[75] I would nevertheless maintain that one can, with reasonable validity, address the manner in which the concept of military potential has evolved across historical eras, with particular attention to the changing role of minerals as ingredients of military potential.

Probably the most significant difference between the new geopolitics of minerals and the old, in the context of military potential, is the extent to which earlier hypotheses were founded on assumptions that were heavily deterministic. Recent analyses of military potential have placed much emphasis on the capabilities of modern industrial societies to utilize substitution and technology to free themselves from the dictates of geography. In the interwar years, however, there was no such stress on voluntarism. Instead, states were held to be truly captives of their resource bases, which were conceived of in static terms. A country either had mineral deposits or it did not; and if it did not, there was not much likelihood of it ever becoming a Great Power. This was held to be so because, as the Great War had convincingly demonstrated, military potential was a direct function of the capacity for industrialization, "and since large-scale industrialization presupposes a ready availability of vast quantities of the basic industrial raw materials, nature, through her unequal distribution of these, has rigidly set a limit to the number of states capable of achieving the status of Great Powers."[76]

The post-Second World War decades have witnessed a markedly different understanding of the role of minerals in overall military potential. Ironically, it was the example of Germany during the war that brought about a reinterpretation of earlier, deterministic assumptions that stressed a strong and direct link between minerals and power. Recall from the preceding section that fear of losing access to needed minerals was a major concern of German foreign policy in the 1930s; both within Germany and elsewhere it was widely assumed that without access to essential minerals, Germany could not hope to become a Great Power.[77] Germany did, of course, acquire substantial mineral holdings through its early conquests in Europe, but the net effect of those conquests was only to reduce, not eliminate, its overall import dependence. Thus it was with a sense of incredulity that postwar students of military potential pondered the German wartime experience. Contrary to what the First World War had "predicted," the experience of Germany in the Second World War seemed to indicate that access to minerals was not, after all, vital for waging a major war. Technology and substitution, both of which assumed a greater degree of administrative skill than had been present in the Germany of 1914–18, were held to have been instrumental in Germany's fighting for as long as it had, given its relatively meagre mineral endowment. Significantly, if Germany could have accomplished so much with so little, then the dependence-minimizing options seemed to be promising indeed for more well-endowed countries like the United States, which emerged from the war in 1945 facing potential supply shortages in nonfuel minerals for the first time in its history.[78]

In a celebrated article that appeared in the inaugural volume of *World Politics,* Edward S. Mason drew an analogy between what the Germans had accomplished and what he thought the United States and other industrialized powers could achieve. Noting that although Germany's consumption of essential minerals had remained constant from 1938 to 1944, German military production had actually increased by 300 to 400 per cent, Mason concluded that "it is quite clear. . . that Germany managed to fight a first-class war on very small quantities of 'essential' raw materials. . . . The moral, for our purpose, seems to be that the potentialities of raw material substitution and replacement in a modern economy are enormous."[79] Other analysts drew on the German experience to reach conclusions similar to Mason's. The new geopolitics of minerals, it appeared, promised to be substantially different from the old, because industrial and therefore military potential were in the process of being freed from the shackles of geographic determinism.

Mancur Olson, jr., was one of the new breed of analysts who minimized the contribution of minerals to military potential. Earlier, deterministic statements of that relationship were examples, said Olson, of the "physiocratic fallacy," in that they proceeded from the erroneous assumption that all wealth flowed from the production of primary goods. Olson's thesis was not that minerals were irrelevant to defence; it was rather that "the experience of the two world wars and a glance at the opportunities for substitution reveal that shortages of primary products need not always be fatal to a nation at war."[80] Far less qualified was the view articulated a decade later by Charles L. Schultze. Writing a few short months before the oil crisis of the autumn of 1973, Schultze advanced the proposition that "the national security of the United States depends in no important way on securing access to raw materials, markets, or sea lanes abroad, and securing or protecting such access cannot reasonably be used as the rationale for a foreign policy. . . . "[81]

Schultze's argument has merit if, and only if, national security is conceived of in the narrow sense of physical security. Clearly the most dangerous challenge the United States faces in a military sense is the destructive capability of the other superpower's nuclear arsenal. The same is true for the Soviet Union. In a major nuclear war between the superpowers, mineral reserves cannot constitute anything but a trivial asset, if they are an asset at all. As the First World War *seemed* to indicate, wars of attrition required substantial military potential in the form of a capacity for industrialization. Whether the Second World War—or at least the German experience in that war—contradicted the lesson of 1914–18 remains an open question (although frankly I am sceptical of the Mason thesis). What cannot be questioned, however, is that if a Third World War were to involve nuclear weapons, it would not be a war of attrition at all. And in *that* sense, minerals would hardly matter.

But if, as I suspect, military potential is enmeshed in the same kind of conceptual broadening process that has seen national security come to mean security in an economic as well as a physical sense, then surely the military potential of stronger economies—no matter how it is measured or what it signifies—has to be greater than that of weaker economies, all other things being equal.[82] According to the broader view of national security, a NATO alliance not beset with supply problems for oil and other strategic minerals must be a stronger NATO than one beset with such difficulties. The point is that while the new geopolitics of minerals is indeed less deterministic than the old insofar as the relationship of minerals to military potential is concerned, it remains the case that issues of minerals access possess meaning in the *military* context. The experience of Western industrialized states in the years since 1973 has led analysts of minerals questions to draw back from the more sanguine assumptions of the years from 1945 to 1973. It has not proved possible, despite the very impressive gains brought about by technology, for modern economies to reduce very much their need for imports of certain essential minerals.

Individual minerals may become irrelevant for military purposes as a result of technological developments. An outstanding example of this is seen in the case of natural nitrates, which were rendered dispensable as a result of breakthroughs achieved by German chemists who, stimulated by the British disruption of Germany's Chilean nitrate supply during the First World War, succeeded in synthesizing nitrates economically, a success that ultimately doomed the Chilean nitrate industry. But to be sustainable over the long term, substitution made possible by technology must be economic, or at least not terribly uneconomic. In this regard the German interwar experience with synthetic fuel production is instructive. Although technology enabled Germany to satisfy nearly half its domestic oil consumption from coal by the late 1930s, it was at a heavy price (about four times the cost per barrel of imported oil)—a price that redounded to the detriment of overall German industrial performance, and hence military potential.[83]

Nor is economics the only drawback to the more widespread use of what one geologist has scornfully termed the "technical fix."[84] Even assuming that economical substitutions are possible technology is a two-edged sword. It may eliminate dependence on some minerals, but usually at the cost of creating dependence on others. As Nazli Choucri and Robert North have argued, "the more advanced the level of technology... the greater the variety and quantity of resources needed by that society."[85] An illustration of this tendency was provided by the U.S. experience during the interwar period, when a search for mineral substitutes for items that were on the strategic list uncovered thirty-four new materials (among them beryllium, lithium, and magnesium), many of which were produced outside the United States.[86]

A further instance of the limited capability of technology to find substitutes is the continuing problem that advanced industrial societies, Canada included, have encountered in trying to reduce their dependence upon imports of certain essential minerals. One of the striking similarities between the new geopolitics and the old consists in the inability of states to eliminate their need for particular minerals. Two important examples were strategic to most industrialized states during the interwar period and remain so today: manganese and chromium, both essential for steelmaking purposes, neither with an economical substitute (indeed, for manganese there is no substitute at all).[87] The list of such hard-to-replace items could be expanded, with oil being an obvious inclusion.

THE ISSUE OF SCARCITY

Technology may have limits, but it should be stressed that the underlying problem of strategic minerals—that is, the very reason they *are* strategic—is not that they are on the verge of depletion, but rather that they are differentially distributed throughout the world. If the pattern of global minerals distribution were somehow more uniform than it is, the question of access would, in theory, be less an international political issue and more a purely domestic one, as each country sought to satisfy consumption from its own reserves. Actual physical or geological scarcity has not been a serious problem to date, and in this respect the old and new geopolitics of minerals are again similar. Paradoxical as it might seem, and despite the gargantuan consumption of minerals by the industrialized and industrializing world since the end of the Second World War, "reserves of nearly all mineral commodities are larger today than in the early postwar period."[88] However, if physical depletion is no closer today than it was a half-century ago, the *perception* that it is a growing danger has been more pronounced in the years since 1973 than in the interwar years. In the earlier period there was, to be sure, intermittent concern (particularly in the immediate aftermath of the First World War) over the physical supply of certain minerals, especially oil. Perhaps more so than anywhere else, there was in the United States in the early 1920s a perception that oil reserves could not last much beyond another decade. Some students of minerals issues even predicted that "our children will in all probability see the end of the petroleum industry."[89] Ultimately, the fear that oil reserves were about to be exhausted proved to be self-correcting, for it motivated the American government to practice "resource diplomacy," thereby helping American companies establish their presence in oil provinces outside the western hemisphere. So intensive and successful was the search for new oil fields (both in the United States and elsewhere) that by the end of the 1920s the "menace" of physical depletion of oil had been put to rest, at least for several decades.

By the early 1930s, no informed student of minerals would have deemed the world mineral problem to be one of scarcity. Rather, glut seemed to be plaguing mineral production. Because of improvements in the technology of mineral extraction, the real price of minerals tumbled throughout the 1920s, and their market was characterized by oversupply, despite rising demand during the decade. The onset of the Depression caused demand to fall, making a bad situation worse for producers of minerals and other commodities.[90] In 1937, the Raw

Materials Committee of the League of Nations reported that to the degree the world had a minerals problem at all, it was chiefly a function of the inability of consumers to pay for them, not of the world to produce them.[91] Analysts in Great Britain and elsewhere did not fail to note the incongruity between the global oversupply of minerals and the clamant demands of Germany for a more "equitable" distribution of territory. "Among the many irrational features of international affairs today," wrote H.D. Henderson, "there is none more ironical than the voicing of the demand for more 'living-space' by the leader of a great European industrial nation at this particular juncture of the world's history. For never was living-space a less real problem for the people of Western Europe."[92]

The response of Germany (and to a lesser extent the other "have-nots") to the observation that minerals were so abundant that their acquisition had never before been *easier* was to point up the deficiencies of trade as a means of remedying the access problem. In an ideal world, stated Hjalmar Schacht, trade could resolve the access question, just as it had in the era before the Great War, when Germany and other minerals-deficient countries procured their supplies in free international markets. But the global trade regime prevailing in the 1930s was a far cry from that of the prewar period, a situation that to Schacht suggested that "it is either silly or cynical... for foreign commentators to declare that Germany can buy raw materials in the world market at will." This was impossible, according to Germany's leading economist, because Germany lacked foreign exchange, and it lacked foreign exchange because it was becoming increasingly harder for its manufactures to penetrate foreign markets in the protectionist environment.[93]

Economists in Britain and other "have" countries were more than a little naive in expecting international trade to do for minerals consumers in the protectionist 1930s what it had been able to do in the earlier, more liberal era that Asa Briggs characterized as "the *belle époque* of interdependence."[94] On the other hand, German (and Italian and Japanese) demand for minerals in the 1930s was in large measure a function not of the dictates of normal peacetime economies but rather of economies rapidly preparing for war. How else can we explain the anomaly of "have-not" economies, all of them well-launched on ambitious rearmament programs, consuming many more minerals in the late 1930s than they did in the more prosperous previous decade.[95] In any case the debate over trade as a means of settling access problems totally overlooked what should have been obvious to everyone: that trade itself, as Albert O. Hirschman has brilliantly argued, cannot lead to the depoliticization of minerals questions precisely because trade was, is, and probably always will be an eminently political process. It is so because, whether intended or not, it inevitably affects the power position of states. The effect is twofold: because trade can enhance a state's military potential by supplying essential minerals, it was said by Hirschman to possess a property known as the "supply effect"; and because it could serve as a direct source of power, through the fostering of asymmetrical dependencies, it possessed an "influence effect."[96]

I will have some further comments about trade as a means of ensuring access, but for the moment let us return to the question of scarcity as it has been formulated in the years since 1973. The argument that minerals are becoming less abundant globally takes two distinct forms: the first and more common variant is that depletion, whether in the physical or economic sense, is the principal threat to future supply; the second, which has gained plausibility in the past few years, is that scarcity will not be a function of either physical or economic depletion, but rather will have political causes.[97]

In the years since 1973, much more so than in the interwar period, there has been a quickened sense of anxiety about the possibility that global mineral reserves might be depleted. There is, of course, nothing new about the notion that non-renewable resources must, in a finite world, sooner or later become exhausted. Depletion—whether in the physical sense of things actually running out or in the economic sense of their becoming too expensive for the world to use—has been a theoretically interesting proposition since the time of Malthus and Ricardo.[98] The germane question, and the one for which no one has been able to supply a definitive answer, concerns the amount of time it will take before either economic (Ricardian) or physical (Malthusian) scarcity sets in. In the early 1970s, it began to appear that Ricardian scarcity was closer to reality than the most optimistic (or "cornucopian") viewpoint had held it to be. Shortages of minerals were in fact starting to crop up by late 1973, as accelerating demand among OECD consumers temporarily outran supply. The OPEC cartel was in the process of shocking world oil consumers with its unprecedented use of "resource power." And the Club of Rome had begun to publicize its dramatic findings that nonrenewable resources were rapidly disappearing.[99]

This is not the place to detail the methodological problems associated with the Club of Rome findings as published in the controversial work *Limits to Growth*.[100] However, one central fallacy of that report needs to be pointed out: the assumption that *reserves* are the most important aspect of global mineral supply. The concept of reserves is a dynamic one; reserves may indeed decline, as the Club of Rome report noted, but they can also increase. Whether dynamic or not, they are not the most relevant conceptual category around which to base a series of assumptions about the probability of scarcity. Reserves simply mean the quantity of minerals in deposits that can be profitably exploited under current economic and technological conditions.[101] Far more important conceptually than reserves are the earth's total *resources,* for the former are but a subset of the latter. Put differently, resources become reserves through a combination of discovery and improvements in either technology or price or both. Copper provides an example of the distinction between reserves and resources. A century ago, the average grade mined was about 3 per cent; by 1960, it was 0.72 per cent. In current terminology, only the 3 per cent ores would have been classified as reserves in 1889, while all ores of lower copper content would have been resources.[102] Thus one can account for the otherwise paradoxical tendency of copper reserves to expand at the same time the consumption of copper has been increasing, a situation characteristic of the post-Second World War decades. Although "known" global reserves of copper were 100 million metric tons in 1945 and consumption was 93 million tons between 1945 and 1970 alone, by the end of the 1970s world reserves stood at more than 300 million tons.[103]

Total global mineral resources are truly, as geologist James Boyd described them, "large enough to stagger the imagination."[104] And it would take a feverish imagination indeed to conjure up a probable Malthusian future. But is a Ricardian future as improbable? And if not, how far away is it? All that can be said of this is that the scholars are divided. Minerals economists tend to be more optimistic than geologists about the prospect of staving off a Ricardian scenario.[105] In any case, hardly any knowledgeable student of minerals, whether economist or geologist, envisions the onset of Ricardian scarcity until the next century at the earliest. And all would agree that whether or not economic scarcity does become manifest even then depends upon whether "the race between the cost-decreasing effects of new technology and the cost-increasing effects of depletion is won by the latter."[106]

Far more problematical is the prospect that access will become more difficult as a result of politically induced scarcity. Political scarcity can be a function either of the withdrawal of capital investment on the part of multinational mining companies frightened by increased "resource power" in many parts of the Third World, or of supply disruptions that are either an incidental consequence of political turmoil in a producing country (as happened with cobalt in Zaïre in the late 1970s), or an intended consequence of Soviet attempts to render Western economic security more tenuous. The potential disruption of supply whether intended or unintended will be discussed in a subsequent chapter; suffice it to note in this regard that there was growing concern in the West a few years ago that these might be the most likely kinds of supply disruptions in the 1980s.

Here I would like to address briefly the possibility that political scarcity may be brought about as a result of increasingly assertive LDC (less developed countries) governments attempting to extract more economic rent from multinational mineral producers operating within their boundaries. Here is a further way in which the new geopolitics of minerals differs sharply from the old, for in the interwar period many of the mineral-producing regions were outright colonies of European consuming states, and those that did have legal sovereignty were (except for Mexico and Bolivia in the late 1930s) unwilling or unable to challenge the terms governing the operations of foreign extractive enterprises.

With rapid decolonization in the decades after the Second World War, and with the declining ability of the United States to preserve its hegemonic position in world politics, economic power seemed to be shifting toward the developing states; this was especially so by the mid-1960s.[107] Their exercise of "resource power" was given an apparently powerful fillip when OPEC launched its successful price action in 1973, and for a time it appeared that cartels in other minerals would make supply increasingly costly and risky.[108] One effect of LDC assertiveness was "an enormous shift in the location of new mineral activity," which by the mid-1970s was increasingly taking place in countries considered more hospitable to private foreign capital—countries like the United States, Canada, Australia, and South Africa.[109] During the period from 1966 to 1972 American mining and smelting investment in developing countries amounted to some 40 per cent of such investment in developed countries (mostly Canada and Australia); by the end of 1977, the developing countries' share had declined to only 32 per cent of that of the developed countries.[110] Nor was there anything exceptional about the behaviour of American-based multinationals, for mining firms domiciled in other consuming countries likewise undertook a relative shift in the locus of their operations.[111]

By the mid-1970s, people were beginning to think that scarcity was more likely to be caused by political than by economic developments in future—primarily political developments attending the climb up the "learning curve" by more assertive LDC governments anxious to exert greater control over their mineral wealth.[112] Whatever the particular modalities chosen by the LDC governments to assert their resource power (embargoes, cartels, and unilateral price administration schemes were some of the possibilities mentioned), mineral experts in the West were becoming increasingly convinced that "we should . . . look more to the political context than to economic theories to assess the present and potential difficulties in international transactions in raw materials."[113] But the recession of the early 1980s led to a drastic and rapid reassessment of the postulated link between political forces and mineral scarcity. Indeed, for some minerals (such as copper) a common argument was that political manipulation (for reasons related to balance of payments and job creation) was a principal source of glut![114]

28

CONCLUSION

Despite the important ways in which questions of mineral access in the years since 1973 differ from those in the interwar period, a strong undercurrent of continuity crosses the two historical eras. Access to minerals continues to be ultimately a function of political processes, and because of this the access question remains today what it was in the 1930s, a matter of geopolitical concern. It has proven impossible for the international political and economic order that emerged from the Second World War to bring about a depoliticization of minerals, despite some optimistic assertions in the early 1960s that increasing interdependence among nations would do just that.[115] Indeed, to the extent that interdependence must mean vulnerability interdependence, a thesis provocatively advanced by David Baldwin,[116] it connotes not a *solution* to the access problem but a confirmation of its most worrisome feature from the perspective of the industrialized countries, namely, the vulnerability of consumers. I shall return to this point in the concluding chapter; for the moment, let us explore a set of concerns, both international and domestic, that animated Canadian mineral policymaking in the years since 1973.

NOTES

1 Issues get "politicized" when they become subject to agitation and controversy, and subsequently are raised to the top of various national and international policy agendas. Robert O. Keohane and Joseph S. Nye, *Power and Interdependence: World Politics in Transition* (Boston: Little, Brown 1977), 33.

2 C.K. Leith, *World Minerals and World Politics: A Factual Study of Minerals in their Political and International Relations* (New York: Whittlesey House, McGraw-Hill 1931), 104.

3 Japan is perhaps the best example of mineral deprivation. It has been termed a "minerals museum" because it contains mineral deposits in amounts sufficient for museum exhibition and little else. International Economic Studies Institute, *Raw Materials and Foreign Policy* (Washington: IESI 1976), 15.

4 Hanns W. Maull, *Raw Materials, Energy and Western Security* (London: Macmillan/International Institute for Strategic Studies 1984), 7.

5 For a discussion of this approach, see Sylvia L. Thrupp, "Diachronic Methods in Comparative Politics," in *the Methodology of Comparative Research*, ed. Robert T. Holt and John E. Turner (New York: Free Press 1970), 343–58; and Arend Lijphart, "Comparative Politics and the Comparative Method," *American Political Science Review* (Sept. 1971):689–91.

6 At least in Anglo-American precincts of the discipline, for as John Child and others have noted, elsewhere the "geopolitical" tradition retains its allure. See John Child, "Geopolitical Thinking in Latin America," *Latin American Research Review* 14 (1979):89–111; Child, *Geopolitics and Conflict in South America: Quarrels among Neighbors* (New York: Praeger 1985); Judith Ewell, "The Development of Venezuelan Geopolitical Analysis since World War II," *Journal of Interamerican Studies and World Affairs* 24 (Aug. 1982)295–320; Stephen M. Gorman, "Geopolitics and Peruvian Foreign Policy," *Inter-American Economic Affairs* 36 (Autumn 1982):65–88; John D. Young, "L'explication inter-théorique en relations internationales: Quelques jalons pour une synthèse du réalisme structurel américain et de la géopolitique française contemporaine," *Etudes Internationales* 18 (June 1987):305–28; and Patrick O'Sullivan, *Geopolitics* (New York: St. Martin's 1986).

7 Two interesting studies of *Geopolitik* and its relationship to geopolitics, both written during the Second World War, are Andrew Gyorgy, *Geopolitics: The New German Science,* University of California Publications in International Relations, vol. 3 (Berkeley: University of California Press 1944); and Johannes Mattern, *Geopolitik: Doctrine of National Self-Sufficiency and Empire,* Johns Hopkins University Studies in Historical and Political Science, series 60, no. 2 (Baltimore: Johns Hopkins University Press 1942). A prewar and more sympathetic treatment of the work done by Karl Haushofer's Geopolitical Institute at Munich is provided in Richard Hartshorne, "Recent Developments in Political Geography, II," *American Political Science Review* 29 (Dec. 1935):960–4.

8 Ray S. Cline, *World Power Assessment, 1977: A Calculus of Strategic Drift* (Boulder, CO: Westview Press 1977), 3.

9 Ladis K.D. Kristof, "The Origins and Evolution of Geopolitics," *Journal of Conflict Resolution* 4 (Mar. 1960):34.

10 K.J. Holsti, "Retreat from Utopia: International Relations Theory, 1945–70," *Canadian Journal of Political Science* 4 (June 1971):165–77.

11 Harold J. Barnett, "The Changing Relation of Natural Resources to National Security," *Economic Geography* 34 (July 1958):188–201.

12 John H. Herz, "Rise and Demise of the Territorial state," *World Politics* 9 (July 1957):473–93.

13 Colin S. Gray, *The Geopolitics of the Nuclear Era: Heartland, Rimlands, and the Technological Revolution* (New York: Crane, Russak 1977), 12. Also see, by the same author, *Maritime Strategy, Geopolitics, and the Defense of the West* (New York: National Strategy Information Center 1986); and "Keeping the Soviets Landlocked: Geostrategy for a Maritime America," *National Interest* 4 (Summer 1986):24–36.

14 Nicholas John Spykman, *America's Strategy in World Politics: The United States and the Balance of Power* (New York: Harcourt, Brace 1942). The other classics of geopolitical literature are Alfred Thayer Mahan, *The Influence of Seapower upon History, 1660–1783* (Boston: Little, Brown 1897); and Halford Mackinder, *Democratic Ideals and Reality: A Study in the Politics of Reconstruction* (New York: Henry Holt 1942).

15 Bohdan O. Szuprowicz, *How to Avoid Strategic Materials Shortages: Dealing with Cartels, Embargoes, and Supply Disruptions* (New York: John Wiley & Sons 1981), ix.

16 An interesting discussion of the resurgence of geopolitics is found in Leslie W. Hepple, "The Revival of Geopolitics," *Political Geography Quarterly* 5 (Oct. 1986):S21–36.

17 Harold and Margaret Sprout, "Geography and International Politics in an Era of Revolutionary Change," *Journal of Conflict Resolution* 4 (Mar. 1960): 152.

18 W.B. Gallie, "Essentially Contested Concepts," in *The Importance of Language,* ed. Max Black (Englewood Cliffs, NJ: Prentice-Hall 1962), 123. Also see William E. Connolly, *The Terms of Political Discourse,* 2nd ed. (Princeton: Princeton University Press 1983), Ch. 1: "Essentially Contested Concepts in Politics."

19 Klaus Knorr, *The War Potential of Nations* (Princeton: Princeton University Press 1956), 35–7.

20 In the early postwar period iron and coal were generally considered to be of "basal" importance to industrial capacity, and hence to military potential. In the words of one writer, distribution patterns of iron and coal deposits had "repeatedly changed the balance of power throughout the world." Edwin C. Eckel, *Coal, Iron, and War: A Study in Industrialism Past* and Future (New York: Henry Holt 1920), 96.

21 Quoted in P.H. Frankel, *Essentials of Petroleum: A Key to Oil Economics,* new ed. (London: Frank Cass 1969), 3.

22 A contemporary popular treatment of the topic is found in Ludwell Denny, *We Fight for Oil* (New York: Alfred A. Knopf 1928). Contemporary scholarly treatments include: Leith, *World Minerals and World Politics;* Leith, "Mineral Resources and Peace," *Foreign Affairs* 16 (Apr. 1938):515–24; and Norman Angell, *Raw Materials, Population Pressure and War,* World Affairs Books, no. 14 (Boston: World Peace Foundation 1936). For a recent scholarly discussion, see Stephen D. Krasner, *Defending the National Interest: Raw Materials Investments and U.S. Foreign Policy* (Princeton: Princeton University Press 1978), 106–19.

23 For an analysis of America's relatively favourable position with respect to mineral and other raw material supplies, see Brooks Emeny, *The Strategy of Raw Materials: A Study of America in Peace and War* (New York: Macmillan 1934).

24 Franklin P. Huddle, "The Evolving National Policy for Materials," *Science* 191 (20 Feb. 1976):654.

25 Alfred E. Eckes, jr., *The United States and the Global Struggle for Minerals* (Austin: University of Texas Press 1979), 43.

26 Army and Navy Munitions Board, Memorandum of 7 Jan. 1939; cited in Spykman, *America's Strategy in World Politics*, 293.

27 Quoted in Percy W. Bidwell, *Raw Materials: A Study of American Policy* (New York: Harper and Bros./Council on Foreign Relations 1958), 32–3.

28 U.S. Federal Emergency Management Agency, *Stockpile Report to the Congress: October 1981–March 1982* (Washington: Sept. 1982), 27.

29 National Strategy Information Center, *Strategic Minerals: A Resource Crisis* (Washington: Council on Economics and National Security 1981), 34.

30 The definitional problem is discussed in some detail in U.S. General Accounting Office, *Report to the Secretary of the Interior: Actions Needed to Promote a Stable Supply of Strategic and Critical Minerals and Materials* (Washington: June 1982).

31 United Kingdom, House of Lords, Select Committee on the European Communities, *Strategic Minerals*, sess. 1981–2, 20th report (London: Her Majesty's Stationery Office 1982).

32 Alan Archer, "Definition of Strategic Minerals and the Means Currently Available to the United Kingdom Government to Identify Strategic Sources and Requirements," in *Availability of Strategic Minerals* (London: Institution of Mining and Metallurgy 1980), 2–3.

33 Hans H. Landsberg, *Minerals in the Eighties: Issues and Policies* (Oak Ridge, TN: Oak Ridge National Laboratory, Program Planning and Analysis 1982), 20–1.

34 Phillip Crowson, *Non-Fuel Minerals and Foreign Policy* (London: Royal Institute of International Affairs 1977), 3.

35 V. Anthony Cammarota, jr., "America's Dependence on Strategic Minerals," in *American Strategic Minerals*, ed. Gerard J. Mangone (New York: Crane, Russak 1984), 30.

36 Arnold Wolfers, " 'National Security' as an Ambiguous Symbol," *Political Science Quarterly* 67 (Dec. 1952):481–502.

37 Wolfram F. Hanreider, "Dissolving International Politics: Reflections on the Nation-State," *American Political Science Review* 72 (Dec. 1978):1276–87.

38 Interview with Jonathan Power, *Manchester Guardian Weekly* 7 Mar. 1982, p. 8. Others adopting an inclusive interpretation of national security include Maull, *Raw Materials, Energy, and Western Security*, Ch. 1: "Minerals, Markets and Security"; Lester R. Brown, *Redefining National Security*, Worldwatch Paper no. 14 (Washington: Worldwatch Institute 1977), 6; and Richard N. Cooper, "Natural Resources and National Security," *Resources Policy* 1 (June 1975):192–3. For a recent theoretical treatment of national security, see Barry Buzan, *People, States, and Fear: The National Security Problem in International Relations* (Brighton, Sussex: Wheatsheaf Books 1983).

39 Few would dispute Robert Lieber's claim that "oil is a resource... nearly as essential as food or water." Robert J. Lieber, "Cohesion and Disruption in the Western Alliance," in *Global Insecurity: A Strategy for Energy and Economic Renewal*, ed. Daniel Yergin and Martin Hillenbrand (Harmondsworth, Middlesex: Penguin Books 1982), 347.

40 U.S. Executive Office, *National Materials and Minerals Program Plan and Report to Congress* (Washington: Apr. 1982), 12.

41 John D. Morgan, "Future Demands of the United States for Strategic Minerals," in *American Strategic Minerals*, 60.

42 Amos A. Jordan and Robert A. Kilmarx, *Strategic Mineral Dependence: The Stockpile Dilemma*, Washington Papers, vol. 7, no. 70 (Washington: Center for Strategic and International Studies, Georgetown University 1979), 18–19; Hans H. Landsberg and John E. Tilton, with Ruth B. Haas, "Nonfuel Minerals," in *Current Issues in Natural Resource Policy*, ed. Paul R. Portney (Washington: Resources for the Future 1982), 91–95. I return to this discussion in Ch. 8.

43 John I. Cameron, "Nickel," in *Natural Resources in U.S.-Canadian Relations*, vol. 2: *Patterns and Trends in Resource Supplies and Policies*, ed. Carl E. Beigie and Alfred O. Hero, jr. (Boulder, CO: Westview Press 1980), 87; U.S. Bureau of Mines, *Mineral Commodity Summaries, 1985* (Washington: Department of the Interior 1985), 106.

44 John M. Dunn, "American Dependence on Materials Imports: The World-Wide Resource Base," *Journal of Conflict Resolution* 4 (Mar. 1960):118.

45 T.S. Lovering, *Minerals in World Affairs* (New York: Prentice-Hall 1943), 237.

46 Archer, "Definition of Strategic Minerals," 2.

47 Though it is not, to be sure, uncommon for a country to import a strategic mineral and export it again, whether in modified form or as a simple transshipment.

48 T.D. Weldon, *The Vocabulary of Politics* (Harmondsworth, Middlesex: Penguin Books 1953), 26–7.

49 Szuprowicz, *How to Avoid Strategic Materials Shortages*, 1.

50 Brian J. Skinner, "A Second Iron Age Ahead?", *American Scientist* 64 (May-June 1976):258–69. The "strategic" nature of iron ore has been highlighted in the debate in Sweden on whether that country's iron ore exports to Germany prolonged the Second World War. The thesis that they did is argued in Rolf Karlbom, "Sweden's Iron Ore Exports to Germany, 1933–1944," *Scandinavian Economic History Review* 13 (1965):65–93. Rebuttals include Alan S. Milward, "Could Sweden Have Stopped the Second World War?" and Jorg-Johannes Jager, "Sweden's Iron Ore Exports to Germany, 1933–1944," both in *Scandinavian Economic History Review* 15 (1967):127–47.

51 Michael Howard, *The Franco-Prussian War: The German Invasion of France, 1870–1871* (New York: Macmillan 1961), 40–1. German statesmen actually would have preferred to receive Belfort instead of the Lorraine iron ore fields as a prize of war, but in the face of strenuous French opposition to the transfer of the former, they settled for part of Lorraine. But so poorly formed was their knowledge of the Lorraine fields that the Germans left more than half of the Lorraine deposits in French hands. In any event, not until the discovery of the basic Bessemer, or Thomas-Gilchrist, process in 1879 would the high-phosphorus Lorraine ores become practical for steelmaking. Eckel, *Coal, Iron, and War,* 56–8.

52 Leith, "Mineral Resources and Peace," 515–16.

53 Robert Strausz-Hupé, *Geopolitics: The Struggle for Space and Power* (New York: G.P. Putnam & Sons 1942), 99–100.

54 The meaning of international equality in the contemporary context is explored in Robert W. Tucker, *The Inequality of Nations* (New York: Basic Books 1977).

55 R.R. Kuczynski, *"Living-Space" and Population Problems,* Oxford Pamphlets on World Affairs, no. 8 (Oxford: Clarendon Press 1939), 5.

56 Patrick Salmon, "British Plans for Economic Warfare against Germany, 1937–1939: The Problem of Swedish Iron Ore," in *The Second World War: Essays in Military and Political History,* ed. Walter Laqueur (London: Sage 1982), 31–49.

57 Moritz J. Bonn, *The Crumbling of Empire: The Disintegration of World Economy* (London: George Allen & Unwin 1938), 209; David L. Gordon and Royden Dangerfield, *The Hidden Weapon: The Story of Economic Warfare* (New York: Harper & Bros. 1947), 8.

58 C.K. Leith, J.W. Furness, and Cleona Lewis, *World Minerals and World Peace* (Washington: Brookings Institution 1943), 47.

59 Leith, "Mineral Resources and Peace," 519–21; Robert C. North, "Toward a Framework for the Analysis of Scarcity and Conflict," *International Studies Quarterly* 21 (Dec. 1977):569–91.

60 Emeny, *Strategy of Raw Materials,* 23–4; J. Hurstfield, "The Control of British Raw Material Supplies, 1919–1939," *Economic History Review* 14 (1944):26–7.

61 Hjalmar Schacht, "Germany's Colonial Demands," *Foreign Affairs* 15 (January 1937):228.

62 Leith, Furness, and Lewis, *World Minerals and World Peace,* 48.

63 Lovering, *Minerals in World Affairs,* 84.

64 Eckes, *United States and the Global Struggle for Minerals,* 58.

65 James A. Miller, Daniel I. Fine, and R. Daniel McMichael, *The Resource War in 3-D: Dependency, Diplomacy, Defense* (Pittsburgh: World Affairs Council of Pittsburgh 1980); U.S. House, Committee on Foreign Affairs, Subcommittee on Africa, *The Possibility of a Resource War in Southern Africa,* 97th Cong., 1st sess. (Washington: U.S. Government Printing Office, July 1981). For a critical analysis of this perspective, see Jock A. Finlayson and David G. Haglund, "Whatever Happened to the Resource War?" *Survival* 29 (Sept./Oct. 1987):403–15.

66 See in particular two articles by Robert W. Tucker: "The Purposes of American Power," *Foreign Affairs* 59 (Winter 1980/81):241–74; and "Oil: The Issue of American Intervention," *Commentary* 59 (Jan. 1975):21–31. Also relevant is Geoffrey Kemp, "Military Force and Middle East Oil," in *Energy and Security,* ed. David A. Deese and Joseph S. Nye, A Report of Harvard's Energy and Security Research Project (Cambridge MA: Ballinger 1981), 365–85; and David G. Haglund, "The Question of Persian Gulf Oil and U.S. 'Vital' Interests," *Middle East Focus* 7 (Sept. 1984):7–11ff.

67 For an assessment of likely Soviet energy needs in the 1980s, see Thane Gustafson, "Energy and the Soviet Bloc," *International Security* 6 (Winter 1981/82):65–89.

68 This thesis was advanced in Robert Moss, "Reaching for Oil: The Soviets' Bold Mideast Strategy,"

Saturday Review (4 Apr. 1980):14–22; and Edward Friedland, Paul Seabury, and Aaron Wildavsky, *The Great Détente Disaster: Oil and the Decline of American Foreign Policy* (New York: Basic books 1975), 50.

69 Robert L. Pfaltzgraff, jr., "Resource Issues and the Atlantic Community," in *Atlantic Community in Crisis: A Redefinition of the Transatlantic Relationship*, ed. Walter F. Hahn and Robert L. Pfaltzgraff, jr. (New York: Pergamon Press 1979), 299. American concern for the security of sea lanes is conveyed in U.S. Department of the Navy, Chief of Naval Operations, *U.S. Lifelines: Imports of Essential Materials—1967, 1971, 1975—and the Impact of Waterborne Commerce on the Nation* (Washington: U.S. Government Printing Office 1978).

70 Ruth W. and Uzi B. Arad, "Scarce Natural Resources and Potential Conflict," in Ruth W. Arad et al., *Sharing Global Resources* (New York: McGraw-Hill 1979), 71–2.

71 Venezuelan Ministry of Energy and Mines, *Carta Semanal*, no. 1328, 15 Feb. 1985, p. 7.

72 Preface to Gray, *Geopolitics of the Nuclear Era*, vii.

73 "Scarce Natural Resources," 104.

74 Klaus Knorr, *Military Power and Potential* (Lexington, MA: D.C. Heath 1970), 15. Also see the same author's earlier work, *War Potential of Nations*, 40–60, for a conceptual analysis of military potential.

75 Ray S. Cline has devised a formula for measuring the perceived power of states, even though he concedes that some of his variables are impossible to quantify. The formula states that $Pp = (C + E + M) \times (S + W)$, where Pp = Perceived Power, C = Critical Mass (or Population plus Territory), E = Economic Capability, M = Military Capability, S = Strategic Purpose, and W = Will to Pursue National Strategy. Cline, *World Power Assessment*, 34. For an interesting review of various scholars' efforts to operationalize power, see James Lee Ray, *Global Politics*, 3rd ed. (Boston: Houghton Mifflin 1987), Ch. 6: "Comparing States and Foreign Policies."

76 Emeny, *Strategy of Raw Materials*, 1. Also see George Otis Smith, ed., *The Strategy of Minerals: A Study of the Mineral Factor in the World Position of America in War and in Peace* (New York: D. Appleton 1919), 26; Russell N. Fifield and G. Etzel Pearcy, *Geopolitics in Principle and Practice* (Boston: Ginn 1944), 37–8; and Leith, *World Minerals and World Politics*, 142.

77 C.W. Wright, "Germany's Capacity to Produce and Consume Metals," *Mineral Trade Notes*, Special Supplement no. 4 (Washington: U.S. Bureau of Mines, Nov. 1936), 34.

78 Eckes, *United States and the Global Struggle for Minerals*, 121–4; Dunn, "American Dependence on Materials Imports," 106–7; Michael B. Stoff, *Oil, War, and American Security: The Search for a National Policy on Foreign Oil, 1941–1947* (New Haven: Yale University Press 1980), 209.

79 Edward S. Mason, "American Security and Access to Raw Materials," *World Politics* 1 (Jan. 1949):151–3.

80 Mancur Olson, jr., "American Materials Policy and the 'Physiocratic Fallacy'," *Orbis* 6 (Winter 1963):680.

81 Charles L. Schultze, "The Economic Content of National Security Policy," *Foreign Affairs* 51 (Apr. 1973):523.

82 This, of course, is the argument currently being made by Paul Kennedy and David Calleo, among others, about the security consequences of relative economic decline. See Paul Kennedy, *The Rise and Fall of the Great Powers* (New York: Random House 1987); and David P. Calleo, *Beyond American Hegemony: The Future of the Western Alliance* (New York: Basic Books 1987).

83 Emeny, *Strategy of Raw Materials*, 127–9; Lovering, *Minerals in World Affairs*, 167.

84 Preston E. Cloud, jr., "Realities of Mineral Distribution," *Texas Quarterly* 11 (Summer 1968):108.

85 Nazli Choucri and Robert C. North, "Dynamics of International Conflict: Some Policy Implications of Population, Resources, and Technology," in *Theory and Policy in International Relations*, ed. Raymond Tanter and Richard H. Ullman (Princeton: Princeton University Press 1972), 87–8. Also see Andrew Scott, *The Dynamics of Interdependence* (Chapel Hill: University of North Carolina Press 1982).

86 Eckes, *United States and the Global Struggle for Minerals*, 54–5.

87 Harry N. Holmes, *Strategic Materials and National Strength* (New York: Macmillan 1942), 36–38; G.A. Roush, *Strategic Mineral Supplies* (New York: Macmillan 1939), 31–69, 97–129; Leonard L. Fischman, *World Mineral Trends and U.S.Supply Problems* (Washington: Resources for the Future 1980), 15–16; Michael W. Klass, James C. Burrows, and Steven D. Beggs, *International Minerals Cartels and Embargoes: Policy Implications for the United States* (New York: Praeger 1980), 135–6; U.S. Congress, Office of Technology Assessment, *Strategic Materials: Technologies to Reduce U.S. Import Vulnerability* (Washington: U.S. Government Printing Office 1985), 27.

88 John E. Tilton, *The Future of Nonfuel Minerals* (Washington: Brookings Institution 1977), 9.
89 Eckel, *Coal, Iron, and War,* 118.
90 J.W.F. Rowe, *Primary Commodities in International Trade* (Cambridge: Cambridge University Press 1965), 79–83.
91 Eckes, *United States and the Global Struggle for Minerals,* 73.
92 H.D. Henderson, *Colonies and Raw Materials,* Oxford Pamphlets in World Affairs, no. 7 (Oxford: Clarendon Press 1939), 30.
93 Schacht, "Germany's Colonial Demands," 229.
94 Quoted in Kenneth N. Waltz, *Theory of International Politics* (Reading, MA: Addison-Wesley 1979), 140.
95 Herbert Feis, "Raw Materials and Foreign Policy," *Foreign Affairs* 16 (July 1938):579.
96 Albert O. Hirschman, *National Power and the Structure of Foreign Trade* (Berkeley: University of California Press 1945), 14–15. For other discussions of German utilization of trade as a political weapon in the 1930s, see Cleona Lewis, *Nazi Europe and World Trade* (Washington: Brookings Institution 1941); and Herbert Feis, *The Changing Pattern of International Economic Affairs* (New York: Harper & Bros. 1940; reprint ed., Port Washington, NY: Kennikat Press, 1971).
97 John E. Tilton and Hans H. Landsberg, "Nonfuel Minerals: The Fear of Shortages and the Search for Policies," in *U.S. Interests and Global Natural Resources: Energy, Minerals, Food,* ed. Emery N. Castle and Kent A. Price (Washington: Resources for the Future 1983), 48–80.
98 Cooper, "Natural Resources and National Security," 193.
99 Tilton, *Future of Nonfuel Minerals,* 2; IESI, *Raw Materials and Foreign Policy,* 2.
100 Donella H. Meadows et al., *The Limits to Growth* (New York: Universe Books 1972). For critical analyses of this report, see Eric Ashby, "A Second Look at Doom," *Encounter* 46 (Mar. 1976):16–24; and Harold J. Barnett, "Energy, Resources, and Growth," in U.S. Congress, Joint Economic Committee, *Resource Scarcity, Economic Growth, and the Environment,* Hearing before the Subcommittee on Priorities and Economy in Government, 93rd Cong., 1st sess. (Washington: U.S. Government Printing Office 1974), 171–90.
101 G.J.S. and M.H. Govett, "The Concept and Measurement of Mineral Reserves and Resources," *Resources Policy* 1 (Sept. 1974):47.
102 James F. McDivitt, *Minerals and Men: An Exploration of the World of Minerals and Its Effect on the World We Live In* (Baltimore: Johns Hopkins University Press, Resources for the Future 1965), 68–71.
103 Jordan and Kilmarx, *Strategic Mineral Dependence,* 11–12.
104 James Boyd, "Minerals and How We Use Them," in *The Mineral Position of the United States, 1975–2000,* ed. Eugene N. Cameron (Madison: University of Wisconsin Press 1973), 7.
105 T.S. Lovering, "Non-Fuel Mineral Resources in the Next Century," *Texas Quarterly* 11 (Summer 1968):128–9.
106 Tilton, *Future of Nonfuel Minerals,* 92.
107 The "declining-hegemony" thesis is advanced by Krasner, *Defending the National Interest,* 352.
108 For analyses of the viability of "resource power," see Carmine Nappi, *Commodity Market Controls: A Historical Review* (Lexington, MA: D.C. Heath 1979); and Robert L. Rothstein, *Global Bargaining: UNCTAD and the Quest for a New International Economic Order* (Princeton: Princeton University Press 1979).
109 British-North American Committee, *Mineral Development in the Eighties: Prospects and Problems* (London, Montreal, and Washington: British-North American Committee 1976), 14–15.
110 Raymond F. Mikesell, *New Patterns of World Mineral Development* (London, Montreal, and Washington: British-North American Committee 1979), 24.
111 Edward R. Fried, "International Trade in Raw Materials: Myths and Realities," *Science* 191 (20 Feb. 1976):646.
112 A good study of one country's ascent up the learning curve is Theodore H. Moran, *Multinational Corporations and the Politics of Dependence: Copper in Chile* (Princeton: Princeton University Press 1974).
113 Harald B. Malmgren, *The Raw Material and Commodity Controversy,* International Economic Studies Institute Contemporary Issues, no. 1 (Washington: IESI 1975), 6.
114 See Aleksander Markowski and Marian Radetzki, "State Ownership and the Price Sensitivity of Supply: The Case of the Copper Mining Industry," *Resources Policy* 13 (Mar. 1987):19.
115 McDivitt, *Minerals and Men,* 156.
116 David A. Baldwin, "Interdependence and Power: A Conceptual Analysis," *International Organization* 34 (Autumn 1980):471–506.

Part II

2

Canadian Mineral Policy in an International Context: The Experience of the "Boom-to-Glut" Decade, 1973–83

Andrew Fenton Cooper

INTRODUCTION

A considerable body of literature devoted to the question of minerals as crucial components of resource diplomacy has grown up since the 1970s, much of it concentrating on North-South or East-West conflict. The focus has been on commodities as sources of economic power and often also as weapons to advance foreign policy objectives. Without doubt the resource politics of the United States, the USSR, and the OPEC members have received the most intensive treatment. Increasingly, however, attention has also been given to other resource-rich countries, especially those abundant in non-fuel mineral resources. Among such countries Canada is unique.[1] On the one hand, it is an industrialized country and an integral member of the Western alliance; on the other, it depends heavily on resource exports. Canada continues to be a leading producer of many of the basic minerals essential for the running of a modern economy. It is also important in the world market for many of those minerals that may be more narrowly termed "strategic" because they are used for high technology or for military equipment. Canada has a significant share of the world's production of alloy metals and precious metals.[2] In the international politics of minerals, therefore, Canada presents a case of some interest. Reflecting its dual position as a Western country with a large and diverse mineral resource base, Canada has taken on a split personality in the sense of assuming different roles on different issues according to its perceived interest. The purpose of this chapter is to explore more fully this ambiguity, and to situate it particularly within the larger pattern of international minerals developments during the turbulent period that began with the resource scarcity climate of 1973 and culminated in the global mineral glut of 1983.

CANADIAN MINERALS IN THE EAST-WEST AND
NORTH-SOUTH CONTEXT

The Canadian role in the immediate postwar period was straightforward enough: Canada offered the West in general and the U.S. in particular certain "functional" services.[3] A crucial component of this approach was the assumption that whatever supply dislocations or emergencies occurred, Canada would remain not only a safe and plentiful but also relatively cheap resource bank for its allies. It was taken for granted that Canada's mineral resources were capable not only of supporting a much larger domestic industrial output but also of "satisfying any foreseeable demand by countries of the free world."[4] In performing this function Canada was deemed to be fulfilling an important part of its commitment to NATO and NORAD.

This view of Canada as a resource supplier to the West served to both facilitate and legitimize the integration of Canada into a continental trading system in minerals. Such a pattern of development, based on Canada's geographical proximity to the U.S., was justified not only in economic terms but also in terms of the U.S. national security.[5] Motivated by the spectre of mineral shortages during the Korean War, President Truman established a Materials Policy Commission to investigate the resource position of the U.S. Its report, entitled *Resources for Freedom,* reiterated the necessity of a systematic policy for obtaining access to resources in reliable, politically stable nations in order to uphold America's strategic superiority.[6] The enduring importance of Canada to this policy may be judged from the report prepared more than two decades later by the National Commission on Supplies and Shortages:

> Overall, Canada is far and away the United States' principal supplier of non-fuel materials. In 1976, shipments from Canada accounted for one-third of the value of all imports of crude nonfuel mineral ores, concentrates and scrap and for a slightly higher share of semi-processed minerals imports. In dollar value, these imports were about as great as those from all the developing countries of Latin America, Asia, and Africa combined. Of 33 nonfuel minerals imports listed by the Bureau of Mines, Canada is among the principal sources for twenty, Australia for eight, and South Africa for seven.[7]

A key component of this resource strategy was investment in Canada by U.S. mining multinationals in order to enhance security of supply.[8] Through a variety of incentives, including a modification in tax laws, the U.S. government made private foreign investment in mining attractive for American companies; this was justified on the basis that American companies would understandably be more responsive to American resource needs in terms of access and cost. Many American companies, in turn, were attracted to Canada because the risks were thought to be minimal. Investment patterns in minerals from 1959 to 1972 reflect this shift, as half of U.S. investment in this period went to Canada.[9]

The range of mineral options open to Canada began to broaden with the relaxation of the Cold War in the late 1960s and the advent of the resource crisis of the early 1970s. The ascendancy of the Nixon-Kissinger policy of détente allowed Canada much greater leeway in attempting to use its resources to somehow strengthen its international position. The *Limits to Growth* perspective, combined with the action of OPEC and the potential proliferation of non-oil cartels, proved instrumental in generating an ongoing debate in Canada about a new resource agenda in international relations—a debate in which the attainment by Canada of "optimum benefits" from current and future use of its resources was given priority.[10] Part of the discussion on optimizing benefits pertained to the pursuit of economic goals, in particular the question of how much Canada should sell of its resources and at what price in order to obtain advantages in growth, employment, and balance of trade.[11] But the debate on the use of natural resources equally reflected a desire by Canada "to have a greater voice in international economic affairs on a wide range of issues."[12]

Canadian resource diplomacy emerged, then, out of both the East-West and North-South contexts. Neither of these contexts has remained static; rather, both have undergone major transformations since the mid-1970s. The publicity given to the start of a "resource war" between the West and the Soviet bloc for access to the world's raw materials placed renewed emphasis, at the start of the 1980s, on conflict in the East-West context. At the same time, the ability of producer associations to manipulate commodity prices became much reduced by the economic recession. Collective action no longer appeared able to alter prices in the face of declining demand.

Concern about an East-West resource struggle stimulated a renewed consciousness about supplies and the need for "friendly" countries to take up the slack in case of interruption, while from the North-South perspective, predictions of scarcity by the Club of Rome have had to be reversed. The slowdown in the growth of the world economy weakened demand to such an extent that by the mid-1980s the overriding concern in the minerals market was not shortage but oversupply. The intense speculation about the prospects of cartelization in nonfuel minerals has likewise given way to fears about a destructive beggar-my-neighbour policy among producers.

Against this changing background, the opportunities and risks for Canada in international minerals have had to be reassessed. The fundamental question concerns the degree to which the economic potential or political leverage attributed to Canadian minerals in the 1970s has been eroded in the 1980s. In a period of increasingly cutthroat competition in minerals the issue appeared less one of "optimizing" the benefits from resources than of ensuring mere "survival."[13]

OPPORTUNITIES AND RISKS FOR CANADIAN MINERALS

A number of scenarios covering a broad range have been developed concerning a Soviet threat to Western mineral supplies. Some analysts have discerned a Soviet strategy of massive and consistent military and diplomatic expansion.[14] Others have perceived a strategy of opportunism on the part of the Soviets, who, rather than initiating action, were held to be patiently and indirectly responding to the ebb and flow of events in southern Africa.[15] In the latter case, at least, it was suggested from time to time that Canada, as a major exporter of minerals and one that stood out in this regard among the Western allies, might benefit economically from disruptions in the supply of certain selected resources. The best known example of suspected Soviet manipulation of minerals involved cobalt at or about the time of the Shaba invasion in Zaïre in May 1978. A belief spread that the Soviets took advantage of their prior knowledge of the invasion to purchase heavy amounts of the metal on the London mineral market. The ensuing price escalation led the major Western nations to convene a "cobalt consumers meeting" in London in July 1979.[16] In Canada, the cobalt scare gave a boost to the domestic industry (with Sherritt Gordon raising its selling price to U.S. $8.70 a pound in June 1978 from the $7 it had been charging at the beginning of that year).[17] Unlike Zaïre, which in the past provided more than 70 per cent of the world's cobalt supplies, Canada produces cobalt mainly as a by-product of nickel and copper production. Continuing problems in Zaïrean production, however, provided a short-term impetus for technological changes designed to allow Canada to cover more easily any future needs in the aerospace or electrical industries. For example, INCO followed Sherritt Gordon's lead in moving towards the production of electrolytic cobalt, and remains well placed to become a major actor in this industry.[18]

Where Canada's economic interests really converge with those of its Western allies are in its role as an importer/consumer. For, despite its wealth in mineral resources, Canada is not self-sufficient in every mineral required by modern

economies. To be sure, much of its industrial needs are met by domestic supplies; the steel industry, for instance, is 85 per cent based on Canadian ores. But
many minerals have to be imported. An internal report produced by the Mineral
Policy Sector of Energy, Mines and Resources (EMR) early in this decade found
that Canada was deficient in thirty-three minerals.[19] Some of these, including
phosphate rock and zirconium, exist in Canada but are not mined commercially.
Of the remaining minerals, Canada has small quantities of bentonite and tin,
but they have usually been recovered as a by-product of base minerals.[20] It has no
resources in two—aluminum (bauxite and alumina) and industrial diamonds.
Another mineral, chromium, used to be included in this last category.
Feasibility studies, however, have been done to ascertain whether low-grade
chromium deposits located in the Bird Lake and Euclid Lake areas of Manitoba
are capable of sustaining production.[21]

Canada's own supply chain exhibits certain elements of "criticality" and
"vulnerability" in that the minerals that the country lacks are key ingredients in
the economy and would be difficult to replace if supplies from present sources
were curtailed.[22] Chromium, for example, is a required additive to produce spe-
cialty steel and super alloys. Manganese is important as a hardener for steel. Indeed an EMR spokesman has been quoted as stating that "if ferrochrome were cut
off, the stainless steel industry would stop dead. And if manganese and ferromanganese imports stopped, the raw steel mills would last no more than five
months."[23] An additional cause of concern is the supply of vanadium. Used as an
alloy element in high strength and alloy steel, nearly all of this mineral is purchased from South Africa; industries that would be especially hard hit by a sharp
curtailment in imports include the Steel Company of Canada, Algoma Steel, the
Atlas Steels Division of Rio-Algom, and Sydney Steels.[24]

The ambiguous, "split personality" aspect of the Canadian position becomes
more apparent in the North-South context. A 1970s claim that Canada has
"interests similar to those of other producing countries" has been a credo of several recent Canadian governments.[25] As the OECD's largest supplier of nickel,
zinc, copper, lead, and asbestos (in terms of value), Canada naturally would
stand to gain from any measures that could provide increased returns for its resources. More specifically, Canada appears to have had a common interest with
the less developed countries (LDC's) regarding the further development of
domestic mineral-processing industries. The clearest official expression of this
common cause came in 1974, in a statement by the Canadian Secretary of State
for External Affairs to the Sixth Special Session of the UN's General Assembly:
"We believe that raw-material producing countries have a legitimate interest in
upgrading their resources."[26] Along with the LDC's, Canada has pressed for a
reduction in escalating tariffs and other forms of discrimination against highly

processed materials by the U.S. and Western Europe. One of the striking features of the Canadian economy, uncharacteristic of an industrialized country, has been the dearth of "linkages" between the natural resource sector and industries based on finished products.[27] The degree of vertical integration of the Canadian copper industry is said to be lower than that of other major producers with the exception of Peru and Zaïre. In lead and zinc the degree of integration is also considered low, with Canada ranking only ahead of Peru.[28] An apt illustration of a lack of diversification in specialized materials is found in the case of platinum. Although Canada is the third largest producer of platinum group minerals, it has remained completely dependent on foreign refiners and smelters for the finished form. This failure to build capacity to add value to primary commodities not only limits employment opportunities in Canada but also makes it much more difficult for Canadian mineral producers to cope with an uncertain market.

Canada clearly does not seek or want any radical transformation in the global economic order. Indeed, on all minerals questions it has had constantly to evaluate its interests as both an importing/consuming country and a producing/exporting one. Canada as an exporter might benefit from certain changes in international trading practices that would accord it higher prices and a greater access in mineral markets. Yet as an importer of raw materials it is as interested in low cost as any of its Western allies. Consequently, Canada has seen its fundamental objectives to be the stabilization of world mineral patterns and prices.[29]

Illustrative of this has been the question of international conventions for multinational corporations. Canada has been willing in the past to politicize its own domestic mining industry. It has moved at times to change the rules of the game by which the mining companies operate in terms of economic rent, royalty rates, and greater government control.[30] Nevertheless, it has downplayed the United Nations' Charter of Economic Rights and Duties of the State (1974), which embraces the principle of "permanent sovereignty over natural resources," in favour of the concept of "judicious use of Canadian sovereignty" over resources.[31] Needless to say, Canada opposes any expropriation of foreign-owned assets without compensation, and it likewise is against fundamental changes in the conditions of operation facing Canadian-based mining companies with interests abroad. Projects that have caused concern in this respect include INCO's Indonesian mining operations and Falconbridge's operations in the Philippines and Namibia. The Guyanese takeover of Alcan's bauxite operation is a reminder that Canadian companies are not immune to nationalizations.

Moreover, despite the rhetoric concerning co-operation, Canada did find itself engaged during the 1970s in intense competition with the LDC's over market shares for certain minerals. Although Canada's mineral exports increased in absolute terms during the late 1970s, its relative position as a supplier has suffered noticeable deterioration in recent years. Canada's share of the non-Communist world market for nickel, to take the starkest example, declined from 95 per cent in 1950 to about 60 per cent in 1970 and 43 per cent in 1977.[32] This trend reflects the proliferation of new low-cost mining operations around the world. In 1950 Canada, New Caledonia, and the Soviet Union were the only major sources of nickel. By the late 1970s nickel was produced in more than twenty countries, and output soared. A similar trend has occurred in copper. Chile, Peru, Zambia and Zaïre accounted for nearly 40 per cent of the world copper output by the late 1970s, and since then new mines have continued to come on-stream. Canada likewise lost its pre-eminent position as a silver producer to Peru and the Soviet Union during the 1970s.[33]

It would be wrong to assume that because Canada during the 1970s and early 1980s lost ground to the LDC's in terms of global mineral position, it is at a complete disadvantage to them in terms of economic factors of production. The Canadian mining industry does have several points in its favour. Its technical expertise and skilled labour force are solid attractions. Canada also benefits from relatively cheap extraction costs. For instance, nickel production from sulphide deposits found in Canada provides a competitive edge over the lateritic deposits found in tropical countries. Lateritic ores may be less expensive to develop because they are open-pit operations, but once in place their energy cost is much higher. It is interesting to note that it was this factor that prompted INCO to close the Exmibal mine in Guatemala despite its apparent attractiveness vis-à-vis Canadian mines.

But there is a negative side to Canadian mining. Many of the Canadian ore deposits are simply not as rich as those of the LDC's.[34] Those deposits that are high in ore grade are often found in remote and inaccessible areas, escalating costs for transport and construction and imposing strains on recruitment of labour.[35] To be sure, this problem of rising costs does not in itself distinguish Canada from the LDC's. One thing that does, however, is that Canada lacks the compensation of access to low-interest loans from such organizations as the International Monetary Fund (IMF) and the World Bank for exploration and development.[36] Indeed, the Canadian mining industry has more than once "complained that foreign aid programmes have created unfair competition" for it.[37]

The competitiveness of Canadian mining is also hampered by a number of constraints imposed by government for social policy ends. These constraints, for the most part not found in the LDC's, include strict environmental controls, worker health and safety legislation, the settlement of native claims, and land-use regulations. Still, the difficulties of the Canadian mining industry in the early 1980s could not be laid entirely—or even mostly—at the doorstep of government. The major contributing factor remained the lack of order in the international marketplace. In the past large companies involved in producing a particular commodity restricted output in times of poor demand. This means of controlling prices has been eroded, and it has not been replaced by any other effective mechanism. In 1970 INCO retained about 50 per cent of the world nickel market, with another 40 per cent of world supply being sold at the official producers' price by Falconbridge, Société Le Nickel, Western Mining, and others, leaving only approximately 10 per cent for the free market. By mid-1982, in contrast, more than 40 per cent of world supplies were priced at free market levels.[38] In a similar fashion, the basic producer price in zinc and the North American producer price in copper have collapsed.

This situation has been exaggerated by the mounting pressure placed on the system by the LDC's. Highly sensitive to export earnings, these countries have shown an unwillingness or an incapacity to curtail output in line with the overhanging markets; moreover, new producers have continually tried to break into the market. Peru, for example, announced plans in the late 1970s to double copper supplies despite a Western overcapacity at the time of 1.6 million tons. Chile has followed suit. In Brazil the massive Carajás iron ore project (developed with the help of a World Bank loan) has come on-stream. Such producers have an obvious need to ensure a level of production sufficient to cover their overhead costs. Several countries with state-owned or state-controlled corporations have, for their part, a great incentive to maintain sales at almost any price. Many of these countries are "one-crop" economies and are heavily dependent on these products to meet debt payments, expand or maintain employment, and pay for imports.[39] The short-term gain (often facilitated by currency devaluations) is maximized at the expense of long-term stabilization. As the *Financial Post* commented more than a decade ago: "Canada's mining industry, and that of nearly every developed country, is fighting a new kind of trade war that everybody loses, but in which the less developed nations can claim some sort of Pyrrhic victory."[40]

One of the most dramatic signs of the LDC challenge in terms of mineral exports has been the frequent use by many of these countries of countertrade techniques. Certainly the Canadian mining industry has on occasion been "sideswiped" when its competitors in the Third World have engaged in practices of this type. This sideswipe effect may be illustrated with reference to potash and asbestos. In the case of potash, Jordan can be singled out as an international competitor that has cut into Canada's export sales through the utilization of countertrade.[41] In the case of asbestos, Canada has lost market share in India to Zimbabwe.

Other possible scenarios for the future must be taken into account. One of these is that the East-West dimension will meld into the North-South one, as for instance through increased Soviet bloc (including Cuban) output. Already Canada and other producers of nickel face competition from expanding sales by the Soviet Union.[42] Another prospect, of course, is that there will be a new rush of minerals to the international market in the late 1990s and beyond through seabed ventures.

The overall effect of low demand and a large surplus production capacity left Canada in an exposed competitive position during the market slump of the late 1970s and early 1980s. In order to survive as a producer at all, the domestic mining industry had to cut costs. In its most drastic form this response meant closures of high-cost mines. Eight large nickel-copper mines were shut down for at least some time in 1978. Seven big new projects were slowed or halted after being deemed too expensive. In 1977 INCO began a program of cutbacks and continued the process into the 1980s. Falconbridge did the same. Because of Brian Mulroney's role, the most publicized instance of a cutback came when the Iron Ore Company of Canada closed down its operations at Schefferville, Quebec. These closures meant heavy unemployment in the industry. One study established that by early 1983 more than 50 per cent of a labour force of 130,000 or 135,000 previously employed in mining were out of work.[43]

Finally, it appears unlikely that Canada will be able to counterbalance its relatively declining position in the international mineral markets by capturing new markets in processed or refined metals at the expense of the LDC's. As the LDC's move to establish smelters, refineries, and fabricating units at source, there is some basis for claiming that they will have an advantage in these sectors as well. Facilitated by the introduction of the Generalized System of Preferences (GSP), LDC exports of processed and semi-processed metals to the OECD countries have increased substantially in recent years. Furthermore, there is reason to believe that this trend will continue in the future.

THE FUTURE DIRECTION OF CANADIAN MINERALS POLICY

The above discussion suggests a number of questions about the role of Canadian minerals in both the East-West and North-South contexts. Viewing Canada first as a producing/exporting country, one sees that the most pertinent question is whether the political climate in the country during the past decade has undermined Canada's single biggest advantage over the LDC's, namely, reliability of supply. A pessimistic attitude about Canada in this respect has emerged, in some respects because of the perceived balkanization of Canada. Actions such as the Quebec government's takeover of the asbestos industry have led to concern about barriers to investment along regional lines. However, for the better part of a decade—and especially after the advent of the Reagan administration—

attention focused mainly on the question of whether Canada's flirtation with economic nationalism reduced confidence in the country as a safe location of investment and as a supplier of minerals. In the early 1980s some American observers feared that this was the case. An editor of a Washington-based newsletter on resource strategy stated in 1981, for example, that "the developing minerals and energy situation in Canada is such that the reliability of traditionally friendly Canada as a long term source of strategic minerals for America must be questioned."[44] Another U.S. mineral analyst wrote in *Business Week* that economic nationalism in Canada "threatens to revive the doctrinaire demands of the mid-1970s among governments of the LDC's."[45]

Certainly it cannot be disputed that the "Canadianization" policies of the Trudeau government were irritants in Canadian-American relations.[46] The screening of all new Canadian investments, including takeovers, by the Foreign Investment Review Agency (FIRA) was seen by the U.S. as an impediment to resource investment. Although 90 per cent of the cases FIRA reviewed were accepted, there remained a widespread feeling that it discouraged business activity because of delays or unreasonable demands. The Canada Development Corporation's deal with Société Nationale Elf-Aquitaine for an exchange of Texas Gulf shares was viewed as a harbinger of more widespread nationalistic policies in the mining sector along the lines of the National Energy Program. Among the principal properties of Texas Gulf was the rich Kidd Creek mine in northern Ontario.

It may be argued, though, that these "disheartening" signs regarding Canada's reliability as a long-term supplier of minerals have been somewhat exaggerated. The Trudeau government did not try to control or manipulate the mineral trade with the U.S. Nor did Canada discriminate against American companies outside of the oil and gas sector. On the contrary, the Trudeau government repeatedly assured the mining industry in very clear terms that what was applied to the oil and gas industry did not apply to nonfuel minerals.[47] Apropos of this assurance, the president of the Mining Association of Canada remarked to an American audience in 1982 that there is "no reason to doubt that they mean what they say."[48] If Canada appeared generally less attractive to investors and importers in the early 1980s, economic, more than political or strategic factors, have to be taken into account in any explanation. Demand for many minerals was simply not very strong. The change that may now be taking place is perhaps due to Canada's attractiveness as a supplier in more selected items rather than in the traditional base minerals. The development of the Mount Pleasant tungsten-molybdenum mine by the Sullivan Mining Group in the midst of all the cutbacks adds some credence to this argument.

Paradoxically, the most significant (if unintended) consequence of Canadian economic nationalism has been to hinder diversification in investment away from the U.S. to Western Europe, a region that, unlike the U.S., has no great reserves of many of the basic minerals. There were signs in the mid-1970s that European mining companies were growing hesitant about entrepreneurial risktaking in the Third World; given that hesitancy, it is understandable why Canada was considered a potential target for much higher levels in investment. Not only was Canada stable politically, but it had been actively pursuing (since the early 1970s) economic co-operation with Europe as part of the Third Option. Despite the early promise, however, there has been relatively little progress over the past decade with regard to European investment in Canadian mining.

The experience of the Federal Republic of Germany is illustrative. Judging from the fact that a large trade delegation from West Germany was sent to Canada in 1979 to explore the possibilities of achieving greater bilateral co-operation in mineral development, there was good reason to believe that West German mineral importers were initially attracted by conditions in Canadian mining despite the generally higher costs. Indeed, the West German mining industry looked to increase its investment in several projects in Canada. Metallgesellschaft took a 14 per cent stake in Teck's Highmont copper-molybdenum mine.[49] Urangesellschaft, for its part, became involved in two uranium projects in northern Saskatchewan. The rejection by FIRA of Preussag's application to acquire the British Metal Corporation (Canada) in December 1979, however, created a great change in outlook concerning investment in Canada. Reflecting the European sense of insecurity in resources, the West German economic minister at the time stated repeatedly that "a relaxation [of FIRA] would be desirable, as this would improve the framework conditions for investment decisions by German companies."[50]

From the perspective of Canada as a consumer/importer, the issue that must be addressed is how Canada has been affected by the various mineral policy options pursued by its allies. In analysing the options open to the U.S. and Western Europe for securing supplies, it is possible to imagine Canada finding itself handicapped in market terms. One thing is certain: Canada will not be able to rely on any co-ordinated western approach to the question. Some provision has been made for a NATO-directed Central Supply Agency in time of war, but otherwise each country is left to do what it feels is in its own national interest.

The Lomé II and Lomé III Conventions between the European Community and the African-Caribbean-Pacific (ACP) countries have some adverse implications for Canada.[51] Designed by the European Community (EC) as an "insurance" scheme for a number of minerals essential to its member states, Lomé II placed Canada at a double disadvantage. It acted, on one hand, to reduce Canada to the position of a residual supplier of copper and cobalt to the EC.[52] On the other hand, the agreement made it more difficult for Canada to acquire its own raw material requirements from ACP countries. This last point is important with respect to manganese from Gabon and bauxite from Guinea and Sierra Leone.[53] Although the main emphasis of Lomé III is on agricultural development, it does extend the mineral arrangements to include guarantees for private investment in ACP countries. These guarantees are particularly relevant to the smaller EC countries, which, unlike West Germany, France, and Britain, do not have their own investment-protection agreements with most of the individual ACP states.

Policy changes during the Reagan administration concerning national stockpiles of strategic minerals can also be potentially detrimental to Canada. One little-noted danger is that Canada could allow itself to become over-reliant on U.S. stocks—stocks that it seems unrealistic to expect the U.S. would release during an emergency. As former Congressman James Santini has stated: "Any foreign government relying on the mineral stockpiles of the U.S. is investing its expectations in an illusion."[54] A more important threat to Canadian interests stems from recently invoked administration plans to sell off several commodities currently being stockpiled. Nor is it likely that for those commodities where one can expect a build-up of stocks there will be anything like the demand for Canadian minerals that existed in an earlier stockpiling era.

It has been suggested that Canada take steps to ensure the introduction of a comprehensive international minerals policy, one that would allow it to deal with the specific problems facing it both as a producing/exporting and a consuming/importing country. One possible path, mooted a decade or so ago, would be for Ottawa simply to try to steer a middle course, attempting to balance or manoeuvre between Canada's different roles so as not to alienate its Western allies or the LDC's. This approach fits well into the country's older diplomatic tradition of "the helpful fixer." Its advantage in theory would be that it would allow Canada to gain benefits without undue risks. In practice the approach would mean that Canada would continue to support orderly market development in international commodity negotiations. Great stress would remain on the establishment of "international commodity arrangements, in which both national exporters and national importers were represented,"[55] not on confrontations between the two groups.

The limitations of this approach are obvious. In particular, it does not address the possibility that the parties in question may well have irreconcilable interests. For example, in the case of International Commodity Arrangements the LDC's have sought a greater market share, not orderly market development.[56] In this circumstance the only type of agreement acceptable to the LDC's would be one that allowed them first claim to any market growth, whether by special concessions or by the restriction of production and exports of industrial countries such as Canada. Under such arrangements, mining industry spokesmen have warned that "Canada would have to relinquish position in world markets and, in times of oversupply, curtail output and finance surplus production from the developing countries."[57] For its part, the U.S. wants no part of any international agreements other than those dealing with information and technical knowledge.

Given these polarized views, Canada runs the danger of being regarded less as a helpful fixer than as a meddlesome actor. In the past, Canada has shown itself capable of moving from high-minded idealism to hardball politics; notwithstanding its adherence to equitable trading practices, Canada was one of the last of the industrialized countries to comply with the GSP. Likewise, Canada's stands at the United Nations Conference on the Law of the Sea (UNCLOS) have had a large self-serving component. Such an approach, not surprisingly, can lead to resentment rather than appreciation.[58]

One may conclude that the range of choice in a minerals policy lies between a "fallback" policy (with greater attention being paid to the meshing of Canadian and U.S. interests) and a more active, "creative" policy.[59] A requisite feature of the latter course of action would be some form of mechanism to co-ordinate and harmonize the activities of government and business.[60] A glimpse of how a more dynamic policy might work in terms of mineral procurement may be gained from a study of Japanese, French, or West German approaches to mineral policy.[61] By utilizing the same techniques, including concessionary loans for the prospecting costs of Canadian firms, risk sharing, and joint ventures, Canada could not only expand domestic production in selected items, but it could more easily secure its supplies of raw materials such as bauxite, chromium, and manganese found in the Third World. Furthermore, this policy could be fitted into a national industrial strategy. The loss of export markets for Canadian basic minerals could be compensated for somewhat by the export of machinery, equipment, and expertise and general know-how on the one hand, and the establishment of a more diversified domestic refining industry on the other.[62] Such, at least, is the ideal. It remains to be seen what the limitations of these options would be, especially in terms of business reaction to them, to say nothing of market forces.

CONCLUSION

This chapter has sought to supply an overview of the international context within which Canadian mineral policy was made in the critical period from 1973 to 1983. It has identified themes, many of which will be treated in greater detail elsewhere in this volume, that have had a bearing on current and recent attempts by policymakers to ensure that Canada's mineral interests have been articulated and defended. It has not always proved possible for those interests to be successfully prosecuted, for many reasons. Paramount among the obstacles confronting Canadian mineral policy one finds those imposed by the changes in the international system discussed in this and other chapters of this volume. This is not to say that systemic forces strip Canada of all freedom of manoeuvre; they do impose severe constraints, however—constraints that must be borne in mind by all who would write about or make Canadian mineral policy.

NOTES

1 Harald von Riekhoff, "The Natural Resource Element in Global Power Relationships," *International Perspectives* (Sept./Oct. 1974):21–22; Garth Stevenson, "Canada in the United Nations," in *A Foremost Nation: Canadian Foreign Policy and a Changing World,* ed. Norman Hillmer and Garth Stevenson (Toronto: McClelland & Stewart 1977), 169.

2 Government of Canada, *Canadian Minerals Yearbook, 1985: Review and Outlook* (Ottawa: Energy, Mines and Resources Canada 1986).

3 See, for example, John W. Holmes, "Canadian External Policies since 1945," in *The Better Part of Valour: Essays on Canadian Diplomacy* (Toronto: McClelland & Stewart 1970), 5–15.

4 House of Commons, *Debates,* 1 June 1961, p. 5690. See also Gordon M. Grant, "Our Mines Build Foundations for Freedom," *Financial Post,* 8 Mar. 1952.

5 Richard Shaffner, "The Resource Sectors of the United States and Canada: An Overview," in *Natural Resources in U.S.-Canadian Relations,* ed. Carl Beigie and Alfred O. Hero (Boulder, CO. Westview Press 1980), 17.

6 President's Materials Policy Commission, *Resources for Freedom (Washington:* U.S. Government Printing Office 1952).

7 National Commission on Supplies and Shortages, *Government and the Nation's Resources* (Washington: U.S. Government Printing Office 1976). Also see Congressional Research Service, Library of Congress, *A Congressional Handbook on U.S. Materials Import Dependence/Vulnerability. Report to The Subcommittee on Economic Stabilization of the Committee on Banking, Finance and Urban Affairs* (Washington: U.S. Government Printing Office 1981), 22.

8 Robert Gilpin, *U.S. Power and the Multinational Corporation: The Political Economy of Foreign Direct Investment* (New York: Basic Books 1975), Ch. 5. Concessions in terms of tariff rates also had the effect of "achieving an economic integration of North American resources." See House of Commons, *Debates,* 10 Dec. 1947, p. 135.

9 Raymond F. Mikesell, *Nonfuel Minerals: U.S. Investment Policies Abroad,* Washington Papers (Beverly Hills: Sage 1975), 3.

10 Federal and Provincial Mines Ministers, *Towards a Mineral Policy for Canada (Opportunities for Choice)* (Ottawa: Information Canada 1974). See also Carl Beigie, "Optimum Use of Canadian Resources," *Academy of Political Science,* Proceedings, 32 (1976).

11 James Eayrs, "Canada's Emergence as a Foremost Power," *International Perspectives* (May/June 1975):24.

12 Von Riekhoff, "Natural Resource Element," 21.

13 "Message from the Associate Deputy Minister," *Canadian Mining Journal* (Feb. 1983):19.

14 See, for example, W.C.J. van Rensburg and D.A. Pretorius, *South Africa's Strategic Minerals—Pieces on a Continental Chess Board* (Johannesburg: Valiant 1977); Alfred Coste-Fioret, "The Grand Design of the USSR in Africa: To Deprive the West of Its Vital Sources of Supply," *Atlantic Community Quarterly* (Fall 1979):17.

15 M. Crawford Young, testifying on U.S. interests in Africa before the House Subcommittee on Africa, Committee on Foreign Affairs, 18 Oct. 1979. For a Soviet view of these scenarios, see A. Arbatov and

I. Amirov, "Raw Material Problems in Interstate Conflicts," *International Affairs* (Moscow) (Aug. 1984):65–73, 103.

16 A.J. Webb, *Cobalt: Medium Term Outlook for Consumption, Supply and Price* (Ottawa: Department of Energy, Mines and Resources, Mineral Policy Sector 1979).

17 John Soganich, "Sheritt Raises Price for Now-Short Cobalt," *Financial Post*, 3 June 1978.

18 The Economist Intelligence Unit, *World Commodity Outlook 1980, Industrial Raw Materials* (London: The Economist 1979); Albert Sigurdson, "Falconbridge Finds Major B.C. Copper-Cobalt Deposit," *Globe and Mail*, 19 Jan. 1983.

19 R.J. Shank, *Canada's Dependence on Imported Minerals and Metals—The Issues* (Ottawa: Department of Energy, Mines and Resources, Mineral Policy Sector 1981).

20 An exception is Rio Algom's East Kemptville, Nova Scotia, project. The Thor Lake property in the Northwest Territories appears to be an important new source of zirconium, among other strategic minerals.

21 Lawrence Welsh, "Chromium Study Could Create Major Manitoba Steel Project," *Globe and Mail*, 13 Jan. 1983. T.M. Bush, "Regional Mineral Developments," *Canadian Mining Journal* (Feb. 1983):35. See also David G. Haglund, "The Debate over Strategic Mineral Vulnerability: Implications for Canada," *Raw Materials Report* 5 (1987):16–35.

22 See "National Symposium on the Availability of Strategic Minerals," *Mining Journal* (23 Nov. 1979):437; "Strategic Minerals: A More Precise Definition," *Mining Journal* (19 Nov. 1982):7683.

23 Martin Illingworth, "Canada is Vulnerable to Mineral Disruption," *Financial Post*, 7 Feb. 1981. See also D.G. Law-West, "Chromium," *Canadian Minerals Yearbook, 1982*, 12.4.

24 Canada, Department of Energy, Mines and Resources, *Vanadium: An Imported Mineral Commodity*, Mineral Bulletin MR 188 (Ottawa: Minister of Supply and Services 1980). There are plans to extract vanadium from waste at the Suncor Oil sands plant near Fort McMurray, Alberta. "Plant Planned for Rare Metals," *Globe and Mail*, 13 Apr. 1985.

25 Donald S. Macdonald, "Macdonald: Mineral Output May Triple by Year 2000," *Financial Post*, 6 Apr. 1974.

26 Canada, Department of External Affairs, "Notes for a Statement by the Secretary of State for External Affairs, the Honourable Mitchell Sharp," delivered at the Sixth Special Session of the United Nations General Assembly (New York, 11 Apr. 1974), cited in the North-South Institute, *Commodity Trade: Test Case for a New Economic Order* (Ottawa: North-South Institute 1978), 6.

27 P.L. Bourgault, *Innovation and the Structure of Canadian Industry*, Background Studies no. 23 (Ottawa: Science Council of Canada 1972); J. Britton and J. Gilmour, *The Weakest Link: A Technological Perspective on Canadian Industrial Underdevelopment* (Ottawa: Economic Council of Canada 1977).

28 Lawrence Welsh, "Canada's Mining Felt Weakened by Lack of Integration," *Globe and Mail*, 9 Dec. 1981.

29 Macdonald, "Mineral Output may Triple by Year 2000."

30 See Science Council of Canada, *Natural Resource Policy Issues in Canada* (Ottawa: Science Council of Canada 1973).

31 Charles C. Pentland, "Domestic and External Division of Economic Policy: Canada's Third Option," in *Economic Issues and the Atlantic Community*, ed. Wolfram F. Hanrieder (New York: Praeger 1982), 141.

32 Ronald Anderson, "World Mining," *Globe and Mail*, 28 Sept. 1977.

33 Canada, Department of Energy, Mines and Resources, *Canadian Minerals and International Economic Independence*, Mineral Bulletin MR 162 (Ottawa: Minister of Supply and Services 1977).

34 P.C.F. Crowson, "Reversing the Declining Investment in Metals Exploration," *Metals and Minerals* (Mar. 1981). A recent study by Metals and Minerals Research Services found that the average copper ore graded in open pits is 0.38 per cent in Canada compared with 1.02 per cent in Chile and 0.79 per cent in Peru. *The Latin American Threat to North American Base Metals Industries* (London: Metals and Minerals Research Services 1984).

35 Lawrench Welsh, "Mining Industry Cited as Having Disadvantages," *Globe and Mail*, 21 Oct. 1981.

36 J.P. Drolet, "Resource Diplomacy Revisited," a paper presented to the Seminar in Mineral Economics, Department of Metallurgical Engineering, McGill University, 14 Feb. 1977; "Constraints on Canadian Mine Development," *Mining Journal* (May 1984):312.

37 Hon. Judy Erola, "Managing Canada's Resources: A Government Perspective," *CIM Bulletin* (June 1981):41.

38 "Nickel: Problems Remain," *Mining Journal* (25 Mar. 1983):7701.

39 Denis Pirages, *Global Ecopolitics: The New Context for International Relations* (North Scituate, MA: Duxbury 1978), 157. One result of this "unfair" competition has been a protectionist backlash in developed countries.

40 Patrick Bloomfield, "World Metal Trade Seers INCO," *Financial Post*, 29 Oct. 1977. More recently, the *Northern Miner* has stated that "it is really the Third World and developing countries which are killing and taking over our export markets." "Copper Picture Remains Grim," 1 Sept. 1986.

41 See, for example, Andrew McIntosh, "Jordanian Potash Project Will Cut into Sales Growth," *Globe and Mail*, 26 Aug. 1985.

42 Lawrence Welsh, "INCO, Falconbridge Facing Soviet Market Threat," *Globe and Mail*, 2 Oct. 1982. INCO (Europe), with other companies, complained that Soviet nickel was being dumped.

43 Wilfrid List, "More than Half Now Jobless in Canadian Mining Industry," *Globe and Mail*, 2 Feb. 1983. Mulroney has admitted that the "ideal situation" for iron ore production was in Brazil not Quebec. *Where I Stand* (Toronto: McClelland & Stewart 1983), 221–2.

44 Lawrence Welsh, "U.S. Advisor Sees Canada's Politics Undermining Its Reliability as Supplier," *Globe and Mail*, 19 Oct. 1981.

45 Daniel I. Fine, "Canada Adds Fuel to a 'Resource War'," *Business Week*, 27 July 1981.

46 See, for an account of such irritation, Jock A. Finlayson and David G. Haglund, "Oil Politics and Canada-United States Relations," *Political Science Quarterly* 99 (Summer 1984):271–88.

47 Canada, Department of Energy, Mines and Resources, *Mineral Policy: A Discussion Paper* (Ottawa: Energy, Mines and Resources Canada 1981), 66; Jennifer Lewington, 'Mine Study Will Not Mimic Oil Sector,' *Globe and Mail*, 3 Nov. 1981. Even a background study for a U.S. congressional subcommittee suggested "the need to avoid possible exaggeration and over-reaction" concerning Canadian economic nationalism. Congressional Research Service, *A Congressional Handbook on U.S. Materials Import Dependence/Vulnerability*, 166.

48 Special Report on Mining, "Message to U.S.: No NEP for Canadian Mining," *Financial Post*, 6 Mar. 1982. Mines Minister Judy Erola told the 1982 American Mining Congress meeting that "Canada has been a major and reliable source of minerals for the United States for decades. We are proud of that record and we plan to continue to supply minerals for your economy." "Minister Seeks to Calm Fears of U.S. Investors," *Globe and Mail*, 12 Aug. 1982.

49 Lawrence Welsh, "Explorations Planned by Metallgesellschaft," *Globe and Mail*, 7 Apr. 1979; John Schreiner, "Wooing in the West," *Financial Post*, 8 Sept. 1979.

50 Josh Moskau, "Energy Costs Force Change in Export Threat," *Globe and Mail*, 2 Nov. 1981; Josh Moskau, "Investment in Canada 'incredibly repelled' by FIRA," *Globe and Mail*, 19 Oct. 1982.

51 See, for example, Michael C. Webb and Mark W. Zacher, "Canadian Export Trade in a Changing International Environment," in Denis Stairs and Gilbert R. Winham, eds., *Canada and the International Political/Economic Environment*, Research Studies, Royal Commission on the Economic Union and Development Prospects for Canada, vol. 28 (Toronto: University of Toronto Press 1985), 119.

52 The value of Canadian copper exports to EC countries declined appreciably in the mid-1980s. In contrast, a number of ACP countries (most notably, Zaïre) have raised the value of their exports to the Community during the same time period. *1986 International Trade Statistics Yearbook*, vol. 11, *Trade by Commodity* (New York: United Nations 1984), 964. The Japanese strategy of securing essential minerals through long-term transactions may reduce Canada's competitive position even further. The implications for the Canadian mining industry of this strategy stand out clearly when some of the deals negotiated by Japan with LDC's are listed. These deals include buy-back arrangements with Peru (copper ore and concentrates), Chile (iron ore), and Venezuela (aluminum); import compensation arrangements for technical aid with Malaysia (copper blister), and Mexico (copper); and a massive production-sharing joint venture in Brazil. See, for example, James I. Walsh, "The Growth of Development-for-Import Projects," *Resources Policy* (Dec. 1982).

53 Canada, Department of Energy, Mines and Resources, *Annual Review of the Canadian Mining Industry, Chromium, Manganese, 1980* (Ottawa 1980). Also, by the same author, *Annual Review of the Canadian Mining Industry, 1979: Aluminum* (Ottawa: Energy, Mines and Resources Canada 1980).

54 Illingworth, "Canada is Vulnerable to Mineral Disruption." Canada did build up small stockpiles of tin, cobalt, and antimony during the Korean War. These minerals were later placed on the market.

55 Alan R. Winberg, "Raw Material Producer Associations and Canadian Policy," *Behind the Headlines* 34 (Toronto: Canadian Institute of International Affairs 1976): 6.

56 For an excellent analysis of the interests and bargaining stances of LDC s in the commodities area, see

Jock A. Finlayson and Mark W. Zacher, *Managing International Markets: Developing Countries and the Commodity Trade Regime* (New York: Columbia University Press 1988).

57 Lawrence Welsh, "Mining Firms Warned of Competition," *Globe and Mail,* 9 Feb. 1979.

58 See for example, Peyton V. Lyon and Brian W. Tomlin, *Canada as an International Actor* (Toronto: Macmillan 1979), Ch. 9.

59 For an excellent discussion of the impact of the Canada-U.S. free trade agreement on the Canadian mineral industry, see David L. Anderson, "Implications of the Canada-USA Free Trade Agreement for the Canadian Minerals Industry," *Resources Policy* (June 1986).

60 Canada, Department of Energy, Mines and Resources, *A Mechanism to Facilitate Canadian Mineral Industry Involvement Abroad,* Mineral Policy Sector, Internal Report MRI 81/9. See also Patrick J. Caragata, *Natural Resources and International Bargaining Power: Canada's Mineral Policy Options* (Kingston, Ont.: Queen's University Centre for Resource Studies 1984).

61 P.C.F. Crowson, "The National Mineral Policies of Germany, France and Japan," *Mining Magazine* (June 1980).

62 "Mining: The New Economic Order," *Mining Journal,* (20 Dec. 1983):467; Lawrence Welsh, "Joint Ventures Could Spur Mining Exports," *Globe and Mail,* 17 Mar. 1983.

3

Interference or Safety Net: Government and the Canadian Mining Industry

David Yudelman

INTRODUCTION

This chapter draws on a short and selective history of Canadian mineral policy[1] and does not attempt to portray the history of Canadian mining. It does not claim to be comprehensive, although there is a need for a definitive history of both Canadian mining and mineral policy.

The objective of the chapter is twofold: to plug the historical gap in a makeshift and temporary way, possibly encouraging more substantial attempts by others; and, more important, to pass on to those interested in contemporary mineral policy some of the ambiguous lessons of its history. The present state of the industry and its need to take certain measures to survive, let alone prosper, in an international environment unprecedented in its competitiveness call for new approaches and solutions. Nevertheless, however important the call for novelty in policy, it must be pointed out that many of the contemporary issues are over eighty years old and have engaged some of the best minds in Canada for many years. There is much to learn from the successes and failures of the past.

Two major problems beset mineral policy: unfeasible or mutually inconsistent goals, and policy instruments that are inadequate to achieve the goal for which they are designed. Knowledge of the history of mineral policy can help us avoid both problems. While knowing what to avoid does not in itself tell one what to do and how to do it, it is an essential first step.

The fundamental policy issues confronting the Canadian mining industry are relatively few: What is the optimum growth rate and size for the industry? How shall the benefits of mining be distributed within the Canadian economy and society? How shall the costs be distributed? The history of mineral policy demonstrates that it is necessary for governments to have a fairly firm grasp of their priorities if they are to avoid merely contingent and unrelated responses to issues as they arise. Policymakers must plan to prevent fires, not merely rush from one fire to the next. This is not to argue, however, that a policy must be consistent in all respects, or that priorities be rigidly enforced. History shows that even governments that follow the most ordered set of priorities need the political space to enthusiastically embrace contradictory policy imperatives.

It is unrealistic to expect governments to operate continually with all their cards on the table. Moreover, it is possible to argue that government policies are not fully comprehensible or predictable in advance even to governments themselves. This is because they are not merely goals, but goals and instruments interacting over time. It can be argued that a policy is the actual course of action followed by governments over significant periods of time, whose pattern can be identified only by close examination of the interaction between government and other groups, such as the mining industry. This view puts both the historian and policy analyst in a privileged position to contribute to policy formulation: "policy does not seem to be a self-defining phenomenon: it is an analytic category, the contents of which are identified by the analyst rather than by the policy-maker or pieces of legislation or administration. There is no unambiguous datum constituting policy waiting to be discovered in the world. Policy may usefully be considered as a course of action or inaction rather than specific decisions or action, and such a course has to be perceived and identified by the analyst in question. Policy exists by interrogating rather than intuiting political phenomena."[2]

This chapter attempts to identify broad historical trends in Canadian mineral policy, the continuities and changes in the goals of different policy regimes, and the shifting relationship of goals to instruments. It then attempts to identify the emergence of a new mineral policy focused on maturity management. In this way it should pinpoint some of the priority areas—such as regional policy, diversification policy via spinoffs, and integration of mining into a high technology-oriented economic growth policy—while showing how they differ from or are similar to traditional concerns, such as further processing and import substitution.

It is worth repeating that this is a brief history of mineral policy rather than a history of mining. Provincial mineral policies are treated impressionistically, using case studies. There is no in-depth attempt to analyse international political aspects of policy discussed elsewhere in this volume. The chapter does, however, aim to advance our understanding of the international dimensions of Canadian strategic minerals by concentrating on what students of international politics so often omit: the domestic policy context.

FOUNDATIONS OF CANADIAN MINERAL POLICY

Paradoxically, the enduring foundations of Canadian mineral policy were laid down long before mining became a significant factor in the country's economic life. Although Canadian mining did not make a major contribution to the economy until the last hundred years, the origins of the mineral policies that guided its development date back to the earliest European settlements. The colonial and constitutional legacy dating back to the 1700s is important today. Many issues of the early period are relevant today. Their outward manifestation might have changed over time, but their content has stayed surprisingly constant.

The basic question of all mineral policy, the question from which all others flow, is "Who owns the resource?" Historically, the earliest owners of minerals were the kings or monarchs. In Egypt, Persia, and China, for example, the actual miners were slaves or paid servants of the ruler.[3] In Canada, there has been a continuation of monarchical forms of ownership in which the government, or the state it represents, has exerted control over the country's natural resources. The expression "Crown lands" is only one visible form of the durability of monarchical structures. Crown ownership stems from both British and French traditions. French seigneurial and British freehold land systems both distinguish between possession of surface rights and ownership of minerals underground, and these traditions have been transferred to North America.[4] The principle of reservation by the state, for fiscal or public interest reasons, was passed down by repetition in Ontario, substantially unaltered.

Mining developed slowly in the early 1800s, and to encourage exploration governments gradually made miners' access to Crown lands easier. In Ontario, the liberalization of reservation provisions was at first limited to the base ores, though access to the land was made easier for all the minerals. In 1864, however, the first statute governing mining in Canada East and West, the Gold Mining Act, provided for the outright sale of lands containing gold ore, with full title to the gold going to the landowner.[5] In 1866 the Gold and Silver Mining Act included a 2–10 per cent royalty on gold and silver mined, but in 1869 this was repealed by the General Mining Act, which enabled any licensed prospector to obtain full ownership rights to subsurface minerals for $1 an acre. In 1888, five years after the discovery of the major copper-nickel deposits at Sudbury, the Ontario government established a Royal Commission to analyse the province's mineral resources and the part to be played by government in exploiting them.[6] The Commission's report dealt at some length with the issue of who owns the subsurface minerals. It rejected the leasehold form of mining tenure as unacceptable and uncompetitive with the United States system of absolute title: "There are some persons who favour a return to the system of reservations and royalties abandoned and made void by the act of 1869. . . . [A]s long as mineral development in Ontario continues to depend largely upon investments of foreign capital, and especially of American capital, a liberal policy must be followed; mining lands must not be less free here than in the United States."[7]

However compelling these legal and competitive arguments may have been, the Mowat government moved in exactly the opposite direction by reimposing the reservation of minerals on all sales of agricultural land and introducing a new form of tenure, a mineral lands lease. It also proposed a royalty system for various metals. This met with stiff opposition and was postponed for seven years, after which it was restricted to net profit rather than gross income as originally intended. In spite of many subsequent changes to royalty and other provisions of the mining code, the "basic political value," the principle of a public share in natural resources, has continued to apply throughout the twentieth century for Ontario and other provinces, albeit tempered by the ever-present need to encourage the industry's further development.

The relationship of public and private sectors vis-à-vis mineral ownership remains a crucial factor in Canadian mineral policy. Although the issue predates the problem of federal-provincial jurisdiction, many accounts of Canadian mineral policy begin with this problem. Since the 1970s federal-provincial issues have tended to dominate most discussions, and this may account for any imbalance found in recent accounts of Canadian mineral policy.

Whatever their relative importance, there can be little doubt that the three major actors in the process of mineral policy formation are the private sector and the federal and provincial governments. It is vital to understand the constitutional and legal framework in which they operate. The Canadian framework is significantly different from that of most other mining countries:

> A number of major mining countries have federal institutions, since federalism is almost a necessity in countries of large geographical extent, and the larger a country is, the more likely it is to have a resource base for a significant mining industry. In most federations, however, the central government is the legal owner of mineral resources (except to the extent that they are in private hands) and can dispose of these resources with little or no restraint or influence by subnational levels of government. Only Australia shares with Canada the not always enviable distinction of being an exception to this rule.[8]

In Canada, ownership is vested in the provinces. It was entrenched in Section 109 of the British North America Act (BNA Act) of 1867 (replaced by the Constitution Act of 1982), which stated that "All lands, Mines, Minerals, and

Royalties belonging to the several provinces of Canada, Nova Scotia and New Brunswick at the Union, and all sums then due and payable for such lands, Mines, Minerals and Royalties shall belong to the several Provinces of Ontario, Quebec, Nova Scotia and New Brunswick in which the same are situate or arise, subject to any Trust existing in respect thereof, and to any interest other than that of the Province in the same."

British Columbia, Prince Edward Island, and Newfoundland later entered Confederation under similar terms. Alberta, Manitoba, and Saskatchewan were formed out of federal lands, but the mineral rights to these provinces were ceded by the federal government to the provinces in 1930 to maintain balance and equity in the federal system. This was done somewhat reluctantly even though they seemed to have little mineral potential at the time.

The BNA Act of 1867 was intended to entrench federal powers.[9] Because of the rudimentary state of the mining industry in the mid-nineteenth century, Section 109 was not thought to be incompatible with this objective. But when the mining industry expanded rapidly in the twentieth century, Section 109 had the effect of significantly shifting the balance of power towards the provinces. Since 1930 all the provinces have been in similar positions with regard to ownership of land and resources, though the degree of control and its exact forms vary because of historical factors. Over 75 per cent of Canada's provincial land areas are Crown land, and most mineral rights, including the rights to minerals found under private land, belong to the provinces. This is so in spite of the alienation of rights that occurred far more intensively in the early areas of settlement, in Eastern and Central Canada. Federal land holdings in the provinces, by contrast, are under 2 per cent of the total land area. The federal government's mineral ownership rights, then, are overwhelmingly concentrated in the territories, which explains why "Northern mineral policy" became increasingly important to the federal government in the early 1980s, though its rights continue to be challenged in many areas by Native land rights claims.

The actual mechanics of provincial ownership vary from province to province. The principle of provincial ownership itself, however, has been vital because it has been taken by the provinces to imply special rights in the taxation of mining companies and has been used by the provinces as a weapon to limit any federal intervention in resources, whether such intervention has to do with ownership or other issues. Thus in Canada the political expression of the move to community control of natural resources has usually meant a variant of economic nationalism that has been characterized as "economic provincialism."[10]

For all the problems caused by provincial ownership of natural resources, the federal government has an extensive range of powers and levers with which to formulate and implement mineral policy. To start with, it has proprietary rights to minerals in the territories, almost 40 per cent of Canada's land mass, and—a principle established only recently—to offshore minerals. Mining activity is still negligible in both areas but has long-term potential for expansion. The Constitution Act confers a number of legislative prerogatives on the federal government that are not directly connected with mineral ownership but are vital to the process of making mineral policy. The federal government has jurisdiction over "works and undertakings" that extend beyond a single province to constitute interprovincial trade. This jurisdiction, eventually extending over gas and oil pipelines, railways, and waterways, has had important effects on the development of Canadian mining, as has the federal power over international trade and over taxation, "the raising of money by any mode or system of taxation."

The federal government may also exert authority in areas not normally within its jurisdiction, on the basis of acting in what is declared to be the "national interest," "for the general advantage of Canada." Federal authority was exercised over nickel production in both world wars, backed by the threat of this declaratory power. The power was used directly with the enactment of the Atomic Energy Control Act of 1946, which placed the uranium industry under the extensive regulation of the federal government.

The early policy environment of Canadian mining is sometimes characterized as "laissez-faire."[11] This is not accurate, for though it is true that federal and provincial governments eschewed *direct* participation and interference, they did adopt and promote the objectives of encouraging investment, creating new enterprises and jobs, and fostering sources of government revenues. All of this was to be achieved by establishing a climate in which economic growth would be maximized. Mining, which was starved of investment capital and which had failed to develop as quickly as had been hoped, particularly needed such a stimulus. In Ontario the provincial government gradually liberalized the terms of access to its lands in an effort to promote exploration. After 1845, access to lands containing base metals was systematically eased. Areas of claims were reduced, the price per acre cut and licences and fees were reduced or abolished, and the time allowed for development was extended.

Some have interpreted this liberalization as a victory for special interest groups over the interests of society as a whole. H.V. Nelles, for instance, writes critically of "the permissive conditions within which special pleading eroded the power of the state."[12] He does not, however, discuss which policy alternatives might have been more viable. If one wishes to argue against development, one needs to advance alternatives. If not, to criticize governments for acting to liberalize conditions of access is to implicitly set up the counterfactual hypothesis: "If they had not made these concessions, a viable alternative policy was open to them at the time." Such a policy may have been available, but Nelles and others have not elaborated what it was.

Well over a century later, the same dilemma still faces Canadian mineral policy. The debate continues whether the Foreign Investment Review Agency (FIRA)—renamed Investment Canada—frightened development capital away from Canadian mining or was essential to capture the benefits of Canada's resources for society at large. In both the mid-nineteenth and the late-twentieth centuries, the alternatives to encouraging foreign investment have appeared to be either less investment or more government-initiated and managed enterprises. Neither alternative is without drawbacks, and it is a slow, tortuous process to come up with an acceptable blend of the two extremes.[13]

In mineral policy, then, there is a constant tension between emphasizing economic growth on the one hand and focusing on distribution (the division within society of the benefits of economic growth) on the other—a tension that is reflected in and magnified by the issues of nationalism and internationalism. In this regard, the question of further processing of copper and nickel in Ontario in the late 1800s and early 1900s provides both a case study of broad relevance and a portent of things to come in modern Canadian mineral policy.

The easing of conditions of access to and exploitation of mineral ores encouraged land speculation, particularly after 1869, and was partly responsible for the virtual monopoly that the Canadian Copper Company secured in the Sudbury area. This monopoly was accentuated because the workable deposits were so concentrated. After 1891 the Ontario government attempted to increase its revenue from nickel, with little success. Canadian Copper consolidated its position and, in alliance with the Orford Company, persuaded the U.S. government to remove tariff barriers from nickel ore and matte. This opened the U.S. market to Canadian Copper but effectively meant refining plants would be located in the U.S., as a duty of ten cents a pound on refined nickel and nickel oxide was retained.

The strength of both the U.S. government and Canadian Copper-Orford (which merged into the International Nickel Company in April 1902) meant that both the Canadian federal and the Ontario provincial governments could not impose their will on International Nickel at the time. Both governments desperately needed development capital, as well as growth and its resulting increases in employment and revenue. On the other hand, it could be argued that the company missed an opportunity to defuse a situation that was to trouble it for the next twenty years. It soon became clear to Canadian governments that the benefits of a simple "growth policy" were limited, and as a result the 1890s were marked by the struggle to impose further processing in Canada on the producers.

The struggle was orchestrated by the ousted founder of Canadian Copper, Samuel Ritchie, supported by a group of Quebec and Hamilton businessmen. Though unsuccessful in the short term, the consequent publicity created a public climate in Canada distinctly unfavourable to International Nickel. Both the federal and the Ontario governments had been slowly building up expertise of their own, capable of evaluating the conflicting claims of the various business interests; this enabled them to respond supportively to the potential rivals of International Nickel, who were themselves becoming increasingly vocal and involved in the public process of influencing policy. During the early years of the First World War, International Nickel's position on Canadian refining—that it was uneconomical—came under increasing criticism. Both the press and general public complained that the U.S., then a neutral country, was shipping refined nickel, a strategic war material, to Germany, with whom Canada was at war.

In February 1915 the Ontario government appointed the Royal Ontario Nickel Commission, composed of experts on refining nickel. In November 1915 the Imperial Munitions Board conducted an independent study on materials for munitions, concentrating on copper and nickel refining. This resulted in a note in February 1916 from the federal government to International Nickel insisting on the establishment of a nickel refinery in Canada. Partly as a result of the study and of other pressures, a small copper refinery was erected at Trail, B.C., beginning operations in 1916. Finally, in August 1916, International Nickel announced it had selected a site at Port Colborne, Ontario, for a nickel refinery. The refinery was completed less than two years later, in July 1918.

The Royal Commission's findings came out after the decision to establish the Port Colborne refinery had been made, but its mere existence, and the sorts of questions it was considering, undoubtedly influenced International Nickel's decision. The Commission found that refining in Canada would be economical, and that foreign ore producers did not (contrary to International Nickel's argument) constitute a serious potential source of competition to Canadian producers. It refused to recommend that refining in Canada be made compulsory by law, because International Nickel had already started a refinery and because it doubted that the Ontario government possessed sufficient regulatory powers to enforce refining in the province.

From 1912 to 1917, because of the difficulty of separating mining, smelting, and refining profits, an agreement was arranged according to which the company paid a fixed annual Canadian tax of $40,000 even though profits had increased from $3.5 million in 1912 to $11 million in 1916. In 1917, partly for this reason, a new Mining Tax Act was passed by the provincial government that discriminated against the nickel producers, particularly International Nickel. The new tax increased the rate on only nickel and copper from 3 per cent to 5 per cent up to a profit level of $5 million. As profits rose above $5 million, the rate increased further. The Act also permitted the deductibility of taxes paid in Canada and Great Britain, but not the U.S. The tax was made retroactive to January 1916 and International Nickel, after an unsuccessful appeal to the Canadian federal government, was forced to pay $1.3 million in back taxes.[14] Under wartime conditions the company had no alternative supply of ore, and no alternative but to pay.

The effect of the tax (which was reversed in 1924) was to reinforce International Nickel's need to start building refining capacity in Canada, not only to quieten Canadian nationalist opposition but also to avoid double taxation. The latter was particularly important as International had long-term contracts with its customers and therefore could not pass the costs on to the consumer. It became increasingly clear that taxation was a potentially powerful and underutilized instrument of government policy. Unusual and temporary conditions of nationalism and concern over the strategic implications of foreign control during the war had combined to shift the balance against International Nickel; but the resulting increased expertise and capacity of governments to generate policy, and the heightened awareness of the instruments available to them, became permanent influences on the formulation of mineral policy.

Thus another principle of mineral policy was entrenched: that of political intervention when the government and/or "public opinion" judged it to be in the provincial and national interest. From the principle of direct government intervention in times of emergency, such as war, it was but a short step to the principle of intervention at other times when the "national interest" was thought to justify it. Different governments, naturally, utilized the principle in different ways. John Diefenbaker, for example, minimized intervention whereas Pierre Trudeau intensified it.

Though this power had been allocated to the federal government at the time of Confederation, it was used sparingly until the Second World War. The experience of the nickel industry in Canada, however, showed that the principle could become a real threat in practice. Facing this sword of Damocles, the industry has been far more amenable to meeting the government's mineral policy objectives by compromise rather than confrontation.

In the Third World, of course, the concept of intervention in the public interest and the exercise of this concept have become even more important. Mexico, for example, established a Ministry of the National Patrimony to reinforce the principle that all non-renewable resources should directly benefit the nation as a whole.[15] Governments, according to this view, should be managers of resources, rather than mere custodians. Canadian governments have never accepted this view as a general rule but, since the Second World War, have on occasion taken on the role of protector of the national patrimony, the national interest, and national security.

Whatever the stance on the manager/custodian issue has been at any particular time, after the Second World War the mining industry was keenly aware that governments might invoke the national patrimony principle. The climate of mineral policy formation, therefore, was permanently changed by war, burgeoning nationalism, and the growth in the role of the state. The "nickel issue" neatly encapsulates these developments in Canada.

THE MINERAL POLICY OF GROWTH, 1945–70

The years from 1945 to 1970 were characterized both by the growth of governments and by the fairly uniform adoption of growth-oriented mineral policies. Such policies were relatively unchallenged, and there was no need to justify them in terms of Grand Theory or five-year blueprints. Towards the end of this period, however, people began to question the primacy of growth in mineral policy, and there were attempts to formulate a new national mineral policy.

The encouragement of growth that was the overriding principle of post-Second World War mineral policy was interwoven with many related goals. Growth was to be achieved by providing inducements to domestic and foreign companies to invest in Canadian mining. The success of these inducements caused governments to concern themselves increasingly with policy towards foreign investors. As has been shown in connection with the issue of further processing this area was not a new one for mineral policy. But a number of related issues emerged from it, and these need to be understood if we are to fully understand later events. The growth policy that prevailed after the Second World War provides the context for looking at important developments in several fields. These developments were the harbingers of issues that were to rock both governments and the mining industry in the 1970s. Four of the most important were: (1) growth and bureaucratization of government, (2) taxation changes, (3) foreign investment and its multiplier effect, and (4) direct government intervention.

After the Second World War both business and governments accelerated the bureaucratization of their structures and professionalized their operations. Successive federal governments established Crown corporations. The two most important in the area of natural resources were Eldorado Nuclear (1944) and Petro-Canada (1975). The incorporation of public enterprises accelerated after 1960. By 1983, there were 400 wholly owned or controlled federal Crown corporations involved in all facets of Canadian economic life.[16] At the federal government level, the forerunner of what is now the Department of Energy, Mines and Resources was the Geological Survey of Canada, established in 1841 by the first Parliament of the Province of Canada that was created by the 1840 Act of Union.[17] The Geological Survey was greatly expanded after Confederation in 1867. In 1907, in response to the requests of the Canadian Institute of Mining and Metallurgy, the federal government formed the Department of Mines. With a staff of twenty-two, the new department incorporated the Geological Survey and a new Mines Branch and provided services to the private sector—to Canadian prospectors, explorers, and metallurgists, and to those selling minerals.

During the First World War the Department of Mines grew rapidly, responding to the growing demand for war materials in Europe. Research by the department, especially in metallurgy, expanded enormously. The period from the 1920s through the early 1960s saw the bureaucratic fortunes of the department wax and wane; finally in 1966, it underwent a major reorganization, becoming the Department of Energy, Mines and Resources (EMR). The new department was made responsible for the discovery, investigation, development, and conservation of all Canada's mineral and energy resources, including the offshore resources. In addition to the traditional areas of scientific research and data collection, it was made responsible for economic research into markets and potential demand for mineral resources and energy. This new policy responsibility was an important one, and EMR was specifically authorized to carry out interdisciplinary studies in order to develop policies and plans for resource management and conservation.[18] Of course, these studies were expected to take into consideration policies developed by other departments.

Overall, however, as we shall see later, EMR has never been able to formulate mineral policy unilaterally. Within the federal government, a number of other departments and bodies have had a crucial voice in doing this. These include departments such as Finance, Regional Industrial Expansion, External Affairs, Indian Affairs and Northern Development, and Environment; federal regulatory agencies such as the Atomic Energy Board, National Energy Board, and Foreign Investment Review Agency; Crown corporations such as Eldorado Nuclear, Cape Breton Development, and Petro-Canada; and central agencies and committees such as the Prime Minister's Office, the Privy Council Office, and the Cabinet committees responsible for Planning and Priorities, Economic and Regional Development, Social Development, and Foreign and Defence Policy.

And then there are the provinces—major actors—and a large number of competing interest groups, such as local communities, environmentalists, and Native groups. Nevertheless, there is no doubt that EMR's capacity to make policy, whatever its real limitations, was considerably more significant than that of its predecessors, which had been widely regarded as technically oriented service departments, at times too ready to be the mouthpiece of the mining industry within the federal government rather than an independent source of policy advice.[19]

The provinces are able to play a major role in the formulation of Canadian mineral policy by virtue of the powers vested in them by the BNA Act of 1867 and the Constitution Act of 1982. Some of them began to make an important contribution well before the turn of the century; in many respects Ontario's mineral policy provided a model for federal policy during the First World War. Despite its role as a policymaking trendsetter, however, the Ontario government still saw a limited role for its Department of Mines (elevated to a full portfolio in 1919). This was also true of other provincial governments before the 1960s. Government departments dealing with resources tended to be broken down into branches and divisions (such as forests, mines, and petroleum) that were better adapted for co-operating with the private sector than taking independent policy initiatives or developing an overall provincial policy on natural resources. The issues they dealt with were generally technical rather than political: they usually did not deal with contentious questions and policy debates.[20]

Officials and bureaucrats with a high degree of technical knowledge were recruited. Many had worked in the private sector and shared its assumptions and values. Most continued to work closely with former colleagues and circulate freely between jobs in the public and private sectors. However, there was not much liaison with other departments, and many resource departments were isolated from other branches of the bureaucracy. This became very important later, when the provinces began to make significant policy decisions affecting the mining industry. We shall see that in a number of vital cases in the 1970s, the provincial mining departments were bypassed or ignored as was EMR at the federal level.

As we have seen, mineral policy and mining development do not move in tandem. The foundations of Canada's mineral policy were laid down long before a significant mining industry had developed. Conversely the policy clash between federal and provincial governments in the 1970s was foreshadowed by significant structural changes in the mining industry in the 1950s and 1960s. These changes were masked by developments during the Second World War, when Ottawa exercised extraordinary powers over the economy, including the resources used by the military. At the time, the federal government accounted for over 80 per cent of all government expenditure (the provinces and municipalities accounted for the other 20 per cent). This could not be maintained in peacetime, however, and after the war the provinces steadily recovered ground that they had lost to Ottawa.

A major reason for the growing strength of the provinces was the expansion of the resource industries, with the U.S. taking much of the increased production and investing much of the required capital. When American capital threatened to dry up at the end of the 1950s, the provinces began to compete for it by offering subsidies, concessions, infrastructure, and various other inducements. In the 1960s some of the provinces, far from being hostile to the federal role vis-à-vis mineral policy, actually went to Ottawa for advice on developing their own policies. The Atlantic Development Board also requested help. The federal government responded with a series of reports on how the provinces might reorganize their resource departments, what policy opportunities for mining development were available, and how the provinces might develop their own policymaking capacity;[21] ironically, some of this advice helped the provinces in their disputes with the federal government in the 1970s. With or without federal help, however, there would have been provincial policy changes in response to the rapid growth of Canadian mining.

The reports illustrate in a striking way the development of federal thinking on mineral policy, the move away from maximum growth, and the need for a more assertive, "pro-active" governmental presence in the mining industry. They strongly recommend further growth of the mining bureaucracy in the provinces, higher salaries to attract competent professionals from outside the province concerned if necessary, and the reorganization of both the internal structure of the mines departments and their relationship with other provincial departments. In the later reports, on Manitoba and British Columbia, EMR seemed to suggest a duplication of recent internal changes in EMR itself: the fostering of an internal capacity to identify development opportunities, evaluate them for feasibility and social desirability, and implement them through policy programs. Of course, when some of the provinces succeeded in doing the latter, it meant they were moving into space previously occupied not only by the private sector of the industry but by EMR itself. The challenge to EMR from the provinces in the 1970s then, was aided at the start by a paternal federal government.

When this challenge came, it did so primarily in the area of taxation. The need to encourage the development of mines and the difficulty of doing so, both in Canada and internationally, dissuaded governments from taxing mining companies heavily in the early part of the twentieth century. In fact, the federal tax system had long encouraged mining development through a "depletion allowance" (introduced at the same time as the income tax), which reduced the base on which taxable income was calculated. Depletion allowances followed U.S. precedents, as did exploration and development allowances, which treat all exploration and development costs as current and allow them to be written off immediately. The three-year tax exemption introduced in 1936 was unique to Canada, however. It exempted from income tax the profit from new mines during their first three years of production. This meant that the Canadian way of taxing mines—which was otherwise similar in most respects to the U.S. system—gave Canadian producers a competitive edge.[22]

Special taxation treatment continued to be accorded the mining industry through the 1960s, but important opposition to it came as early as the 1957 *Final Report* of the Gordon Commission, which pointed out that the industry was growing and maturing and would not be able to justify its favoured tax treatment indefinitely. In 1962 the Royal Commission on Taxation (the Carter Commission) began a lengthy re-examination of federal tax policy towards the mining industry (among others) that was to challenge the very foundations of the mineral policy of growth that had prevailed since before the Second World War.

Direct government intervention in the mining industry was another development that took shape during the "growth era." There were many reasons for this, but the two major ones were economic and nationalistic. With some exceptions both federal and provincial governments tended to avoid direct intervention until the mid-1960s when they focused on the energy sector.[23]

Canadian mining grew very rapidly in the two decades after the Second World War. By 1967 it was a leading resource industry and, by stimulating secondary and tertiary industry through its multiplier effects, created markets for other industries. As its share of GNP grew, so did its national and regional economic significance.[24] From 1950 to 1970 mineral production grew from 5.8 per cent of GNP to 7.1 per cent, or nearly $5 billion annually. Minerals and mineral products accounted for one-third of Canada's exports by 1970, 43 per cent of revenue freight traffic, and more than 12 per cent of total annual capital investment. They were also the backbone of Canadian infrastructure development.[25] Thus mineral policy was, and is, inextricably tied with overall Canadian economic development policy, with infrastructural policy, and with regional policy. In addition to being involved with the mineral sector for economic development reasons, the federal government participated directly in mineral production for nationalistic and strategic reasons, especially during the Second World War. It did so through the following routes:

(a) *Crown corporations* that gave Ottawa complete ownership and control (e.g., Wartime Metals Corporation, which mined and processed tungsten, magnesium, and molybdenum);

(b) *Crown plants* that were owned by the government but operated by such private companies as Algoma Steel and Dominion Steel and Coal; and

(c) *Crown assets* placed in privately owned and operated companies.

Over $40 million in mining assets were government-controlled by the end of the war, but were largely disposed of within a few years.[26] Eldorado Mining and Refining Company, "a crown Corporation appropriated from private industry in

1944 at the cost of over $5 million" to produce uranium, stayed in federal hands for reasons of "national security." It became the first peacetime company owned by a Canadian government to engage in mineral exploration and development.[27]

From its inception the Canadian mining industry has been dependent on foreign investment and expertise, especially from the U.S. It has also relied (and will continue to rely) heavily on foreign markets for its exports, particularly American markets. Thus the issues of foreign ownership and of further processing that were sharply focused by the debate on the nickel question in the first decades of the 1900s continued to draw the attention of policymakers and analysts after the Second World War.

In 1956, the federal leader of the Progressive Conservative Opposition, George A. Drew, renewed the age-old attack on a policy that allowed the export of unprocessed raw materials, arguing instead for "a national development policy which will develop our natural resources for the maximum benefit of all parts of Canada and encourage more processing in Canada." Was the Canadian mining industry, he asked, being forced into an undesirable and limited role as "hewers and diggers" for the United States?[28]

The following year the Gordon Commission study on Canadian mining expressed similar misgivings about Canadian processing of mineral exports.[29] Nevertheless, the proportion of Canadian copper, lead, and zinc exports in processed form showed a steady decline after 1960, largely because of increased exports to Japan in unprocessed form. Thus the perennial mineral policy issues of foreign ownership and further processing of Canada's minerals remained alive into the 1970s. In that decade, they gained vastly increased attention and became major issues of Canadian public policy. The main question increasingly came down to the deceptively simple query: Were Canadians getting optimal benefit from their resources? This formulation immediately inspired further questions, which were asked but not answered throughout the 1970s and early 1980s: Which "Canadians" does this refer to, and what are "optimal" benefits? Mineral policy, previously largely an area of such quiet consensus that many felt a policy did not exist or need to exist, now became a battleground of federal and provincial governments, as well as the private and public sectors.

THE MINERAL POLICY OF REDISTRIBUTION, 1970–8: GOVERNMENTAL RELATIONS

The worldwide growth in the role of governments in modern economies since the Depression and particularly since the Second World War is well known. Canadian governments have been no exception: the proportion of national income directed through government expanded vastly. Between 1927 and 1977 for example, it rose from 15.2 per cent to 41.1 per cent in Canada.[30] This expansion of the economic role of states has obvious and far-reaching ramifications both for the relationship of government to business and for the process of economic policy formation.

One response to the growth in the scale of government was organizational upheaval. After 1968 the new Prime Minister, Pierre Elliott Trudeau, built up a highly structured and integrated cabinet committee system. This was intended to restore to cabinet ministers power that they had increasingly lost to the deputy ministers as the scale of government expanded. The power, however, tended to shift to the prime minister and his close associates rather than to the cabinet, largely because responsibility was not clearly allocated between the various cabinet committees.[31]

The expanding role of governments has made the relationship between business and government immeasurably more complex. No longer do these two parties necessarily talk the same language. No longer can either automatically assume that it shares basic priorities with the other. After the Second World War there was agreement between business and government on the need to allocate top priority to economic development, but by 1970 a basic change had occurred. The proliferation of newly powerful and articulate interest groups and the expanding role of the state—partially to accommodate them—led to what has been regarded by some as a breakdown in the historic consensus between business and state on material goals and priorities.[32]

The institutional context of this breakdown is of interest. The 1970s witnessed the decline of the policymaking power of the traditional line departments of the federal government, and the replacement of the "mandarin bureaucrat" (the old-style power brokers) by the "bureaucratic technicians."[33] These new bureaucratic generalists ran the powerful cabinet committees and central agencies, which had grown to be so dominant since Prime Minister Trudeau established the Committee on Priorities and Planning in 1968 and entrenched "rational planning" in the federal bureaucracy generally. The committees and agencies were designed to increase collective responsibility and the input of cabinet ministers, but had the effect of drastically curtailing the influence of once omnipotent individual ministers and their deputy ministers while greatly increasing the powers of the political strategists. Power moved to the "person who knows how the system works" as opposed to the "person who is an expert in a substantive area of knowledge."[34]

The mineral policy of growth that prevailed until the 1960s was the product of input from federal departments, provincial governments, and the industry. In the 1960s, however, and particularly after the Trudeau shake-up of the federal bureaucracy in 1968, EMR moved consciously towards claiming for itself a more "pro-active" planning role in mineral policy, a move that corresponded to developments taking place with varying speed elsewhere in the federal bureaucracy. Increasingly called into question was the simple mineral policy of growth, according to which the benefits would trickle down to other groups in Canadian society. Replacing it was the concept of "optimum development," or balanced development, in which government would play an important role in determining which interests should get the fruits of development. The new policy not only was redistributive but also advocated a concentrated effort by government to develop new project ideas and encourage their being put into effect. The change in the perception of government's role from facilitator to active participant, from administration to mineral management policy, could hardly have been more complete.

In November 1969, EMR was asked by the Privy Council Office to prepare a paper on the mining industry to help in the PCO's task of devising various "possible constitutional options." The federal government was growing increasingly concerned at having been excluded from many of the financial benefits of mining's great expansion in the 1950s and 1960s by Section 109 of the BNA Act. While EMR responded to this federal brief, it also chose to use this request from the Privy Council Office as an opportunity to press for wider and more intensive federal efforts in the area of mineral policy, on the assumption that a national mineral policy could be successfully devised only in the context of a national economic development policy. It seized the opportunity to introduce the necessity of a national mineral policy in the federal bureaucracy, and it did so by taking advantage of federal-provincial tensions. A mineral policy was only possible under the leadership and co-ordination of the federal government after intensive consultation with the provinces EMR argued.[35] With hindsight it seems ironic that the only way EMR could get the federal cabinet to take national mineral policy seriously was in the context of federal-provincial relations, for it was on the rocks of this relationship that the quest for a universal policy was to founder in the 1970s.

A second major opportunity to proceed with the formulation of a mineral policy occurred in the autumn of 1970, when Prime Minister Trudeau directed the Minister of Energy, Mines and Resources, J.J. Greene, to review Canada's water needs and energy policy. Greene responded by offering, in addition, to undertake a review and redefinition of Canada's national mineral policies. The rationale for this included a consideration of "managing" foreign investment to obtain higher returns for Canada.[36] This issue had already been the subject of close consultation between EMR staff and Minister Herb Gray's staff in the Department of Industry, Trade and Commerce. Within a week the Prime Minister replied, authorizing EMR to go ahead with the study. He warned that it would be a complex task because of the different policy requirements of different minerals, but said that a comprehensive review of mineral policies (he avoided the singular) would be helpful in providing "a coherence for the total picture."[37]

The report was completed by July 1971. It made explicit its philosophical differences with Canada's past mineral policy of growth in three succinct points:

(1) It recognized that world price mechanisms alone, without government interference, "cannot ensure the optimum allocation of resources to generate the maximum stream of net social benefits to Canadians";

(2) It stressed that the need for co-ordination of all levels of government had increased, and suggested that a "strict adherence to the allocation of powers conferred by the BNA Act" should be modified; and

(3) It suggested that the economic theory of comparative cost advantage (which asserts that trading countries should specialize in producing those commodities in which they have a "comparative advantage" and exchange them for commodities in which they have a comparative cost disadvantage) was based on unrealistic assumptions. "Indeed, adherence to this doctrine has accounted in part for Canada's failure to recognize the opportunities its mineral resources afforded for balanced sectoral and regional growth."[38]

The major thrust of this document was that the federal government should begin to play a much more active role in mineral policy vis-à-vis both the provinces and the industry itself. Some of the provinces were also at this time busily pondering the contributions mining could make to their own needs. Thus, although EMR and the federal government had already privately started challenging the contemporary appropriateness of Section 109 of the BNA Act, there appeared to be a great deal of common ground between the federal and provincial governments on the issue of mineral policy. The previously mentioned federal studies of mineral policy done for various provinces had created a reservoir of goodwill (however temporary), and the two levels of government proceeded to embark on a concerted effort to formulate a national mineral policy.

In early 1973 federal and provincial ministers held a series of meetings aimed at developing greater co-operation between governments in formulating policy. On 13 April 1973 they issued a communiqué agreeing on the development of a formal mechanism for consultation, which, they argued, was "essential for the formulation of mineral policies that are national in scope." They also authorized the publication of a document, "Mineral Policy Objectives for Canada," which was to form the basis for future ministerial discussions.[39] Significantly, the goals and objectives presented in this document are almost identical to those suggested in EMR's internal "Progress Report on National Mineral Policy Objectives," issued in July 1971. The only changes are some minor shifts in emphasis and the addition of one objective: to "strengthen the contribution of minerals to regional-national development."

In late November 1973, a Canadian Ministerial Conference on Mineral Policy was created to formalize previous arrangements for intergovernmental consultation on mineral policy. The Ministerial Conference defined itself largely as a consultative and consensus-building body that could not deal with all issues of joint concern, and care was taken to emphasize that policy decisions remained the responsibility of individual governments. The ministers agreed that the conference be chaired jointly by the federal minister of Energy, Mines, and Resources and the provincial minister hosting the annual Provincial Mines Ministers Conference.

The first meeting of the Ministerial Conference on Mineral Policy took place on 6 December 1974. The ministers considered four basic scenarios, or options, for alternative mineral policies.[40] *Option One* was a policy of continuing, as in past decades, to encourage maximum mineral production. It emphasized the need for a favourable investment climate and it presupposed (a) that the market system satisfactorily distributed benefits from minerals, (b) that economic development based on minerals automatically arose when and where it was economically feasible, and (c) that government support of the mineral industry would generate the best possible benefits for Canadians.

Option Two called for the encouragement of economic diversification and growth through increased mineral processing and mineral-based manufacturing in Canada. It addressed itself to the need for both regional development and linkage of the mining industry to other sectors of the economy. It presupposed that appropriate policies would achieve greater mineral processing, fabricating, mineral-based manufacturing, and intersectoral linkages over the long term through a mixture of private and public investment. It also assumed that Canada could develop a self-sustaining, diversified industrial structure beyond the year 2000 that would become less dependent on its mineral resources as a main vehicle for development.

Option Three argued for obtaining the highest possible net financial returns to Canadians from minerals—returns for *all* Canadians, not just the mining companies. The additional revenues, naturally, would be distributed by governments, both federal and provincial, "in support of other priorities and alternative economic and social opportunities." This option presupposed that governments could obtain increased net revenues from minerals—through such means as higher taxes, royalties, reduced government expenditures in support of the industry, public equity participation, or higher export prices—without disproportionate effects on mineral sector development; that governments' shares of these revenues would be redistributed effectively in support of other priorities according to the objectives of each government; and that postponed development would permit higher returns from minerals in the future.

Finally, *Option Four* advocated a policy of conserving mineral resources for long-term domestic requirements. This option drew strength from the Club of Rome[41] and OPEC-induced panic about world supply that was current at the time. It presupposed that Canada was in danger of depleting its minerals too rapidly; that minerals left in the ground would not become obsolete through new discoveries elsewhere, substitution, or technological change; that postponed development would permit better benefits from minerals in the future; and that other economic activities would compensate, both nationally and regionally, for delayed growth in the mineral sector if further mining development were postponed.

Towards a Mineral Policy for Canada was clear on the necessity of choosing a particular option rather than merely adopting all of them. However, only Option One, the traditional mineral policy of growth that had been dominant in the 1950s and 1960s, was apparently rejected. The other three options were by nature redistributive, and *all* were endorsed. Significantly, there was a slight preference for Option Two, the policy of economic diversification and growth, which was also a mineral policy with a long history in Canada.

Some of the reasons for avoiding a clear decision on policy direction are only too obvious. Most obvious of all was the division of jurisdiction between the federal and provincial governments. Although the Ministerial Conference was successful in bringing about a degree of consultation between federal and provincial governments, it was not successful in achieving an integrated mineral policy. It achieved a consensus on aims—one of its prime goals—but not a consensus on priorities. Avoiding choices in this way and concentrating on general aims on which diverse groups would agree resulted in little really being accomplished. Although the consensus-building function of the Ministerial Conference should not be belittled (it could have become significant if it had not been so gratuitously shattered by external factors in the next three years), it stopped short of the crucial choices demanded in the formulation of a mineral policy.

The very definition of "mineral policy" adopted by *Towards a Mineral Policy for Canada* embodied all the tensions and ambiguities that resulted in its ducking the task it had set itself. Mineral policy was argued to be "the sum of government decisions and actions that influence the mineral system, and the way in which the system itself affects the economy and the society in general. Its elements are diverse and continually changing."

All elements of *strategy* (which are normally contained in the concept of "mineral policy"), all indications of creating a hierarchy of priorities (which the document claimed to be doing), are completely absent from this definition. Not surprisingly, then, the promised priorities did not emerge. But at least the document did recognize that, though various policy options existed, some or all of them were contradictory or inconsistent. Thus the mere process of detailing the options and emphasizing that a choice would have to be made constituted progress of sorts. As Donald Macdonald put it the same year, it recognized that the present situation—operating hand to mouth in an ad hoc fashion—was "no longer good enough."

The opportunity to go on at this stage and make choices between the various options was, however, never followed up. Instead, EMR embarked on a major series of nineteen detailed specific studies, most of which were published in 1976. They dealt with diverse topics such as individual commodities (asbestos, copper, gypsum, iron ore, nitrogen, phosphate, potash, sulphur, and zinc), labour needs, women in mining, the environment, and energy needs.[42]

Whatever its merits as a source of detailed information about Canada's mineral industry, the EMR series was of little significance in the quest for a comprehensive mineral policy incorporating an ordered set of priorities. It was essentially background work that appears to have been published once it became clear that the general process of federal-provincial collaboration in formulating a national mineral policy had stalled or perhaps even died. A large part of the reason for this failure was undoubtedly the formidable obstacle posed by the political and constitutional realities of the federal-provincial relationship in Canada (which will be discussed in the following section). But these realities were not the only forces at work. There was also a failure of political will on the part of both politicians and bureaucrats, who were to some extent responsible for allowing the genuine clashes of interest in the mineral sector to submerge what were potentially far larger shared interests in the health and ordered development of Canadian mining. This failure turned out to be an expensive one for governments, the industry, and Canadians generally. The turmoil and internecine conflict created confusion and instability in the industry, frightened off investors, and resulted in missed or delayed opportunities.

MINERAL POLICY OF REDISTRIBUTION, 1970–8:
REVENUE AND TAXATION

The strong growth of the mining industry from 1945 to 1970 was of great significance to federal and provincial governments, who were themselves growing during the same period. Mining became important both as an employer and as a source of revenue. The industry continued to grow in the 1970s, and did so until the downturn of the early 1980s. But this growth was deceptive, for it depended largely on higher prices and inflation rather than on increases in physical production. To be sure, some sectors of the mining industry, such as coal, uranium, and potash, did increase output significantly, but most showed either slow or no growth at all in terms of volume. There was a second difficulty: the nonfuel mining industry was increasingly overshadowed by the OPEC-influenced boom in the oil and gas sector. Metals, in particular, showed a decline in relative importance: as late as 1960 they accounted for nearly 57 per cent of the value of all Canadian mineral production; by 1982, however, they constituted only some 21 per cent.

Thus it can be argued that the 1970s represented a period of overall physical stagnation and even *decline* in the industry, with the exception of potash, oil, gas, and other energy-related minerals such as uranium and coal. The decline was masked by higher prices and steeply escalating inflation. In retrospect, the industry was less able than it appeared to survive a frontal fiscal assault. Moreover, as I stated earlier in this chapter, mining developments and mineral policy do not move in tandem. The strength of nonfuel mining in the 1950s and 1960s led to government policies in the early 1960s designed to deal with what was increasingly regarded as a "mature" industry, one no longer in need of special incentives. These policies, most notably in the area of taxation, were not fully implemented until the mid-1970s, by which time the condition of the industry was very different. This policy lag also occurred in the fuels sector, where federal energy policy responded to the boom of the mid-to-late 1970s with the National Energy Program in 1980, a policy designed for a growing, not a slowing, sector. Provincial energy policy, reflecting a relatively less complex balance of interests, responded faster, with Alberta taking unilateral action to extend the royalty concept in the early 1970s.

There were three basic protagonists in the revenue and taxation issue: the producing companies, the federal government, and the provincial governments. All played a crucial part in the development of mineral policy from 1970 to 1978, and for convenience their interaction will be considered together. The major struggle for the maximum possible share in the rewards from Canadian mining was reflected in the new emphasis on a mineral policy of redistribution rather than one of growth. Let us first briefly recount the struggle for revenue share, and then examine the policy implications underlying the struggle.

The tax concessions made to mining from 1936 to the mid-1950s, initially renewed annually, were made permanent by the federal budget of 1955. As a result, the mining industry incorporated this favourable tax regime into its long-term planning, and large investments were made whose viability depended on its continuance.[43] By the early 1960s the mining industry saw itself as enjoying very favourable tax treatment.[44] So, too, did others—increasingly as the decade wore on. The Carter Commission, with a general brief to make recommendations to improve tax laws and administration, noticed the generous treatment offered to mining and widened the scope of its inquiry to examine the issue. Its report, released in February 1967, focused on mining taxation among other things, but its recommendations—opposed by both the industry and the provinces—were thought at the time too controversial to be implemented. In essence, the Commission advocated a concept of "tax neutrality," according to which all sectors of the economy should be taxed at equal rates. Mining, it was argued, was undertaxed. More than two years later, on 7 November 1969, a watered-down version of the Carter Report's proposals was published in a federal government White Paper, which was sharply criticized and withdrawn for further review. Finally, Bill C-259, a proposal to amend the Income Tax Act, was introduced on 18 June 1971 and became law on 1 January 1972.

The new Act's ramifications for the mining industry were extensive. The following were some of its major provisions:

(1) The three-year tax exemption for mines, initiated in 1936, was to be phased out effective in 1974;

(2) The exemption from taxation of prospectors' and grubstakers' profits, initiated in 1941, was to be phased out effective in 1971;

(3) The automatic depletion allowance of 33⅓ per cent, initiated in 1934–5, was replaced with an earned depletion allowance of 33⅓ per cent for mine and processing facilities effective in 1977;

(4) Deductions for domestic exploration and development costs were left unchanged at rates up to 100 per cent, and extended to foreign operations as well;

(5) The federal government would terminate the deductibility of provincial mining taxes and royalties in computing federal taxes effective in 1977.

This last provision was especially significant. Deductibility had been in effect since the Second World War, allowing deductions so long as provincial mining taxes and royalties conformed to various conditions and giving the federal government de facto control of provincial fiscal policies. Its termination would have the effect of uncoupling the federal and provincial tax systems, giving the provinces more autonomy. At the same time, to compensate for the heavier tax burden on the mining industry, the federal government cut its tax on mining income by 15 percentage points.

Soon after, a number of provinces, encouraged by the commodities boom of 1972–4, substantially increased provincial mining taxes and royalties. The federal government responded in two 1974 budgets to the threat of a substantial erosion of its tax base by advancing the effective date of nondeductibility and earned depletion from 1977 to 1974. In effect, the federal government, having at first made fiscal concessions to the provinces, felt compelled to withdraw some of them when the provinces were not content with the concessions and attempted to further augment their share by increases in direct provincial taxes and royalties.

The commodities boom of 1972–4 upset the temporary alliance of industry and provinces against the federal government. The provinces' race to increase their share of "windfall" profits, combined with the new federal taxation regime, had a drastic effect on mining taxation. From 1969 to 1975 the effective tax rate on manufacturing declined by 16 per cent (from 38.6 to 32.5 per cent) while that for mining increased by 101 per cent (from 20.7 to 41.8 per cent).[45]

Some of the measures taken by the provincial governments were far more drastic than the federal measures had been. Indeed, while the provincial *changes* received an angry reception from the industry, some of the provincial mineral policy *proposals* positively frightened and disrupted it. The most famous, or notorious, of these was Eric Kierans' *Report on Natural Resources Policy in Manitoba*.[46] The Kierans Report was written for and published by the government of Manitoba in the spring of 1973 with virtually no participation by its Department of Mines, Resources and Environmental Management.[47] To this day, mining industry audiences react emotionally to its mere mention.

The Report focused on the analysis of mining profits and the potential benefits to Manitoba of establishing Crown corporations. It recommended that the Manitoba government make the public sector responsible for all future mining development to ensure that the value of its depleted resources remained in Manitoba. Specifically, it urged the creation of Crown corporations for mining. Manitoba did not follow all of Kierans' recommendations, but it did increase its mining tax rate and supplement it with a system of royalties.[48] The Report left a legacy of controversy and bitter criticism.[49] Though for the most part not implemented, it created a lasting impression by voicing the previously unutterable. In some ways it made the industry more placatory and prepared to envision changes, provided they were less radical than those Kierans had advocated.

The industry, understandably, blamed the provincial governments more than the federal government for the substantial tax increases of the mid-1970s. It continued to press for lower federal tax rates, however. By the middle of the decade, relations between the federal and provincial governments, as well as the relations of the mining industry with both levels of government, reached their nadir while effective tax rates were reaching their peaks. It was generally recognized that the governments had to compromise on revenue shares to avoid irreparable harm to the industry, and 1976 and 1977 saw dramatic rollbacks. These years also saw a move toward increased consultation between the three parties. Among the results of the tax jurisdiction wrangle was the further slowing of the momentum towards a national mineral policy that had been present since the early 1970s. In late January 1978 federal and provincial mines ministers met for the first time since 1974. They agreed on the need for co-operative action by both levels of government to enhance the contribution of the resource industry to Canada's economy, but they disagreed on their respective resource tax jurisdictions. The following month, the First Ministers' Conference announced a tax review by federal and provincial officials for finance and resource ministers. The review was completed and presented as a discussion paper at the First Ministers' Conference on the Economy, 27–9 November 1978.

The review did not confine itself to narrowly defined taxation issues and constituted an impressive recognition by governments of the industry's problems. It stressed that only a healthy industry would be a reliable source of revenue, and unlike the dominant government view of the previous decade, did not regard mining as largely a milch cow, a potential source of revenue to finance other sectors of the economy. Though it was not intended as an exercise in mineral policy formulation, the priorities outlined by the report had definite policy implications. The priorities are particularly striking when compared to the actual tax changes of the previous six years, and can be summarized as follows:[50] stability and certainty in the tax system; recognition in the tax system of the cyclical nature of the mining industry; adequate levels of capital investment, growth, and development; an acceptable federal-provincial division of revenues; greater harmony and less complexity in tax systems; the encouragement of further processing in Canada; and consistency of the tax system with national priorities.

The Taxation Review was officially forwarded to the ministers on 1 November 1978. Two weeks later the federal Minister of Finance, Jean Chrétien, assured the mining industry in his budget speech that the federal government would co-operate with the provinces on taxation and ensure that the industry benefited as a consequence. He made a number of fairly important taxation concessions to the industry at the same time, proposing that the write-off for development expenditures on mining be increased from 30 per cent to 100 per cent and significantly increasing the items that could be deducted under the "earned depletion" and development provisions. Early the following year, the Federal-Provincial Working Group on the Mineral Industry was set up to continue to work towards federal-provincial co-ordination in mineral policy.[51]

Chrétien also assured the provinces that the federal government would not step into any tax space that might be vacated by any province. Some of the provinces responded to this and to other developments by significant rollbacks in taxation, largely through the removal or cutting of graduated or incremental taxes on mining. But the industry had by 1979 (and in spite of the growing concern of governments for its health) only regained some of the ground it had lost in the mid-1970s.

At this juncture it would be useful to take a second look at some of the assumptions underlying the intergovernmental battles of the 1970s. In particular, we might seek an answer to this question: Why was there a recognition, at the beginning of the 1970s, of the need to change the mineral policy of growth? Not, obviously, because Canadians generally wanted to slow or reverse that growth. Environmentalists, for example, wanted only to control the growth and clean it up. Even conservationists merely wanted to synchronize growth with long-term proven reserves. Besides, neither the environmentalists nor the conservationists were making Canadian mineral policy. The real issue appears to have been who was to share the fruits of growth and in what measure, rather than whether growth was desirable.

The federal and provincial governments decided in the early 1970s that the central goal of a new mineral policy should be to "obtain optimum benefit for Canada from present and future use of minerals." This innocuous statement masked potential struggles over power and wealth; it also concealed a real move toward a quite different brand of mineral policy. To decode the new policy one has to ask what "optimum" (as opposed to "maximum") meant, and what "Canada" (as opposed to Canadian citizens, producers, consumers, miners, and governments) denoted.

On the most obvious level, the goal of obtaining maximum benefit for Canada reflects the enduring theme of nationalism in mineral policy, which had ebbed and flowed since the late 1800s. By the 1960s the growth of large multinational firms in the mining industry in particular was seen as a "great challenge to government at all levels."[52] It was strongly argued by governments that they had to develop the capability, both in data-gathering and analysis as well as in policy formulation, to handle this challenge.

Confronting foreign multinationals is usually a politically easy and popular policy to follow, especially so long as the confrontation is largely limited to words and does not lead to large-scale divestment and unemployment. In this case, while the multinationals were subjected to insults for the benefit of the Canadian electorate, the actual effect on them of mineral policy in the 1970s amounted to mere pinpricks. In 1971 Canada established a system of foreign direct investment regulation through the Foreign Investment Review Act and Foreign Investment Review Agency. Until 1980 it was seen as only a minor irritant and condoned explicitly on occasion by the U.S. government.[53]

Indeed, the important changes being made at the time in the tax system had the effect of entrenching the large integrated mining companies (which most of the foreign companies are at the expense of the smaller companies (which are overwhelmingly Canadian).[54] To take just one example: the abandoned three-year tax exemption was lamented by all in the industry, but the provision had been relatively more favourable to the extraction of small- and medium-sized ore bodies because of their shorter life. The new system was designed to provide for full capital cost recovery prior to the payment of profit-based tax, rather than the exemption of profits themselves from tax. This favoured those firms most able to use the available tax shelters, namely, the large integrated mines which had other sources of income against which the tax write-offs could be applied. In effect, this was a policy decision to favour the large companies over their smaller counterparts.[55]

If the changes in mineral policy damaged the mining companies, they wreaked havoc on federal-provincial relations. The various mineral policy suggestions being published at the time studiously attempted to be inoffensive to both levels of governments. To do this they had to avoid the real issues of mineral policy in the early 1970s, because the issues were highly contentious and required debate as well as compromise on basic principles. At least two such issues were major: the federal-provincial jurisdictional dispute, particularly as it affected taxation; and the continuing struggle over what share of mining's revenues should go to the federal and provincial governments, what share to the industry, and what share to other interests.

In both cases, the central policy objectives of federal and provincial governments were to optimize their own benefits from the present and future use of minerals by a policy of redistribution. This is not to say that the policies were aimed cynically at self-aggrandizement and were indifferent to encouraging growth, though it must be pointed out that they were self-serving enough. Each level of government no doubt believed that its objectives would optimize the situation for Canada—or Ontarians, or citizens, or the poor or unemployed, or any number of groups that make up "Canada."

TABLE 1: Tax and royalty rates on mining: 1969—75 (Percentage)

	Federal	Provincial		
Year	Income	Income	Royalties	Total
1969	10.0	2.7	7.7	20.7
1970	11.4	3.1	7.0	21.7
1971	8.4	2.5	7.5	18.5
1972	11.5	3.5	10.2	25.4
1973	9.4	2.6	7.4	19.5
1974	14.8	5.1	16.4	36.7
1975	14.4	5.5	21.1	41.8

Source: Statistics Canada, Department of Finance, cited in E.P. Neufeld, "Federal-Provincial Resource Taxation Review," Doc. No. 800-9/018 (Ottawa 1978), 31. The above refers to both metal and non-metal mines.

The jurisdictional dispute appears to have emerged because, with the expansion of governments, revenue sources became ever scarcer and governments' revenue thirst ever more insatiable. As we have seen, one of the ironies of intergovernmental relations was that some provincial governments learned from their federal counterpart how to walk on their own feet, thereby undercutting the dominance over mineral policy that the federal government was attempting to establish. As Table 1 indicates, the mining industry did experience a marked increase in its tax burden during the early 1970s.

What exactly the federal and provincial governments ultimately did with the revenue they were battling each other to obtain remains a moot point; but there is some evidence of a shift by both levels of government to favouring manufacturing and the processing of metals over mining in the mid-1970s, when mining taxes were said by many in the industry to be nearly a third higher than taxes on manufacturing.

The federal-provincial conflict over mining taxation, as I have noted, was eventually eased on the initiative of the mining industry, whose advocates persuaded the two levels of government to come to the bargaining table at the intergovernmental resource ministers' meeting on 20 January 1978. In retrospect, it seems evident that the great 1970s mining-revenue grab constituted a striking instance of the tension between the concrete needs of the moment and the longer-term principles that underlie mineral policy. If policy fails to take into account the concrete interests vying for scarce resources, it becomes either an irrelevant abstraction or dangerously divorced from reality. On the other hand, if it moulds itself to the shifting tides of everyday events it becomes a mere summary of these events. First the federal government, then its provincial counterparts, decided in the early 1970s to redistribute mining revenue in a fundamental way. But they overreached, partly through conflict between the different levels of government, partly through an inadequate grasp of what was feasible at the time. To ensure the survival of threatened sections of the industry, they had to make a partial but significant retreat. This retreat, however, was not accompanied by the development of any new strategy, and led to policy responding in an ad hoc way as events unfolded.

By the mid-1970s the federal and provincial governments and the mining industry had drifted into an abyss that might have been avoided had there been a coherent mineral policy to draw on. The collapse of the commodity boom would have created problems, but the fiasco resulting from the many conflicting mineral and tax policies of the mid-1970s greatly exacerbated matters. Only the exhaustion and desperation of failure later brought governments and industry together again to compromise their incompatible goals.

The positive aspects of the new situation emerged slowly. The dominance of redistributive issues from 1970 to 1978 was supplanted by a rekindled concern for the health of the industry that generated the revenue and employment in the first place. Governments and the industry became aware of their mutual interests. There was a new determination to lay down a stable taxation and general mineral policy regime in which the industry might re-establish its strength. This did not mean a return to the old mineral policy of growth. A policy favouring resource-led economic growth and emphasizing regional development now began to emerge, borrowing freely from the mineral policies of growth and redistribution but attempting to avoid old mistakes and recognize new realities. Further progress, however, was halting and not without setbacks.

RESOURCE POLICY AND MINERAL POLICY SINCE 1978:
MANAGING "MATURITY"

For a few years after 1978 Canadian governments returned to what might be called the traditional policy of resource-led economic development. Mineral policy was dominated by resource policy as well as by industrial strategy and regional policy as a whole, and I will discuss it here in this broader context. A primary concern of governments has been the necessity of encouraging Canadian industry in general to export more. There are two ostensibly complementary policy responses to this: breaking down the artificial protection accorded Canadian manufacturing by tariff and non-tariff barriers and following one's comparative advantages; or enforcing a policy of further processing of natural resources before export, even if this entails the adoption of a comprehensive "industrial strategy."[56]

What began to emerge after 1978, in fact, was a new blend of these two options. Policies began to focus again on generating economic growth by concentrating on Canada's supposed comparative advantages in resources; but these policies displayed important differences from the traditional policy of growth. Instead of generating economic development merely by providing the conditions for resource-led growth, federal and provincial governments leaned increasingly towards direct intervention in and the forced growth of resource industries. They also increasingly rejected the trickle-down theory of the redistribution of the wealth generated by resources (according to which profitable companies create new or better-paid jobs that in turn generate higher government revenues and capacity to undertake social programs) in favour of governments' taking over the redistributive role themselves. This subtle, but important, shift of emphasis is well illustrated by the two alternatives sketched in a 1980 EMR *Discussion Paper on Coal*. The document was specific to coal policy, but its preoccupation with government intervention in a resource industry to achieve macroeconomic and regional policy goals had broad implications.[57]

The push for more government intervention in the late 1970s and early 1980s was greatest in three energy minerals: oil, natural gas, and coal. With the price of oil still rising steeply and demand seemingly inexhaustible, this was where the real revenue potential lay. Mining, having undergone a debilitating three-cornered federal-provincial-private sector struggle over taxation from 1968 to 1978, was not a high priority area for accelerated government intervention. But energy was, and for those making energy policy, EMR became "*the* place to be in the great Ottawa bureaucratic structure, the place where key policy was being made."[58] The new group of "super-bureaucrats" in the department all recognized the importance of resources in the Canadian economy, as had earlier poli-cymakers; but they drew very different conclusions about the desirable role of government in dealing with the resource industries, particularly the energy fuels. The result, of course, was the National Energy Program (NEP) of 1980, discussed elsewhere in this volume.

It cannot be overemphasized that energy lay at the heart of this new focus on resource-led growth and that the Liberal federal government always denied that it was planning a NEP for other resource sectors. In the sense that the government was not planning on "using the full arsenal of interventionist weapons, from corporate takeovers, to buy-in provisions, massive changes in tax and ex-penditure revenues and direct regulation," its assurance can be taken at face value. Notwithstanding the limitation of the "full arsenal" to the energy sector, it should be pointed out that there are other less direct methods of intervention, some of which appeared to be potentially applicable to such other sectors as agri-food, fisheries, forestry and mining—"applicable" in the sense that they held out the prospect of achieving greater Canadian "value added," enhancing interna-tional trade prospects, and even encroaching on provincial jurisdiction.[59]

Many of these policy issues and priorities receded into the background with the plummeting of the price of oil and the general economic crisis of 1982–3. About $22.3 billion of energy megaprojects were cancelled and much of the re-maining $19.2 billion were delayed or scheduled for reconsideration.[60] There was a definite shift to what has been called "the ethos of small-scale development," and a general shift in energy politics to a far less interventionist line on deregula-tion, oil and gas incentives, and Canadianization. The Liberals began to overhaul the NEP in 1983–4, and the new Conservative federal government merely ac-celerated the process.

This withdrawal from megaprojects and the selective use of the "full arsenal of interventionist weapons," while modifying the resource-led growth strategy advanced by the federal government in November 1981, does not necessarily negate the central principle of emphasizing Canada's comparative advantage in resources where it exists, or the possibility of using this as the basis of economic development policy.

It must be conceded, however, that the method of doing this has yet to be worked out in concrete terms: EMR and the other resource departments—with the possible exception of forestry—have largely failed to map a strategy for putting themselves at the centre of economic growth policy. Interestingly, from the late 1960s to the late 1970s there was a tendency for policymakers and analysts alike to view Canadian mining as a "mature industry." By this they meant an industry that could stand alone without government incentives, one that could even generate resources to help other sectors of the economy. In the early 1980s the term "mature industry" was transformed by some to "sunset industry." Thus, mining became grouped with a number of dying industries (such as footwear and clothing) targeted by policymakers to be phased out with the minimum possible fuss and pain.

It can be argued, however, that "maturity" in the case of the mining industry implies neither independence from the policy environment and government support nor the inevitability of decline and death. It may be true that Canadian mining is not likely to grow again with the adolescent vigour of the 1950s and 1960s, but it is equally true that the mining industry is a long way from its dotage. In such a situation, the term "maturity" takes on a new meaning, and a policy of "managing maturity" is neither one of milking a self-sufficient industry for the benefit of other sectors of the economy or society nor one of gently laying a dying industry to rest.

Canadian mineral policy in the 1980s has to deal with an industry that has ended its rapid growth phase but is still vigorous and demonstrably able to adapt to the extreme competitiveness of its new international environment. In other words, mineral policy has to avoid the peril of either excessive subsidization or enervating neglect. Since 1982 makers of mineral policy have been wrestling with this new conception of a "mature industry" as it applies to Canadian mining. Thus far their success has been mixed, as is clearly evident in the major EMR policy report of March 1982, *Mineral Policy: A Discussion Paper*.[61]

The *Discussion Paper* contains a wealth of detail about Canada's mining industry and much valuable analysis of particular problems it experiences. In terms of a coherent discussion of Canadian mineral policy, however, it is largely a failure. It contains no major new initiatives. Even worse, though it explicitly claims to reflect "the themes and priorities identified in the economic development document" (published with the budget in November 1981), the *Discussion Paper* actually devotes virtually no attention to following up and buttoning down the very explicit commitments to resources made by the cabinet.[62]

Much of the mining industry, which expects EMR to actively promote its health, regarded this as a serious missed opportunity.[63] It is only fair to point out, however, that while some industry disappointment with the *Discussion Paper*'s failure is justified, some of it also stems from a yearning for the Golden Age of the seemingly unending expansion of the Canadian mining industry. When a sector of the economy is expanding, policy has to meet the challenge of managing growth by co-ordinating the development thrust. But when the sector has reached maturity or is contracting, policy has to meet new challenges by co-ordinating a concerted trade and competition thrust. When the days of seemingly limitless expansion and market outlets are over, mineral policy has to change its focus to the problems of selling what is coming into the market from productive capacity that is already installed.

In the case of Canadian mining, the mineral policy shift to managing maturity (sometimes loosely called "adjustment policy") can be seen in the heavy and perhaps justifiable new emphasis on international marketing, market access, and productivity. This new emphasis has been accelerating rapidly since the extreme depression in the industry in 1982–3 and the lack of policy direction in the *Discussion Paper*. Whether Canadian mining has actually reached a state of maturity, and whether this means that policy should now de-emphasize the encouragement of growth, are highly contentious issues.

What are the central policy elements of managing maturity in the mining industry? At least four can be distinguished: (1) research and development, (2) trade and competition, (3) diversification and procurements, and (4) regional policy.

The first two, though not uniquely a response to maturity (both contain elements of the older mineral policies of growth and redistribution), have become fairly unambiguous components of mineral adjustment policy. They are, moreover, relatively uncontentious areas in that federal and provincial governments, corporations, and labour are largely in agreement on all the basic issues. The role of governments in these areas is that of a service organization, a role generally acceptable to all parties. The area of diversification and procurement and that of regional policy are, however, far more contentious and ambiguous, and have profound implications for development policy as well as adjustment policy. Although one can say that these four elements constitute an embryonic mineral policy, there is not yet anything that one can call a *national* mineral policy. The hard choices on detailed priorities, on who are to be winners and loser, have not yet been made. Nor has an overall strategy been articulated.

Nevertheless, it is reasonable to predict that these four elements will constitute an important part of any new policy. The variations possible under the rubric of managing maturity remain enormous, but it is important to note that the old policies that served for so long in Canada—policies focused on nationalism, growth, or redistribution—have been superseded. This is so in spite of the fact that problems similar to those from the past occur in the present and will continue to do so in the future. The governments, the companies, and labour will continue to debate such issues as tax and the optimal division of mineral revenues, as they always have. But they do so now within a new framework of managing maturity that, although it leaves room for large and crucial variations in detailed policies, at least provides the mineral policymaking process with parameters and a direction.

CONCLUSION: THE AMBIGUOUS LEGACY

Three basic mineral policies have been identified in the post-1945 period: the mineral policy of growth, 1945–70; the mineral policy of redistribution, 1970–8; and the post-1978 mineral policy of managing maturity. There is considerable overlap between these three policies and each contains elements of the others, but the orientation of each policy is strikingly different. Moreover, while perennial themes and concerns run through the three—size of the industry, distribution of its benefits and costs—the central thrust and emphasis of each is distinct.

The policy of growth, for example, focused on quantitative expansion first and foremost, with the belief that private sector capitalist enterprise was the optimal means of growth and that its benefits would be equitably distributed to society as a whole in the form of more jobs, growing wages, and higher government revenues from mining. The policy of growth was ambivalent towards government intervention in mining. While it encouraged maximum government intervention in sharing the development costs of mining (by providing infrastructure and fiscal incentives), it called for minimum intervention in the distribution of mining's benefits, trusting more to the efficient operation of the free market.

The policy of redistribution, on the other hand, was almost unequivocally interventionist. It focused on maximizing the financial benefits of mining and, while it did not oppose growth, its policy instruments tended to have an inhibiting effect. Although it was not properly speaking a policy of managing maturity, it conceived of the industry as being "mature" enough to stand alone without government support. Historically, it has gone even further and operated on the assumption that mining is in the position to render direct support to other industries. Thus, the mineral policy of redistribution laid most emphasis on increasing the tax burden of mining capital and capturing its "economic rents," and channelling the proceeds via government revenues to other areas of the economy and society. This was done, for example, by increasing government incentives to other industries and increasing the regulation of environmental and social aspects of mining.

As I have mentioned, the notion of "maturity" on which the post-1978 mineral policy is based considers Canada's mining physically adult. Its rapid growth phase is now over. This does not mean that it will never resume growing or that rapid growth in specific sectors (such as gold production) is impossible. It does mean that, at least for the short to medium term, mineral policy no longer has as its prime focus the management and co-ordination of growth. The industry's physical maturity means that much of its future development depends on the more efficient and co-ordinated use of its resources in a highly competitive world. One clear implication of this, with utmost relevance to this volume, is that more so than at any other time, Canadian mineral policy will be constrained and conditioned by the international aspects of mineral production and trade.

NOTES

1 David Yudelman, *Canadian Mineral Policy Past and Present: The Ambiguous Legacy* (Kingston, Ont.: Queen's University Centre for Resource Studies 1985).

2 Hugh Heclo, "Policy Analysis: Review Article," *British Journal of Political Science* 2 (1972):83–108.

3 W.G. Jeffery, "Mining Legislation and Administration in Canada," Mineral Policy Sector Internal Report MR181/5 (Ottawa: Department of Energy, Mines and Resources 1981), 2.

4 H.V. Nelles, *The Politics of Development: Forests, Mines and Hydro-Electric Power in Ontario 1849–1941* (Toronto: University of Toronto Press 1975), 2–3.

5 Nelles, *Politics of Development*, 21–3.

6 Ontario, *Report of the Royal Commission on the Mineral Resources of Ontario and Measures for Their Development* (Toronto 1890). The Commissioners comprised a Member of Parliament, two bureaucrats, an academic, and an "explorer-miner."

7 Ontario, *Report of the Royal Commission*, 305–6.

8 Garth Stevenson, "The Process of Making Mineral Resource Policy in Canada," in *Natural Resources in U.S.-Canadian Relations*, ed. Carl E. Beigie and Alfred O. Hero, jr., vol. 1: *The Evolution of Policies and Issues* (Boulder, CO: Westview press 1980), 168–9.

9 See Gerard V. La Forest, *Natural Resources and Public Property under the Canadian Constitution* (Toronto: University of Toronto Press 1969), 27–47; Wendy MacDonald, *Constitutional Change and the Mining Industry in Canada* (Kingston, Ont.: Queen's University Centre for Resource Studies 1980); and Garth Stevenson, "Federalism and the Political Economy of the Canadian State," in *The Canadian State: Political Economy and Political Power*, ed. Leo Panitch (Toronto: University of Toronto Press 1977), 76–7.

10 Stevenson, "The Process of Making Mineral Resource Policy," 169–70.

11 Jeffery, "Mining Legislation," 8–9.

12 Nelles, *Politics of Development*, 20–1.

13 For a recent ttempt, see David L. Anderson, *Foreign Investment Control in the Canadian Mineral Sector: Lessons from the Australian Experience* (Kingston, Ont.: Queen's University Centre for Resource Studies 1984).

14 O.W. Main, *The Canadian Nickel Industry: A Study in Market Control and Public Policy* (Toronto: University of Toronto Press 1955), 84–8.

15 W.G. Jeffery, "Mineral Policy Alternatives: A Background Essay," Energy, Mines and Resources Internal Report MRI 81/4 (Ottawa 1981), 3–4.
16 Roy Romanow, "The Justification and Evolution of Crown Resource Corporations in Saskatchewan," in Mining Law in Canada, ed. Richard Bartlett (Saskatoon: Law Society of Saskatchewan 1984), 47.
17 Roy M. Longo, ed., Historical Highlights of Canadian Mining (Toronto: Pitt Publishing 1973), 108ff.
18 Longo, Historical Highlights, 113.
19 Western Miner, 33 (Feb. 1960).
20 Stevenson, "The Process of Making Mineral Resource Policy," 173–4.
21 For example: Mineral Resources Division, Department of Mines and Technical Surveys, Mineral Resource Development: Province of Newfoundland and Labrador, Mineral Resources Internal Report MRI 288/66 (Ottawa: May 1966); Mineral Resources Division, Department of Energy, Mines and Resources, Mineral Resource Development: Province of New Brunswick, MRI 340/67 (Ottawa: Sept. 1967); Mineral Resources Division, Department of Energy, Mines and Resources, Mineral Resource Development: Province of Nova Scotia, MRI 368/68 (Ottawa: June 1968); Mineral Resources Branch, Department of Energy, Mines and Resources, Mineral Industry Development in Manitoba to 1980, MRI 381/68 (Ottawa: Oct. 1968); Mineral Resources Branch, Department of Energy, Mines and Resources, Mineral Resources Management in British Columbia, MR 415/69 (Ottawa: Sept. 1969).
22 John David, Mining and Mineral Processing in Canada (Ottawa: Queen's Printer 1957), 357.
23 Patrick James Caragata, "Non-Fuel Minerals and Canadian Foreign Policy: Negotiating from Strength and Weakness" (Ph.D. dissertation, University of Toronto 1980), 115.
24 J.P. Drolet and R.B. Toombs, "The Influence of the Mineral Industry on the National Economy" (Paper presented to a Royal Society of Canada Symposium on Earth Sciences in Canada, June 1967).
25 W. Keith Buck, "Factors Influencing the Mineral Economy of Canada: Past, Present and Future," MR106 (Ottawa: Department of Energy, Mines and Resources, Mineral Resources Branch 1970), 2.
26 Margot J. Wojciechowski, Federal Mineral Policies, 1945 to 1975: A Survey of Federal Activities that Affected the Canadian Mineral Industry (Kingston, Ont.: Queen's University Centre for Resource Studies 1979), 7.
27 Wojciechowski, Federal Mineral Policies, 7; Caragata, "Non-Fuel Minerals and Canadian Foreign Policy," 115.
28 House of Commons, Debates 9 July 1956, pp. 5779–80; Donald J. Patton, "The Evolution of Canadian Federal Mineral Policies," in Natural Resources in U.S.-Canadian Relations, 1:208.
29 Davis, Mining and Mineral Processing in Canada, 326.
30 David C. Smith, ed., Economic Policy Advising in Canada (Montreal: C.D. Howe Institute 1981), 3.
31 Hugh G. Thorburn, Planning and the Economy: Building Federal-Provincial Consensus (Ottawa: Canadian Institute for Economic Policy 1984), 62.
32 Russell Harrison, Chairman of the Canadian Imperial Bank of Commerce, addressing a management conference at the University of Western Ontario, Jan. 1983, as reported in the Globe and Mail, 12 Jan. 1983.
33 Richard D. French, How Ottawa Decides: Planning and Industrial Policy Making, 1968–1980 (Ottawa: James Lorimer 1980), 22.
34 James Gillies, Where Business Fails: Business-Government Relations at the Federal Level in Canada (Montreal: Institute for Research on Public Policy 1981), 106.
35 W. Keith Buck and R.B. Elver, "An Approach to Mineral Policy Formulation," Mineral Information Bulletin MR108 (Ottawa: Department of Energy, Mines and Resources, Mineral Resources Branch 1970).
36 Department of Energy, Mines and Resources, "Progress Report on National Mineral Policy Objectives," MR1487/71 (Ottawa: July 1971), Appendix A: "Terms of Reference."
37 Energy, Mines and Resources, "Progress Report," Appendix A.
38 Energy, Mines and Resources, "Progress Report," Appendix D: "Background Note on Minerals and National Goals," 2–3.
39 "Mineral Policy Objectives for Canada: A Statement by Federal and Provincial Ministers Responsible for Mineral Policy" (Ottawa: 1973).
40 Towards a Mineral Policy for Canada: Opportunities for Choice (Ottawa: Information Centre 1974), 20.
41 See Donella H. Meadows et al., The Limits to Growth: A Report for the Club of Rome's Project on the Predicament of Mankind (New York: Universe Books 1972).
42 Andrew J. Freyman, "Mineral Policy: The Last 20 Years," in CRS Perspectives, Sept. 1982, 2.

43 M.W. Bucovetsky, "The Mining Industry and the Great Tax Reform Debate," in *Pressure Group Behaviour in Canadian Politics,* ed. A. Paul Pross (Toronto: McGraw-Hill Ryerson 1975), 93.

44 Caragata, "Non-Fuel Minerals and Canadian Foreign Policy," 130.

45 Caragata, "Non-Fuel Minerals and Canadian Foreign Policy," 140.

46 Published in Winnipeg, 1973.

47 Stevenson, "The Process of Making Mineral Resource Policy," 176.

48 James T. Cawley, "The Metallic Minerals Royalty System of Manitoba," in *Rate of Return Taxation of Minerals,* Proceedings no. 1, Centre for Resource Studies (Kingston, 1978), 71–81.

49 Hedlin Manzies and Associates, *An Analysis of the Kierans Report on Mining Policy* (Prepared for the Mining Association of Manitoba, 1973); G. Anders, "Rent, Communal Property and Economic Nationalism" (Toronto: Ontario Ministry of Natural Resources 1973); Charles H. Pye, *Profitability in the Canadian Mineral Industry* (Kingston, Ont.: Queen's University Centre for Resource Studies 1981), 43–4.

50 Douglas Brown and Julia Eastman, with Ian Robinson, *The Limits of Consultation: A Debate among Ottawa, the Provinces and the Private Sector on an Industrial Strategy* (Ottawa: Science Council of Canada 1981), 117ff.

51 Michael J. Prince and G. Bruce Doern, *Federal Policy and the Role of Enterprise in the Mining Sector,* Working Paper no. 31 (Kingston, Ont.: Queen's University Centre for Resource Studies 1984), 22.

52 Department of Energy, Mines and Resources, "Mineral Management and Federal-Provincial Relations," MR1 1436/70 (Ottawa: Mineral Resources Branch, April 1970), 23.

53 Anderson, *Foreign Investment Control in the Canadian Mineral Sector,* 1.

54 Caragata, "Non-Fuel Minerals and Canadian Foreign Policy," 132.

55 L. Gonzague Langlois, "Juniors Spur Exploration in Quebec," *Northern Miner,* 21 June 1984, p. C7.

56 Glen Williams, "Trade and Promotion and Canada's Industrial Dilemma: The Demise of the Department of Industry, Trade and Commerce," in *How Ottawa Spends Your Tax Dollars 1982: National Policy and Economic Development,* ed. G Bruce Doern (Toronto: James Lorimer 1982), 117–23.

57 Department of Energy, Mines and Resources, *Discussion Paper on Coal,* 80 IE (Ottawa: 1980), 43.

58 Peter Foster, *The Sorcerer's Apprentices: Canada's Super-Bureaucrats and the Energy Mess* (Toronto: Collins 1982), 74.

59 G. Bruce Doern, ed., "Liberal Priorities 1982: The Limits of Scheming Virtuously," in *How Ottawa Spends Your Tax Dollars 1982* (Toronto: James Lorimer 1982), 21.

60 Jennifer Lewington, "Megaprojects Replaced by More Modest Proposals," and "Energy Politics' Shift to the Right Is Accelerating," *Globe and Mail,* 1 June 1984.

61 Department of Energy, Mines and Resources, *Mineral Policy: A Discussion Paper,* Report MP81-IE (Ottawa: 1982).

62 In the November 1981 budget document, *Economic Development for Canada in the 1980s,* the Liberal government made it plain that it saw Canada's leading economic priority to be "the development of Canada's rich bounty of natural resources."

63 For a detailed treatment of the mining corporations' reactions to the *Discussion Paper,* see David Yudelman, *Canadian Mineral Policy Formulation: A Case Study of the Adversarial Process,* Working Paper no. 30 (Kingston, Ont.: Queen's University Centre for Resource Studies 1984).

Part III

4

Canada as a Strategic Mineral Importer: The Problematical Minerals

Jock A. Finlayson

INTRODUCTION

The international politics of natural resources was one of the many interesting topics that successfully competed for the attention of international relations scholars in the decade of the 1970s.[1] Growing interest in the politics and economics of international resources trade stemmed from such diverse sources as the sharp increases in petroleum prices engineered by OPEC; the oil embargo instituted by Arab petroleum producers during the 1973 Middle East war; the rapid rise in virtually all primary commodity prices during the 1972–4 period; the formation and strengthening of producer cartels for such commodities as copper, bauxite, iron ore, and natural rubber; and increasing concern about the depletion of essential non-renewable mineral commodities.[2] By the end of the 1970s, the marked deterioration in East-West political relations, the Soviet and Cuban interventions in Africa after 1975, and the invasions of Zaïre's mineral-rich Shaba province by Katangan rebels in 1977 and 1978 (perhaps with outside support) led many analysts and policymakers in various Western countries to conclude that the West was increasingly vulnerable to drastic price increases and interruptions in the supply of so-called "strategic" or "critical" mineral commodities. With the election of Ronald Reagan in 1980, the possibility that the Soviets might seek to deny the West access to Africa's plentiful mineral supplies began to be taken quite seriously.[3] At the same time, France, West Germany, Japan, and Britain also evinced increasing concern about their vulnerability to both curtailments in the supply of important minerals and rapid increases in the prices of such minerals through producer collaboration.

However, several developments in the 1980s served to attenuate interest in the question of strategic minerals shortages. The world recession of 1981–2 unleashed a devastating onslaught on commodity prices and led to sustained downward price pressures and global oversupply of numerous mineral commodities throughout most of the 1982–6 period. The ascension to power of Soviet General Secretary Mikhail Gorbachev ushered in an era of friendlier East-West relations that caused many observers to pay less attention to the West's dependence on mineral imports from potentially unstable or unreliable suppliers. Finally, the efforts of Third World commodity producers to boost raw materials prices and institute new intergovernmental schemes to regulate international commodity markets utterly failed to change the way in which these markets operated, with the result that by the mid-1980s Western analysts were no longer expressing concern about developing countries' "commodity power."[4] Despite these events, the fact remains that in the 1970s and the very early years of the present decade, the West's potential vulnerability to interruptions in the supply of critical raw materials was viewed by several governments and many scholars as an important issue.

Because Canada is in the fortunate position of being more richly endowed with most mineral resources than its Western allies, it is not surprising that—with the notable exception of oil—there has been relatively little public or official concern about this country's reliance on mineral imports. The major contribution made by the mineral extraction and processing industries to Canada's national income and balance of payments indicates that government attention should quite properly be directed primarily towards promoting the country's interests as a minerals *exporter*. Nonetheless, fear of instability in both international minerals markets and supplier countries prompted various federal government departments in the late 1970s and early 1980s to examine the extent and implications of the country's dependence on foreign sources for all or a large part of its requirements of several minerals and metals. Reflecting this concern, this chapter concentrates on assessing Canada's vulnerability as an importer of nonfuel minerals. It first provides an overview of Canada's dependence on imports of such minerals. Following this is a more detailed examination of several specific cases where Canada may be vulnerable to supply interruptions caused either by instability in exporting countries or by actions such countries take to engineer large price increases. Finally, an analysis of the major policy options and difficulties facing Canada as an importer of nonfuel minerals will be offered.

OVERVIEW OF CANADIAN NONFUEL MINERAL IMPORTS

In 1985 imports of nonfuel crude and fabricated minerals cost Canada approximately $7.5 billion, up from $6.9 billion in 1984.[5] In the same year exports of nonfuel minerals and metals totalled $15.7 billion (vs. $15.6 billion in 1979). The United States was by far the most significant market for Canadian nonfuel minerals in the 1980s, accounting for close to 60 per cent (by value) of exports; the EEC received some 15 per cent and Japan just under 10 per cent of exports. About 65–70 per cent of Canadian mineral imports also come from the United States, although in many cases raw materials processed in the U.S. prior to shipment to Canada actually originate in third countries.

A breakdown of the nonfuel mineral import data reveals that the single most important category is *fabricated* (smelted, refined, and semi-manufactured) ferrous and nonferrous minerals, the import of which required outlays of $6.3 billion in 1985.[6] This reflects two things: first, that Canada must import many metals and fabricated materials whose constituent ores are not mined domestically; and second, that Canada also imports substantial quantities of metals and materials whose ores *are* mined within the country. Column three of Table 1 lists nearly thirty minerals not produced in Canada by the early 1980s and whose fabricated forms are generally only available to Canadian consumers through imports. Many of the minerals listed in the second column of Table 1 are also imported in processed forms owing in part to the inadequate scale of domestic mine production; tin is an example that will be considered in more detail in this chapter.

Also interesting are those mineral ores mined in significant quantities within the country, and often even exported in large volumes, but which are imported as metals and other fabricated materials. Tungsten is a good example. In its fabricated forms (particularly ferrotungsten and tungsten carbide), it is widely used for manufacturing cutting edges on machine tools because of its hardness, as an alloy constituent in the production of high-speed and tool-and-die steels, and in a variety of other super- and non-ferrous alloys.[7] Canada is in fact one of the major non-Communist producers of tungsten concentrates, accounting for about seven per cent of world mine output. According to the U.S. Bureau of Mines, Canada also has the second largest tungsten reserves in the world (the People's Republic of China has the bulk of known world reserves).[8] Despite this relative abundance, however, during the mid-1980s Canada annually spent some $7 million on imports of ferrotungsten carbide (rotary rock) drill bits, and some $14 million on imports of tungsten carbide tools (all largely purchased from the U.S. and the UK).[9] Among the several other minerals produced and exported as

TABLE 1: Sources of minerals and metals for Canadian needs

Essential minerals produced in Canada (surplus exported)	Minerals produced in Canada but not in right form (or deficit imported)	Minerals not presently produced in Canada (imports)
Arsenic	Antimony	Aluminum (bauxite and alumina)
Asbestos	Ball clay	Beryllium
Barium	Bentonite	Boron
Bismuth	Cesium	Bromine
Cadmium	Columbium	China clay (kaolin)
Calcium	Diatomite	Chromium
Cobalt	Fire clays	Corundum and emery
Common clays & shales	Gallium	Diamond (industrial and natural)
Copper	Gem stones (cottage	Feldspar
Ferosilicon	industry grade)	Flourine (fluorspar)
Gold	Iridium	Fuller's earth
Gypsum	Mica	Garnet
Helium	Palladium	Gem stones (high quality)
Indium	Platinum	Germanium
Iron	Pyrophyllite	Hafnium
Lead	Rare earths	Iodine
Lime	Rhenium	Kyanite
Magnesium	Rhodium	Lithium
Molybdenum	Rubidium	Manganese
Nepheline syenite	Ruthenium	Mercury
Nickel	Tantalum	Natural graphite
Potash	Thallium	Perlite
Radium	Tin	Pumice
Salt	Titanium	Strontium
Sand and gravel	Tungsten	Thorium
Selenium		Vanadium
Silicon		Vermiculite
Silver		Zirconium
Sodium sulphate		
Stone		
Sulphur		
Tellurium		
Uranium		
Zinc		

Sources: Department of National Defence Canada, Operation Research and Analysis Establishment, Directorate of Strategic Analysis, *Economic and Strategic Significance of Canada's Pacific Seaborne Trade* (Ottawa: November 1981), 107; and EMR, *Canadian Minerals Yearbook, 1985* (Ottawa: EMR 1986)

ores or concentrates but imported in fabricated form are nickel (of which Canada is the second largest producer and the largest exporter in the world), titanium (of which Canada mines a considerable volume although it meets all its metal and titanium dioxide needs through imports), and platinum (of which Canada is the third largest producer and exporter in the world although it imports certain platinum metals).[10] These trade patterns are examples of the kind of situation that has stimulated the arguments of the Science Council of Canada and economic nationalists opposed to the export of unprocessed raw materials.[11]

Canada also imports several non-metallic minerals in both crude and fabricated forms, with the most important being phosphate rock, essential for the production of fertilizers and largely imported from the U.S.; fluorspar, used in the chemical industry and in the production of artificial cryolite (needed for the electrolytic reduction of alumina to aluminum) and imported mostly from Mexico and Western Europe; industrial diamonds, used for drills and other industrial purposes and imported mainly from the U.S. (although they likely originate in raw form in Zaïre, South Africa, or the Soviet Union); and bentonite, primarily used in this country as a binder in the pelletizing of iron ore concentrates, and also mainly imported from the United States.[12]

It is evident that Canada is in a relatively favourable position compared to its allies with respect to the nine strategic minerals that have often been considered to pose the most serious security-of-supply problems for the NATO countries and Japan. In nickel, tungsten, and platinum Canada is basically self-sufficient, at least with respect to the crude forms of these minerals, and enjoys substantial

TABLE 2: Estimated import dependence of the United States, the EEC, and Japan: Imports as a percentage of consumption in the late 1970s and early 1980s

	U.S.	EEC	Japan
Bauxite and alumina	85	85	100
Chromium	90	100	100
Copper	13	95	98
Iron ore	30	80	95
Lead	10	70	78
Manganese	98	100	98
Nickel	70	100	100
Phosphate	exporter	99	100
Platinum group	90	100	100
Tin	82	88	98
Tungsten	57	99	98
Vanadium	30	99	100
Zinc	62	80	80

*Due to conflicting data and occasional uncertainties (e.g., whether scrap and recycled material are included), no claim is made that the table provides a precise picture of actual import dependence in any single year.

Sources: A Jordan and R. Kilmarx, *Strategic Mineral Dependence*, 18,34; "Availability of Strategic Materials," *Aviation Week and Space Technology*, 5 May 1980, p. 52; *Mineral Commodity Summaries*, 1986 (Washington: Bureau of Mines, Department of the Interior)

reserve bases as well. Japan and the European Community are totally dependent on external sources for these important commodities, while the United States also must meet most of its requirements through imports (see Table 2). Indeed, Canada itself supplies close to 40 per cent of U.S. and European Community nickel imports and significant shares of their tungsten requirements as well; it also sells nickel and tungsten to Japan.[13] As I have noted, Canada does rely on other countries for certain fabricated forms of nickel, tungsten, and platinum, but these imports tend to come from the U.S. and Western Europe rather than from potentially unreliable or unstable sources.[14] In the case of copper, another crucial mineral, Canada imports only minor amounts of semi-processed copper and is in fact a major world exporter, accounting for about 10 per cent of European Community and a quarter of U.S. imports.[15] Canada is also essentially self-sufficient in cobalt, a mineral whose supplies have at times been vulnerable to disruption because of Zaïre's role as the predominant producer and exporter.[16]

This leaves only four of the nine strategic minerals included in Tables 4 and 5: chromium, manganese, bauxite, and tin. In all these cases Canada's high degree of import dependence (see Table 3), combined with the economic importance of these minerals and their possible vulnerability to supply manipulation and/or interruption, justifies a closer examination.

TABLE 3: Canadian imports of selected minerals and materials in late 1970s and early 1980s

Commodity	Per cent Canadian consumption provided by imports	Principal uses
Alumina	45	to make aluminum
Bauxite	100	to make alumina
Bentonite	75	drilling muds
Beryllium	100	nuclear springs, specialty instrument
Chromium (ores and ferrochromium)	100	specialty steels, refractories
Fluorspar	100	aluminum, plastics, steel flux
Industrial diamond	100	cutting tools
Manganese	100	essential for steel
Mercury	100	caustic soda, paper industry
Phosphate rock	100	fertilizers
Platinum group metals (finished forms only)	100	cutting edges, catalysts
Tin	95	containers and cans
Titanium (metals and dioxides)	100	jet engines, pigments, steels
Vanadium (oxides and metal)	100	specialty and other steels, oxidation catalysts
Zirconium (zircon and alloys)	100	nuclear industry, abrasives

Sources: *Canada's Dependence on Imported Minerals and Metals—The Issues,* Energy, Mines and Resources Canada, Internal Report, Mineral Policy Sector, MRI 81/7 Ottawa: Aug. 1981); other internal EMR data provided to the author; *Mineral Commodity Summaries, 1986* (Washington: Bureau of Mines, Department of the Interior)

TABLE 4: Distribution of world reserves of selected strategic minerals, 1985*

Commodity	Percentages of major countries
Bauxite	Guinea—25.4; Australia—19.8; Brazil—12.5; Jamaica—8.6; India—5.1; Guyana—3.9
Chromium	South Africa—84.0; Zimbabwe—11.1; Soviet Union—1.9; Turkey—1.1
Cobalt	Zaire—25.0; Cuba—21.7; New Caledonia—10.3; United States—10.3; Zambia—6.5; Philippines—4.8; Canada 3.1
Copper	Chile—18.4; United States—17.1; Australia—7.8; Soviet Union—6.8; Zambia—6.4; Peru—6.1; Zaire—5.7; Canada—4.4
Manganese	South Africa—70.8; Soviet Union—20.8; Australia—4.0; Gabon—3.7; Brazil—1.5
Nickel	Cuba—22.5; New Caledonia—15.3; Canada—13.3; Soviet Union—7.3; Indonesia—5.2; Australia—4.8; Philippines—4.6
Platinum group metals	South Africa—80.8; Soviet Union—16.7; United States—1.3; Canada—0.7
Tin	Malaysia—37.0; Indonesia—22.7; Thailand—9.0; Australia—6.0: Bolivia—4.6; United Kingdom—3.0; China—2.6; Soviet Union—2.6; Brazil—2.3
Tungsten	China—35.5; Canada—19.3; Soviet Union—14.1; United States—8.4; Australia—4.0

*See the discussion of the concept of mineral reserves in the text.
Source: *Mineral Commodity Summaries* (Washington: Bureau of Mines, Department of the Interior 1986)

CANADIAN IMPORT VULNERABILITY: SPECIFIC EXAMPLES

As I have mentioned, Canada is more fortunate than most other Western countries in being able to meet its requirements for a great many crude minerals through domestic mine production. Like its allies, however, it depends on only a few foreign sources for minerals such as chromium, manganese, tin, and bauxite. Hence it must share the insecurity of the Western world regarding access to adequate supplies in the future. These four commodities are discussed next. Because the potential difficulties facing importers of chromium and manganese are largely traceable to the role of African suppliers (particularly the Republic of South Africa), these two metals are considered together.

The African Connection: Chromium and Manganese

The concentration of world production and reserves of chromite ore and, to a lesser extent, manganese in the Republic of South Africa, combined with the importance of these minerals in certain industrial uses, has led several Western gov-

TABLE 5: Shares of world mineral production, 1985 (based on actual mine production)*

Commodity	Percentages of major producers
Bauxite	Australia—35.4; Guinea—15.7; Brazil—7.9; Jamaica—6.9; Soviet Union—6.0; Yugoslavia—4.0: Greece—3.9
Chromium	Soviet Union—31.1; South Africa—31.1; Albania—9.4; Turkey—6.6; Zimbabwe—4.7 Indian—4.7; Philippines—2.8
Cobalt	Zaire—51.2; Zambia—14.2; Soviet Union—8.5; Canada—6.3; Cuba—5.1; Australia—4.3
Copper	Chile—16.5; United States—13.4; Canada—9.1; Soviet Union—7.7; Zaire—6.9; Zambia—6.1; Peru—5.1
Manganese	Soviet Union—42.6; South Africa—14.7 Brazil—9.3; Gabon—8.9; Australia—8.1; China—7.0; India—5.4
Nickel	Soviet Union—24.0; Canada—23.7; Australia—9.9; Indonesia—8.5; New Caledonia—5.3; Cuba—4.9
Platinum group metals	Soviet Union—50.0; South Africa—43.2; Canada—4.7
Tin	Malaysia—19.9; Soviet Union—17.4; Indonesia—9.9; Thailand—9.9; Bolivia—9.4; Brazil—8.9 China—7.4; Australia—4.5
Tungsten	China—29.9; Soviet Union—20.1; Canada—6.6; Republic of Korea—5.8; Australia—4.4; Bolivia—3.8; Portugal—3.1; Austria—3.1

*Note that mineral production rankings do not necessarily reflect countries' importance as exporters.
Source: *Mineral Commodity Summaries* (Washington: Bureau of Mines, Department of the Interior 1986)

ernments to establish or seriously consider establishing stockpiles in the past decade. Along with cobalt (of which Zaïre is the dominant exporter) and platinum (in which South Africa and the Soviet Union together dominate the global production) chromium and manganese are the nonfuel minerals that have been of most concern to policymakers in importing countries.[17] Both are unquestionably among the most essential metals. "Chromium is unique among metals in its ability to resist oxidation and corrosion, and it is also able to withstand stress at high temperatures."[18] It is "irreplaceable in stainless steels and high temperature resistant alloys, two classes of materials that are vital to the technological well-being" of modern industrial economies. Worse still, "there are no known . . . substitutes likely to be developed in the foreseeable future."[19] Chromium is indispensable in petrochemical processing and in the manufacturing of jet engines, turbines, precision tools, and nuclear reactors. As Table 4 makes clear, South Africa and Zimbabwe are completely dominant in terms of reserves of chromite (the ore); in terms of exports (not production), South Africa typically accounts for 25–30 per cent, the Soviets for around 25 per cent, and the Philippines, Zimbabwe, Turkey, Albania, and India for much smaller shares. The Soviet Union has tended to be a "sporadic contributor to the world market, taking advantage of a sort of 'dealer's' price opportunity in times of market tightness."[20] It halted all exports to the U.S. in the 1950s, and has at times sharply curtailed exports since then, apparently because of the vicissitudes of domestic output and a deteriorating ore grade. South Africa is actually a much larger presence in the market than its share of chromite exports suggests because it has increasingly opted to process more of its mine output into ferrochromium prior to sending it abroad. In the early 1980s it accounted for more than half of global ferrochromium exports.[21]

Like chromium, manganese is crucial in the production of steels, which accounts for some 90 per cent of its consumption. In fact, "there is little, if any, steel production which does not make use of substantial quantities of manganese."[22] It is added to steel furnaces in order to "scavenge" out the impurities, and it has no known substitute for this purpose.[23] It is also alloyed with steel to impart toughness and durability. Although substituting other materials for manganese is more feasible than doing the same for chromium, the costs associated with suddenly having to do so would be high and the consequences serious for the steel and allied industries.[24] The Soviet Union is by far the largest producer of manganese ore, followed by South Africa, Brazil, and Gabon (see Table 5). However, owing to domestic and Warsaw Pact requirements, little Soviet ore is now exported to the free market. Thus South Africa and Gabon have loomed large in the global export picture, accounting for roughly 35 per cent and 20 per cent, respectively. Other important exporters are Brazil, Australia, and India, although the latter has of late restricted its ore exports in an effort to conserve its rapidly dwindling reserves for domestic use.[25] In addition to South Africa, major exporters of *ferromanganese* include France, Norway, and Japan, which process imported ores both for domestic use and for sale abroad. The United States has reduced its domestic processing capacity and increasingly relies on imports of ferromanganese.[26] The Soviet Union and South Africa together account for the bulk of estimated world reserves, suggesting that South Africa will in the future play an increasingly important role as a provider of this mineral to Western countries.[27]

Table 6 provides data on the sources of Canada's imports of crude and fabricated chromium and manganese. A very important point to note is that *all of the ores and most of the metals imported from the United States and other NATO countries are re-exports, they do not originate in these countries.*[28] This makes it somewhat difficult to determine the original sources of Canada's imports. A number of metals imported into the country have been processed in the United States or elsewhere prior to their export here. In some cases, crude or fabricated minerals are simply bought by a U.S. broker before being sold to Canadian entities. With respect to chromium and manganese, the dominant position of South Africa, the Soviet Union, and a few other countries as exporters of *ore* strongly suggests that the bulk of Canadian requirements is met ultimately by these sources. Thus, like its allies Canada may be vulnerable to interruptions in the supply of these essential commodities; it cannot really protect itself from contingencies by purchasing these minerals from other sources.

How probable is it that some type of major supply interruption will face Canada and other importers in the foreseeable future? Although chromium and manganese have been regarded by those few Canadian policymakers concerned with security-of-supply issues as the most serious problems facing the country, it

TABLE 6: Main sources of Canadian imports of chromium and manganese, 1984*

Commodity	Country	Per cent of total imports by value
Chromium in ores/concentrates	United States	32.7
	South Africa	28.7
	Turkey	17.6
	Philippines	17.5
	Cuba	3.4
Ferrochromium	United States	45.7
	South Africa	34.1
	Sweden	16.2
	Zimbabwe	4.0
Manganese in ores/concentrates	Gabon	67.1
	Brazil	12.8
	United States	10.2
	South Africa	6.9
Ferromanganese	United States	45.6
	West Germany	20.9
	South Africa	19.6

*Note that ultimate sources often differ from recorded sources.
Source: EMR, *Canadian Minerals Yearbook, 1985*

is far from certain that any interruption in supplies must occur.[29] Despite the urgency that has periodically characterized discussions of strategic minerals in certain quarters, political analysts should recognize that unpleasant scenarios may well never unfold on the world stage.[30] On the other hand, the concentration of production, exports and—a crucial point in terms of the future—reserves in a few countries does indicate that political instability in leading supplier countries could pose dangers for importers.

Concern about chromium focuses primarily on the future stability of South Africa. South Africa is not only the major supplier of both chromite ore and ferrochromium to the Western world but also possesses, in conjunction with Zimbabwe, over "95 per cent of the world's reported reserves. . . and about 97 per cent of the additional known resources."[31] (A mineral's identified resource base consists of all known economic *and* subeconomic deposits.)[32] South Africa also warrants attention in connection with future supplies of manganese to Canada and other importers. It supplies close to 40 per cent of the ores imported by the West, and accounts for a smaller but growing share of the Western world's imports of ferromanganese.[33] Moreover, because it possesses the bulk of non-Communist world reserves (see Table 4), South African exports are likely to satisfy an increasing share of the non-Communist world's manganese needs. Also significant is the high-grade ore content of South African deposits and the prospect that "many of the lesser manganese producing countries will have depleted their reserves by the end of the century."[34] A second African state whose export policies and future stability must also be considered when assessing the future security of manganese supplies is Gabon, which recently has accounted for around 15–20 per cent of world ore exports.

Two kinds of supply disruption are possible in the future. Deliberate embargoes or partial curtailment of exports of chromium could occur if the key suppliers decided to press for a much higher market price for their non-renewable reserves. In the 1960s and early 1970s, the Soviet Union and Turkey at times took advantage of the fact that their high-grade metallurgical chromite ore was required for the major uses of chromium; since such ores were not available in sufficient quantities elsewhere, they were able to demand a premium on the market by tacitly co-operating to restrict supplies.[35] More recently, however, technological developments have made possible the use of other ores (particularly those found in South Africa) in the production of ferrochromium, the basic intermediate product for the manufacturing of stainless and other steel alloys. Thus the market power of Turkey and the Soviet Union has been undercut.[36] South Africa has to date not sought to exploit its market position to force prices up, although theoretically it could, in collaboration with the Soviets, precipitate a sharp price rise through reduced exports. Pretoria may possibly be reluctant to incur the political opprobrium of its Western customers that would surely result if it engaged in cartel-like behaviour. More to the point, though, the government apparently believes that South Africa's "large mineral reserve position. . . [is] best exploited by sufficient price restraint so as not to stimulate conservation and substitution on the part of consumers and increased production on the part of higher cost suppliers."[37] Despite the concern of some analysts about chromium suppliers, the 1981–2 recession did not spare the chromium market, although prices did not fall as drastically as those of many other minerals.[38]

Deliberate action by one or more of the major suppliers of manganese to the Western world to curtail exports is also highly improbable. Brazil and Australia are unlikely to participate in producers' attempts to restrict supplies, partly because they are anxious to increase their share of the markets for bauxite, manganese, and other minerals, and partly too because of their unwillingness to act in an unfriendly fashion towards close political allies and economic partners.[39] South Africa has similar motives for refraining from taking action to increase prices drastically. South Africa could conceivably seek to punish its Western critics by reducing exports of manganese, chromium, and other important minerals, but in fact its current plans anticipate a major *increase* in production of both manganese and chromium, a policy that is "hardly consistent with supply restriction."[40] The small share of South Africa's (and also Australia's and Brazil's) foreign exchange earnings accounted for by exports of manganese strongly suggests that incurring the political antipathy of the West and encouraging efforts to improve substitution and to expand high-cost production elsewhere are costs that would outweigh any short-term economic gains that might accrue from establishing a manganese cartel or curtailing exports.

On the other hand, Gabon, which unlike the other producers obtains a large share of its export earnings from manganese, might expect significant economic gains from the formation of an explicit manganese cartel designed to engineer large price increases. However, Gabon's ambitious plans to expand mine output and the major investments it has already made in improved transportation facilities indicate that it would be reluctant to abandon its goal of a greater market share. Moreover, without South Africa's co-operation a manganese cartel would be doomed, particularly in light of that country's dominant reserve position in the non-Communist world.[41] The land-based producers of manganese are also aware that severe upward price pressure will only intensify the search for seabed manganese nodules and improve the prospects for the economic recovery and sale of these resources.[42]

Disruption of chromium and manganese deliveries could result from political instability and turmoil in South Africa. Much scholarly ink has been spilt in the past ten years over the contentious question "how long will South Africa survive?"[43] No attempt to grapple with this difficult topic can be undertaken here, but it is reasonable to think that growing dissatisfaction among the disenfranchised elements of the South African community (the Blacks, Coloureds, and Indians who together comprise close to 85 per cent of the population) is virtually certain to cause more and more politically motivated acts of sabotage and terrorism against industrial, military, and other targets that symbolize the exclusive power and privilege enjoyed by the minority white regime. Unsupported by external allies, domestic insurgent groups would be no match for the powerful and recently much strengthened South African security forces.[44] Nonetheless, attacks on the transportation infrastructure, power plants, factories, and mining and processing facilities could certainly lead to at least partial and temporary interruptions in mineral production and exports. Also possible is the prospect of black opposition groups receiving significant support from other states in the region, and perhaps from the Soviet bloc as well. If this should happen, conflict between Pretoria and its neighbouring states (including perhaps a Marxist and black-ruled Namibia) could well occur, with incalculable consequences.[45] That many of South Africa's major mineral deposits are located in the northeast of the country, close to Zimbabwe and Mozambique, cannot be reassuring to anxious importers.[46]

A fear voiced by some observers in the late 1970s and early 1980s was the possibility that the Soviet Union could seek to deny the West access to southern Africa's minerals by exerting greater diplomatic, economic, and military influence in the region.[47] According to one alarmed Hudson Institute analyst, "the Soviets are seeking, in the long term, to deny the Western economies the resources of the Southern African region, a course which imposes a more diminished burden on Soviet foreign policy than a classical imperialist assault."[48] One bleak scenario had the Soviets simultaneously fomenting revolution in South Africa, gaining leverage over neighbouring black African states, and imposing—perhaps with the imprimatur of the United Nations—a naval blockade to interdict shipments of South African raw materials to the Western capitalist economies.[49] It was also noted that if the Kremlin could somehow control the whole of southern Africa, it could then put in place a "strategic materials supercartel," since more than half of the global output of some fifteen important strategic minerals comes from the Soviet bloc and this area of Africa.[50]

Another prospect that could lead to problems of supply involves the imposition of a United Nations embargo of South Africa, possibly accompanied by other economic and diplomatic sanctions. A major Resources for the Future study of future minerals availability judged this the most likely cause of a prolonged interruption in chromium and manganese supplies to the West.[51] In spite of their dependence on South Africa's mineral wealth, Canada and other Western nations may eventually conclude that their wider interests are best served by co-operating with a sanctions policy against an unpopular "pariah state."[52] However, the history of UN sanctions against Rhodesia after 1965 strongly suggests that ingenious importers can find ways of purchasing a desired commodity from an embargoed state.[53] The United States, of course, explicitly decided with the passage of the "Byrd Amendment" in 1971 simply to ignore the UN embargo and import chrome from Rhodesia, but other countries—including the Soviet Union, which resold Rhodesian chromium on the world market at a premium—also continued to trade with the white regime.[54] Western governments would have incentives to look the other way if business firms and brokers continued to import minerals from South Africa if some type of embargo were in effect.

It is of course impossible to know how or whether the tragic problems posed by the apartheid regime in South Africa will be resolved. Nor can it be said with certainty that upheaval in this mineral-rich region would necessarily lead to prolonged disruptions in mineral supplies, although a prudent policymaker would be unwise to assume that there would be none. It seems clear, however, that Western importing countries have reason to concern themselves about the future availability of chromium and manganese from South Africa and contiguous producing states. Canada, because of its total dependence on imports of these two minerals, cannot ignore events in this potentially very unstable area of the globe.

Bauxite: A Mineral Cartel?

Although aluminum is among the most plentiful metallic elements in the crust of the earth, bauxite is currently by far the most important and economically exploitable aluminum-bearing ore. Largely found in areas characterized by wet, tropical climates, it is usually mined in open-pit operations. After being washed, crushed, and then dried, bauxite is refined into alumina (aluminum oxide), which is then transported to a smelter, where aluminum is produced by subjecting the alumina to an electrolytic process that is highly energy-intensive. Four to five tons of bauxite ultimately yield one ton of aluminum metal.[55] The Western market economies are the major producers and consumers of aluminum, but with the exception of Australia, the OECD countries mine little bauxite. Historically the alumina-refining process has also been carried out in the developed countries that are the major producers of aluminum metal. More recently there has been a growing trend toward refining alumina within the countries in which the bauxite is mined, but at present relatively little aluminum is produced in the countries that are the major suppliers of the primary ore.

Another central feature of this industry is the presence of six large, vertically integrated multinational companies that control most of the non-Communist world's bauxite, alumina, and aluminum production. Although the influence of these firms (Aluminum Company of America; Alcan Aluminum, a Canadian firm; Reynolds; Kaiser Metals; Péchiney, which is French; and the Swiss company, Aluswisse) has been somewhat reduced because of the entry of new competitors and the partial nationalizations of bauxite mines and alumina refineries in several countries, they nonetheless continue to enjoy very strong market positions, especially at the stage of aluminum production.[56] The marketing skills and financial resources of these multinational firms have succeeded in vastly increasing the demand for aluminum metal, which is used in almost every industry and sector of the economy and is now second only to steel as the most widely used metal.

Australia and Guinea are the world's two most important producers of bauxite; they also possess the largest reserves (see Tables 4 and 5). Jamaica, which used to be the major producer, has seen its share decline in the face of the rapid development of the Australian and Guinean industries. A number of other developing countries also produce smaller quantities of bauxite, and several of them are very dependent on exports of the commodity for foreign-exchange earnings. Australia's share of world *exports* of bauxite is considerably smaller than its production share because increasing amounts of bauxite are refined into alumina prior to export.[57] The approximate export shares of other countries in the early 1980 were: Guinea, 25 per cent; Jamaica, 21 per cent; Guyana, 15 per cent; Surinam, 9 per cent; Greece, 4 per cent; Dominican Republic, 3 per cent; Yugoslavia, 2.5 per cent; Haiti, 2.5 per cent; Indonesia, 1.5 per cent; and Sierra Leone, Brazil, and Ghana, less than one per cent.[58] (Brazil's share has since increased to more than 10 per cent.)

With respect to alumina, Australia was the largest exporter, accounting for roughly 34 per cent, followed by Jamaica (22 per cent), Surinam (about 10 per cent), and Hungary, the U.S., and Guinea (5 per cent). It is important to note that many of the Western countries import bauxite and refine it into alumina for domestic use, not for sale abroad. For example, the United State produces over 15–18 per cent of the world's alumina, Canada just under 4 per cent, West Germany slightly less than 5 per cent, Japan about 6 per cent, and other West European countries smaller shares. The U.S., West Germany, France, Italy, and a few other Western countries (but *not* Canada) do export some of this alumina, but together they account for less than 20 per cent of alumina exports.[59]

In the case of trade in aluminum, the Western market economies are still predominant, and it is here that Canada occupies a prominent position as an exporter. Canada and Norway are the two largest exporters of aluminum, each typically responsible for 12–15 per cent of world exports. Other Western exporters include the Netherlands, West Germany, the UK, France, the United States, and Australia.[60] Canada and Norway enjoy a cost advantage in the provision of the huge volumes of electricity required to sustain an internationally competitive aluminum industry. Other Western countries are also major *producers* of aluminum. The world's largest producers in the early 1980s, in descending order, were the United States, the Soviet Union, Japan, and West Germany, followed by Canada and Norway. Only in the latter two, however, was production primarily for export rather than domestic consumption.[61]

Most of Canada's aluminum exports go to the United States; indeed, some two-thirds of U.S. aluminum imports come from its northern neighbour. Smaller quantities of various fabricated forms of aluminum metal go to Japan, Western Europe, and a few developing countries.[62] Two companies are involved in aluminum production in Canada. The Aluminum Company of Canada (Alcan) is by far the more important, operating four smelters in Quebec and one in British Columbia that together comprise about 85 per cent of Canadian smelter capacity. Canadian Reynolds Metals Company also operates a smelter in Quebec and accounts for the remainder of capacity. The latter company is a wholly owned subsidiary of the American firm Reynolds Metals, while Alcan is approximately 40 per cent Canadian-owned and apparently controlled by Canadian management.[63]

Table 7 lists the sources of Canada's bauxite and alumina imports. Of interest is the fact that Canada imports almost all its bauxite—none is mined in this country—from developing countries, particularly Brazil, Guinea, Guyana, and Surinam. Little is bought from Australia, the world's largest producer. In fact, relatively stable trade patterns have tended to develop between bauxite exporters and importers over the past twenty years because individual alumina plants depend upon particular types of ore mixes, and also because of the vertically integrated nature of the industry and the cost advantages associated with obtaining the mineral from nearby suppliers. The United States, for example, is very dependent upon the type of bauxite mined in the Caribbean countries, which are its closest suppliers. Canada, on the other hand, uses so-called trihydrate bauxite in its alumina plants, and this is found in a number of countries in Africa and the Western Hemisphere, as well as in Australia.[64] For supplies of alumina, Canada basically depends on other Western countries and on Jamaica. It is of course true that the United States and other developed countries (except Australia) that are alumina exporters obtain their bauxite elsewhere. This indicates that when discussing security-of-supply issues in connection with the aluminum industry, the proper focus is on the possibility of disruptions in deliveries of bauxite.

Considerable interest in the availability of bauxite supplies was shown by many analysts as a result of the creation in 1974 of the International Bauxite As-

TABLE 7: Main sources of Canadian imports of bauxite, alumina, and tin, 1984*

Commodity	Country	Per cent of total imports by value
Bauxite ore	Brazil	52.6
	Guyana	18.0
	Guinea	8.0
Alumina	Jamaica	37.5
	Australia	22.0
	Japan	19.8
Tin (blocks, pigs, and bars only)	United States	36.5
	Brazil	22.9
	The Netherlands	13.1
	Singapore	12.2
	Bolivia	10.7

*Note that ultimate sources often differ from recorded sources.
Source: EMR, *Canadian Minerals Yearbook, 1985*

sociation (IBA), a producers' group that in the eyes of some has many of the trappings of a cartel.[65] The Jamaicans, under Prime Minister Michael Manley, were the strongest proponents of a bauxite cartel, although there was also sympathy for such an organization among the governments of Surinam, Guyana, and Guinea. Initial members included Jamaica, Australia, Guinea, Guyana, Sierra Leone, Surinam, and Yugoslavia. Joining shortly thereafter were the Dominican Republic, Haiti, Ghana, and Indonesia. The IBA accounts for roughly 75 per cent of world bauxite production and for a smaller but still substantial share of alumina exports.[66] Jamaica was also the first producing state to overturn the existing taxation and regulatory rules governing the operations of the multinationals. In 1974 it partially nationalized the bauxite mines and increased bauxite production and export levies more than 700 per cent (from about U.S.\$1.77 to over U.S.\$15 a ton). Surinam, Guyana, Haiti, the Dominican Republic, and Guinea subsequently imposed tougher fiscal conditions on the aluminum firms' operations, although none increased levies and taxes to the same extent as Jamaica.[67]

All of these Third World bauxite producers hoped to emulate the recent and spectacularly successful resource pricing policy put into effect by OPEC; at the same time, the sharply higher prices they had now to pay for petroleum imports because of OPEC's success provided an additional motivation to obtain a greater return for exports of a non-renewable mineral of vital interest to the West. The changed fiscal regime imposed by the Third World bauxite exporters, combined with partial nationalizations of mines, did succeed in increasing the revenues accruing to the governments of producing countries, particularly Jamaica. The vertically integrated aluminum companies reluctantly accepted the new policies, since they did not want to jeopardize their sources of bauxite. In most cases they retained managerial control and partial ownership of mines and refineries, and they felt they could pass along the cost of higher bauxite levies because of the industry's oligopolistic structure and the fact that even at the higher price levels bauxite still constitutes only a small part of the cost of aluminum metal.[68]

Bauxite is one of the most important minerals imported by Canada. Were supplies to suddenly disappear, the aluminum industry would be unable to operate. However, in spite of the actions by various IBA members to extract greater revenues from companies involved in mining bauxite, there has never been any suggestion of an IBA embargo or a curtailment of exports to Western importers.[69] The IBA has sought on several occasions since late 1977 to agree to a minimum price for exports of bauxite and alumina, but these minimum levels have typically been close to prevailing market prices and, more importantly, *no collective effort to vary supplies in support of a price floor has been undertaken.*[70]

For several compelling reasons, Canada and other importers are not likely to face deliberately planned reductions in bauxite exports. First, the suppliers who have generally been the most militant and imposed the toughest conditions on the companies (Jamaica, Surinam, Guyana) have seen their market shares decline precipitously because the multinationals have shifted investment to more hospitable countries, in particular Australia and Guinea. Second, Australia, the number one source of bauxite, has exhibited little interest in forcing up market prices because it enjoys low production costs and is not prepared to threaten close political allies with reductions in bauxite or alumina deliveries. Along with Guinea and Brazil (which has not joined the IBA but which has substantial bauxite reserves and ambitious plans to develop them), Australia is anxious to increase its market share, a policy that is not compatible with much higher prices. Also significant is the fact that these three countries have been more lenient in their treatment of the multinational aluminum firms than have Jamaica, Guyana, and others. Third, bauxite producers are aware that importing countries have available essentially limitless quantities of non-bauxite, aluminum-bearing ores that they could exploit if the cost of bauxite were to rise significantly. Although it could take up to two years to switch over to producing alumina from non-bauxitic ores, the long-term impact of such a technological development on producing countries would be devastating. Thus while future hikes in bauxite prices certainly cannot be ruled out, deliberate embargoes or reductions in exports are extremely unlikely, and the magnitude of any price increase is constrained by the availability of other sources of aluminum.[71]

The possibility that bauxite exports might be reduced as a consequence of political instability or civil strife within the countries in which it is mined must also be considered. It is noteworthy that four developing countries (Guinea, Jamaica, Guyana, and Surinam) currently account for about half of world bauxite exports. That internal turmoil could engulf one or more of these countries is not inconceivable. However, as noted previously, Canada is more fortunate than the United States in that it is mainly dependent on a type of bauxite found in more regions of the world, whereas the U.S. has traditionally relied mostly on so-called "Jamaican-type" bauxite, which is only mined in the Caribbean area.[72]

Moreover, it is highly likely that Canada will import relatively less bauxite and more alumina in the future, as bauxite mining countries seek to refine increasing amounts of their ores. This trend will reduce Canada's dependence on traditional bauxite suppliers while heightening its reliance on Australia and Jamaica, the largest suppliers of its alumina imports (see Table 7). In addition, as Brazil, Indonesia, and other new bauxite producers cut a wider swath in the world market, the prospect of lessening dependence on a small number of traditional suppliers becomes more feasible. In the past few years, for example, Brazil has grown to become Canada's biggest supplier of bauxite. If the Canadian aluminum industry began to fear for the stability and reliability of its current sources of bauxite, it would likely undertake a concerted effort to diversify. It must also be stressed once again that future technological developments may make possible the production of alumina from non-bauxite materials such as clays, anorthosite, and alunite. Alcan has conducted research into the possibility of using other materials.[73] Finally, while internal strife in a given country could lead to temporary supply interruptions, it is improbable that more than one major bauxite exporter would be facing such a situation at any one time. Since most Third World bauxite suppliers are very dependent on selling this commodity abroad to earn foreign exchange, governments in these countries would surely seek to resume exports as soon as practicable.[74]

Tin: Scarcity and Potential Cartelization

The last of the strategic minerals for which Canada must depend on foreign sources is tin. It is included in many analysts' lists of potential problem minerals largely because it is almost exclusively mined in developing and Communist countries (see Table 5). A handful of countries accounts for the bulk of world mine output: five countries alone (Malaysia, Thailand, the USSR, Bolivia, and Indonesia) are responsible for more than 65 per cent. Because the Soviet Union and other non-Third World suppliers mine tin for domestic use, export concentration is even greater than production statistics would indicate. In the early

1980s, four countries accounted for almost 70 per cent of world exports: Malaysia (29.1 per cent), Bolivia (10.7 per cent), Thailand (14.1 per cent), and Indonesia (13.8 per cent).[75] These developing countries not only mine the basic tin ore (cassiterite), but also smelt the vast majority of the world's tin metal. This contrasts sharply with the case of bauxite and aluminum. Minor producers of tin metal include Brazil, Australia, the United Kingdom, Spain, the United States, Nigeria, and Zaïre; the first two are likely to become significant exporters in the decades ahead because of their large and mostly underdeveloped deposits (Table 4).[76] Tin has more numerous and more readily usable substitutes than most of the other strategic minerals considered here, but it is nonetheless regarded as an essential industrial raw material by most analysts. Its most important use, accounting for some 40 per cent of consumption, is as a coating on steel strips to form tinplate; it is also used in solders and in the chemical industry.[77] A significant share of the Western world's tin requirements is satisfied through secondary recovery, and if the primary metal were unavailable, secondary sources would presumably become even more important.[78]

Canada currently meets a tiny share of its tin requirements through recovery of the ore as a by-product of base-metal mining and milling, but since the country has no smelting capacity this small quantity must be shipped elsewhere. It is difficult to determine the ultimate sources of Canada's imports because Canadian buyers tend to purchase the metal from U.S. metal merchants who arrange for transshipment through New York; thus the United States is predominant in the import statistics.[79] However, because the U.S. is also largely dependent on imports and obtains some 60 per cent of its tin from Southeast Asian suppliers and most of the rest from Bolivia, Canada must also be assumed to be dependent on these same sources.[80] Curtailment of tin exports from Asian producers following the Japanese occupation during the Second World War forced Canada, the United States, and other importers to rely on Bolivia and minor producers such as Nigeria and the Belgian Congo, as well as to exploit subeconomic domestic deposits. This experience, combined with the sharp escalation in tin prices early in the Korean War, promoted the United States to include tin in its list of strategic commodities to be stockpiled. Huge quantities of the metal were purchased by the U.S. in the early 1950s, and before long Washington's tin stockpile was large enough to satisfy several years of U.S. requirements.[81] Although other countries stockpiled minor amounts of tin, only the U.S. has bought the metal on a large scale. Washington has significantly reduced the size of its tin stockpile since the late 1960s, but Congress has refused to permit the disposal of much of the "excess" metal for fear of adverse consequences on American defence preparedness; as a result the U.S. still possesses sufficient tin to meet the nation's needs for several years.[82]

Tin is the only mineral commodity to have been subject to an inter-governmental, producer-consumer commodity control agreement designed to ameliorate market instability. The first such agreement was negotiated in 1953 and came into effect three years later; successor agreements were renegotiated at five-year intervals until 1985, when the scheme collapsed. Through the employment of a buffer stock and, when necessary, export controls, the tin control schemes have aimed to reduce price fluctuations and, perhaps more importantly, they have provided an essentially guaranteed minimum price to the producers, virtually all of which are developing countries.[83] Canada has been a signatory to all the postwar tin agreements, as have most major importing countries (except the U.S. before 1976) and all the important exporters. One might expect that the existence of this co-operative, producer-consumer institution would ease the anxieties of importing countries about the security of future supplies. Occasionally in recent years, however, certain tin exporters—particularly Bolivia, which depends on the commodity for up to 70 per cent of export earnings—have threatened to withdraw from the agreement because of dissatisfaction with its operation, and to press for a producers' cartel.[84] In 1980–1, despite the generally poor state of the metals market, the tin price held up remarkably well, reportedly as a result of secret large-scale interventions by Malaysia and other producing countries to force prices up.[85] In addition, very few new, exploitable deposits of tin have been found in recent decades; as a result there is some concern about the adequacy of supplies into the next century.[86] This relative scarcity, combined with the concentration of production and exports, could make possible the formation of an effective tin cartel, at least in the short run. This cartel in turn could seek to reduce exports in order to push up the market price.

The likelihood of this occurring is slim, however. Several factors militate against a deliberately planned effort by producers to follow an OPEC-type pricing and supply policy. First, as noted earlier, tin has several acceptable substitutes that, in the event of a major price increase, would probably be used in various industries (for example, aluminum, glass, and paper can replace tin cans in the packaging industry). Such substitution would not be without its costs, but at some point it would clearly become the preferred strategy of tin consumers.[87] Second, several importing countries, including Canada, have deposits of tin ore that have not been vigorously exploited for economic and technical reasons. Once again, sharply higher prices and/or threats of disruptions in deliveries by tin exporters would precipitate greater interest in expanding indigenous production. In Canada's case, several projects are currently under way that promise to make the country more self-sufficient in tin by the 1990s.[88] Third, some countries that are currently not major actors in the tin market do possess significant reserves that are likely to be exploited on an increasing scale, particularly if prices rise significantly. Australia and Brazil are two such countries, and they are known to be hostile to cartel pricing policies.[89] Thus, while tin prices may well rise as a result of periodic shortfalls in supply (and perhaps occasional market manipulation by major exporting countries), a purposeful policy of reducing deliveries to importing countries should not be expected of the tin exporters.

Tin exports could also be threatened by domestic strife in producing countries or by interstate conflicts. Bolivia has had output reduced by both strikes by tin miners and the political chaos endemic to that unfortunate land. One pessimistic scenario involves the development of serious difficulties in the operation of Malaysia's tin-smelting capacity, particularly the mammoth Penang smelter. Since Malaysia accounts for up to 50 per cent of the non-Communist world's tin metal exports, the prolonged incapacitation of its smelting facilities would cause problems for importing countries.[90] It must also be stressed that an interstate conflict in Southeast Asia that engulfed one or more of the area's tin exporters could also lead to reduced tin deliveries. In this connection, the possibility of a Vietnamese incursion into Thailand warrants mention.

However, bouts of political instability in Malaysia, Indonesia, and Thailand have had no significant impact on the availability of tin. Except perhaps for Bolivia, these countries also appear to be more stable now than during the 1950s and 1960s. On balance, the prospect of serious interruptions in tin supplies to Canada and other import-dependent countries must be judged more remote than prospects for disruptions in chromium and manganese supplies.

Other Minerals

The minerals I have just discussed are considered by most analysts as strategic metals for which the Western nations, including Canada, are mainly dependent on "foreign" sources of supply—"foreign" meaning non-Western countries. Canada must also rely on external sources for a variety of other mineral raw materials; as Table 3 makes clear, tin, bauxite, chromium, and manganese are by no means the only ones in which the country is entirely import-dependent. In 1981 the Department of Energy, Mines and Resources analysed Canada's potential vulnerability with respect to imports of some of these other minerals.[91] Its brief analysis suggested that because most of Canada's imports of minerals listed in Table 3 come from the United States and other Western countries (a designation that includes Australia but *not* South Africa), the threat of supply disruptions is significantly reduced. For example, most of this country's imports of bentonite, feldspar, titanium metal, vanadium, and phosphates come from the United States, a major producer of these minerals. For zirconium, essential in the nuclear industry, the largest source of imports and the world's largest producer is Australia, also considered a "safe" supplier.[92] Industrial diamonds are an exception in that world supplies largely originate in southern Africa and the Soviet Union (although once again Canada's imports are routed through the United States and other Western countries). However, the development of synthetic diamonds, which are acceptable substitutes in all of the uses of industrial diamonds except hardrock and cement core drilling, indicates that consumers' stocks could be utilized for these particular purposes if exports are curtailed.[93] It must be stressed that equanimity regarding the future availability of minerals from Canada's allies could be dispelled if, for example, certain of these countries decided to restrict or eliminate exports in order to conserve supplies for domestic use. But barring such an occurrence, obtaining these minerals should not be difficult in the future.

CONCLUSION: SOME POLICY CONSIDERATIONS

Only recently has the Canadian government begun to exhibit interest in the future availability of nonfuel imports. The Department of Energy, Mines and Resources (EMR) is the key agency in the development of mineral policy for the country, and various officials from there have been involved in exploring the dimensions and implications of Canadian dependence on external supplies of certain minerals. In early 1980 EMR surveyed a large number of experts in order to set priorities and criteria for future detailed examinations of specific Canadian mineral imports. The survey's results led to the establishment of three "priority groups" of imported minerals and metals.[94] The four minerals selected for closer inspection in this paper (chromium, manganese, bauxite, and tin) were all included in EMR's "highest priority" group. Subsequently the department recommended that chromium and manganese be singled out for urgent attention because of the potential unreliability of major suppliers and the critical need for these raw materials in various industries.[95] Other Canadian government departments with some interest in this issue are External Affairs and Defence, although little in the way of published discussions or analyses has emerged from them.[96]

Clearly, Canada is less vulnerable than its allies to interruptions in mineral supplies. Some commodities that are of great concern to other Western countries are not problems for Canada because the country is totally or largely self-sufficient; cobalt, platinum, and nickel are examples. However, if Canada's main trading partners were faced with serious and prolonged mineral supply shortages, Canada would suffer indirectly from their direct misfortune; this country's comparative mineral resource wealth cannot really insulate the country from problems caused by possible shortages afflicting other western countries.

Governments anxious to lessen their nations' vulnerability to disruptions in the supply of mineral raw materials have several options available. It must be stressed that some policies designed to cope with perceived security-of-supply problems will be incapable of dealing with sudden, unanticipated interruptions in mineral deliveries, while others will be specifically addressed to such short-term difficulties. This distinction between short- and long-term perspectives must be borne in mind when assessing various policies to reduce national vulnerability.

Import Diversification

Perhaps the best strategy for nervous mineral importers is to encourage the development of additional mineral deposits throughout the world. Dispersal of sources of supply will, among other things, moderate the impact of production disruptions in any single exporting country *and* make more difficult the establishment of exporters' cartels. For example, the Western world's sporadic concern over possible interruptions in cobalt deliveries because of political instability in Zaïre, the predominant producer, would presumably be substantially reduced if other countries also became major producers. Similarly, the consequences for the world chromium market of severe turmoil in southern Africa would be less disastrous if there were more major exporters of that essential commodity. It is not surprising that analysts who have examined the West's susceptibility to cut-offs in exports of cobalt and chromium have recommended that other foreign suppliers be encouraged to expand their output.[97] Economists also underline the critical importance of diversifying the sources of a commodity to reduce the likelihood and effectiveness of cartels.[98] The 1976 proposal of the United States to create an International Resources Bank to help fund mineral exploration and development in the Third World was clearly motivated by a desire to increase and diversify supplies of key minerals.[99] However, as noted previously, Western companies involved in the nonfuel mineral sector have since the late 1960s shifted much of their investment capital out of developing countries as a result of numerous nationalizations and episodes of instability.[100] The political and social environment in many areas of the world is simply not propitious for the investment of hundreds of millions of dollars in mining projects, particularly when foreign-owned enterprises are involved. Nonetheless, the emergence of Brazil, Australia, and a few other countries as major exporters of certain strategic minerals, combined with the possibility that China may also enter world markets in a more vigorous way, offers some prospect for supply diversification over the longer term.

Substitution, Recycling, and Technological Improvements in Resource Use

When a mineral's real price rises, a certain amount of substitution is bound to occur even without any active measures by governments. Price escalation will also encourage efforts to improve recycling and to economize on the intensity of resource use. There are, of course, limits to the extent of substitution that can occur for most minerals. In some cases no known substitutes exist. Cobalt, for example, is indispensable in the manufacturing of jet engines and high speed tools.[101] At the same time, it is always true that a material can be replaced in at least some of its applications.[102] Cobalt again is an example. After the invasions of Zaïre's Shaba province in 1977 and 1978, consumers moved to replace cobalt with other metals in high-temperature super-alloys wherever possible, and this, in conjunction with the recent recession, depressed the market for the commodity.[103] Another interesting example is bauxite, which can be replaced by non-bauxitic ores in the making of aluminum. Aluminum itself must compete with other metals and materials in most of its uses. The resort to substitutes is not a solution to the problem of mineral import vulnerability and is not likely to offer immediate relief in the event of a sudden reduction of supplies, but "the possibility of substitutes represents a real threat at any time to the effective maintenance of substantially higher prices."[104] The prospect that synthetic and natural substitutes will be developed thus acts to check the enthusiasm of mineral producers for cartels and embargoes.

Increasing secondary mineral production can also help to lessen the costs imposed by interruptions in mineral exports. Secondary production entails "collecting, sorting, transporting, and processing scrap, either new scrap generated in the manufacturing process or old scrap recovered from finished products that have been used and discarded."[105] The costs associated with recycling scrap vary widely from case to case. In the United States more than 40 per cent of the iron, copper, and lead used in final goods is recovered, as is 16–17 per cent of the aluminum and zinc, and some analysts argue that industrial economies can be run largely on recyclable materials.[106] However, recycling is practiced extensively where it is already economical to do so, and substantial increases would be costly.[107] Recycling would nonetheless offer some help in mitigating the consequences of curtailments in mineral deliveries, and it certainly becomes more feasible as mineral prices rise.

While recycling can help to meet national mineral requirements if imports are disrupted, better and more efficient use of resources and the employment of technology to develop substitutes can lessen reliance on foreign sources for vital materials. According to one economist, "the most important factor alleviating resource scarcity is increases in resource productivity stemming from capital accumulation and technical progress."[108] It is not difficult to find examples of how technological advances have altered patterns of mineral use. The twentieth century has witnessed tremendous improvements in mining techniques and in metallurgy that have extended the life of mineral reserves and made possible the economic exploitation of progressively lower grade ores. Ferdinand Banks notes that thanks to increasing productivity and the application of more sophisticated mining techniques, "the real cost of obtaining copper from ore with a copper content of 0.5% is no higher today than it was a century ago, when ore content averaged 6%."[109] The development of electrolytic plating has greatly reduced the amount of tin needed to manufacture the tin can, while the introduction of synthetic rubber has fundamentally changed the market for elastomers.[110] In the steel industry, the ability to substitute one material for another in the production of many steel alloys mitigates the consequences of being unable to acquire a particular mineral or metal or of being able to purchase it only at a much higher price. Analysts concerned about dependence on external supplies of strategic minerals often call for government policies to encourage the substitution of relatively abundant and secure materials for scarce and expensive materials, to foster the development of technologies that increase productivity and economize on the intensity of resource use, and for subsidies for recycling and other efforts to improve secondary recovery.[111] With the partial exception of greater recycling, these policies will not significantly lessen the vulnerability of importing countries in the short term, but they should certainly do so over a longer period.

Exploiting Domestic Deposits

Although many countries that import strategic minerals and metals could theoretically choose to replace a portion of such imports with subeconomic domestic reserves, it is obvious that high (perhaps very high) economic costs would be incurred by a conscious strategy of mineral self-reliance. Economists tend to be very critical of this kind of approach to the problem of mineral import dependence, arguing that countries "should rely on imports for their mineral requirements that cannot be supplied domestically at competitive world prices."[112] Yet for policymakers worried about the threat of mineral supply interruptions, subsidizing the development of domestic deposits may seem an attractive option in certain cases and even a necessity in others. But this strategy will be feasible only to the extent that a country actually possesses domestic resources of sought-after minerals. The American government has provided subsidies to the domestic titanium industry in the form of loan assistance and purchase guarantees because of the need for titanium metal in various high-technology weapons applications.[113] The U.S. Defense Production Act permits public subsidization of domestic mining operations where this has been deemed essential to military security and defence preparedness, and there has in this decade been some consideration given to employing this legislative authority in order to facilitate the development of low-grade cobalt and chromium deposits by U.S. mining firms.[114] Canada does have deposits of several minerals currently imported into the country, although most of these are not now commercially viable. Significant resources of chromium exist in Manitoba and the Eastern Townships area of Quebec; in the latter, chromite was actually mined during the Second World War. Low-grade manganese deposits are found in Nova Scotia, New Brunswick, and British Columbia.[115] And, as noted previously, domestic tin reserves and non-bauxitic sources of aluminum are being developed by Canadian mining companies. If government and industry in Canada ever became more concerned about the future availability of, say, chromium and manganese, it might well be worthwhile to explore the possibility of bringing domestic deposits into production with the aid of government subsidies. Provided that such a policy was restricted to a small number of particularly promising cases, it is unlikely that major public expenditures would be required.

The Stockpile Option

Stockpiling minerals and metals is perhaps the most effective means of mitigating the consequences of sudden disruptions in supplies caused by instability in major exporting countries, by embargoes, or by manifestations of cartel behaviour. The United States has had a major stockpile program in effect since the late 1940s, but the acquisition and disposal of materials in the stockpile has been governed by military and national defence criteria and needs. According to some observers, however, a tendency has developed to perceive the U.S. stockpile as also meeting more general economic and industrial security goals.[116] An example of the latter was the disposal of large amounts of tin from the strategic stockpile during the 1960s, which helped to ease an acute world supply shortage.[117] The prospect of additional tin disposals has more recently attenuated the enthusiasm of tin exporters for an explicit cartel. A number of analysts and institutions were recommending in the late 1970s that the U.S. build up an *economic* stockpile in order to provide some protection against shortages of certain materials essential to the smooth functioning of industry.[118] Such a stockpile would contain only a few minerals and metals currently imported from countries deemed unstable or unreliable, with chromium, manganese, cobalt, and platinum the most likely candidates for inclusion. These recommendations, however, have yet to be taken seriously.

Other Western governments have already established economic contingency stocks of certain materials, or else have considered doing so. The French government has for several years been buying a number of minerals and metals for the national stockpile, but details on its composition and the criteria governing its use are very difficult to come by owing to the secrecy surrounding the program. In the early 1980s the British government created a small stockpile that, like the French, was shrouded in official secrecy for no apparent reason. Japan, which is of course much more reliant on mineral imports than most of the Western nations, has apparently decided to stock cobalt, chromium, and several other materials, with both the government and the private sector providing the necessary funding. [119] And Sweden has for some time acquired minerals for both a wartime emergency stockpile and a peacetime contingency stockpile, although the quantities purchased to date are quite minor. [120]

There are no government-financed or government-supported stocks of commodities in Canada at present, although industry does of course maintain inventories of needed materials as a part of normal business operations. The previous analysis identified chromium and manganese as the essential mineral imports most susceptible to supply disruptions, so it is worth examining whether stocking these materials would be desirable. Because the quantities of chromium and manganese imported into the country are not great and they can be stored without serious deterioration, it may not be costly to acquire, with limited government financial support, contingency stocks. It is estimated that the cost of purchasing the equivalent of one year's imports of these two commodities would be around $70 million, with additional costs being incurred through the provision of stockpile facilities. [121] (A recent U.S. report recommended the acquisition of peacetime contingency stocks sufficient to satisfy up to two years of consumption requirements for chromium and twelve to eighteen months for manganese.)[122] However, private stockholdings of manganese ore are already quite significant, suggesting that any government purchases could be restricted to ferromanganese. [123]

It is unlikely that any stockpile initiatives will be taken at the governmental level to address the questions posed by Canada's vulnerability to interruptions in supplies of chromium, manganese, or other materials unless or until some kind of actual supply shortfall occurs. By then, however, it may be extremely expensive to build up contingency stocks. For the moment, it is apparent that security-of-supply issues have been stirring little anxiety and even less curiosity in the makers of Canadian mineral policy and in the country's mineral producers.

NOTES

1 Zuhayr Mikdashi, *The International Politics of Natural Resources* (Ithaca, NY: Cornell University Press 1976).

2 Kenneth W. Clarfield et al., *Eight Mineral Cartels* (London: Metals Week 1975); P. Connelly and R. Perlman, *The Politics of Scarcity* (London: Oxford University Press 1975); Donella H. Meadows et al, *The Limits to Growth* (New York: Universe Books 1972); Charles River Associates, *International Minerals Cartels and Embargoes* (New York: Praeger 1980), hereinafter cited as *International Minerals Cartels;* C. Fred Bergsten, "The Threat From the Third World," *Foreign Policy* 14 (Summer 1973):102–24; and Ruth and Uzi Arad, "Scarce Natural Resources and Potential Conflict," in Ruth and Uzi Arad et al., *Sharing Global Resources* (New York: McGraw-Hill for the Council on Foreign Relations 1979).

3 Senator Sam Nunn and D. Bartlett, *NATO and the Soviet Threat* (Washington: U.S. Government Printing Office, Jan. 1977); W.C.J. Van Rensburg, "Africa and Western Lifelines," *Strategic Review* 6 (Spring 1978):41–50.

4 On the declining interest in raw materials issues in the 1980s, see Jock Finlayson and David Haglund, "Whatever Happened to the Resource War?," *Survival* 29 (Sept./Oct. 1987):403–15.

5 Energy, Mines and Resources Canada, *Canadian Minerals Yearbook, 1985* (Ottawa: EMR 1986), Tables 1 and 2; and G.R. Peeling, "Canada's Non-Fuel Mineral Trade and the International Scene," *Canadian Mining Journal* (Feb. 1984):26–7. Unless otherwise noted, all dollar amounts are in Canadian currency. Totals exclude scrap.

6 EMR, *Canadian Minerals Yearbook, 1985,* Table 2.

7 EMR, *Canadian Minerals Yearbook, 1985,* Ch. 63.

8 U.S. Bureau of Mines, *Mineral Commodity Summaries, 1986* (Washington: Bureau of Mines, Department of the Interior 1986), 171 (hereinafter cited as *Mineral Commodity Summaries*).

9 EMR, *Canadian Minerals Yearbook, 1985,* Ch. 63.

10 EMR, *Canadian Minerals Yearbook, 1985,* Ch. 63. See also Canada, Department of National Defence, *Economic and Strategic Significance of Canada's Pacific Seaborne Trade* (Ottawa: Operational Research and Analysis Establishment, Directorate of Strategic Analysis, Department of National Defence, Nov. 1981), 36–7 and 50.

11 See, for example, the following study by the Science Council of Canada: *The Weakest Link: A Technological Perspective on Canadian Industrial Underdevelopment* (Ottawa: Oct. 1978).

12 EMR, *Canadian Minerals Yearbook, 1985.* See also DND, *Economic and Strategic Significance,* 21, 24–7, 113, 122, 131, and 134.

13 *Mineral Commodity Summaries,* 108, 170; Paul Cheesewright, "Raw Materials: Europe's Age of Anxiety," *OPTIMA* 28 (Aug. 1979):165.

14 DND, *Economic and Strategic Significance,* 147.

15 *Mineral Commodity Summaries,* 42; DND, *Economic and Strategic Significance,* 128–9.

16 DND, *Economic and Strategic Significance,* 33–4.

17 W.C.J. Van Rensburg, "Global Competition for Strategic Mineral Supplies," *Resources Policy* 7 (Mar. 1981):7ff.; and interviews with officials in the Department of Energy, Mines and Resources, Mineral Policy Sector, Dec. 1981.

18 DND, *Economic and Strategic Significance,* 25.

19 National Materials Advisory Board, Commission on Sociotechnical Systems, National Research Council, *Contingency Plans for Chromium Utilization: Report of the Committee on Contingency Plans for Chromium Utilization* (Washington: National Academy of Sciences 1978), 1 (hereinafter cited as *Contingency Plans*). See also DND, *Economic and Strategic Significance,* 25; and J. Nutting, "Cobalt and Chromium," in J. Nutting et al., *Future Metal Strategy* (London: Metals Society 1980), 106–8.

20 *World Mineral Trends and U.S. Supply Problems* (Washington: Resources for the Future 1980) (hereinafter cited as *World Mineral Trends*).

21 *World Mineral Trends,* 216, 454; *Mining Journal,* 4 Jan. 1980, 7.

22 *World Mineral Trends,* 163. See also P.L. Dancoisne, "Manganese," in Nutting et al., *Future Metal Strategy,* 72–8.

23 Charles F. Park, *Earthbound: Minerals, Energy and Man's Future* (San Francisco: Freeman, Cooper 1975), 58.

24 *World Mineral Trends,* 163; *International Minerals Cartels,* 171.
25 *World Mineral Trends,* 218–20.
26 *World Mineral Trends,* 219.
27 *World Mineral Trends,* 297–8.
28 DND, *Economic and Strategic Significance,* 25, 27. EMR, *Canadian Minerals Yearbook, 1985,* Chs. 18, 38.
29 Interviews. Also see Energy, Mines and Resources Canada, *Chromium: An Imported Mineral Commodity,* Mineral Bulletin MR196 (Ottawa: Minister of Supply and Services 1983).
30 See, for instance, Van Rensburg, "Global Competition for Strategic Mineral Supplies"; Herbert Meyer, "How We're Fixed for Strategic Minerals," *Fortune,* 9 Feb. 1981, 68–70; and David Kroft, "The Geopolitics of Non-Energy Minerals," *Air Force Magazine* (June 1979):78–9.
31 *World Mineral Trends,* 484
32 *Mineral Commodity Summaries,* 182–4.
33 *World Mineral Trends,* 220–1, 494; *International Minerals Cartels,* 165.
34 *Mining Journal,* 12 June 1981, 454.
35 *World Mineral Trends,* 487–8; *International Minerals Cartels,* 46.
36 *International Minerals Cartels,* 46
37 *World Mineral Trends,* 448.
38 *Mining Journal,* 6 Nov. 1981, 345–7.
39 *World Mineral Trends,* 494; *International Minerals Cartels,* 47–81.
40 *World Mineral Trends,* 495. See also reports on South Africa's plans to expand its mine output of chromium and manganese in *Mining Journal,* 4 Jan. 1980, and 12 June 1981, pp. 453–4.
41 *World Mineral Trends,* 495–6; *International Minerals Cartels,* 48.
42 Judith Kildow, ed., *Deepsea Mining* (Cambridge, MA: MIT Press 1980), especially the articles by Jane Z. Fraser, "Resources in Seafloor Manganese Nodules," 41–83, and Lance Antrim, "The Role of Deepsea Mining in the Future Supply of Metals," 84–106.
43 On South Africa's future political stability, see I. William Zartman, "Negotiations in South Africa," *Washington Quarterly* 11 (Autumn 1988):141–58. Also see, Richard E. Bissell and Chester A. Crocker, eds., *South Africa into the 1980s* (Boulder, CO: Westview press 1979); Robert A. Jaster, *South Africa's Narrowing Security Options,* Adelphi Paper no. 159 (London: International Institute of Strategic Studies, Spring 1980); L.H. Gann and Peter Duignan, *South Africa: War, Revolution, or Peace?* (Stanford: Hoover Institution Press 1978); and R.W. Johnson, *How Long Will South Africa Survive?* (London: Macmillan 1977).
44 Gann and Duignan, *South Africa: War, Revolution, or Peace?,* 47–9; Jaster, *South Africa's Narrowing Security Options;* and Chester Crocker, "Current and Projected Military Balances in Southern Africa," in Bissell and Crocker, eds., *South Africa into the 1980s.*
45 Ibid., 97–8; W.C.J. Van Rensburg, "Africa and Western Lifelines," *Strategic Review* 6 (Spring 1978): 46–8.
46 Amos A. Jordan and Robert A. Kilmarx, *Strategic Mineral Dependence: The Stockpile Dilemma,* Washington Papers, vol. 7 (Beverly Hills: Sage Publications 1979), 26; and *Mineral Supplies from South Africa,* Economist Intelligence Unit, Special Report no. 59 (1978), Chs. 1 and 2.
47 W. Scott Thompson and Brett Silvers, "South Africa in Soviet Strategy," in Bissell and Crocker, eds., *South Africa Into the 1980s,* 133–58; Van Rensburg, "Africa and Western Lifelines," 41–50; Bohdan Szuprowicz, *How to Avoid Strategic Minerals Shortages* (New York: Wiley 1981), 135–40; Kroft, "The Geopolitics of Non-Energy Minerals," 78–9.
48 William Schneider, cited in the *Foreign Affairs Research Institute Report,* Oct. 1978, "The Growing United States Dependency on Imported Strategic Raw Materials,"
49 Charles Perry, *The West, Japan, and Cape Route Imports: The Oil and Non-Fuel Mineral Trades* (Cambridge, MA: Institute for Foreign Policy Analysis 1981); Van Rensburg, "Africa and Western Lifelines," 48.
50 Szuprowicz, *How to Avoid Strategic Minerals Shortages,* 135ff.
51 *World Mineral Trends,* 486–7, 494–5.
52 Robert Harkavy, "The Pariah State Syndrome," *Orbis* 21 (Fall 1977): 623–50. A very useful discussion of Western options with respect to South Africa can be found in James Barber and Michael Spicer, "Sanctions Against South Africa: Options for the West," *International Affairs* 55 (July 1979): 385–401.

53 James Barber, "Economic Sanctions as a Policy Instrument," *International Affairs* 21 (July 1979):374–5; and Harry Strack, *Sanctions: The Case of Rhodesia* (Syracuse, NY: Syracuse University Press 1978). See also, on the utility of sanctions in general, Margaret P. Doxey, *Economic Sanctions and International Enforcement* (London: Oxford University Press 1971); and Douglas G. Anglin, "United Nations Economic Sanctions against South Africa and Rhodesia," in *The Utility of International Economic Sanctions,* ed. David Leyton-Brown (London: Croom Helm 1987), 23–56. For a less pessimistic assessment of the effectiveness of sanctions, see David A. Baldwin, *Economic Statecraft* (Princeton: Princeton University Press 1985).

54 *World Mineral Trends,* 212–13; Jordan and Kilmarx, *Strategic Mineral Dependence,* 27; Park, *Earthbound,* 69–70.

55 Clarfield et al., *Eight Mineral Cartels,* 115–16; Carmine Nappi, *Commodity Market Controls* (Lexington, MA: Lexington Books 1979), 121.

56 Nappi, *Commodity Market Controls,* 129–30; Marian Radetzki, "Market Structure and Bargaining Power: A Study of Three International Mineral Markets," *Resources Policy* 4 (June 1978):116–17; Ferdinand E. Banks, *Bauxite and Aluminum: An Introduction to the Economics of Nonfuel Minerals* (Lexington, MA: Lexington Books 1979), 70–74.

57 Banks, *Bauxite and Aluminum,* 64.

58 World Bank, *Commodity Trade and Price Trends* (Baltimore: Johns Hopkins University Press 1981), Table 10. Figures are averaged over the period 1977–9.

59 Banks, *Bauxite and Aluminum,* 46, 65; *World Mineral Trends,* 225.

60 *World Mineral Trends,* 22; Banks, *Bauxite and Aluminum,* 67.

61 Nappi, *Commodity Market Controls,* 128.

62 *World Mineral Trends,* 226; EMR, *Canadian Minerals Yearbook, 1985,* Ch. 6.

63 G. Ninacs, "Aluminum," *Canadian Mining Journal,* Feb. 1980, pp. 1, 6–8.

64 *World Mineral Trends,* 222–4.

65 Clarfield, *Eight Mineral Cartels,* 113–40; C. Fred Bergsten, "The New Era in Commodity Cartels," *Challenge* (Sept.–Oct. 1974).

66 Mikdashi, *The International Politics of Natural Resources,* 112; Isaiah A. Litvak and Christopher J. Maule, "The International Bauxite Agreement: A Commodity Cartel in Action," *International Affairs* 46 (Spring 1980):306–7.

67 Nappi, *Commodity Market Controls,* 123; Banks, *Bauxite and Aluminum,* 69.

68 Banks, *Bauxite and Aluminum,* Ch. 4; *International Minerals Cartels,* 44–45; Nappi, *Commodity Control in a Partially Nationalized Industry,* Technical Paper no. 21 (Institute of Latin American Studies, University of Texas at Austin 1979); A.A. Francis, *Taxing the Transnationals in the Struggle Over Bauxite* (The Hague: Institute of Social Studies 1979).

69 Banks, *Bauxite and Aluminum,* 68.

70 Nappi, *Commodity Market Controls,* 125; *Mining Journal,* 26 Dec. 1980, 527, and 18 Dec. 1981, 457–8.

71 Litvak and Maule, "The International Bauxite Agreement," 308–11; Banks, *Bauxite and Aluminum,* 68–9; *World Mineral Trends,* 504–6; *International Minerals Cartels,* 110, 119–20.

72 *World Mineral Trends,* 224.

73 Interviews with officials in the Mineral Policy Sector of the Department of Energy, Mines and Resources, Ottawa, Dec. 1981.

74 *World Mineral Trends,* 507–8.

75 World Bank, *Commodity Trade and Price Trends, 1985,* Table 8.

76 *Mineral Commodity Summaries,* 167.

77 D.A. Robins, "Tin," in Nutting et al., *Future Metal Strategy,* 64–5.

78 *Mineral Commodity Summaries,* 166–7.

79 EMR, *Canadian Minerals Yearbook, 1983–84.*

80 *Mineral Commodity Summaries,* 166.

81 William Fox, *Tin: The Working of a Commodity Agreement* (London: Mining Journal Books 1974), 228–40.

82 Jordan and Kilmarx, *Strategic Mineral Dependence,* 42–59.

83 For a detailed discussion of the history of the postwar tin agreements, see Fox, *Tin;* and Jock A. Finlayson and Mark W. Zacher, *Managing International Markets: Developing Countries and the Commodity Trade Regime* (New York: Columbia University Press 1988), Ch. 3.

84 See, for example, *Far Eastern Economic Review*, 21 Jan. 1977, 97–98; and 1 May 1981, 46–7; *Latin American Commodities Report*, 8 May 1981; and *Mining Journal*, 12 Feb. 1982, 119.

85 *Mining Journal*, 4 Dec. 1981, 424; and *Latin American Commodities Report*, 28 Aug. 1981.

86 Rex Bosson and Benison Varon, *The Mining Industry and the Developing Countries* (New York: Oxford University Press 1977), 223; and Ruth and Uzi Arad, "Scarce Natural Resources and Potential Conflict," 35–6.

87 EMR, *Canadian Minerals Yearbook, 1985*, Ch. 61.

88 Energy, Mines and Resources Canada, *Tin in Canada: Potential for Future Production* MRI /81/3 (Ottawa: EMR, Mineral Policy Sector, Jan. 1981).

89 *Mineral Commodity Summaries*, 167; *Latin American Commodities Report*, 19 June 1981.

90 J. Thoburn, "Policies for Tin Exporters," *Resources Policy* 7 (June 1981): 75–7.

91 Energy, Mines and Resources Canada, *Mineral Policy: A Discussion Paper* (Ottawa: Minister of Supply and Services, Dec. 1981), 23–4 (hereinafter cited as *Mineral Policy*).

92 *Mineral Policy*, 27–31.

93 *Mineral Policy*, 30–2.

94 Energy, Mines and Resources Canada, *Imported Mineral Raw Materials: Guidelines for Research Policy* MRI 80/8 (Ottawa: EMR, Mineral Policy Sector, May 1980).

95 *Mineral Policy*, 31–3.

96 With the exception of the Department of National Defence study, *Economic and Strategic Significance*, 18–30.

97 *International Minerals Cartels*, 143, 199.

98 John E. Tilton, *The Future of Nonfuel Minerals* (Washington: Brookings Institution 1977), 82–3; Raymond Mikesell, *New Patterns of World Mineral Development* (Montreal: British-North America Committee 1979), 7; Bosson and Varon, *The Mining Industry and the Developing Countries*, 126–7.

99 On U.S. commodity policy in the 1970s, see J. Robert Vastine, jr., "United States International Commodity Policy," *Law and Policy in International Business* 9 (1977).

100 Mikesell, *New Patterns of World Mineral Development*, 24–9.

101 Park, *Earthbound*, 70.

102 Tilton, *Future of Nonfuel Minerals*, 22–3; Nathan Rosenberg, "Innovative Responses to Material Shortages," *American Economic Review* 63 (May 1973): 111–18; Benison Varon and Kenji Takeuchi, "Developing Countries and Non-Fuel Minerals," *Foreign Affairs* 52 (Apr. 1974): 507.

103 J. Allum, "Recession in West Hits Cobalt Users," *South Magazine* (Mar. 1981): 67–9.

104 Varon and Takeuchi, "Developing Countries and Non-Fuel Minerals," 507.

105 Tilton, *Future of Nonfuel Minerals*, 17.

106 Figures taken from Ferdinand Banks, "Natural Resource Availability: Some Economic Aspects," *Resources Policy* 3 (Mar. 1977): 6. See also Tilton, *Future of Nonfuel Minerals*, 17–18; and Richard Lecomber, *The Economics of Natural Resources* (New York: Wiley 1979), 136–7.

107 Lecomber, *Economics of Natural Resources*, 136. For an argument that there are serious limits to the contribution that can be made by recycling, see D.W. Pearce and I. Walter, *Resource Conservation: The Social and Economic Dimensions of Recycling* (New York: New York University Press 1977).

108 Lecomber, *Economics of Natural Resources*, 17.

109 Banks, "Natural Resource Availability," 3–4; Tilton, *Future of Nonfuel Minerals*, 14–15.

110 Tilton, *Future of Nonfuel Minerals*, 15; Lecomber, *Economics of Natural Resources*, 17–18.

111 *International Minerals Cartels;* Tilton, *Future of Nonfuel Minerals*, 104–5; Jordan and Kilmarx, *Strategic Mineral Dependence*, 36–9; Banks, "Natural Resource Availability," 4–6.

112 Mikesell, *New Patterns of World Mineral Development*, 7.

113 Jordan and Kilmarx, *Strategic Mineral Dependence*, 37.

114 *Mining Journal*, 27 Nov. 1981, 407–8.

115 *Mineral Policy*, 31. For a further discussion of this, see David Haglund's Ch. 8 in this volume, "Current Issues in the International Politics of Strategic Minerals and their Implications for Canada."

116 Jordan and Kilmarx, *Strategic Mineral Dependence*, 64–5.

117 Fox, *Tin*, Ch. 15.

118 Jordan and Kilmarx, *Strategic Mineral Dependence*, 66–7; National Commission on Supplies and Shortages, *Government and the Nation's Resources* (Washington: U.S. Government Printing Office 1976), 134–40; Comptroller-General of the United States, *U.S. Dependence on Imports of Five Critical Materials: Implications and Policy Alternatives* (Washington: U.S. Government Printing Office 1976);

International Minerals Cartels, 14–16.
119 See Haglund, Ch. 8 in this volume.
120 Swedish Futures Secretariat, *Resources, Society and the Future* (New York: Permagon Press 1980), 131.
121 *Mineral Policy*, 32.
122 *International Minerals Cartels*, 15.
123 *Mineral Policy*, 32–3.

5

Canadian Participation in the International Energy Agency: A Decade of "Collective Security" in Oil

David Blair

INTRODUCTION

The period of surplus oil production during the mid to late 1980s has made discussions of oil crisis management appear somewhat irrelevant. With world surpluses amounting to more than 25 per cent of oil consumption in the advanced industrialized countries, the chances of an oil shortage in the immediate term seem slim. One should recall, however, that the oil market was also relatively calm before the oil crises of the 1970s. Unforeseen events rapidly altered the market situation, setting the stage for the supply disruptions and oil price shocks that followed. Paradoxically, the relatively low price levels that accompanied the oil glut of the late 1980s have increased the prospects for oil crises in the 1990s. These lower prices make the development of high-cost non-OPEC oil production capacity less attractive, raising the likelihood of greater dependence on OPEC oil in the future.[1] Oil crises in the 1990s are by no means inevitable, however, as long as the lessons of the recent past are not forgotten. It seems judicious during the period of abundant supply to review the history of oil security measures and to consider the adequacy of existing preparations for possible disruptions.

One of the ways in which Canada has attempted to reduce its oil import vulnerability is by collaborating with other import-dependent Western countries in collective arrangements designed to prevent or to lessen the impact of supply disruptions on any single country. The main assumption underlying these arrangements is that oil import vulnerability can be reduced more effectively if Western oil-importing countries act jointly rather than try to deal with the problem independently. The first part of this chapter will review the collective measures developed in the wake of the supply disruptions of the 1970s and 1980s, explain how these measures are intended to operate, and discuss some of the problems that may reduce their effectiveness. Canada's interests in participating in the emergency preparedness system of the International Energy Agency are identified in the second part. The third part of the chapter evaluates Canada's commitment to "collective security" in oil and attempts to explain Canadian oil import security policy. Finally, I will suggest ways in which Canada's oil emergency preparations can be improved.

EMERGENCY PREPARATIONS OF THE INTERNATIONAL ENERGY AGENCY

Shortly after the October 1973 oil embargo, price increases, and production cuts, the U.S. Secretary of State, Henry Kissinger, called for the establishment of an energy action group of major Western industrialized countries. In a speech delivered in London on 12 December 1973, Kissinger stressed the need for a co-ordinated response to the energy problem in such areas as energy conservation, alternative energy sources, and research and development.[2] This initiative was undertaken to serve a number of U.S. foreign policy interests. There was a desire to seize upon the issue of the energy crisis in order to reassert American leadership in the West and to buttress Western alliance solidarity. The Secretary of State also wanted to end competition for supplies among the major oil-importing countries, which led to bilateral deals with OPEC countries that drove up the world price of oil. He was concerned that the shock of rapidly rising oil prices might result in protectionist policies and threaten what was left of the postwar liberal economic order. In addition, Washington wanted to head off a possible shift in Western European and Japanese foreign policies toward the Arab position in the Arab-Israeli dispute, since this would complicate American mediation efforts in the region. Finally, it was hoped that a common consumer stance would lessen the West's vulnerability to pressure from oil-exporting countries, and prevent any future embargoes.[3]

The initial European and Japanese response to American overtures for Western energy co-operation was one of wariness. The French in particular were concerned that such an approach would antagonize OPEC and permit the U.S. to interfere in the making of European energy policies. At a European Community summit meeting following Kissinger's London speech, ministers agreed on the importance of entering into negotiations with oil-exporting countries and chose the OECD rather than any new energy action group as the most suitable forum for major oil-importing countries to study energy problems.[4] Nevertheless, Western European governments accepted President Nixon's invitation to an energy conference in February 1974 that included the United States, Canada, Japan, and the European Community.

One week before the Washington Energy Conference, the nine EC countries worked out a common position in which they committed themselves to resist moves to create any permanent institutions for consumer co-operation.[5] However, during the conference the European delegates, with the exception of the French, moved closer to American proposals for a consumer coalition as the tensions of the oil crisis began to ease. The Europeans soon realized that oil import vulnerability could not be reduced effectively without the co-operation of the United States. As the largest importer of oil, the United States could contribute more than any other Western country to a stable world oil market. Indeed, as one observer has pointed out, "Europe needed American leadership and the discipline which only the U.S. could enforce as an alternative to its own lack of leadership and lack of mutual trust. Furthermore, since any future crisis-sharing would require the collaboration of the international oil industry and restraint among all major importers, only a framework which included the U.S. and Japan made sense."[6]

At the end of the conference, a communiqué was issued calling for an emergency oil allocation plan, as well as greater co-operation in such areas as alternative energy sources, energy conservation, and research and development. All participants in the conference, except France, agreed to establish an Energy Coordinating Group (ECG) to work out an agreement based on the measures outlined in the communiqué. Despite the altered position of its EC partners, France remained opposed to the American proposals and refused to participate in the ECG.

In the fall of 1974, the ECG produced the Agreement on an International Energy Program (IEP), which set out the details of an emergency oil-sharing scheme. On 19 November 1974, sixteen OECD countries signed the agreement, establishing the International Energy Agency (IEA) as an autonomous body within the framework of the OECD to implement the provisions of the program. In addition to emergency preparations, areas of concern in the IEA included: long-term co-operation in reducing excessive dependence on oil; an information system on the international oil market involving consultation with oil companies; co-operation with oil-producing and other consuming countries; and co-ordination of research and development policies of member countries.

The central feature of the IEA is its emergency oil-sharing system, which provides for a collective response by member countries to short-term emergencies where members suffer a petroleum supply shortage. An emergency management manual setting out detailed rules and procedures for the sharing system was approved by IEA members in 1976. The system involves demand-restraint measures, the controlled draw-down of emergency reserves, and the reallocation of supplies available to the group. When the IEA Secretariat makes a finding that the normal level of oil supplies of one or more members has fallen short by at least 7 per cent, for whatever reason, the emergency scheme is to be activated. In this case the normal level is considered to be the average level of supplies during the most recent twelve months. Activation of the system can be prevented only by a very large majority of member countries voting in the Governing Board, which is the executive body of the IEA.[7] The fact that activation of the emergency cannot be blocked easily by member governments has been considered one of the virtues of the scheme. During the 1973 oil embargo, certain non-embargoed European countries attempted to protect themselves by vetoing the activation of an OECD emergency oil-sharing system and by opposing any European Community allocation schemes.

Whenever the group suffers an overall supply shortfall greater than 7 per cent but less than 12 per cent, member countries are to cut back oil consumption by 7 per cent. For group shortfalls of 12 per cent or more, demand is to be reduced by 10 per cent. Each IEA member is required to maintain emergency reserves equal to ninety days of its net imports; each draws down its emergency reserves at a certain rate, depending on its share of the group's emergency reserve commitments and on the size of the group supply shortfall. Members have a supply right equal to the normal level of consumption minus the demand restraint rate and emergency drawdown obligation rate. If the actual level of supplies available to a country (including actual net imports and normal domestic production) is higher than the country's supply right, then the country has an obligation to make supplies equal to the amount of the difference available for reallocation. If a country's actual level of supplies falls short of its supply right, then it is entitled to receive supplies from other member countries in an amount that will bring its actual level up to the supply-right level.

Whenever any single IEA member sustains a supply shortfall of more than 7 per cent but less than 12 per cent, that country must cut back its oil consumption by 7 per cent. For shortfalls of 12 per cent or more, it must reduce consumption by 10 per cent. Any shortfall over the 7 per cent or 10 per cent demand-restraint level will be made up by other IEA members either through demand-restraint measures or by drawing down emergency reserves. The obligation to allocate this amount of oil is shared by the other members on the basis of their oil consumption. The emergency sharing system can also be activated whenever a major region of a member country whose market is incompletely integrated suffers a shortfall of more than 7 per cent. In this case, the region will be treated as a separate member, as will that part of the country concerned that does not suffer a shortfall over 7 per cent.[8] Quebec and the Maritimes are considered a major region, known as "Canada East," because they rely on imported oil for most of their requirements and because western Canadian oil cannot replace all of these imports in case of an emergency.

The co-operation of the oil industry is vital to the functioning of the IEA emergency system. The oil companies remain in control of the logistics system in emergency allocations, and redirect supplies under the guidance and supervision of the IEA. The companies also provide the Secretariat with information on current and projected levels of oil imports, exports, production, and stocks whenever an emergency appears imminent. The governments of participating countries report information on the same subjects to the Secretariat. The oil companies and governments consult and advise the IEA Secretariat in its management of emergencies. In normal times the Standing Group of Emergency Questions (SEQ), composed of government representatives and serviced by the Secretariat, reviews and assesses each country's emergency preparations to ensure their adequacy.

The emergency oil-sharing system of the IEA can enhance the oil security of importing countries in four ways. First, by appearing to provide an effective defence against oil embargoes, the system may act as a deterrent to oil exporters who may be contemplating the imposition of an embargo on an IEA member. It is often difficult to determine the effectiveness of a measure intended as a deterrent, since it is not always clear whether or not the restraint of the targeted country is due to that particular measure. However, it seems reasonable to assume that in most cases a country considering some punitive action such as an embargo will take into consideration the likelihood of the contemplated action succeeding. If some factor exists that threatens to reduce or eliminate the effect of an embargo, then the attractiveness of such an option is likely to be diminished. Thus the existence of the IEA emergency system might be expected to weaken the desire of oil-exporting countries to impose embargoes on IEA members. This may help to explain why no major embargo was ever imposed on oil-importing countries after the creation of the Agency, even though Arab countries have had many reasons for wanting to do so—and, during the 1970s, had a favourable climate for contemplating such a move.

Second, if the emergency system functions as it is supposed to, consumers in any member country should not suffer a supply shortage greater than the 10 per cent maximum demand-restraint requirement, even if all of a particular country's imports are cut off. An added advantage of the IEA system is that any member country whose domestic oil production is suddenly disrupted (for example, due to sabotage, technical problems, or natural disasters) is eligible to receive supplies from other IEA members, since activation of the allocation scheme is tied to oil *supplies* and not just imports. This feature is of particular interest to large oil producers such as Canada.

Third, the contribution of the IEA allocation scheme to the oil-import security of Western countries has grown over the past few years as a result of changes in the structure of the world oil market. Prior to 1975 the multinational oil companies were able to manage any oil-supply disruptions, including the 1973 oil embargo, with little outside help. However, with the share of the multinationals in world trade declining from 78 per cent in 1974 to about 40 per cent by the 1980s, the ability of these companies to control the allocation of supplies in any emergency has diminished. The IEA allocation system has an advantage over a purely multinational oil-company allocation in that it can co-ordinate a far larger share of total world oil trade, since it includes the growing number of independent and state-owned oil companies that purchase their supplies directly from oil exporters.

The fourth way in which the IEA sharing system can enhance oil security for member countries is by forestalling upward pressure on world oil prices. If countries do not have to secure their imports by competing for bilateral oil-supply deals with oil producers or by bidding on the spot market during supply disruptions, then rapid price increases such as the ones experienced in 1973–4 and 1979 can be avoided. It must not be overlooked, the present glut notwithstanding, that price can be a major factor in oil-import security, given the economic damage that large price increases can inflict upon an importing country.

While the IEA emergency oil-sharing system seems impressive in its extensive preparations, there are several factors that may reduce its effectiveness in providing oil-import security. The first set of problems is of a technical nature. The oil-sharing system is an extremely complex arrangement, involving twenty-one countries and more than fifty companies. With the rise in direct sales of crude oil by producing countries to refiners in importing countries, it has become necessary to include more oil companies in the IEA emergency scheme, which makes the allocation of supplies more difficult to co-ordinate. Each refinery can handle only certain grades and qualities of crude, so that supplies have to be shifted around to get the right type of oil to the right locations. This whole exercise is complicated by the growing number of restrictions written into supply contracts with oil-producing countries. Restrictions may be placed on the destination of supplies, or on the resale or exchange of oil between companies. Thus, the flexibility of reallocation is further hampered by the need to find supplies that are free of such restrictions.

The problem of complexity has been dealt with to some extent by conducting test runs of the emergency system every two to three years. During the third such test, conducted in late 1980, considerable confusion was experienced in the early weeks of the exercise. However, due to the lag time of about four to six weeks between the loading of crude on tankers and its delivery at the ports of most IEA countries, this initial chaos should not threaten the successful operation of the system. These test runs help to point out the various technical problems that could arise in an actual emergency allocation, and thus permit participants in the system to work out solutions to these problems. In the spring of 1983 a fourth test run was held using a new computer system that had been developed to facilitate the matching of oil supplies with oil supply need. This particular test run served to boost the confidence of participating countries in the emergency scheme, as the computer system demonstrated its ability to increase the efficiency of IEP supply allocations.[9]

The emergency system does not include a mechanism for setting prices of oil delivered in reallocations, and it is possible that disputes may arise over this issue. There appears to be a conflict between the IEP agreement and the IEA Emergency Management Manual concerning the principle to be used in pricing supplies allocated in an emergency. While the agreement states that prices shall reflect comparable commercial transactions, the manual favours the allocation of oil at term, or contract, prices rather than at the prevailing spot market prices. Members have been unable to resolve their differences on the pricing issue, although provisions have been made for the mediation of pricing disputes. The IEA has also created a special arbitration commission to handle cases where the mediation process has not succeeded.[10] The pricing issue should not prevent the emergency system from functioning, at least in serious disruptions, since participating countries are likely to be much more concerned with obtaining supplies than with price. However, in low-level disruptions or in isolated supply shortfalls, price disputes may impede informal efforts to allocate supplies. In such cases government pressure on oil companies may be required to ensure that allocations are carried out.

Another potential obstacle that the IEA scheme faces is U.S. antitrust legislation, which may prevent American oil companies from providing information or participating in an emergency allocation. This legislation has created an air of uncertainty among American oil companies over the legal limits of their cooperation with the IEA.[11] The provision of accurate data on a continuing basis is vital to the functioning of the IEA sharing system, and without special legal protection from Congress extending immunity from antitrust laws these companies have declared that they would stop providing such data. Immunity is usually granted to companies for fixed periods of time whenever it is requested by the administration, but the ad hoc nature of this clearance has created some doubt among participating countries about the ability of American companies to co-operate in future supply emergencies. A more automatic granting of antitrust clearance is considered desirable by many IEA countries, but no change in procedure has been introduced by the U.S. government.

There is also a possibility that the emergency scheme may be hampered by inadequate emergency oil reserves. All IEA members normally carry the required "90 days of net imports" level of emergency reserves. But the definition of emergency oil reserves under the IEP agreement includes industry working stocks that must be maintained in order for refineries to be fully operational.[12] Because a large part of the emergency reserves stored in IEA countries consists of working stocks, the actual level of stocks that can be used in an emergency may be well below ninety days of net imports. However, the level-of-stocks problem should not pose a serious impediment to the emergency system. Most IEA countries import oil from a variety of sources, so it is unlikely that net imports would be totally cut off in a supply disruption. If emergency reserves minus working stocks are somewhat less than the ninety-day level, there should still be enough oil in reserve to handle the partial import shortages that are most likely to occur.

An additional problem for the emergency oil-sharing system is the fact that the trigger level for activation of the system may become obsolete. A supply shortfall of 7 per cent is the trigger level set out in the IEA agreement, but this provision is based on the assumption of continually increasing, or at least stable, demand. When world oil demand declines, as it did during the 1980s, activation of the sharing system is no longer automatic.[13] Under this formula, IEA countries were in a triggering situation for some time, even though supplies were more than adequate to meet demand. In the event of a serious general supply shortage there would probably not be much difficulty in activating the system, but in more borderline shortages the absence of a clear trigger level may cause problems. Some new method of calculating supply shortages seems to be desirable, perhaps one based on current and expected import levels rather than on the level of imports over the preceding year.

Another problem with the trigger level is that even in times of increasing or stable demand, supply shortages below 7 per cent may be sufficient to cause a serious disruption in the oil market and lead to large, rapid price increases. A 7 per cent shortfall was set as the trigger level because this was the degree of supply shortage in the 1973–4 oil crisis. In 1979 the Iranian revolution resulted in a 5 per cent world supply shortfall, which led to a doubling of the world price for oil. The macroeconomic impact of this second oil price shock in western countries was almost as severe as that brought about by the larger supply shortfall of 1973–4, and had serious consequences for Western alliance relations as well.[14]

A number of collective measures were introduced by the IEA in an effort to arrest the spiralling of world oil prices that attended the Iranian crisis. An agreement was reached in March 1979 to reduce oil consumption in IEA countries as a group by 5 per cent, but there was no commitment at this time to country-specific targets.[15] After oil prices continued to rise, major oil-importing countries became more interested in collective measures. Country-specific import targets were adopted for 1979, 1980, and 1985 by the seven major industrialized countries at the Tokyo economic summit. These targets were reconfirmed at the December 1979 IEA ministerial meeting and individual targets for the other IEA countries were set for 1980 and 1985.[16] Energy ministers of the IEA countries also committed themselves to meet promptly in the event of any major change in the world oil supply situation to decide on corrective action, including the adjustment of import ceilings. This measure was intended to ensure that any overall supply shortfall under the 7 per cent level would be met by an equivalent cutback in demand, shared proportionately among IEA members. Thus, it was hoped that competitive bidding under tight market conditions and the resulting oil price increases could be prevented.[17]

At the May 1980 ministerial meeting, IEA countries repeated their commitment to the import ceilings and agreed to adopt additional demand-restraint measures whenever a tight market situation appeared imminent. Moreover, a system of yardsticks was approved to measure progress in achieving the import goals, based on estimates of each country's future oil requirements. Following the outbreak of the Iran-Iraq war in September 1980, ministers of IEA countries agreed to consider the possible use of import ceilings, but there seemed to be little enthusiasm for this measure as a means of handling supply disruptions. After 1980 the idea of import targets was dropped, even by the United States, which had been one of its strongest proponents. Because of the need for consensus in the IEA, the import ceilings were generally set very high, so that they could be easily met. Hence, the setting of import targets was not particularly meaningful or useful in the management of low-level oil supply disruptions.[18]

Another measure introduced in 1979 was the establishment of a registry of world spot market transactions. The summit countries agreed to this measure in Tokyo in an attempt to prevent spot market prices from spiralling out of control by bringing greater "transparency" to the market. After the other IEA members approved the scheme, a registry was set up, although its usefulness was extremely limited. Most of the data were at least a month old when they were reported, and only a small percentage of transactions were actually recorded. Because of the need for confidentiality the available figures were not very useful for analysis.[19]

The commitment by ministers to meet as soon as there was a major change in the world oil supply situation was a somewhat more effective measure in dealing with supply shortages under 7 per cent. When prices on the spot market began to rise less than a week after the outbreak of the war between Iran and Iraq, an emergency meeting of the IEA Governing Board was held. Government representatives agreed to "urge and guide" oil companies to refrain from making any abnormal spot market purchases and to absorb shortfalls by drawing down stocks held above the emergency reserve level.[20] When the energy ministers of IEA countries met in December 1980, they reaffirmed their decision to monitor closely the oil market situation, to continue the drawing down of stocks, and to encourage oil companies "at an appropriately high level" to refrain from making unusual spot market purchases.[21]

Through the winter of 1980–1 the oil spot market stayed relatively calm and oil companies drew down stocks at a rate of 2.5 million barrels a day, instead of the normal drawdown rate of 900,000 barrels a day. The market situation was helped by stepped-up production in certain OPEC countries, by the gradual return of exports from Iran and Iraq, and by a 6 per cent decline in world oil demand because of a combination of slower economic growth and increased conservation.[22] By March 1981 world oil production had surpassed demand, creating a glut on the market that intensified in subsequent years. While many oil industry officials insisted that their decision to refrain from making spot market purchases and to draw on their record high oil stocks was taken purely on business grounds, in the opinion of a number of government and Secretariat officials the IEA played a useful role in maintaining market stability during the Iran-Iraq war. The IEA pronouncements and government consultations with oil companies shortly after the outbreak of the war were felt to have helped set a psychological climate that encouraged restraint on the spot market.[23] The importance of psychological forces in the world oil market was demonstrated in 1979, when the atmosphere of uncertainty grew into a panic that led to a scramble for supplies.

During the Iranian revolution and following the outbreak of the Iran-Iraq war, the IEA developed a new approach to isolated or localized supply disruptions. When Sweden and Italy suffered shortages of more than 7 per cent for limited periods in 1979, the Secretariat consulted with the governments of these countries and persuaded them to work out their problems with the oil companies.[24] Sweden's shortfall was due to the fact that it traditionally purchased its supplies on the spot market, and because of domestic price controls companies were reluctant to import oil at the much higher price that was being demanded by suppliers. The shortage in Italy was due to a scandal in the state-owned oil company, ENI, which led to the cancellation of a supply contract by Saudi Arabia. In both cases the supply shortages were temporary, and the Secretariat felt that the situations could be resolved more easily through informal arrangements with oil companies than by triggering the emergency oil-sharing system.

There were supplies available on the world market at the time and all that was needed was a means of directing them to the countries with the most severe shortfalls. The Secretariat was also concerned that activation of the formal allocation system might intensify the crisis atmosphere and lead to even more vigorous competition in the spot market.[25]

This response to individual countries' supply shortfalls of more than 7 per cent demonstrated that the emergency oil-sharing system was really intended to deal with large, generalized supply shortages. Most IEA countries shared the feeling that localized shortages could usually be handled with less complication and probably greater efficiency through informal measures. This approach was endorsed at the December 1980 ministerial meeting, where it was agreed that when a country suffered a relatively severe loss of oil supplies, the Secretariat would consult with the countries concerned and with oil companies. Taking these consultations into account the Secretariat would then propose possible measures that could be adopted by countries and companies to correct the imbalances.[26] If informal measures were unable to solve serious supply problems in one or a few member countries (for example, if there were no extra supplies that could be redirected to the countries concerned), then the formal sharing system could still be activated.

Turkey lost about 70 per cent of its oil imports in late 1980 when the oil pipeline from Iraq was cut off by the war between Iraq and Iran. After consulting with oil companies, the IEA Secretariat arranged for supplies to be sent to Turkey. This arrangement was held up because of Turkey's unwillingness to pay the price that was being asked for this oil; eventually it became superfluous when the pipeline reopened in January 1981.[27] While the issue of price remains a potential impediment to IEA action, the Secretariat has demonstrated its usefulness in directing shipments of oil to the hardest-hit countries in limited supply disruptions. As long as disputes over price can be overcome (and they need not be a major obstacle in every supply allocation), the Secretariat can prevent sudden pressure on the spot market that may lead to a large, disruptive increase in world oil prices.

After fighting in the Iran-Iraq war intensified in early 1984, agreement was reached in the IEA on procedures for carrying out a number of so-called "co-ordinated early response measures" (CERM), which included feeding oil from emergency stocks into the world market and restraining oil demand as soon as any shortage of world oil supplies occurred. This move followed the Reagan administration's decision to quickly release supplies from its Strategic Petroleum Reserve in case of an interruption of oil imports before the disruption actually made itself felt. This meant that IEA members were now committed to taking concrete, co-ordinated action in the early stages of a supply disruption in order to calm oil markets and to prevent the panic buying that could touch off yet another oil price spiral.[28] An operations manual was put together, and CERM was tested for the first time in January and February 1988.

The IEA's experimentation with these various emergency measures since 1979 has broadened the range of crisis situations in which collective action may be taken. The development of new ideas and responses could prove to be the most effective way of dealing with future disruptions, which may take on totally unexpected forms. Different responses will be required depending on the circumstances and the particular countries involved. The IEA provides a framework in which such ad hoc measures can be developed.

In addition to the technical problems that have just been discussed, a second set of potential problems may prevent the IEA from increasing the oil-import security of its members. These problems are essentially political in nature. While technical problems may hinder the smooth functioning of the emergency oil-sharing system or of alternative measures worked out in the IEA, they will probably not prevent the exercise of collective action by major oil-importing countries. This assessment is shared by some very critical analysts of the emergency preparations of the IEA.[29] The greatest threat to the collective management of oil supply disruptions will come from a loss of political will on the part of member countries to co-operate in emergency situations. Members may decide not to participate in collective arrangements for a number of reasons. Certain IEA countries may refuse to co-operate in an emergency allocation if one or more members are embargoed as a result of some politically motivated action. An example of this kind of situation is the embargo imposed by Iraq on oil exports to Canada in 1979 after the Conservative government expressed its intention to move the Canadian embassy in Israel from Tel Aviv to Jerusalem. A number of Canada's IEA partners felt that this action was inspired by a desire to increase domestic political support for the government, and if the embargo had spread to other oil-exporting countries there were indications that some IEA countries would not provide oil for reallocation to Canada.[30]

A more serious case of countries withdrawing from an IEA-sponsored supply allocation could occur if the United States were to take some action in the Middle East or adopt some policy that resulted in an embargo on oil exports to the U.S. If America's allies in the IEA are not consulted before such an action is taken, or if they are profoundly opposed to the action, certain IEA countries may be unwilling to suffer any loss of supplies through an emergency reallocation. Some countries may also fear that by providing supplies to the United States they will be identified with American policies and hence become the target of an embargo themselves. This problem might be avoided if other IEA members are consulted before any participating country takes actions that could result in its being embargoed by oil exporters; but as the U.S. raids on Tripoli and Benghazi indicated, consultation, particularly with respect to activities in the realm of Arab policy and politics, is less than perfect even among members of military alliances—and the IEA is far from being a military alliance.

Countries may decide not to co-operate with other IEA members if they feel that they cannot trust these other members to fulfil their commitments, or if it is believed that supplies could be secured more effectively through independent action. Robert Jervis has noted that the chances of achieving co-operation among members of a group of countries will be increased by anything that decreases the incentives for defecting by increasing the costs of mutual non-cooperation, or by anything that increases the incentives to co-operate by increasing the gains of mutual co-operation. The gains from co-operation are increased if each member of the group comes to value positively the others' well-being.[31] There is good reason to believe that in the case of oil trade, IEA countries have a better appreciation than ever before of their mutual interests in collectively managing oil supply disruptions. Most IEA governments have recognized that all Western countries were harmed by the competition for supplies in both the 1973–4 and 1979 oil crises, and the way in which they handled the disruption resulting from the Iran-Iraq war (and the favourable outcome of that experience) bodes well for the collective management of future oil supply disruptions.

Britain was one of the first IEA members to demonstrate actively an appreciation for the value of consumer co-operation in supply crises. During the 1979 disruption the British government, even though it was in the midst of an election campaign, refused to redirect North Sea oil exports to the British market. Despite the fact that Britain was experiencing significant oil supply shortages, Energy Minister Tony Benn argued that the country had an interest in keeping the price of oil low because of the effect that a price shock would have on world trade.[32] Even France, one of the most vigorous proponents of independent action during the supply crises of the 1970s, has come to support the strategy of collective action.[33] Although it has officially remained the only major Western oil-importing country without IEA membership, France now co-operates de facto with the agency's emergency sharing system due to that system's overlapping relationship with the EC sharing mechanism, in which France is a participant.

Domestic political pressure may also force some governments to withdraw from collective arrangements during supply disruptions. This pressure may be particularly acute if consumers in a particular country are required to cut back their energy use by 7 or 10 per cent even though the country is not directly affected by a supply disruption. In countries that allocate some domestic production to other IEA members, there could be strong opposition to giving up domestic öil during a supply crisis. However, there is a good chance that this opposition would be overshadowed by the general crisis atmosphere that would grip most Western countries during a serious supply shortage, particularly if the disruption were presented to domestic groups as a threat to national security or economic well-being. If the situation were explained in these terms, then governments might find it somewhat easier to justify the need for joint action with military allies and major trading partners.

The political problems enumerated above are not likely to prevent the most important member of the IEA, the United States, from participating in a collective response to future oil supply disruptions. The IEA was largely an American creation, and the U.S. has a special strategic interest in maintaining alliance solidarity among Western countries and in protecting Western economic security. With the participation of the largest oil-importing country more or less assured, the prospects for the successful functioning of the IEA emergency mechanisms are reasonably favourable.[34] Moral suasion may be effective in ensuring the participation of hesitant IEA members, although it would probably be insufficient to prevent the withdrawal of countries that became strongly opposed to the collective management of supply crises. The IEA should be able to carry out its emergency plans if one or several relatively minor members decide not to participate, although the system's effectiveness would obviously be greatly diminished if one of the major oil-importing countries, such as Germany or Japan, withdrew.

IEA EMERGENCY MEASURES AND CANADIAN INTERESTS

Because its oil imports cannot readily be replaced by domestic oil at tolerable costs, Canada can be considered vulnerable to external instability in the supply and price of these imports.[35] Even though Canada officially regained oil self-sufficiency in 1983, this condition really only meant that there were no *net* imports of oil. However, certain regions of the country are still dependent on imported oil that may not easily be replaced by domestic oil if supplies are cut off. In a 1986 study of Canada's oil prospects, the National Energy Board predicted that Canada would continue to import oil into the twenty-first century (and would continue being a *net* importer of light and medium crude), regardless of whether world oil prices were high or low.[36] In addition, as long as domestic oil prices are tied to world prices, Canada will continue to be sensitive to price fluctuations resulting from supply disruptions. Thus, Canada will have an ongoing interest in enhancing oil import security.

Canada's overriding interest in oil import security is composed of two main elements. The first is its interest in ensuring continuous supplies of imported oil. The IEA security-of-supply arrangements involve both costs and benefits for

Canada. Many of the benefits of these arrangements are the same for Canada as for the other IEA members. The deterrent effect of the IEA may prevent Canada from being the target of a serious embargo, or from losing supplies indirectly through a reallocation by multinational companies in response to punitive actions against other major oil-importing countries. Some may point out that this did not happen in the case of the 1979 Iraqi embargo. However, because Canada imported relatively little oil from Iraq the embargo cannot be regarded as a serious punitive action, but rather a symbolic gesture to register disapproval of Canadian policies. It could equally be argued that the existence of the IEA deterred other Arab countries from joining the embargo and causing a serious supply shortfall.

Canada's membership in the IEA increases the probability that Canadian consumers would not suffer a shortage of more than the 10 per cent maximum demand-restraint level, even if all of the country's imports were cut off. According to IEA regulations, Canadians need not suffer any shortages if the government decides to use available shut-in domestic oil or emergency stocks above the ninety-day level to make up the demand-restraint requirement. A temporary loss of 10 per cent would be an inconvenience to most Canadians, but it would not be as damaging as a total cut-off of imports, which by the late 1980s were about a third of Canadian oil requirements, and which under even the most optimistic price scenarios will still be around a quarter of domestic requirements by the year 2000. Canada could receive from other importing nations supplies of oil that it might not otherwise be able to obtain in a supply shortage. And, as was mentioned earlier, Canadian refineries would be eligible to receive supplies from other IEA members if for some reason domestic oil production were cut off.

Canada is in a better position than most IEA countries under the emergency oil-sharing system insofar as its supply situation is concerned. The proportion of supplies that Canada must be prepared to give up in an emergency reallocation is much smaller than for most other IEA members. Emergency reserves are based on net imports, and because Canada has been a net exporter since 1983, it is not technically required to hold any emergency reserves under the IEP agreement. The majority of IEA countries depend on imports for most of their oil supply requirements, so they are required to carry large emergency stocks, thus making available a much larger percentage of their total oil supplies for reallocation. When discussing "giving up" or "making available" oil supplies, it must be remembered that consumers in IEA countries ideally can only suffer a maximum shortage of 10 per cent. Supplies given up for reallocation would come partly from demand restraint and partly from emergency reserves. If Canada had to give up the maximum amount of supplies required under the IEA emergency system, this would represent less than 10 per cent of its total supplies, since any available emergency stocks or surplus oil production capacity would not need to be given up for reallocation. Japan and certain European countries, on the other hand, are required to make available the equivalent of about 90 per cent of their total supplies during an emergency.

Because the IEA emergency oil-sharing system includes oil imported by independent and government-owned oil companies, it promises to be a much more effective allocator of supplies than the multinational oil companies. If Canada reduces its reliance on multinational companies for oil imports, either through government-to-government deals or direct purchases by refiners, then the IEA will provide protection for these "non-multinational" oil imports. Should any of these imports be cut off by a limited supply disruption, the IEA Secretariat may be able to redirect supplies to Canada. The ability of the IEA to bring greater stability to the international oil market is very much in Canada's interest. By heading off a scramble for supplies in limited disruptions, the IEA can prevent certain countries, including Canada, from being left unnecessarily short of supplies.

The major cost involved in Canada's IEA membership is the possibility that the government would be required to cut back consumer demand by at least 7 per cent and to give up oil supplies even though the country may not be affected directly by a supply disruption. The probability of Canada losing supplies in an emergency reallocation is quite high because a greater percentage of other members' oil supplies consists of imports. Since other IEA members are likely to suffer more serious shortages than Canada in future disruptions, Canada will probably be required to give up supplies under most scenarios. This situation could be politically difficult for the government, although, as noted earlier, any supply shortage serious enough to trigger the IEA emergency system would likely be interpreted as a threat to Western security. The government would probably be able to justify the giving up of supplies as a part of Canada's contribution to the defence of the West. Canadians have shown themselves willing in past crises to come to the aid of countries with whom they share many common values and to whom they are tied economically, socially, and culturally. The potential domestic political cost of Canada's IEA membership could also be reduced if it is explained to Canadians that because the country relies on multinational oil companies for almost all of its oil imports, Canada would lose supplies through a reallocation by these companies even if Canada were not an IEA member. With IEA membership, the Canadian government at least has some voice in how supply reallocations are conducted and knows in advance how supply disruptions will affect the Canadian supply situation.

The second main element of Canada's interest in oil import security is price stability. The oil price shocks of 1973–4 and 1979 fuelled inflation and caused an economic recession in Canada and in other Western economies. The world recessions that followed the two crises led to reduced economic activity and higher unemployment in Canada as its export markets contracted. The serious economic impact of these oil price shocks underlines the fact that price is a crucial part of any country's oil import security. Canada is a trading nation, very much dependent on the health of the world economy, and any economic disruption stimulated by rapid oil price increases would ultimately harm the country's economic security.

The ability of price shocks to damage economic security in turn has consequences for military security and political stability. Economic disturbances resulting from rapid increases in the price of oil may result in social tensions and perhaps even domestic political unrest. Increasing economic burdens on governments may lead to lower spending on defence, and protectionist measures adopted to deal with growing economic problems could threaten to reduce the cohesion of the Western alliance.

The IEA arrangements to maintain oil price stability can be viewed, then, as serving a vital Canadian security interest. The costs involved in these arrangements are essentially the same as the costs involved in the management of supply problems, since price moderation is dealt with by regulating demand. It may be argued that price moderation is not necessarily in Canada's interest since rapid price increases make the exploitation of high-cost domestic oil reserves feasible. However, if the price of oil increases too much too quickly, economic recession, stepped-up conservation efforts, and fuel switching may result. This will weaken the demand for oil and drive down prices, making many high-cost energy development projects economically unviable. In the 1980s the collapse of world oil prices caused considerable economic hardship for Canadian oil-producing regions and for the oil industry in Canada. Hence, as an oil-producing country, Canada is vulnerable not just to rapid price increases but also to a rapid decline in the price of oil.

CANADA'S COMMITMENT TO COLLECTIVE ARRANGEMENTS

The federal government strongly supported the concept of a collective approach to reduce oil-import vulnerability following the October 1973 oil embargo. President Nixon's invitation to the Washington Energy Conference was readily accepted, and Canada worked with eleven other countries in the Energy Coordinating Group through much of 1974. The IEA agreement was signed by Canada on 18 November 1974. An Energy Supplies Allocation Board (ESAB) was set up during 1974 and became the government body responsible for the allocation of supplies in an emergency and for implementing demand-restraint measures as required by the IEA agreement.

Although the government favoured membership in the IEA, its commitment to collective arrangements as a means of enhancing oil-import security was increasingly neglected in the late 1970s. Canada maintained the level of emergency reserves required under the emergency plan of the IEA during the mid to late 1970s, but these reserves were not all held in eastern Canada, where they would be needed if oil imports were ever disrupted. Because no oil pipeline existed east of Montreal, Maritime refiners would have to be supplied during winter months by tankers travelling through the Panama Canal. However, the maximum rate of transport by this means during the 1973–4 crisis was only 50,000 barrels a day—less than 10 per cent of total crude import needs in the period between 1976 and 1979.

A further problem with Canada's emergency preparations was that emergency reserves were based on *net* imports of oil. The net import figure was misleading because it implied that in case of an emergency the oil that was being exported could be used to replace imports. Most of Canada's oil exports went to the western United States and, like emergency reserves, could not readily be transported to the oil-importing regions of Canada. Moreover, the exports were mostly heavy oil that eastern Canadian refineries could not handle. Because of these serious constraints on the degree to which either standby production capacity or emergency reserves in western Canada could be used to protect the vulnerable eastern refineries, the level of emergency reserves in Canada was inadequate. Consequently, in a severe generalized oil supply disruption, consumers in eastern Canada could suffer much greater shortages than their counterparts in other IEA countries. The most serious case of neglect in Canada's participation in the IEA emergency arrangements was the disbanding (temporarily, as it developed) of the Energy Supplies Allocation Board in June 1976. This meant that Canada's ability to allocate supplies and direct demand-restraint measures under the IEA emergency oil-sharing system was seriously impaired.

During the 1979 Iranian crisis the Canadian government devoted much greater attention to collective arrangements in an effort to reduce oil-import vulnerability. The Energy Supplies Emergency Act (1979) was introduced in Parliament, authorizing the re-establishment of ESAB. The board members were appointed in December 1979 and after several months of consultation with provincial governments and with the petroleum industry, ESAB produced a detailed set of regulations governing the allocation of petroleum products in Canada. At the various IEA meetings that followed the outbreak of the Iranian revolution, the government also agreed to restrain Canada's demand for world oil supplies. After the March 1979 IEA Governing Board meeting, Energy Minister Gillespie said that Canada would reduce its imports by 5 per cent, or 8,000 barrels a day, by stepping up western Canadian production. Before the 1979 Tokyo summit meeting, Prime Minister Clark asserted that Canada was not interested in agreeing to any mandatory measures to cut back imports, although he did agree to a net import target of 150,000 barrels a day for each of 1979 and 1980, in addition to a goal of 600,000 barrels a day for 1985.[37] While the 1979 target was not met, primarily because exports of light crude had ended, in December 1979 the Conservative energy minister expressed confidence that imports would be under the 1980 target as a result of slow economic growth. Canada was also able to follow the guidelines set out in the October 1980 IEA communiqué calling upon participating countries to persuade companies to stay off the spot market and to draw down stocks.

As tension in the world oil market diminished during 1980, the Canadian government once again seemed to lose interest in its IEA commitments. The government's National Energy Program (NEP), presented in October 1980, dealt with collective arrangements on 1 page of a 115-page document, even though one of the NEP's three stated policy objectives was energy security. The white paper admitted that only a portion of emergency reserves would be available in a supply disruption and noted that additional inventories would give Canada greater protection in emergencies: "The federal government wishes to *increase* oil storage in Canada, to increase our resilience to interruptions. This would provide additional insurance for the nation, and ease concerns in areas still heavily dependent on oil."[38]

The NEP document further stated that early discussions would be held with oil refiners to examine the possibility of voluntary stockbuilding. As the white paper pointed out, the refining industry lacked the commercial incentive to carry the large inventories necessary to ensure adequate emergency reserves. Nevertheless, the government did not mention the possibility of a government-owned or government-financed emergency oil reserve, nor did it deal with the need to locate storage facilities in eastern Canada, where they were most likely to be needed.

For several years following the appearance of the NEP, no progress was made in establishing adequate emergency reserves. After Canada became a net exporter of oil in 1983, it was no longer required under the IEP agreement to hold any emergency reserves at all, even though in Canada's case, as I indicated earlier, being a net exporter did not mean that the country was invulnerable to an interruption in its oil imports. By 1987 Canadian oil stocks (almost all of which were held by private companies) were the equivalent of seventy-nine days of forward consumption, lower than most other IEA countries. Moreover, only about 10 per cent of these stocks were available for use in an emergency, since most were composed of "working stocks" that had to be maintained in the system for operations purposes. In addition, it was not clear whether the federal government had the authority to force these companies to release their stocks unless an emergency were declared.[39] Consequently, it may not be possible to use most of Canada's stocks in an IEA-co-ordinated early response measures exercise.

During the 1980s the government argued that oil made available by demand-restraint measures, emergency reserves, and shut-in production could be transferred to eastern Canada primarily through oil swaps with the United States. This strategy was pursued during the 1979 oil crisis when surplus production in Alberta was exported to the western U.S. while an equivalent amount of oil originally destined for the United States was diverted to eastern Canadian refineries. In April 1979 a number of oil-swap proposals were turned down by the National Energy Board because the level of shut-in production capacity turned out to be far less than had been estimated.[40] There is no guarantee that such oil-swap arrangements will be possible in future emergencies, even if there are extra supplies available in western Canada. It might be difficult for a U.S. administration to justify giving up oil destined for the densely populated northeastern region in exchange for extra supplies in western states that are already supplied by domestic oil.

The problem of insufficient emergency reserves appears even more serious because in a pre-emergency situation the federal government does not have the authority to implement some of its obligatory demand-restraint plans. Also, the cost of increasing shut-in production capacity has been calculated as five times greater than building a stockpile, and using existing surge production capacity would require the agreement of the producing provinces. In both cases, the problem of transporting increased domestic production to the oil-importing regions remains.[41] Thus, Canada may not be able to rely on these alternatives to an adequate emergency stockpile to the extent that the government has claimed.

In 1987 the Department of Energy, Mines and Resources produced a discussion paper on energy security in Canada, in which a number of the foregoing problems with Canada's emergency preparations were pointed out. This paper noted that given the international dimension of the problem of oil-import vulnerability, collective security with other IEA members provided an effective way to ensure Canada's oil security, particularly in protecting Canada from excessive price shocks. The paper held that the most appropriate and cost-effective means of enhancing Canada's emergency preparedness for the collective management of short-term disruptions would be demand-restraint measures and emergency stocks, while allocation and rationing could be useful in a severe or prolonged disruption. The creation of government-owned stockpiles located in eastern Canada was strongly favoured in the report. Despite the agreement of federal and provincial energy ministers in January 1987 that Canada's energy security could be jeopardized by a period of low oil prices, which would lead to a significant increase in oil imports, the Canadian government hesitated to act on EMR's proposals.[42]

An examination of international forces as well as domestic conditions over the past several years suggests a number of reasons why Canada participates in the IEA, as well as why its preparations for collective action have been deficient. Some of the literature on collective-goods theory is useful in explaining Canada's behaviour with regard to the IEA. Russett and Sullivan observe that states seek to join together to produce a collective good "when they are faced with external diseconomies which they cannot handle as individual actors."[43] A collective good is defined by the properties of "indivisibility" (which means that once the good is provided, one individual's consumption does not detract from another's) and "non-appropriability" (which means that the provider of the collective good cannot exclude others from the good's benefit even though a user refuses to pay user fees). While pure collective goods and pure private goods represent two ends of a spectrum, goods located in the middle of the spectrum are usually referred to as "impure" collective goods.[44]

The supply provisions of the IEA emergency arrangements can be regarded as an impure collective good. The good provided by these arrangements is security of supply, or the likelihood consumers will suffer no more than a 10 per cent loss of oil, as long as countries maintain adequate emergency reserves. Although the consumption of the good by one IEA member does not reduce its availability to other members (in the sense that all can enjoy the same measure of supply security), the good is appropriable, since those oil-importing countries that do not join the IEA will have no opportunity of receiving supplies from other members in an emergency. On the other hand, the price effect of the IEA arrangements can be considered as closer to the "pure collective good" end of the spectrum. Price stability resulting from IEA actions is indivisible, and all oil-importing countries can benefit from it even if they are not IEA members and do not contribute to the costs of providing the good.

Mancur Olson has commented with respect to the provision of collective goods that "rational collective behaviour does not spontaneously lead to a rational collective outcome."[45] For example, although Canada has a strong interest in the existence of the IEA, as a rational individual actor it may not be in Canada's interest to participate in the organization. Canada will benefit to some extent from the operation of the emergency oil-sharing system in any future supply disruptions because the system can prevent competition for supplies that may strain alliance relations and cause economic problems for Canada's trading partners. However, it would seem to make sense from a supply standpoint for Canada to participate in the emergency oil-sharing system only if there were a good chance that Canada would receive supplies in an emergency. As has been seen, this is not very likely to happen. In most scenarios of oil supply disruptions Canada would be required to give up supplies for reallocation. Canada's contribution is not crucial to the operation of the IEA scheme and its absence would not make much difference in the management of supply disruptions. As far as its supply situation is concerned, Canada may be better off outside the IEA, as long as multinational companies do not reallocate more oil destined for Canada than the IEA would, and as long as supplies not imported by multinationals are not disrupted.

Canadian participation in the IEA is not necessarily logical with respect to the price effect of collective arrangements either, according to the theory of collective goods. As Loehr points out, countries receive benefits from the provision of collective goods whether they are organization members or not.[46] While countries have an interest in receiving the benefits of a collective good, it is not in the interest of the individual to assume any of the cost itself.[47] Similarly, although Canada has a definite interest in oil price stability, it does not have an interest in paying the cost of IEA membership. Because the size of Canadian imports as a proportion of total world trade is marginal, the country's non-participation in the IEA would have little or no effect on the ability of collective arrangements to stabilize oil prices. Canada would continue to benefit from oil price stability without having to pay the costs of participation.

Why, then, is Canada a member of the IEA? Collective goods theory postulates that rational, self-interested individual actors will not act to achieve their common group interests unless there is coercion or unless some separate incentive distinct from the achievement of the collective good "is offered to members of the group individually on the condition that they help bear the costs or burdens involved in the achievement of the group objectives."[48] The most commonly used incentive is the offer of non-collective (or private) goods. This tactic was used by the United States in 1974 to induce Western oil-importing countries to co-operate in an emergency oil-sharing scheme. Some of the non-collective goods offered were an oil market information service, a standing group on co-operation with oil-producing countries, and the placing of American domestic oil production within the emergency sharing system.[49] These concessions explain to a large extent the shift in the positions of the European and Japanese governments on consumer co-operation as a means of dealing with oil import vulnerability. Canada's decision to join the IEA was also influenced by the opportunity to gain access to information on oil companies and to expertise in energy research and development. Membership in the IEA provided a useful listening post and offered the possibility of influencing the policies of other Western oil importers.

Another non-collective good provided by IEA membership is prestige or social standing.[50] Canada's desire to be seen as a co-operative, mature member of the Western system may, to a certain degree, account for its participation in the collective arrangements of the IEA. By sharing some of the burden of providing the collective good, Canada may have been attempting to "purchase" the private goods of respectability and credibility among other major industrialized countries, and to avoid a reputation as a "free rider."

Two other international considerations influenced the government's decision to join the IEA. Only days before expressing his support for a proposal put forward by U.S. Secretary of State Kissinger for energy co-operation among OECD countries, Canada's Secretary of State for External Affairs, Mitchell Sharp, had voiced concern over solidarity in NATO, which was being strained by disagreements between the United States and certain European countries over the oil crisis.[51] Participation in the IEA enabled Canada to help restore alliance cohesion, thereby serving a major foreign policy interest.

The second international consideration was that in an emergency situation where American oil supplies were seriously curtailed but Canadian supplies were unaffected, there could be strong moral (and perhaps material) pressure on Canada to share its oil with the United States. The Nixon administration had already been urging Canada to enter a continental energy pact with the U.S. during the early 1970s, and Canada had assiduously resisted these overtures. When questioned about comments by the U.S. Secretary of the Interior that an integrated continental energy policy was essential to avoid fuel shortages in certain regions of the United States, Canadian Energy Minister Donald Macdonald replied in January 1973: "If Secretary Morton is suggesting in reference to a continental energy policy that we should enter into an arrangement whereby there would not only be a pooling of the assets of the continent but a pooling of the shortages as well, clearly that is a policy which this government would not intend to follow."[52]

American pressure for a bilateral oil-sharing arrangement could be resisted by Canada if it joined a multilateral body that included the United States. In future supply disruptions Canada could claim that it was already helping out the American supply situation through its participation in IEA arrangements. The amount of oil that Canada would be required to share under the IEA emergency system could be less than the amount the United States might request if Canada were not an IEA member. In addition, by joining the IEA a good deal of domestic tension caused by a public perception of American "control" of Canadian resources could be avoided.

Collective goods theory may also be useful in accounting for the inadequacy of Canadian preparations for an emergency allocation by the IEA. The theory holds that there is a tendency for those states that place a higher value on the collective good to be willing to bear a disproportionately high share of the burden of providing the good.[53] This implies that states placing a lower value on the collective good would bear a disproportionately low share of the burden. Because imports make up a much smaller proportion of total oil supplies for Canada than for most other IEA countries, the value that the Canadian government places on oil import security is likely to be much less than for countries almost totally dependent on imported oil. This may explain in part why, when Japan and most European members were fully prepared to implement IEA emergency measures, the Canadian government allowed its powers to restrain demand and allocate oil products to expire and why it has failed to maintain adequate emergency reserves.

While international forces played an important role in influencing Canadian behaviour with respect to the IEA, they were by no means the only determinants of this behaviour. One of the shortcomings of applying collective goods theory to international politics is that it often assumes that governments act to maximize the "national interest." Even if a national interest can be assumed to exist there is no guarantee that governments will always act to maximize it. Indeed, governments often act to serve the interests of certain segments of the population or to serve their own interests.[54] Canadian interests do not necessarily correspond with the Canadian government's interests. Any attempt to explain Canada's commitment to collective arrangements for reducing oil import vulnerability must take into consideration the domestic preoccupations of the federal government.

Following the oil crisis of 1973–4, energy matters in general, and the question of the future availability of oil in particular, became highly politicized issues. The initial public reaction to this crisis, as is the case in most national crises, was to demand that the government take some action. The period following the Arab oil embargo was marked by a proliferation of new energy policies and oil policies in Western countries, as governments made efforts to show their electorates that they were doing something about the energy problem. By gaining inclusion in the IEA, the Canadian government was able to demonstrate its determination to increase oil-import security.

The opportunity to gain access to information on oil company operations by joining the IEA arose at a time when the Canadian government was especially interested in acquiring greater knowledge about an increasingly important industry. A report presented by Energy, Mines and Resources in June 1973 advised state participation in the oil industry, largely in order to give the government a better idea of how that industry operated.[55] This was one of the main reasons later given by the government for establishing Petro-Canada. Membership in the IEA permitted the Canadian government to balance its window on the domestic operations of oil companies with a window on their international operations.

Domestic factors played a more crucial role in the government's neglect of emergency preparations. After the Arab embargo was lifted in early 1974, world oil prices levelled off, and during the mid to late 1970s they even declined in real terms. The diminished crisis atmosphere over energy matters in most OECD countries was even more pronounced in Canada due to the existence of price controls, which until 1979 kept the domestic price of a barrel of oil around five dollars below the world price. At a time when the Japanese and Europeans were making vigorous efforts to cut back oil consumption, price controls helped to make Canadians the highest per capita consumers of energy in the world.[56] The low level of public concern over the country's growing vulnerability to future supply disruptions was reflected in the government's neglect of emergency preparations. When the Energy Supplies Emergency Act (1974) was allowed to lapse in 1976, a single question was asked in the House of Commons about whether legislation would be reactivated, but no further discussion of the matter ensued at that time.[57]

Energy once again became a highly politicized issue with the 1979 supply disruption resulting from the Iranian revolution. As noted earlier, the Canadian government responded by re-establishing the Energy Supplies Allocation Board prior to calling a general election. Although energy became a major issue during the election campaign, collective arrangements to reduce oil-import vulnerability were barely mentioned. The Conservative party proposed a policy of oil self-sufficiency, and subsequent Canadian energy security policy was largely based on this objective. After regaining power in February 1980, the Liberal government pledged to make Canada self-sufficient in oil by 1990, and the National Energy Program's energy security provisions were primarily geared towards ending dependence on oil imports. With the collapse of oil prices in the second half of the 1980s, the Mulroney government was forced to reassess this goal. The level of subsidization that would be required to develop the additional oil reserves needed to make Canada truly self-sufficient in oil appeared prohibitive given the growing concern over budget deficits. The market-oriented emphasis placed on economic policy by the Conservative government also seemed to militate against such a high degree of state intervention. Nevertheless, domestic political considerations ultimately contributed to the government's decision, in the run-up to the 1988 federal election, in favour of funding certain energy "megaprojects," especially Hibernia oil development.

The problem of insufficient emergency oil reserves in eastern Canada has remained, chiefly as a result of two domestic factors. First, the media and members of Parliament have been unaware of the problems involved in transporting western Canadian oil to the east during an emergency, in including industry working stocks in the definition of emergency reserves, and in basing these reserves on net imports. Government statistics have until recently indicated that emergency reserves are more than sufficient, and there has been little questioning of this assertion. Second, partly because of the lack of awareness about the reserves problem and partly because of diminishing public concern over energy security caused by the recent world oil surplus, the Canadian government has had little political incentive to pay the costs of adequately preparing for another oil crisis. An important factor in any attempt at collective action is the need that governments have for domestic political benefits. Some analysts have even argued that co-operation is feasible only if governments perceive that they will be better able to deal with domestic problems or to gain support from certain domestic interests and minimize opposition from others.[58] In the case of emergency reserves, the Canadian government is not going to profit politically by expending revenue to build oil stocks that are not likely to be needed immediately. In contrast, the expenditure of resources on a popular policy such as the Canadianization of the oil industry promised to provide, at least for a time, more immediate political support for the last Liberal government, eager to gain favour with what it considered to be an increasingly nationalistic electorate.[59]

CONCLUSION

Following its experience in the early stages of the Iran-Iraq war, many observers saw the IEA as a highly useful instrument for reducing the vulnerability of Western oil-importing nations, not only to large-scale disruptions in oil supply but also to more limited supply interruptions.[60] The effectiveness of this instrument depends to a large extent, however, on the preparedness of member countries. Hence, every possible effort should be made to ensure that Canada is fully prepared to participate in the collective management of oil supply disruptions. The foregoing examination of the factors contributing to the Canadian government's neglect of its IEA commitments indicates how Canada's emergency preparations may eventually improve. The theory of collective goods holds that countries that value a certain collective good highly will be prepared to share more of the burden of providing the good.

Since Canada's imports of oil (particularly light and medium crude) are likely to make up a larger proportion of the country's total oil consumption during the 1990s and into the twenty-first century even if oil prices are relatively high, one would expect a higher value to be placed on the provision of oil import security, and the government may finally be prepared to establish adequate emergency reserves in eastern Canada.[61] In addition, the United States has been putting pressure on its IEA partners to move faster in building up their emergency oil stockpiles.[62] This pressure will probably continue as the concept of "burden sharing" gains popularity in academic and political circles in the United States. The collective goods literature posits that coercion by the leader of a group may help to ensure that the good is provided. Since the U.S. is likely to become more reliant on imported oil in the future, the value it places on these collective arrangements is also likely to increase, as is its willingness to enforce compliance with IEA procedures by other members of the group.

Despite the national interest that would appear to be served in adequately preparing to participate in collective emergency arrangements, and the international pressure that can be expected to be put on Canada to make such preparations, it is difficult to envisage the Canadian government moving in this direction unless it perceives that there will be domestic political benefits in doing so.

The government may be induced to act if pressure from organized interests and/or the attentive public increases. Public concern about oil import vulnerability may increase as domestic, high-cost oil production declines in a climate of persistent glut. At the moment, however, it is the same climate of glut that most contributes to the current public mood of confidence that oil security, which seemed so imperilled in the 1974–83 decade, has been achieved for good. As anyone familiar with the plight of the Alberta economy can testify, however, the oil "problem" has taken on a far different meaning for many Canadians in the late 1980s from what it possessed a decade or so ago.[63]

NOTES

1 Thomas D. Mullins, "The Security of Oil Supplies," *Survival* 28 (Nov./Dec. 1986):509–23; Edward L. Morse, "After the Fall: The Politics of Oil," *Foreign Affairs* 64 (Spring 1986):792–811; and Daniel Yergin, "Energy Security in the 1990s," *Foreign Affairs* 67 (Fall 1988):110–32.

2 Philip Connelly and Robert Perlman, *The Politics of Scarcity: Resource Conflicts in International Relations* (London: Oxford University Press 1975), 104. Also see, for a good analysis of energy shortages and alliance politics during the post-Second World War period, Ethan B. Kapstein, *Allies without Energy: The Politics of Fuel Shortage since 1945* (New York: Oxford University Press 1989).

3 Wilfrid L. Kohl, "The International Energy Agency: The Political Context," in *Oil, the Arab-Israel Dispute and the Industrial World: Horizons of Crisis*, ed. J.C. Hurewitz (Boulder, CO: Westview Press 1976), 247–8; Mason Willrich and Melvin A. Conant, "The International Energy Agency: An Interpretation and Assessment," *American Journal of International Law* 71 (1977):201.

4 Connelly and Perlman, *Politics of Scarcity*, 104; Ethan B. Kapstein, "Alliance Energy Security, 1945–1983," *Fletcher Forum* (Winter 1984):107–12.

5 Wolfgang Hager, "Western Europe: The Politics of Muddling Through," in *Oil, the Arab-Israel Dispute, and the Industrial World*, 42.

6 Hager, "Western Europe," 42.
7 *Agreement on an International Energy Program,* Articles 12–13, 62.
8 *Agreement,* Articles 1–24.
9 Interviews with Canadian government officials and with IEA officials.
10 For a more detailed discussion of this commission, see Philippe Manin, "Le Centre pour le Règlement des Différends de l'Agence Internationale de l'Energie," *Annuaire Français de Droit International,* 2301–49; United States, General Accounting Office, *Determination of Oil Price in the International Emergency Sharing System: An Unresolved Issue,* Report to Senator Howard M. Metzenbaum, 11 Nov. 1982 (GAO/ID-83-15); and J. Wallace Hopkins, "Le système international de répartition d'urgence de l'aie: conclusions d'un récent exercice," *L'Observateur de l'OCDE,* no. 110 (May 1981); 8.
11 Interviews with Canadian and U.S. government officials.
12 David A. Deese and Linda B. Miller, "Western Europe," in *Energy and Security,* ed. David A. Deese and Joseph S. Nye (Cambridge, MA: Ballinger 1981), 193.
13 As mentioned earlier in the text, activation is automatic to the extent that the system comes into operation once the Secretariat has made a finding that a 7 per cent reduction has occurred or can reasonably be expected to occur, and if the activation is not overridden by a "special majority" veto. See the *Agreement on an International Energy Program,* Ch. 4.
14 Economists have not agreed (and probably never will) on the precise extent to which the two oil price shocks were directly responsible for such macroeconomic problems as economic recession, inflation, and unemployment. See, for example, Knut Anton Mork, "The Economic Cost of Oil Supply Disruptions," in *Energy Vulnerability,* ed. James Plummer (Cambridge, MA: Ballinger 1982); Sylvia Ostry, John Llewellyn, and Lee Samuelson, "Le coût du deuxième choc petrolier OPEP II," *l'Observateur de l'OCDE,* no. 115 (Mar. 1982), 40–3; International Energy Agency, *Energy Policies and Programmes of IEA Countries: 1980 Review* (Paris: OECD 1981), 11–12; *The Economics of the Oil Crisis,* ed. T.M. Rybczynski (London: Macmillan 1976); *Higher Oil Prices and the World Economy: The Adjustment Problem,* ed. Edward R Fried and Charles L. Schultze (Washington: Brookings Institution 1975). However, even if these problems were largely created by the reaction of economic policymakers to oil price shocks, there is no guarantee that elected officials will be convinced to take a more economically rational, although politically costly, course of action in response to future emergency situations. Hence, the macroeconomic fallout of large oil price increases could very well be the same as in the past, whether for economic or political reasons.
15 IEA Press Release (79) 4, 2 Mar. 1979.
16 IEA Press Release (79), 29, 10 Dec. 1979.
17 *Petroleum Intelligence Weekly,* 17 Dec. 1979.
18 Interview with IEA official.
19 Interview with IEA official.
20 *The Times* (London), 17 Nov. 1980; *Petroleum Intelligence Weekly,* 6 Oct. 1980.
21 IEA Press Release (80) 20, 9 Dec. 1980.
22 *New York Times,* 15 Nov. 1980.
23 Interviews with Canadian and American government officials and with IEA officials; Edward L. Morse, "Energy Security and International Preparedness," *Current Policy,* no. 272 (Washington: United States Department of State, 23 Mar. 1981), 3; Daniel Badger and Robert Belgrave, *Oil Supply and Price: What Went Right in 1980?* (London: Policy Studies Institute 1982).
24 Interview with IEA official.
25 *New York Times,* 10 Dec. 1980.
26 IEA Press Release (80) 20, 9 Dec. 1980.
27 Interview with IEA official.
28 For a more comprehensive discussion of the 1984 Stockdraw Decision, see Glen Toner, "The International Energy Agency and the Development of the Stocks Decision," *Energy Policy* 15 (Feb. 1987):40–58.
29 Willrich and Conant, "International Energy Agency," 221.
30 Interview with Canadian government official.
31 Robert Jervis, "Cooperation under the Security Dilemma," *World Politics* 30 (Jan. 1978):167–214.
32 *The Guardian,* 27 Mar. 1979.
33 Robert J. Lieber, "Cohesion and Disruption in the Western Alliance," in *Global Insecurity: A Strategy for Energy and Economic Upheaval,* ed. Daniel Yergin and Martin Hillenbrand (Boston: Houghton Mifflin 1982), 337–8.

34 Despite the proclaimed hostility of the Reagan administration to government intervention in the market, the administration did assert its commitment to the collective management of major and limited oil-supply disruptions. See, for example, Senate testimony given by administration officials on 14 July 1981: "International Energy Agency and Global Energy Security Matters," *Hearings Before the Committee on Governmental Affairs, Subcommittee on Energy, Nuclear Proliferation, and Government Processes, United States Senate,* 97th Cong., 1st sess. (Washington: U.S. Government Printing Office 1981). By 1984 the administration had shifted from the major opponent to the major supporter of a co-ordinated stock drawdown in pre-emergency situations. See Toner, "International Energy Agency," 50–5.

35 A country can be considered "vulnerable" when the costs of pursuing alternatives to imported oil are not tolerable. See Robert O. Keohane and Joseph S. Nye, *Power and Interdependence: World Politics in Transition* (Boston: Little, Brown 1977), 13.

36 Canada, Energy, Mines and Resources, *Energy Security in Canada: A Discussion Paper* (Ottawa: EMR 1987), 25–8.

37 *Globe and Mail,* 27 June 1979.

38 Energy, Mines and Resources Canada, *The National Energy Program 1980* (Ottawa: Minister of Supply and Services 1980), 89.

39 *Energy Security in Canada,* 51–2.

40 *Financial Post,* 16 Feb. 28 Apr. 1979; *Globe and Mail,* 16 May 1979.

41 *Energy Security in Canada,* 44, 55.

41 *Energy Security in Canada,* 1–2, 59, 94.

43 Bruce M. Russett and John D. Sullivan, "Collective Goods and International Organization," *International Organization* 25 (Autumn 1971):849.

44 Todd Sandler and Jon Cauley, "On the Economic Theory of Alliances," *Journal of Conflict Resolution* 19 (June 1975):331–2.

45 Mancur Olson, "Increasing the Incentives for International Cooperation," *International Organization* 25 (Autumn 1971):873.

46 William Loehr, "Collective Goods and International Cooperation: Comments," *International Organization* 27 (Summer 1973):428.

47 Mancur Olson, *The Logic of Collective Action* (Cambridge, MA: Harvard University Press 1965), 11.

48 Olson, *Logic of Collective Action,* 2.

49 Willrich and Conant, "International Energy Agency," 220.

50 Russett and Sullivan, "Collective Goods," 856.

51 *International Canada* 4 (Dec. 1973):335–6.

52 *Ottawa Citizen,* 12 Jan. 1972.

53 Mancur Olson and Richard Zeckhauser, "An Economic Theory of Alliances," *Review of Economics and Statistics* 48 (Aug. 1966):272; Russett and Sullivan, "Collective Goods," 854.

54 Joe Oppenheimer, "Collective Goods and Alliances: A Reassessment," *Journal of Conflict Resolution* 23 (Sept. 1979):396–8.

55 Energy, Mines and Resources Canada, *An Energy Policy for Canada, Vol. I* (Ottawa: Information Canada 1973), 120–4.

56 Z. Charles Slagorsky, *Energy Use in Canada in Comparison with Other Countries* (Calgary: Canadian Energy Research Institute 1979), 21.

57 Canada, House of Commons, *Debates,* 30 Jan. 1976, p. 10, 485.

58 Edward L. Morse and Thomas Wallin, "Demand Management and Economic Nationalism in the Coming Decade," in *Challenges to Interdependent Economies: The Industrial West in the Coming Decade,* ed. Robert J. Gordon and Jacques Pelkmans (New York: McGraw-Hill 1979), 16.

59 The Liberal party adopted a nationalistic energy policy during the election of 1980 after the release of a series of opinion polls indicating that the Canadian electorate had become much more nationalistic in recent years. See Heather Robertson, "The New Patriots," *Today Magazine,* 25 Apr. 1981. Three years later the majority of Canadians still supported the NEP's goal of "Canadianization" of the oil industry. It is for this reason that the Conservative opposition restrained itself from attacking the Canadianization provisions of the NEP, and it also helps to explain why the Canadian government was adamant about retaining this part of the policy, despite strong U.S. opposition to it. See Jock A. Finlayson and David G. Haglund, "Oil Politics and U.S.-Canada Relations," *Political Science Quarterly* 99 (Summer 1984):271–88.

60 For example, Badger and Belgrave, *Oil Supply and Price;* Lieber, "Cohesion and Disruption in the Western Alliance," 334; Joseph S. Nye, jr., "Energy and Security in the 1980s," *World Politics* 35 (Oct. 1982):130–1.

61 *Energy Security in Canada,* 26–7.

62 The U.S. urged other IEA members to do this at the May 1987 IEA ministerial meeting (interview with Canadian government official; *International Herald Tribune* 12 May 1987).

63 The U.S. is similarly experiencing recession in oil-producing regions that recently enjoyed vigorous growth. See "Oil Prices Cast a pall over Prudhoe Bay," *New York Times,* 27 July 1986.

Part IV

6

Canadian Strategic Minerals and U.S. Military Potential: National Security Implications of Bilateral Mineral Trade

David G. Haglund

INTRODUCTION

Two basic themes seem to permeate most discussions of the relative resource positions of Canada and the United States. The first is that Canada's role in the international division of labour is that of "hewer of wood, drawer of water." Accordingly, Canada makes its way in the world by supplying the more industrialized states with the vital raw materials they need to fuel their development, while Canada's own development is retarded. Those concerned with Canada's over-reliance on exports of raw materials see great danger ahead. In the words of Maurice Lamontagne, spoken more than a decade ago but no less relevant today, "if we continue to rely on our resource industries as the prime mover to sustain the national economy and to provide more jobs directly and indirectly, our nation will eventually lose its economic viability and might even become a ghost country."[1]

The second theme is that it is the United States, certainly more than any other single country but also more than all other countries put together, that intentionally or otherwise poses the greatest risk to Canadian economic viability in the long term. It does so, according to this view, because of its outsized demand for Canadian resources. Indeed, the obverse of Canadian profligacy in the export of minerals and other forms of raw materials is American gluttony in their consumption. To those who hold this point of view, the primary danger is that the United States, through its voracious appetite for Canadian resources, will so deplete Canadian reserves that not enough raw material wealth will remain to sustain Canada's own development—in effect, Canada will become Lamontagne's "ghost country." As Stephen Clarkson put it some years ago: "Having thrived on selling off its resources, Canada now confronts the problem of their depletion."[2]

Like other countries that are well endowed with raw materials, Canada has experienced in the past few decades periodic upsurges of "resource nationalism," excrescences of what Abraham Rotstein, himself an economic nationalist, labels the "homestead mentality."[3] In addition to a sense of acute anxiety about the presumed squandering of one's birthright, resource nationalists have focused on the *political* costs associated with becoming too much of a source of supply for any single country. That is, the concern is that a too great American dependence upon Canada for any mineral or other resource might eventually present intolerable constraints upon Canadian foreign (and even domestic) policy. Thus, to many who contemplate the relative resource position of Canada and the United States, importations from the former by the latter carry not only potentially onerous economic costs but political ones as well. Perfervid imaginations have even conjured up scenarios of Americans resorting to force to acquire vitally needed industrial inputs from Canada, and at least one Canadian novelist has made a mark for himself by specializing in this genre.[4] Nor has resource nationalism been absent from the most recent federal election campaign, in which frequent reference was made to a Canadian-American Free Trade Agreement as a conduit for the "selling out" of Canadians' resource heritage.[5]

It is not my purpose to dwell upon the economic argument that Canadian mineral reserves are in danger of depletion in large measure because of past exports to the United States. There is a vast literature on the question of mineral scarcity in Canada and elsewhere, and it is beyond the scope of this chapter to do other than remark that though in a physical sense it is evident that non-renewable resources must, by definition, eventually become exhausted, it is far from clear *when* such exhaustion must occur and it is even less clear to what extent exports render a country's reserves position more tenuous than it would otherwise be.[6] It must be recalled that what are ultimately important are resources, not reserves, and to the extent export-led development stimulates the growth of reserves, as it almost always does, a case can be made that, paradoxical as it might seem, to export is actually to build reserves.[7] To be sure, there are certain examples, among which perhaps the most relevant in the Canadian context is conventional crude oil, where exportation and reserve growth have appeared to be antithetical, but this is by no means the general pattern. The case of iron ore suggests it is the exception; Canada, though it typically exports some three-quarters of the iron ore it produces, would almost certainly have had much smaller reserves of iron ore now without the export-oriented development of the post-Second World War decades.[8] What is true for iron ore is also true for a host of other nonrenewable resources, among which must be placed nickel, uranium, copper—and even natural gas.[9] To repeat, non-renewable resources must be depleted by the production process; but reserves, which are simply the quantity of minerals in known deposits that can be profitably exploited under current economic and technological conditions, need not decline. Indeed, they usually do not—at least in all but the long term. Despite the millions of tons extracted by the world's mineral producers in the past three decades, the indisputable fact is that "reserves of nearly all mineral commodities are larger today than in the early postwar period."[10]

In the section on uranium, I will explore the economic dimensions of Canadian-American strategic mineral trade; for the moment, however, I wish to concentrate on the politico-strategic aspects of such trade. If the two themes outlined above—whose implication is that American dependence upon Canadian resources is large and growing—have any real-world relevance, then one would expect to find that Canadian strategic minerals have a relationship to American military potential that is by no means unimportant. Indeed, *if* the two themes reflect reality and not outdated perception, then one is tempted to suggest that as the United States economy becomes more dependent upon Canadian mineral imports, American military potential is also influenced by imports of Canadian strategic minerals. In this chapter I will test the assumption that Canadian strategic minerals are indeed highly important (and becoming even more so) to overall U.S. military potential. By analysing the three most important strategic minerals in recent bilateral trade—nickel, petroleum, and uranium—I will seek to determine the qualitative degree to which we can legitimately speak of Hirschman's "supply effect" of American imports from Canada. In addition, I will also seek to ascertain whether Canada's strategic mineral exports to the United States possess an "influence effect."[11] That is to say, does Canada gain economic and political "leverage" (even if only implicitly) over the United States as a result of its supplying that country with necessary industrial inputs on a large scale?

Internationally traded minerals become strategic in two general ways: by having narrow military applications that are deemed to be essential to national defence, and by having broader economic importance, hence security implications in the larger sense. In the following inquiry I am guided by both understandings of strategic minerals. The three cases I have chosen to isolate can be classed as strategic minerals under either of the two meanings, but two of them, nickel and uranium, have had implications for military potential in the narrower sense, while petroleum chiefly related to the broader meaning of military potential and national security.

In using the case study approach, one must exercise a certain amount of arbitrariness. By definition, the case study implies the exclusion of other, often numerous, subjects of inquiry. To so exclude is not illegitimate (indeed, it is necessary), but it does pose problems. The biggest problem, of course, is choosing the criteria that govern inclusion. In this chapter, I have deemed the most important consideration to be that the Canadian mineral in question must at some time have been a strategic mineral whose consumption requirement in the United States was filled substantially by imports from Canada and other countries. The mineral must have had either narrow military uses or broader security implications. Natural gas fits the criterion of security implications in the broader sense, but it has been excluded from this study because, unlike that of crude oil, its consumption in the United States has never been largely satisfied by imports. This may happen yet, but to date natural gas imports have never constituted more than about 5 per cent of overall U.S. consumption. Crude oil, on the other hand, has been a very important mineral import in the United States. Although American dependence on imports has been levelling off until very recently (and is now about 35 per cent), in 1977 they accounted for nearly one-half of the oil consumed by that country.

A further consideration that has guided my choice of minerals has been the extent to which certain ones have been considered to be more essential than others. Essentiality is contingent on several factors, one of which is the feasibility of import replacement, either through the encouragement of domestic production (including recycling) or substitution by another mineral. Nickel is a very difficult mineral for the United States to do without, and in wartime has been indispensable. Domestic production (barring the advent of fairly economic seabed mining, to be discussed later) cannot possibly replace imports, for the domestic reserve base is simply not available in the United States.[12] Tungsten, on the other hand, is a mineral that has more ample substitution possibilities, and though the United States has been dependent upon imports for more than half its consumption in recent years (and dependent upon Canadian tungsten for about 10 per cent of consumption), tungsten has several substitutes, especially molybdenum, of which the United States is a net exporter.[13] Iron ore is like nickel in having very limited substitution possibilities; how could it be otherwise, when more than 95 per cent of the metal produced in the world is steel, an alloy that is mainly iron? Iron ore is another mineral the U.S. imports from Canada; over the past five years, some 20 per cent of American consumption has been supplied that way.[14] But unlike nickel, iron ore is a mineral in which the United States could be self-sufficient, thanks to the development of technologies that permit the beneficiation of the low-grade taconite ores with which the United States is well endowed—although there would, to be sure, be some costs involved in self-sufficiency.[15]

Ultimately, I have concentrated my attention on nickel, oil, and uranium because these three commodities have been generally regarded for several decades, in the case of nickel for nearly a century, to be the most important strategic minerals in U.S.-Canadian trade. If Canada has been a contributor to American military potential, it has been so in no small measure because of its shipments of nickel, oil, and uranium. And if Canada has possessed leverage over the United States, it has been in part because of the "influence effect" of these three minerals.

NICKEL

The chronological and perhaps even logical place to begin our case studies is with nickel. In its early years of commercial production, in the late nineteenth century, nickel was in many ways like uranium in its early years: the initial demand for each metal was almost exclusively a function of military requirements. Nickel's attributes—strength, hardness, toughness, ductility, corrosion-resistance, and ability to maintain strength under high heat—made it extremely attractive for military users. Its value is enhanced by the fact that it can impart these attributes to its alloys. Especially significant for the future of nickel markets was the development of armoured plating made of nickel steel (to which were added small amounts of chromium and, subsequently, molybdenum), an alloy that was easily able to withstand bombardment from naval guns that were capable of shattering plates made of iron or carbon steel. After 1890 the navies of the world quickly took note of the properties of the new alloy, whose effect was demonstrated most profoundly in the Spanish-American War. During that conflict, American warships clad in nickel steel demolished the Spanish fleet without the loss of a single ship—and with total casualties of only one dead and seven wounded at the battles of Manila Bay and Santiago de Cuba.[16]

Canada was not the first country to embark upon the commercial production of nickel. The French colony of New Caledonia did so in 1875, and for the next thirty years remained the world's leader producer. But the discovery of the incredibly rich Sudbury deposits in 1883 meant that henceforth New Caledonia would encounter growing competition from Canadian ores. By 1910, Sudbury was producing twice as much nickel as New Caledonia, and the gap between the world's two leading producers continued to widen. During the First World War, one province, Ontario, and one company, International Nickel, were supplying 86 per cent of the world's nickel.[17] As INCO had no refining capability in

Canada for most of the war (the Port Colborne, Ontario, refinery came on-stream only late in 1918), all of Canada's nickel was shipped to INCO's Bayonne, New Jersey, refinery for further processing. Apart from strengthening the bilateral trading pattern, which in any case would have been very strong even if all Canadian nickel had been refined domestically, the lack of refining capability had political implications: during the early months of the war, and again in 1916, it became apparent that some Canadian nickel was finding its way from the United States to Germany.[18]

With the war's end, the market for nickel, heretofore almost exclusively a military commodity, collapsed. However, an aggressive marketing campaign on the part of INCO led to the adoption of nickel in numerous civilian uses—so numerous, in fact, that by the mid-1930s it was being argued by some in the company that the mineral's military days were in the past and that henceforth civilian consumption would constitute the predominant demand pressure. The prediction was premature, for by the late 1930s it was once again clear that nickel sales were being largely determined by military purchasing. As the 1930s was also a period when thinking about strategic materials was very much in fashion, both within the military and the more general world of business and academic life, the example of nickel not only demonstrated the manner in which strategic and critical minerals were conceived but also pointed up some important ways in which certain Americans perceived the Canada-U.S. relationship. In his classic 1934 study on America's overall materials position—a position he found to be unsurpassed by any country, hence a position that by itself came close to making America the world's premier military power—Brooks Emeny took it as a given that Canadian nickel was virtually synonymous with American nickel. Due to the concentration of the world's nickel supply in Canada, Emeny regarded the United States as being "in a position to control physically 90 per cent of the world's production." To ensure itself limitless access to Canadian nickel, all the United States had to do was to keep Canada at minimum "coldly neutral" during any war in which the U.S. was involved. "Such being the case, it is apparent that the procurement of nickel in time of war presents no real problem; and except for the fact that the principal source of supply comes from a foreign, though immediate neighbor, it would not even rank as a strategic mineral."[19]

What Emeny was saying was that the United States was dependent, but not vulnerable, with respect to nickel. It was not vulnerable because one could only with great difficulty imagine a situation in which Canada would embargo its nickel exports to the United States. And since likelihood of supply disruption was implicitly a principal distinguishing characteristic of strategic minerals,

Emeny regarded nickel as not genuinely strategic. For even assuming the worst case of Canadian-American conflict, nickel supply could still be assured "through a seizure if necessary of Canadian sources."[20]

The onset of war in 1939 saw the nickel market revert to its pre-1918 pattern. Canada supplied nearly all the nickel used by the Allies, and though no one in Washington had the slightest concern about Canadian *willingness* to provide the war effort with nickel, there was some concern about Canadian *ability* to do so. Accordingly, during the war American planners, for the first time since the introduction of nickel into the technology of warfare some fifty years before, began to contemplate building up non-Canadian sources of supply. The result was that government funds were poured into Cuban nickel-producing facilities. By war's end, lateritic deposits worked by the Nicaro Nickel Company were producing an amount of nickel equivalent to 30 per cent of U.S. prewar consumption.[21]

What happened after the First World War did not recur after the Second World War. The world did not disarm, and nickel did not lose its market. Indeed, nickel experienced a rebirth as a strategic mineral due to the Korean War (and the Cold War in general), as well as the discovery that nickel alloys were essential to the development of the newest military technology, the jet engine. Far from diminishing in importance, by the early 1950s, nickel had come, in the words of a 1954 U.S. Defense Department report, "the closest to being a true 'war metal.' It deserves first priority among materials receiving conservation attention. Since the start of the Korean War, nickel has remained the world's most critical material; this condition is likely to continue for some time."[22]

As it had done in the Second World War, the United States in the 1950s attempted to diversify away from its excessive reliance upon INCO, which at the start of the decade was still producing nearly 90 per cent of the non-Communist world's nickel.[23] The diversification impetus came from two sources: the desire to increase the overall supply of nickel available to the United States and the desire to reduce American dependence upon INCO. As difficult as it may be to imagine in today's economic climate, when until very recently the biggest problem with nickel seemed to be its oversupply,[24] in the United States (and other Western consuming countries) during the 1950s there was an acute perception that nickel shortages were likely to last for years to come, given the competition between military and civilian users of the highly regarded metal.[25] The diversification strategy was fairly successful, and both aims were to a large extent achieved. The tight supply situation that characterized the Korean War years was alleviated as a result of the expansion of production capacity both in Canada and Cuba; by 1957 non-Communist world nickel supply had increased by 50 per cent over the 1950 total, rising from 200 to 300 million pounds. And while global production was increasing, the relative share of INCO was declining, with the result that American dependence upon the Canadian company was reduced from nearly complete at the start of the decade to 65 per cent by 1957.[26]

It bears emphasizing that it was the dependence of the United States upon INCO's nickel that proved so worrisome to planners in Washington; as far as *Canadian* nickel was concerned, there did not seem to be any sense of concern about the continued high level of dependence. As they had in the interwar period, American analysts in the 1950s and 1960s continued to regard Canadian supply as practically equivalent to domestic supply, and consequently did not attempt to extrapolate from the condition of dependence a situation of vulnerability.[27] It is true that Cuban lateritic deposits were once again brought into production with American subsidies during the 1950s, but the overwhelming share of the monies allocated under the Defense Production Act of 1950 were expended on the expansion of Canadian production capacity, with most of the contracts being awarded not to INCO but to Falconbridge and Sherritt Gordon.[28]

One of the ironies of Canadian-American nickel relations is that once an expansion and diversification of worldwide nickel supply was accomplished, and American dependence upon INCO and Canada somewhat reduced, there appeared for the first time a tendency on the part of some strategic minerals analysts to consider nickel one of the minerals in which the United States was *vulnerable.*[29] Vulnerability is a qualitative assessment that differs from dependence in that it is contingent upon not only the overall proportion of domestic consumption satisfied by imports, but also judgments about the probability of those imports being subject to supply disruptions—whether resulting from cartels, wars, disinvestment, or civil unrest. As American dependence upon Canada declined, some began to think that such dependence made the U.S. more vulnerable.[30]

It is not easy to account for the tendency, especially noticeable by the start of the 1980s, to regard the United States as vulnerable in nickel. It may be, as one analyst has suggested, that Washington feared a Canadian-led nickel cartel, similar to the uranium cartel in which Ottawa had such a visible role.[31] Or quite possibly it was worried that Ottawa (perhaps joined by the producing provinces, Ontario and Manitoba) would again attempt, as in the early 1970s, to capture more "economic rent" from the nickel producers, thereby creating a poor climate for investment in new exploration, with negative consequences for Canada's reserves position.[32] It is even conceivable that a new mood of isolationism was sweeping the United States at the start of this decade, engendering an ideological desire for a return to the lost days of mineral self-sufficiency.[33] Most likely, however, the placing of nickel in the vulnerable category was nothing more than a lumping together into one category, for the sake of analytic orderliness, of all the minerals for which the United States is significantly dependent upon imports. In short, the question of dependence alone seems to have taken precedence over the more difficult, but fundamentally more valuable, issue of vulnerability. Not all analysts committed this error, but enough did so that it was common to find studies that presented solutions to the American "problem" with nickel supply.[34] The truth of the matter is that the U.S. has *no* fundamental problem with its nickel supply today, notwithstanding the recent temporary tight situation.

The United States, which over the past five years has been reliant on Canada for nearly 30 per cent of its total nickel consumption, *might* be said to be vulnerable with respect to other strategic metals. Among these, two of the most important are manganese and cobalt, each of which performs essential metallurgical and chemical functions. The problem with both is not one of economic scarcity but rather the perceived political reliability of the major sources of supply. In each case, the major supplier is an African country: Zaïre of cobalt and Gabon of manganese. In the past decade, the principal Western consuming nations have occasionally evinced anxiety about the long-term stability of their African suppliers. The United States relies on imports for 100 per cent of its manganese consumption, and 92 per cent of its cobalt. More than 50 per cent of America's imported manganese comes from Gabon and South Africa, and nearly 40 per cent of its cobalt from Zaïre.[35] The relevance of this particular American dilemma to Canada (which is a marginal source of cobalt supply for the U.S. but which itself relies totally on imports for manganese) is that both cobalt and manganese are present in the polymetallic nodules found in various parts of the deep seabed. The problem from the Canadian point of view is that nickel, too, is found in these "manganese" nodules (along with copper, molybdenum, and vanadium). Thus any large-scale American seabed mining—even if it were primarily intended to reduce American vulnerability in cobalt and manganese—could have serious effects upon the land-based Canadian nickel industry.[36]

Ultimately, seabed mining will only proceed (whether within a U.N. sanctioned regime or not) if its economics appear attractive. If such production is economic at 1990s price levels for nickel and other minerals contained in the nodules, then seabed mining may take place on a significant scale. Whether the economic criterion can be met depends on future price levels and improvements in technology. Although no one can predict what these will be a decade hence, prior to the recession of the early 1980s a consensus seemed to have developed among students of the issue that, in the words of V.E. McKelvey, "prospects seem reasonably good for production of nickel, copper, cobalt, and possibly manganese, molybdenum, and vanadium from nodules on the deep ocean floor in the northeastern equatorial Pacific by 1990."[37] Today, however, analysts are *much* less optimistic about the economic viability of deep seabed mining, at least for the rest of this century.

Should seabed mining ever take place, the long-term effect on Canadian-American nickel trade could be profound. Some experts expect that the United States would not only eliminate its import-dependence in nickel, manganese, cobalt, and copper, but even become a net *exporter* of these metals.[38] One could expect a continuation and even acceleration of the long-term trend that has seen the United States gradually reduce its dependence on imports of Canadian nickel. It seems clear if this occurs the relevance of Canadian nickel exports to overall American military potential will continue to diminish, if not disappear altogether.

OIL

I have dwelt at some length upon nickel not only because nickel was widely considered to be the most strategic of all metals (it has recently been challenged for that ranking by chromium, cobalt, manganese, platinum, and uranium), but also because Canadian exports figured largely in overall American military potential for such a long time. Whatever similarities exist between nickel and oil, a long history of this country as a major source of U.S. imports is not one of them. Indeed, the United States itself was a dominant source of Canadian oil supply for more than half this century. Canada has been a net exporter of crude oil to the United States only since 1955.[39]

Canadian and American oil interests have rarely coincided during the post-Second World War decades. Originally, the most salient bilateral oil issue was whether the United States would make available to Canada as much oil as Canada wanted. In the late 1950s and through the 1960s, Canada switched from trying to convince the Americans to sell it more oil to trying to persuade them to buy more Alberta oil. Finally, by the early 1970s, it was Washington's turn to be the supplicant, when confronted with the unpleasant reality of its growing dependence upon foreign (especially Middle Eastern) oil.[40]

Oil, much more so than either nickel or uranium, is strategic in the broad understanding detailed in Chapter 1. While it also has narrow strategic meaning, for the most part its relationship to national security stems from its overall importance to the functioning of modern industrialized economies. Because it is the most essential fuel, states have tended to lavish upon it the kind of attention given to only a few nonfuel minerals. Most typically this attention takes the form of "policy" of one sort or another—and policy usually implies that special consideration be accorded to nonmarket factors and forces in the allocation of available supply. In the case of the United States, official oil policy in the post-war decades has undergone radical shifts, most of which have affected Canadian interests. During the mid-1950s pressure began building in the U.S. to restrict cheap imported oil. The restrictionist forces were obviously supported by domestic economic interests, particularly the independent producers who had no foreign reserves under their control. But it would be wrong to identify restriction solely, or even chiefly, with economic protectionism; for the case against imports was made clearly and loudly by members of the American national security bureaucracy.

Imports, declared the Office of Defense Mobilization in 1957, were a threat to national security and should be reduced. A special investigatory committee created by President Eisenhower recommended that the major oil companies "voluntarily" restrict their imports, a measure that went into effect in July 1957. Though the measures were only "voluntary," Canada's oil producers stood to be seriously injured if quotas were applied against them, for Alberta oil could not compete with cheaper foreign oil. This was why the province's producers were unable to penetrate eastern Canadian markets. In fact, there was only one market outside of western Canada in which Alberta oil was cost-competitive, the American one. Thus Canadians were quick to react to the implication that somehow their oil sales to the United States constituted a risk to that country's security. Opposition spokesman Lester Pearson reminded Americans of something that analysts of the nickel supply issue had long taken for granted, that Canadian source of supply was practically synonymous with domestic American source of supply: "Oil in Alberta is as safe from hostile interference, and as available for United States use, as oil in Oklahoma."[41]

Canada did manage to escape inclusion in the import restriction measure introduced in 1959, the Mandatory Oil Import Program. The grounds for the Canadian, or "overland" exemption were mainly security and political ones.[42] Nevertheless, throughout the 1960s protectionist forces continued to oppose imports of Canadian oil. By the late 1960s, American "policy" on oil imports could be said to exist only in a rudimentary sense. Though the Cabinet Task Force on Oil Imports created by President Nixon in 1969 (and headed by then Labor Secretary George Shultz) advocated that the United States resolve its growing supply problem with oil by importing more, there was an important minority, spearheaded by the Secretaries of the Interior and Commerce, in favour of stricter import quotas. The President acted on neither recommendation, but instead let American policy drift until the oil supply situation became fairly acute shortly thereafter.

By the early 1970s, with the domestic reserves of oil declining and imports rising, and with a cabinet divided over which course to take, a viable alternative to either laissez-faire or autarky seemed to present itself: the "Canadian option." Canada was in any event by now a major factor in the American oil market, with exports of one million barrels a day (MBD) making it second only to Venezuela as a source of American imports. The appeal of Canadian oil was twofold: as Lester Pearson and other Canadians had argued, the security advantages of Canadian as opposed to other foreign oil seemed so obvious as to hardly require stating; and, happily, Canada seemed to be a country literally brimming with oil.

Havelock Ellis once remarked that optimism flourishes best in lunatic asylums. Had he been alive a decade and a half ago, he might have added, "and in the boardrooms of the North American energy establishment," for on either side of the border extravagant (and in retrospect, crazy) claims were being made by otherwise knowledgeable experts about Canadian energy reserves. In 1971 the U.S. National Petroleum Council, an advisory body of oil industry executives, informed President Nixon that Canada, given its vast reserves of oil, could be selling the United States more than 2 MBD [!] by 1985.[43] The Council was not working in a vacuum; fanciful as its projections now seem (given that total Canadian *production* does not even approach 2 MBD), they were based on reserves data emanating from official Canadian sources, which in turn were being supplied with information by the mostly foreign-owned private oil sector. For instance, both the Canadian Petroleum Association and the Canadian Geological Survey estimated that Canada had more than 120 billion barrels in potential reserves of *conventional* oil, to say nothing of the hundreds of billions of barrels thought to be contained in non-conventional sources.[44] According to the National Energy Board's annual report in 1969, such reserves would be capable of sustaining exports to the United States in the range of 2 to 2.5 MBD by the mid-1980s.[45] Is it any wonder, then, that the Minister of Energy, Mines and Resources, Joe Greene, could confidently (some would say recklessly) claim in June 1971 that, based on current levels of domestic consumption, Canada had enough oil to last another 923 years?[46]

Just as some Americans were starting to get used to the idea that Canada could become an even greater source of imported oil, Ottawa began to reconsider the entire question of oil supply and export potential. Although this reconsideration actually predated the great OPEC price rise of autumn 1973—in fact Canada had begun to reduce its exports to the U.S. in June—it did not attract much attention in Washington until events later in the year. When it was learned that not only was Canada to cut back its exports to the U.S., but it would actually raise the price Americans would have to pay for Canadian oil to world levels, many in the American capital concluded that Canada had "pulled an OPEC" on its best friend. Some even went so far as to suggest that while the Arab oil producers might be following the dictates of self-interest, the Canadian action bordered on betrayal.

In time, the furor abated. It took a while, but eventually American officials (not all of whom had in any case subscribed to the Canada-OPEC analogy)[47] were brought around to the realization that Canada was soon going to encounter oil supply difficulties of its own and would be unable to help Americans much in their bid to reduce their dependence upon Middle Eastern oil. By 1976 a student of Canadian-American oil relations could rightly state that "no informed observer still expects that Canadian energy resources can be a major remedy for the United States energy shortage. Americans realize they must look elsewhere to supplement their own supplies. Canada's contribution must be rather small."[48] That the Canadian contribution would not be as large as before became widely accepted in the U.S.; what was more of a surprise was how quickly Canada would cease being an overall net exporter of oil and start being a fairly large net importer.

It was commonly argued at the start of the current decade that Canada was not really very dependent upon imported oil, and thus was one of the "happy few" OECD countries (with Britain and Norway) that did not have to worry about where the next barrel would come from.[49] In reality, Canada by the end of the 1970s was already significantly dependent upon imported oil to satisfy domestic consumption, and until the recession of the early 1980s appeared to be becoming more so. In 1980 it was importing some 425,000 barrels a day, or about 23 per cent of domestic consumption.[50] Given that 1981 was both the year of worldwide oil glut and demand-reducing economic recession, one would have expected Canada, like the United States and other Western consuming countries, to reduce its dependence upon foreign oil. In fact, it did just the opposite: overall demand did decline, but domestic production declined even further, causing a consumption gap that was closed by an increase in imports, which were nearly 3 per cent higher at the end of 1981 than a year before. At that time, Canada was importing some 437,000 barrels a day and producing a further 1.39 MBD; this gave the country an "import quotient" of about 24 per cent.[51] Oil imports did decline, it is true, after 1982, and by mid-decade accounted for less than 20 per cent of consumption.[52]

Canada has in the past few years once again become a net exporter of crude oil and continues to be a net exporter to the United States, though hardly to the extent of twenty years ago. In its peak export year, Canada sent 1.3 MBD to the United States, an amount that constituted more than a fifth of total American imports of 6.3 MBD.[53] Recently, it has been selling to the United States nearly 500,000 barrels a day, much of it conventional heavy crude that has no ready markets within Canada. It is difficult to determine whether that figure will change much in the next few years; perhaps it is safest to say that in the medium term Canadian oil supply will remain less than crucial to U.S. requirements. Given that the United States now imports 6 MBD,[54] it can be seen that Canada is not an indispensable source of crude oil, accounting for perhaps 8 per cent of total imports and only about 3 per cent of total consumption.

One can only speculate whether Canada might re-emerge as a major supplier of oil to the United States. Were it to do so, it would most certainly not be before the late 1990s at the earliest, and even then it would depend (assuming, of course, that Ottawa once again decided to approve large-scale oil exports and that Washington opted to increase its imports of Canadian oil) upon good fortune in tapping the immense resources thought to be found in the "Canada Lands," especially the Atlantic Grand Banks and the Beaufort Sea/Mackenzie Delta area. However problematical the production prospects for frontier oil might be, it is even less likely that the non-conventional heavy oil deposits that were once thought to be irresistibly tempting to the United States will turn out to be much of a factor in American oil supply.[55] As the shelving of two major Alberta oil-sands developments (Alsands and Cold Lake) has indicated, non-conventional oil production is extremely capital intensive. Given that the United States itself possesses non-conventional oil resources in abundance (in oil shale), there is no reason to imagine that U.S. heavy oil production would be less practicable than similar Canadian production. Nor is there any reason to assume that, even should Canadian oil-sands production be more economical than U.S. oil-shale production, Washington would refrain, notwithstanding the free trade agreement with Canada, from supporting the costlier domestic development with a variety of protectionist measures in the name of national security. The memory of the loss of Canadian oil in the 1970s should be a powerful disincentive to the United States' once again planning to get a significant amount of its imported oil from north of the border. As one American oil analyst observed some time ago, in a study of the possible implications for American oil supply of Canadian and Venezuelan heavy oil development, "hemispheric supply" in and of itself is no guarantee of security of supply. "We once thought that Canadian crude was the most reliable of all imports; it turned out not to be so."[56]

The recent U.S. import experience with Canadian nickel has recurred all the more strongly in the case of Canadian oil. There has been a reduction in dependence upon Canada, associated with the appearance of new foreign sources of supply and accompanied by an uncertain promise of eventual domestic self-sufficiency. The difference between the two minerals is that in nickel's case the process is in a relatively early stage, and only deep seabed mining holds out the prospect of America ceasing to be a major purchaser of Canadian nickel over the medium term. Canada may be a declining source of nickel supply to the United States, but it is still that country's most important supplier. In oil, Canada can only be considered marginal to American supply. While it is true that the U.S. has in recent years greatly reduced its vulnerability to supply disruptions of oil coming from the Middle East, it has done so largely by a combination of policies detailed below. What is significant is that this reduction in vulnerability has occurred without much recourse to a "Canadian option."

There are five principal vulnerability-reducing strategies open to consumers of oil and other strategic minerals: (1) *stockpiles* can be amassed to lessen the costs of short-term supply disruptions (and even serve as a deterrent in some circumstances), (2) *import diversification* toward more stable producers can be pursued, (3) *domestic production* can be increased by a variety of methods, (4) *substitution* of some other mineral for crude oil can be adopted by those countries with an adequate resource endowment, and (5) *conservation* measures can be applied more vigorously.

I should briefly like to review American policy in these areas. For decades *stockpiling* has been a preferred way to reduce vulnerability to supply disruption in the entire range of strategic minerals, at least in the United States.[57] Though not a problem-free option, stockpiling has attracted support even from those liberal economists, such as Hans Landsberg, who wish to see market distortions minimized by whatever policies governments adopt in responding to vulnerability concerns. Stockpiling, it is argued, theoretically has the potential to be nearly self-financing, and it is in any event less costly to consumers than a policy of creating domestic productive capacity through subsidization of high-cost producers.[58] The United States started stockpiling various commodities during the Second World War and now has a Strategic Stockpile of some ninety-four materials (eighty-four of which are metals or nonfuel minerals) valued at some $10.5 billion.[59]

The most strategic of all minerals, oil, was not included in the strategic stockpile. To remedy this anomalous situation, the United States in 1975 created the Strategic Petroleum Reserve (SPR), a stockpile of crude oil that is planned to hold, in salt caverns and mines in Texas and Louisiana, 750 million barrels of oil at an initial estimated cost of at least $40 billion—by far the most ambitious and expensive stockpile in history.[60] Plagued with problems in its early years, the SPR contained 534 million barrels of oil as of 30 September 1987, and was being filled at a rate of 73,000 barrels a day.[61] It is now more than half-filled. When full, it is expected to have a drawdown capacity of between 4 and 5 MBD— roughly 75 per cent of total American crude oil imports at present. Oil can be taken out of the SPR at the rate of nearly 3 MBD,[62] an amount far in excess of U.S. imports from the Persian Gulf.

Import diversification is another option the United States has pursued in reducing its vulnerability to Persian Gulf supply disruptions. That the United States and other countries have been able to shift their purchases of oil toward other producers is a reflection of the "oil proliferation" the world has experienced in the last fifteen years.[63] As a result of significant new production from countries that at the start of the 1970s were either minor exporters or net importers, the relative importance of both OPEC and the Gulf oil-producing states has diminished markedly. Whereas ten years ago OPEC accounted for half the world production of 60 MBD, today its share of global production is approximately a third. In 1973 Gulf producers alone accounted for 21 MBD; today, these same countries produce less than 11 MBD of crude oil.[64]

Indicative of the shift of U.S. imports away from the Persian Gulf is the fact that by the mid-1980s the United Kingdom was supplying more oil to the American market than was Saudi Arabia! But the central element in the U.S. diversification strategy has been Mexico, now the country's principal foreign supplier of oil, responsible for sending some 800,000 barrels a day to the American market.[65] What many in the United States have been advocating since the mid-1970s (and what not a few in Mexico have feared) seems to be happening: the United States is overcoming its dependence on Middle Eastern oil with Mexican "help."[66]

In addition to stockpiling and import diversification, the United States has been able to minimize its vulnerability to oil supply disruption by relying on *domestic production*. With domestic production of nearly 8.7 MBD in 1986, the United States was second only to the USSR in the production of crude oil.[67] There is no reason to expect major additions to reserves and increased production over the short term, but most analysts remain fairly confident about the country's ability to sustain current production levels. Assuming major increases in world oil prices, the United States would have the option to *substitute* for crude oil by switching to coal- and shale-based oil production. One casualty of the oil glut in the early 1980s was the ambitious synthetic fuel program mandated by the Energy Security Act of 1980: $88 billion was to be lavished on substitutes for conventional crude oil, and in 1987 the U.S. was supposed to be producing 500,000 barrels of oil a day from coal and shale. But by 1984 only two synfuels plants were still under construction, with a combined planned capacity of only 10,000 barrels a day.[68]

Finally, there is *conservation*. Although it is less easy to substantiate statistically the degree of vulnerability reduction provided by this option, many analysts are convinced that it has been the real success story of the past few years insofar as weaning the West from Persian Gulf oil is concerned. Writes Daniel Yergin: "[B]y far the most important and powerful form of adjustment has been on the demand side, in terms of greater energy efficiency. Indeed, it has proved much more potent than most analysts would have expected even in the middle 1970s."[69] A useful way to gauge conservation is the "coefficient of energy use," which measures the rate of increase in energy use and the rate of increase in the level of economic activities. During the early postwar era of cheap oil and rapid growth, it was not uncommon for advanced industrial economies to have a coefficient greater than 1, which meant that energy (usually oil) consumption was increasing at a rate greater than the rate of growth of the gross domestic product.[70] By the end of the 1970s, most OECD countries had reduced their energy-use coefficients to between 0.6 and 0.9, and by the early 1980s the average OECD coefficient had declined to 0.34.[71] The United States has benefited more, in absolute terms, from this trend than any other OECD country, given its large consumption of oil—particularly in the transportation sector, where substantial fuel savings have been made in the past few years as a result of the shift towards more energy-efficient vehicles.

URANIUM

Canadian uranium is similar to nickel and oil in the sense that it has been both indispensable (during the 1940s and 1950s) to the American nuclear weapons program and subsequently irrelevant to the functioning of the American economy.[72] That is, Canada's uranium has in the post-Second World War decades gone from being essential in the narrow understanding of military potential to redundant in the broad understanding. Whether Canadian uranium will remain marginal to American economic well-being during the late 1980s and into the 1990s is a question currently attracting much attention in both countries.

Uranium is a good example of how technology converts an otherwise useless commodity into a prized, indeed strategic, mineral. It is not the only one to have undergone this technological conversion from dross into what David A. Baldwin has termed a "power resource,"[73] for all minerals were at one time or other items without value. But in the case of uranium the transformation has been so recent and the implications so great that one can with justification refer to it as not only one of the world's most strategic minerals but also one of its most controversial.[74] The production of uranium had an uncontroversial beginning during the 1930s in both the United States and Canada, where it was a by-product of the mining of other, more highly regarded items. In the U.S., vanadium producers sold what uranium they could find a market for, and discarded what they could not sell; in Canada, radium and silver miners stockpiled their uranium for lack of anything better to do with it.[75]

The wartime "Manhattan Project," which resulted in the 1945 development of the atomic bomb, employed uranium originating in Canada and the Belgian Congo (now Zaïre).[76] From that time until the early 1960s, Canadian uranium was highly essential to American military potential in the narrowest usage of that term. The expansion of both Canadian and American production capability was almost entirely a function of the need for uranium to manufacture nuclear warheads, chiefly for the arsenal of the United States but also for Great Britain's. So long as the U.S. Atomic Energy Commission (AEC) had a policy of letting highly attractive purchasing contracts to North American producers, uranium mining enjoyed prosperity. The peak year for Canadian production was 1959, when the AEC purchased 13,500 tons of uranium oxide (U_3O_8, otherwise known as "yellowcake") out of a total Canadian production of 16,000 tons. Not only was Canada's mining industry highly dependent upon the American market, but the U.S. weapons program was significantly dependent upon Canadian uranium oxide, which in 1959 accounted for 40 per cent of all the uranium consumed in the United States.[77] In that year AEC purchases from Canada netted the latter $331 million, which made uranium the most valuable metal produced in the country and the number two mineral (after petroleum). Because of a virtually non-existent domestic market, it was Canada's most important mineral export in that year.[78]

Nineteen fifty-nine was a watershed year in Canadian uranium production. Although it represented the peak of Canadian output for the U.S. nuclear weapons program, it was also the year in which both the United States and the United Kingdom announced that they would be phasing out their purchases of uranium for arms building. Because there was no alternative source of demand during the early 1960s, the loss of the military purchases dealt a severe blow to the Canadian uranium industry, which accounted for nearly 40 per cent of world production by the 1950s. In the words of Ted Greenwood, "total collapse of the Canadian industry was averted only by the creation of a government stockpile program in 1963."[79]

Canadian uranium mining received a further shock later in the 1960s, when Washington announced that after 1966 no foreign uranium would be enriched in the United States for domestic end uses. Although Canadian and other foreign uranium could continue to be enriched by the AEC for sales abroad, the effect of the American embargo was to close most of the world's new non-military market for uranium during the late 1960s and early 1970s. (Canada has no enrichment facilities of its own, and though the CANDU reactor does not use enriched uranium, light-water reactors, the predominant type used internationally for generating electricity, do.) The world uranium market throughout the 1960s was moribund. In the early 1970s, however, there was a resurgence of interest in uranium as a fuel for generating electricity, stimulated by the dramatic increases in the price of oil and other energy commodities.[80]

The renewed concern for secure access to energy supplies at reasonably stable prices led Washington to phase out its embargo on uranium imports for the domestic commercial market. During the early 1970s, and especially in the wake of the first oil price crisis, a common assumption of American energy planners was that domestic reserves of uranium would soon be insufficient to supply what all assumed would be an ever-growing market for the mineral in the United States. Writing in 1973, Vincent E. McKelvey stated that U.S. reserves of uranium "are sufficient to last about another decade."[81] Some saw in the rapidly changing American supply situation a chance for Canada again to capitalize on its uranium assets (namely, rich and abundant ores and a reputation as a stable source of supply) and recapture its former position in the U.S. market.[82] By the late 1970s, however, the allure of nuclear power had greatly diminished, due in no small measure to the mounting public concern about the safety of power plants especially in the aftermath of the accident at Three Mile Island. Projections of uranium demand made early in the 1970s had become dreadfully obsolete by the end of the decade, and it no longer seemed that the United States (or any other important consumer of uranium) would have a supply problem in the 1980s. Indeed, if there was a supply problem for the uranium industry as a whole, it was one of too much, not too little, of the mineral.

By mid-1985 uranium was again caught up in the protectionism issue in the United States. More than any other mineral commodity in bilateral trade, it has been targeted for import restrictions. The uranium case illustrates how national security considerations can influence trade policy, and thus deserves to be treated at some length. It is no doubt prudent for analysts to be somewhat sceptical of protectionist arguments premised on national security considerations. Still, it would be foolish to imagine that the national security case for import relief is everywhere fallacious, for two related reasons. The first has to do with the debate over proper government policy regarding access to strategic minerals. As I mentioned in Chapter 1, it is commonly conceded that industrialized states depend upon having reasonably secure access to essential raw materials (minerals above all) if they are to maintain their economic and, ultimately, military vitality. Although the exact nature of the relationship between mineral availability and national security is open to some dispute, few would argue that the former is irrelevant to the latter. Instead, students of international policies tend to argue that while dependence (or interdependence) can bring economic gain, it often does so at a high political cost. In the words of one prominent international relations theorist, "states seek to control what they depend on or to lessen the extent of their dependency. This simple thought explains quite a bit of the behavior of states: their imperial thrusts to widen the scope of their control and their autarkic strivings toward greater self-sufficiency."[83]

"Autarkic strivings" are not limited to minerals, however, and this brings us to the second reason for taking seriously protectionist arguments premised on security considerations. It is more relevant perhaps to downstream stages of the fabrication process than to minerals issues, but it is nonetheless worth introducing here. There is a growing concern in the U.S. that the country's industrial base is eroding, both as a result of the natural workings of interdependence and liberalized trade and because of the spread of unfair trading. Though most economists would adjure an attentiveness to the principle of comparative advantage, on the reasonable grounds that high per capita income is the truest measure of national and international economic well-being, national security analysts do worry about the strategic implications of interdependence. One such analyst, Paul Seabury, dismisses as beside the point much of the current American debate between "neomercantilists" and "free traders." According the Seabury, "the necessity for a U.S. industrial policy arises not from domestic economic considerations—however large these may currently loom—but rather from strategic-military concerns. As the only genuine guarantor of security for both itself and the Free World as a whole, the United States simply cannot afford to allow its industrial base to wither away."[84] While it would be incorrect to suppose that every trade issue is suffused with genuine security implications, it would be unwise not to recognize the increasing appeal of arguments linked to the goal of preserving what is sometimes referred to as the "defense industrial base."[85]

It is an irony of bilateral uranium trade that there should be any security concern about imports of Canadian uranium. For several decades, Canadian sources have generally been regarded as being equivalent to U.S. domestic supply insofar as emergency planning and industrial preparedness questions are concerned.[86] For example, the inventory objectives of the U.S. strategic stockpile for a broad range of minerals are determined through an evaluation procedure that makes provisions not only for U.S. domestic production prospects, but also for those in "strategically accessible" countries, and in this category no country seems as strategically accessible to the U.S. than Canada.

What, then, accounts for the recent disquiet over the reliability of Canada as a uranium supplier?[87] The disquiet is related to the dual strategic nature of uranium, namely, that it is both an important energy mineral and an indispensable military one. Admittedly, uranium does not constitute a major share of total energy consumed in the Western industrialized countries: at the start of this decade, OECD members were getting less than 4 per cent of their total energy from nuclear power plants (versus nearly half their energy from oil), and while the proportional OECD consumption of uranium is expected to double by 2000, it will continue to lag far behind that of the fossil fuels.[88] Nevertheless, nuclear fuel is economically important, because it is a significant source of electricity in several parts of the world. The province of Ontario, for example, now generates more than a third of its electricity in nuclear power plants, and by the year 2000 nuclear power is projected to account for more than 60 per cent of the province's electricity. Overall, neither Canadian nor American electricity-generating patterns reflect such a heavy reliance on nuclear power; at present each country counts on nuclear power for slightly less than 13 per cent of its electricity output.[89]

Still, the role of uranium in U.S. electricity generation should not be minimized. At the moment, uranium is second only to coal as a domestic fuel for the purpose, and by 1990 is expected to account for nearly 20 per cent of America's supply of electricity.[90] It is in this context, much more than in connection with weapons building, that one often hears the domestic protectionist forces expressing their misgivings about uranium imports on the basis of security considerations. The argument is advanced that should U.S. uranium producers be put out of business or reduced to insignificance, there would be nothing to check future price gouging on the part of supplier countries such as Canada, and this would be extremely damaging to U.S. economic security. In this regard, one often hears references made to Canada's participation in the uranium cartel of the early 1970s, the clear implication being that it cannot be counted on to refrain from exploiting its leverage over helpless American consumers.[91] Just as during the early 1970s the creation of a national oil company was urged to enable Ottawa to get a "window" on the oil industry and presumably exert some control over upward price movements, so today American uranium producers are urging that domestic (though not state-owned) mining be kept viable to prevent uranium prices from rising to extortionary levels.[92]

In addition to economic security arguments, a military security argument is sometimes made against excessive levels of uranium imports. It is not so much that the U.S. worries about fissionable material for nuclear warheads; there are thousands of warheads already in the American arsenal (many fabricated originally with Canadian uranium), and though they might have to be reconstructed from time to time, it is not because their U-235 or plutonium content has dissipated. By any reckoning, these materials have an extremely long "shelf life."[93] Moreover, the U.S. has massive stockpiles of uranium, estimated to be in the range of 150 million pounds of U_3O_8—stockpiles that have enabled the U.S. government to abstain from any uranium purchases, for *any* purposes, since 1970.[94] In addition to the stocks of U_3O_8, the enrichment facilities operated by the Department of Energy (DOE) also possess immense holdings of depleted uranium ("depleted" in the sense that its U-235 content is less than that found in natural uranium); it is possible that in future the depleted UF_6 (uranium hexafluoride) tailings might be recycled through the DOE's gaseous-diffusion plants in place of fresh natural uranium feed.[95] This last possibility occasions from time to time some anxiety in Canada that Canadian uranium might be getting applied to military purposes, in violation of the country's tough policy governing nuclear exports, as well as of a bilateral treaty with the U.S. forbidding non-peaceful applications of Canadian uranium by the U.S.[96] It is hard to find any basis for these fears at the moment, for the U.S. is neither "stripping" any depleted tailings for enrichment feedstock nor enriching any natural uranium for weapons purposes.[97]

Occasionally, some in Washington will raise the possibility that the U.S. Navy may not in future have a secure source of fuel for its nuclear-powered vessels if the productive capacity of the domestic uranium mining industry continues to erode. Today this industry hovers on the verge of extinction because of its inability to compete with the incredibly rich ore grades of Saskatchewan mines.[98] For the moment, government stocks continue to provide for the fuel needs of the nuclear navy; but there is some dispute in Washington over how much longer the stockpile disposals can continue. It is difficult to arrive at an accurate figure for such a sensitive matter as the Navy's consumption of nuclear fuel. Officials at the Department of Energy estimate that current annual military (mostly naval) demand in the U.S. is about 2 million pounds of U_3O_8; however, sources in the uranium industry challenge this estimate and argue instead that military consumption averages between 5 and 6 million pounds a year.[99] They also maintain that the stockpile will be exhausted sometime during the 1990s. The DOE officials do not foresee such a rapid depletion of stocks, nor do they evince the same level of concern about Canadian policy regarding the export of uranium for military purposes.[100]

Whether Canadian uranium exports to the U.S. will face a reimposition of protectionism depends in large part upon one major consideration: the fate of the Free Trade Agreement (FTA) with the U.S. This contains a specific prohibition against the use of an enrichment embargo (which is seemingly indicated by a section of the U.S. Atomic Energy Act of 1954).[101] This provision, the infamous section 161(v), mandates that the domestic uranium industry be kept "viable" (a term subject to differing interpretations) if need be by an enrichment embargo on foreign U_3O_8.[102] Canadian uranium currently accounts for a quarter of the feedstock for American enrichment facilities, which can be taken as a rough approximation of the current Canadian share of the U.S. market.[103] It is expected that under free trade, Canadian uranium will have a far larger share of the American market because of the differentials in ore grade between Saskatchewan and U.S.

producers. Even if the FTA does survive reasonably intact, there will be no guarantee of continuing access for Canadian uranium to that market; presumably, however, the case against imports will have to be made much more convincingly than to date.

CONCLUSION

To the extent that one can generalize from three important cases, it seems clear that the relevance of Canadian minerals to the military potential of the United States is not anywhere near as great as it once was. The argument that the United States is becoming ever more dependent upon Canadian strategic minerals reflects outdated perceptions.[104] It certainly was the case that, both during the Second World War, throughout the 1950s, and (in the case of oil) even into the early 1970s, the American economy in general and the American military in particular were becoming more reliant upon Canadian strategic minerals. R.D. Cuff and J.L. Granatstein were surely correct when they wrote of the "self-conscious encouragement by American officials of the development of Canadian raw materials production in the 1950s."[105] Canadian mineral production *was* promoted by Americans concerned with strategic considerations, but recently there has been little such encouragement emanating from Washington, even though certain provisions of the FTA, as noted above, are crafted so as to minimize American apprehensions about security of supply. This does not mean that in the future the United States might not turn again to Canada as a dependable source of strategic minerals. For the present and probably for well into the next decade, however, Canadian strategic minerals will become less relevant to American military potential. Even uranium, where a recent surge in imports could indicate a U.S. *need* for foreign resources, should be approached with caution, for the U.S. continues to have vast resources of uranium that, with a modest degree of protection, could be brought quickly into production.[106]

Two implications flow from such a statement. So far, I have concentrated my analysis on the "supply effect" of Canadian strategic mineral exports to the United States. It is now time for a word about the "influence effect" of such exports. The influence effect, to return to Hirschman, is another way of expressing the "gains from trade" accruing to country B as a result of its imports from country A.[107] It is in part, but only in part, a function of the level of dependence of country B on the exports of country A. What is also required is an intention, whether realized or not, on the part of the exporting country to manipulate its trade ties with the importing country so as to achieve maximum political leverage over its trading partner—leverage which ultimately stems from the credibility of a threat to interrupt the flow of exports. This kind of effect has been achieved by states in different eras; the Germans accomplished it before the Second World War with their bilateral trade campaigns directed toward Balkan and Latin American countries, and more recently the Arab oil-producing states succeeded in bringing about a shift in the Middle East policies of some important OECD consumers.

In the case of Canada, it seems logical that because of the reduction in U.S. dependence upon Canadian strategic minerals, there must necessarily be a reduction of whatever influence effect these exports possessed. More importantly, even when American dependence upon Canadian strategic minerals was a good deal greater than today, there was never any explicit attempt on the part of Ottawa to exploit that dependence. To be sure, there were occasional musings on the part of some Canadians in 1973–4 that perhaps the country had a trump card to play in its dealings with the U.S.—the latter's need for Canadian resources, especially oil.[108] But never have such sentiments been reflected in government policy.

Ottawa, for example, never even *contemplated* exploiting American dependence upon Canadian nickel to achieve non-nickel-related purposes. There were some in and out of Parliament in the 1930s who proposed export controls over nickel in order to modify the behaviour of other governments, but the mooted controls were intended to restrain Germany, not any other country and least of all the United States.[109] Even during the Vietnam War, arguably a highly unpopular war in Canada, when there was a great deal of opposition to Canadian participation in continental defence production schemes, hardly any voices were raised to protest against what was in a real sense the more important trade, that in strategic minerals.[110] In contrast, the Swedes have undergone, since the end of the Second World War, a great deal of introspection over the possibility that their exports of iron ore to Germany might have prolonged the war.[111]

There are two major reasons why Canada has refrained from exercising strategic minerals leverage against the U.S. In the first place, rarely have Ottawa and Washington been in conflict on major international issues since 1940. Ottawa would no sooner have countenanced the cessation of nickel exports to the United States in the Second World War and the Korean War than it would have denied nickel to its own defence establishment. Even during the Vietnam War, Canada, however much it might have rhetorically opposed certain U.S. strategies, basically agreed with the goal of containment and was certainly supportive of American global policies. The nickel "weapon" would have been meaningless in any event, given the huge stockpile of the mineral that the U.S. had built during the 1950s.

In addition to its basic agreement with American foreign policy objectives since the Second World War, Canada has had more self-interested reasons to avoid using minerals leverage against the United States. Canada has traditionally sought to avoid "linkage politics" in its dealings with Washington, for the good reason that given the asymmetrical interdependence of the Canadian-American relationship, such an approach could entail enormous economic and political costs.[112] To refer to a commonly employed metaphor in Canadian-American relations, nothing so deters a mouse from running up the nose of an elephant as the thought that the elephant might reciprocate.

The prospect of the elephant running amok is involved in the second implication of the diminished relevance of Canadian strategic minerals to the United States. Notwithstanding any reduction in leverage, it can be argued that Canada benefits politically from the fact that the United States does not need its minerals as much as before. Certainly, Canada stands a bit smaller in the eyes of the Americans, who no longer see themselves as terribly dependent upon Canadian oil or other commodities. But is this so bad? Resource nationalists, in particular, might rest easier with the knowledge that, for the time being at least, the United States is not lurking about, waiting to gobble up Canadian resources—and Canadian sovereignty in the bargain.

NOTES

1 Maurice Lamontagne, "Scientific Research and Canadian Economic Viability." (Paper presented to the Second Biennial Conference of the Association for Canadian Studies in the United States, Washington, 31 Mar. 1973).

2 Stephen Clarkson, *Canada and the Reagan Challenge: Crisis in the Canadian-American Relationship* (Ottawa: Canadian Institute for Economic Policy 1982), 287.

3 Abraham Rotstein, "Canada: The New Nationalism," *Foreign Affairs* 55 (Oct. 1976):97–118. An example of the resource nationalist, or "homestead," perspective is Philip Sykes, *Sellout: The Giveaway of Canada's Energy Resources* (Edmonton: Hurtig 1973).

4 See, for example, two works of Richard H. Rohmer, *Ultimatum* (Toronto: Clark Irwin 1973) and *Exoneration* (Toronto: McClelland & Stewart 1974). For a non-fictional rendering of the same theme, see Philippe J. Brossard, *Sold American!* (Toronto: Peter Martin Associates 1971), 81–2.

5 See Christopher Waddell, "Energy Generates Controversy," *Globe and Mail*, 12 Nov. 1988, B2. This issue is intelligently discussed in "A Continental Energy Market?" *Borderlines* 4 (Spring 1988):4–5; and in Marc Gold and David Leyton-Brown, eds., *Trade-Offs on Free Trade: The Canada-U.S. Free Trade Agreement* (Toronto: Carswell 1988), Ch. 7: "Energy and Natural Resources."

6 Richard N. Cooper, "Natural Resources and National Security," *Resources Policy* 1 (June 1975):193.

7 The distinction between resources and reserves is explored in G.J.S. and M.H. Govett, "The Concept and Measurement of Mineral Reserves and Resources," *Resources Policy* 1 (Sept. 1974):46–55.

8 For the development of Canada's iron ore industry and the importance of exports, see *Iron Ore*, Mineral Bulletin MR148 (Ottawa: Energy, Mines and Resources Canada 1976).

9 But for a differing view on the relationship between natural gas exports and reserves, see Bruce F. Willson, *The Energy Squeeze: Canadian Policies for Survival* (Toronto: James Lorimer/Canadian Institute for Economic Policy 1980), 56.

10 John E. Tilton, *The Future of Nonfuel Minerals* (Washington: Brookings Institution 1977), 9. This generalization applies, of course, to Canada also. How reserves are calculated is explained in *Canadian Mines: Perspective from 1980*, Mineral Bulletin MR190 (Ottawa: Energy, Mines and Resources Canada 1981), 12–15.

11 The terms "supply effect" and "influence effect" were employed by Albert O. Hirschman in his masterful study of the political aspects of foreign trade, *National Power and the Structure of Foreign Trade* (Berkeley: University of California Press 1945), 14–15.

12 The only producing nickel mine in the United States is at Riddle, Oregon, where the Hanna Nickel Smelting Co. works some small-scale lateritic deposits. U.S. Bureau of Mines, *Minerals Yearbook, 1983*, vol. 1: *Metals and Minerals* (Washington: Department of the Interior 1984), 632.

13 U.S. Bureau of Mines, *Mineral Commodity Summaries, 1987* (Washington: Department of the Interior 1987), 172–3.

14 U.S. Bureau of Mines, *Mineral Commodity Summaries, 1987*, 78.

15 James F. McDivitt, *Minerals and Men: An Exploration of the World of Minerals and Its Effect on the World We Live In* (Baltimore: Johns Hopkins University Press/Resources for the Future 1965), 30–44; Eugene N. Cameron, "The Contribution of the U.S. to National and World Mineral Supplies," in *The Mineral Position of the United States, 1975–2000*, ed. Eugene N. Cameron (Madison: University of Wisconsin Press 1973), 14.

16 John F. Thompson and Norman Beasley, *For the Years to Come: A Story of International Nickel of Canada* (Toronto: Longmans, Green 1960), 121.

17 George Otis Smith, ed., *The Strategy of Minerals: A Study of the Mineral Factor in the World Position of America in War and Peace* (New York: D. Appleton 1919), 191.

18 Alex Skelton, "Nickel," in *International Control in the Non-Ferrous Metals*, ed. William Y. Elliott et al. (New York: Macmilllan 1937), 141.

19 Brooks Emeny, *The Strategy of Raw Materials: A Study of America in Peace and War* (New York: Macmillan 1934), 74.

20 Emeny, *Strategy of Raw Materials*, 167.

21 Alfred E. Eckes, jr., *The United States and the Global Struggle for Minerals* (Austin: University of Texas Press 1979), 111–12; Percy W. Bidwell, *Raw Materials: A Study of American Policy* (New York: Harper & Bros./Council on Foreign Relations 1958), 148–51.

22 Quoted in Bidwell, *Raw Materials*, 131–2.

23 David A. Hubbard, "Nickel in International Trade" (M.Sc. thesis, Pennsylvania State University 1975), 15. Nicaro could not match the economies of Sudbury production, and in early 1947 was placed in stand-by condition.

24 By the middle of the 1970s, known world reserves amounted to a tonnage 150 times the annual global consumption of nickel. *Canadian Minerals and International Economic Interdependence*, Mineral Bulletin 162: Mineral Policy Series (Ottawa: Energy, Mines and Resources Canada 1976), 29; T.P. Mohide, C.L. Warden, and J.D. Mason, *Towards a Nickel Policy for the Province of Ontario*, Mineral Policy Background Paper no. 4 (Toronto: Ontario Ministry of Natural Resources, Division of Mines 1977), 173. On the recent tightness in global nickel markets, see Laima Dingwell, "Nickel Nears Crunch," *Financial Post*, 23–25 Apr. 1988, 1.

25 By the middle of the decade, some 40 per cent of the non-Communist world's nickel production was earmarked either for direct defence purposes or the American strategic stockpile. Bernard Goodman, *Industrial Materials in Canadian-American Relations* (Detroit: Wayne State University Press 1961), 94–5.

26 Bidwell, *Raw Materials*, 160.

27 John M. Dunn, "American Dependence on Materials Imports: The World-Wide Resource Base," *Journal of Conflict Resolution* 4 (Mar. 1960): 106–22.

28 John I. Cameron, "Nickel," in *Natural Resources in U.S.-Canadian Relations*, vol. 2: *Patterns and Trends in Resource Supplies and Policies*, ed. Carl E. Beigie and Alfred O. Hero, jr. (Boulder, CO: Westview Press 1980), 69.

29 By the late 1970s, the Soviet Union overtook Canada as the world's principal producer of nickel, though Canada regained the lead in 1980. Canada has remained the world's leading exporter throughout, however, given the huge disparity between its consumption and that of the USSR. Energy, Mines and Resources Canada, Mineral Policy Sector, "Statistical Summary of the Mineral Industry in Canada, 1979" (Ottawa 1979), 14–15; Metallgesellschaft Aktiengesellschaft, *Metal Statistics, 1970–1980*, 68th ed. (Frankfurt am Main 1981), 55.

30 Examples of analyses that regarded nickel as a mineral in which the United States was vulnerable include U.S. General Accounting Office, *Report to the Secretary of the Interior: Actions Needed to Promote a Stable Supply of Strategic and Critical Minerals and Materials* (Washington: June 1982), 6–7; Amos A. Jordan and Robert A. Kilmarx, *Strategic Mineral Dependence: The Stockpile Dilemma*, Washington

Papers, vol. 7, no. 70 (Washington: Center for Strategic and International Studies, Georgetown University 1979), 20; and U.S. Department of Defense, Joint Chiefs of Staff, *United States Military Posture for FY 1982* (Washington: U.S. Government Printing Office 1981), supplement, 3.

31 Cameron, "Nickel," 78, 80, 88. For a discussion of Canada's role in the uranium cartel, see Michael Webb's Ch. 7 in this volume.

32 Nickel reserves have remained fairly static since early 1970s, at slightly more than 7 million tonnes. (Tonnes, or metric tons, are equivalent to 1.1 short tons). W.H. Laughlin, *Canadian Reserves as of January 1, 1980*, Mineral Bulletin MR189 (Ottawa: Energy, Mines and Resources Canada 1981), 7.

33 The case that an ideological cleavage was developing a few years ago between the United States and Canada was made in Charles F. Doran, "Left Hand, Right Hand," *International Journal* 36 (Winter 1980–1):236–40. Evidence of a more militant ideological posture regarding minerals can perhaps be seen in the appearance of a Washington newsletter focusing on resource strategy, *Alarm*. According to the *Alarm's* editor, James Miller, "the developing minerals and energy situation in Canada is such that the reliability of traditionally friendly Canada as a long term source of strategic minerals for America must be questioned." *Globe and Mail*, 19 Oct. 1981.

34 A study that did draw a distinction between nickel and minerals in which the United States could properly be said to be vulnerable is Michael W. Klass, James C. Burrows, and Steven D. Beggs, *International Minerals Cartels and Embargoes: Policy Implications for the United States* (New York: Praeger 1980), 6.

35 U.S. Bureau of Mines, *Mineral Commodity Summaries, 1987*, 38, 98.

36 See W.E. Cundiff, *Nodule Shock?: Seabed Mining and the Future of the Canadian Nickel Industry*, Occasional Paper no. 1 (Montreal: Institute for Research on Public Policy 1978). Also see *The Future of Nickel and the Law of the Sea*, Mineral Policy Background Paper no. 10 (Toronto: Ontario Ministry of Natural Resources 1980).

37 V.E. McKelvey, "Seabed Minerals and the Law of the Sea," *Science*, 25 July 1980, p. 471.

38 Michael R. Gordon, "Companies Ready to Stake Out Claims for Mineral Wealth Beneath the Seas," *National Journal*, 9 Aug. 1980, p. 1312.

39 Goodman, *Industrial Materials in Canadian-American Relations*, 143; Peter Foster, *The Blue-Eyed Sheiks: The Canadian Oil Establishment* (Toronto: Collins 1979), 27–8.

40 Robert O. Keohane and Joseph S. Nye, jr., "Introduction: The Complex Politics of Canadian-American Interdependence," in *Canada and the United States: Transnational and Transgovernmental Relations*, ed. Annette Baker Fox, Alfred O. Hero, jr., and Joseph S. Nye, jr. (New York: Columbia University Press 1976), 6; David B. Dewitt and John J. Kirton, *Canada as a Principal Power: A Study in Foreign Policy and International Relations* (Toronto: John Wiley & Sons 1983), 276–312.

41 Quoted in Bidwell, *Raw Materials*, 321.

42 James F. Keeley, "Constraints on Canadian International Economic Policy" (Ph.D. dissertation, Stanford University 1980), 349.

43 "U.S. Energy, Outlook: An Initial Appraisal, 1971–1985" (Washington: National Petroleum Council, Committee on U.S. Energy Outlook 1971) 1:27.

44 Helmut J. Frank and John J. Schanz, jr., *U.S.-Canadian Energy Trade: A Study of Changing Relationships* (Boulder, CO: Westview Press 1978), 4.

45 National Energy Board, *Energy Supply and Demand in Canada and Export Demand for Canadian Energy, 1966 to 1990*, cited in Frank and Schanz, *U.S.-Canadian Energy Trade*, 62.

46 Willson, *Energy Squeeze*, 4–5.

47 Frank and Schanz, *U.S.-Canadian Energy Trade*, 35.

48 Ted Greenwood, "Canadian-American Trade in Energy Resources," in Keohane and Nye, *Canada and the United States*, 110.

49 See, for example, Robert J. Gordon and Jacques Pelkmans, *Challenges to Interdependent Economies: The Industrial West in the Coming Decade*, 1980s Project/Council on Foreign Relations (New York: McGraw-Hill 1979), 80.

50 David G. Haglund, "Canada and the International Politics of Oil: Latin American Source of Supply and Import Vulnerability in the 1980s," *Canadian Journal of Political Science* 15 (June 1982): 278.

51 The 1981 production and import data are contained in National Energy Board, *1981 Annual Report* (Ottawa: Minister of Supply and Services 1982), 33. NEB statistics are expressed in metric, with the principal measure of oil being the cubic metre (m³). (One m³ is roughly equal to 6.3 barrels.)

52 Statistics Canada, "Crude Petroleum and Natural Gas production, January 1985," Catalog 26-006, pp. 8–9.

53 Richard R. Fagen and Henry R. Nau, "Mexican Gas: The Northern Connection," in *Capitalism and the State in U.S.-Latin American Relations,* ed. Richard R. Fagen (Stanford: Stanford University Press 1979), 387.
54 U.S. Department of Energy, Energy Information Administration, *News Releases* (July/Aug. 1988):1.
55 For the thesis that Canadian oil-sands development was being counted upon by some Americans to help the U.S. overcome its dependence upon OPEC, see Larry Pratt, *The Tar Sands: Syncrude and the Politics of Oil* (Edmonton: Hurtig 1976), 50–68ff.
56 James W. McKie, "Heavy Oil: Its Significance for the U.S. Energy Balance," *Journal of Energy and Development* 7 (Spring 1982):158.
57 The classic work on stockpiling remains Glenn H. Snyder, *Stockpiling Strategic Minerals: Politics and National Defense* (San Francisco: Chandler 1966).
58 Hans H. Landsberg, "What Next for U.S. Minerals Policy?" *Resources,* no. 71 (Oct. 1982):9–10. Whether stockpiles do become self-financing or nearly so depends of course on whether they are sold at some future date, and also on the price level of alternative future supplies on the world market. In this instance, "self-financing" becomes a matter of having one's cake *only* if one is prepared to eat it, for unconsumed stockpiles clearly cannot be made self-financing.
59 U.S. Federal Emergency Management Agency, *Stockpile Report to the Congress: April–September 1985* (Washington: Dec. 1985); V. Anthony Cammarota, "America's Dependence on Strategic Minerals," in *American Strategic Minerals,* ed. Gerard J. Mangone (New York: Crane Russak 1984), 29–57; U.S. Bureau of Mines, "National Defense Stockpile Statistics," *Minerals and Materials: A Bimonthly Survey* (Aug./Sept. 1987):14–18.
60 Ruth M. Davis, "National Strategic Petroleum Reserve," *Science* 213 (Aug. 1981):618–22.
61 U.S. General Accounting Office, *Status of Strategic Petroleum Reserve Activities as of 30 September 1987* (Washington: Nov. 1987).
62 U.S. General Accounting Office, *Analysis of Oil Withdrawal and Distribution Tests for the Strategic Petroleum Reserve* (Washington, May 1985), 2.
63 I have borrowed the phrase "oil proliferation" from U.S. Congress, Joint Economic Committee, Subcommittee on Energy, *A Strategy of Oil Proliferation,* 96th Cong., 2nd session (Washington: U.S. Government Printing Office, June 1980).
64 *The Energy Decade, 1970–1980: A Statistical and Graphic Chronicle,* ed. William L. Kiscom (Cambridge, MA: Ballinger 1982), 429; John Evans, *OPEC, Its Member States and the World Energy Market* (Harrow, Eng.: Longman 1986), 655.
65 U.S. Department of Energy, Energy Information Administration, *Monthly Energy Review: December 1983* (Washington: U.S. Government Printing Office, Feb. 1984), 38–39; Amory B. Lovins and L. Hunter Lovins, "The Avoidable Energy Crisis," *Atlantic Monthly,* Dec. 1987, pp. 22–30.
66 American views on the desirability of Mexican oil imports can be found in Richard B. Mancke, *Mexican Oil and Natural Gas: Political, Strategic, and Economic Implications* (New York: Praeger 1979); David Ronfeldt, Richard Hehring, and Arturo Gándara, *Mexico's Petroleum and U.S. Policy: Implications for the 1980s,* Executive Summary for the U.S. Department of Energy (Santa Monica, CA: Rand Corporation, June 1980); Edward J. Williams, *The Rebirth of the Mexican Petroleum Industry: Development Directions and Policy Implications* (Lexington, MA: D.C. Heath 1979); and Richard R. Fagen, "Mexican Petroleum and U.S. National Security," *International Security* 4 (Summer 1979): 39–53. For Mexican nationalist concerns over increased exports to the United States, see John Saxe-Fernández, *Petroleo y Estrategía: México y Estados Unidos en el Contexto de la Política Global* (Mexico City: Siglo Veintiuno 1980).
67 U.S. Department of Energy, Energy Information Administration, *International Energy Annual 1986* (Washington, Oct. 1987), 14.
68 Andy Plattner, "Energy Issues Shoved Onto Back Burner," *Congressional Quarterly,* 29 May 1982, 1249–52; Hans H. Landsberg and Michael J. Coda, "Synfuels—Back to Basics," *Resources* (Feb. 1983):12–14; U.S. General Accounting Office, *The Synthetic Fuels Corporation's Porgress in Aiding Synthetic Fuels Development* (Washington, July 1984).
69 Daniel Yergin, "Crisis and Adjustment: An Overview," in *Global Insecurity: A Strategy for Energy and Economic Renewal,* ed. Daniel Yergin and Martin Hillenbrand (Harmondsworth, Eng.: Penguin Books 1983), 8–9.
70 Arnold E. Safer, *International Oil Policy* (Lexington, MA: D.C. Heath 1979), 16.
71 Robert Stobaugh and Daniel Yergin, "Energy: An Emergency Telescoped," *Foreign Affairs: America*

and the World 1979 58 (1980):584; Peter Odell, *Oil and World Power*, 7th ed. (Harmondsworth, Eng.: Penguin Books 1983), 247.

72 Canada's role in U.S. atomic bomb development in the Second World War is discussed in Robert Bothwell, *Nucleus: The History of Atomic Energy of Canada Limited* (Toronto: University of Toronto Press 1988), Ch. 1; and Ron Finch, *Exporting Danger: A History of the Canadian Nuclear Energy Export Programme* (Montreal: Black Rose Books 1986), Ch. 1.

73 David A. Baldwin, "Power Analysis and World Politics: New Trends versus Old Tendencies," *World Politics* 32 (Jan. 1979):165.

74 Bohdan O. Szuprowicz, *How to Avoid Strategic Materials Shortages: Dealing with Cartels, Embargoes, and Supply Disruptions* (New York: John Wiley & Sons 1981), 27.

75 June H. Taylor and Michael D. Yokell, *Yellowcake: The International Uranium Cartel*, Pergamon Policy Series on U.S. and International Business (New York: Pergamon Press 1979), 23; Ted Greenwood, with Alvin Streeter, jr., "Uranium," in Beigie and Hero, *Natural Resources in U.S.-Canadian Relations*, 345.

76 See Jonathan E. Helmreich, *Gathering Rare Ores: The Diplomacy of Uranium Acquisition, 1943–1954* (Princeton: Princeton University Press 1986).

77 Thomas B. Cochran et al., *Nuclear Weapons Databook*, vol. 2: U.S. *Nuclear Warhead Production* (Cambridge, MA: Ballinger 1987), 79–81.

78 Taylor and Yokell, *Yellowcake*, 28; Hugh C. McIntyre, *Uranium, Nuclear Power, and Canada-U.S. Energy Relations* (Montreal and Washington: Canadian-American Committee 1978), 13–15; Goodman, *Industrial Materials in Canadian-American Relations*, 138.

79 Greenwood, "Uranium," 346.

80 Melvin A. Conant, *Access to Energy: 2000 and After* (Lexington: University Press of Kentucky 1979), 85.

81 Vincent E. McKelvey, "Mineral Potential of the United States," in Cameron, *Mineral Position of the United States*, 78.

82 For this view, see McIntyre, *Uranium, Nuclear Power, and Canada-U.S. Energy Relations*, 36, 48–9.

83 Kenneth N. Waltz, *Theory of International Politics* (Reading, MA: Addison-Wesley 1979), 106.

84 Paul Seabury, "Industrial Policy and National Defense," *Journal of Contemporary Studies* 6 (Spring 1983):6.

85 U.S. Congress, House Committee on Armed Services, *The Ailing Defense Industrial Base: Unready for Crisis*, 96th Cong., 2d sess. (Washington: U.S. Government Printing Office 1980).

86 David G. Haglund, "Canadian Strategic Minerals and United States Military Potential," *Journal of Canadian Studies* 19 (Autumn 1984):5–31.

87 For a thorough discussion of Canada's perceived reliability as a uranium supplier, see Michael Webb's Ch. 7 in this volume.

88 Hanns W. Maull, *Raw Materials, Energy and Western Security* (London: Macmillan/International Institute of Strategic Studies 1984), 50–1.

89 Robert T. Whillans, "Uranium," in *Canadian Minerals Yearbook 1983–1984: Review and Outlook* (Ottawa: Energy, Mines and Resources Canada 1985), 63.8–63.9, 63.16.

90 U.S. Department of Energy, Energy Information Administration, *Commercial Nuclear Power 1987: Prospects for the United States and the World* (Washington, July 1987), 10.

91 Canadian participation in the uranium cartel is detailed in Larry R. Stewart, "Canada's Role in the International Uranium Cartel," *International Organization* 35 (Autumn 1981):657–89.

92 Interview, Washington, 20 June 1985. For the similar argument made regarding Petro-Canada, see Ghislaine Cestre, *Petro-Canada: A National Oil Company in the Canadian Context* (Washington: U.S. Government Printing office 1977), 18–19.

93 See Thomas B. Cochran, William M. Arkin, and Milton M. Hoenig, *Nuclear Weapons Databook*, vol. 1: *U.S. Nuclear Forces and Capabilities* (Cambridge, MA: Ballinger 1984), Ch. 2.

94 Interview, Washington, 28 June 1985.

95 UF_6 is a gaseous form into which U_3O_8 is converted so that it can be passed through the enrichment process. American utilities and many other utilities worldwide require for their light-water reactors "enriched" uranium to sustain a nuclear reaction. This means that the relative distribution of isotopes in natural uranium must be altered so that the proportion of "fissile" U-235 is increased from its naturally occurring 0.711 per cent (by weight) to about 3 per cent; by the same token, the share of U-238 is reduced to approximately 97 per cent of the weight of the enriched product. U.S. De-

partment of Energy, *World Uranium Supply and Demand: Impact of Federal Policies* (Washington: Energy Information Administration, March 1983), 119–20.

96 "Clark Wants Some Evidence Uranium Used for Weapons," *Globe and Mail,* 1 Oct. 1985, A4.

97 Thomas O'Toole, "U.S. $2.6 Billion Poorer as Uranium-Enrichment Plant Is Halted," *Washington Post,* 19 June 1985, A19. A different question is the reprocessing of depleted tailings for making *conventional* weapons. Armour-piercing projectiles are made from such tailings. "U.S. Arms Use Tonnes of Our Uranium: Report," *Gazette* (Montreal), 30 Sept. 1985, A4.

98 See testimony of Robert P. Luke before the Subcommittee on Energy Research and Development, Senate Committee on Energy and Natural Resources, Washington, 9 Mar. 1987, 2–3.

99 Interviews, Washington, 28 June 1985.

100 For an analysis of Canada's policy, see James F. Keeley, "Canadian Nuclear Export Policy and the Problems of Proliferation," *Canadian Public Policy* 6 (Autumn 1980):614–27.

101 The prohibition is contained in Annex 902.5 of the FTA. Canada, Department of External Affairs, *The Canada-U.S. Free Trade Agreement* (Ottawa 1987), 149.

102 See David G. Haglund, "Protectionism and National Security: The Case of Canadian Uranium Exports to the United States," *Canadian Public Policy* 12 (Sept. 1986): 459–72.

103 In 1986 U.S. domestic utilities delivered 12.9 million pounds of foreign uranium to the Department of Energy's enrichment facilities. This amount represented nearly 42 per cent of U.S. utility requirements, and some 59 per cent of *this* amount was accounted for by uranium originating in Canada. U.S. Department of Energy, Energy Information Administration, *Domestic Uranium Mining and Milling Industry: 1986 Viability Assessment* (Washington: Nov. 1987), 66.

104 An example of this anachronistic tendency is Patricia Marchak, *In Whose Interests: An Essay on Multinational Corporations in a Canadian Context* (Toronto: McClelland & Stewart 1979), 109, where it is claimed that Canada's resources "are essential to the growth of U.S. manufacturing establishments and also to the defence industries and military organizations of the United States."

105 R.D. Cuff and J.L. Granatstein, *Ties that Bind: Canadian-American Relations in Wartime from the Great War to the Cold War,* 2nd ed. (Toronto: Hakkert 1977), xix-xx.

106 Haglund, "Protectionism and National Security," discusses the recent downturn in U.S. uranium production.

107 Hirschman, *National Power and the Structure of Foreign Trade,* 18. Also see David A. Baldwin, "Interdependence and Power: A Conceptual Analysis," *International Organization* 34 (Autumn 1980):471–506.

108 For critical assessments of resource diplomacy, see Philip H. Trezise, "The Energy Challenge," in *Canada-United States Relations,* ed. H. Edward English (New York: Praeger 1976), 116; G.J.S. and M.H. Govett, "Mineral Resources and Canadian-American Trade: Double-Edged Vulnerability," *Canadian Mining and Metallurgical Bulletin* 66 (July 1973):70.

109 In March 1934 legislation was proposed, but not passed, calling for the cessation of the export of nickel for war purposes. Main, *The Canadian Nickel Industry,* 118–19.

110 John W. Warnock, *Partner to Behemoth: The Military Policy of a Satellite Canada* (Toronto: New Press 1970), 248–9. The debate over Canada's arms trade with the United States during the Vietnam years is summarized in John J. Kirton, "The Consequences of Integration: The Case of The Defence Production Sharing Agreements," in *Continental Community? Independence and Integration in North America,* ed. W. Andrew Axline et al. (Toronto: McClelland and Stewart 1974), 127–30.

111 The introspection was initiated by Rolf Karlbom's article, "Sweden's Iron Ore Exports to Germany, 1933–1944," *Scandinavian Economic History Review* 13 (1965):65–93. It was Karlbom's thesis that Swedish iron ore exports were of critical importance to Germany's ability to sustain a war economy. This thesis has sparked numerous rebuttals; especially recommended are Alan S. Milward, "Could Sweden Have Stopped the Second World War?" and Jorg Johannes Jager, "Sweden's Iron Ore Exports to Germany, 1922–1933," both in *Scandinavian Economic History Review* 15 (1967):127–37.

112 Peter C. Dobell, "Negotiating with the United States," *International Journal* 36 (Winter 1980–1):25. Also see the analysis of Canadian-American "diplomatic culture" by K.J. Holsti, "Canada and the United States," in *Conflict in World Politics,* ed. Steven L. Spiegel and Kenneth N. Waltz (Cambridge, MA: Winthrop 1971), 375–96. But for a different perspective on linkage, see David G. Haglund, "Unbridled Constraint: The Macdonald Commission Volumes on Canada and the International Political Economy," *Canadian Journal of Political Science* 20 (Sept. 1987):599–624.

7

Canada as an Insecure Supplier: Nonproliferation, Economic Development, and Uranium Export Policy

Michael C. Webb

INTRODUCTION

This chapter examines Canadian uranium export policy from the perspective of uranium as a strategic mineral. Uranium is of special interest because its international trade affects the strategic interests of *both* consumers and producers more than trade in any other mineral. The fact that uranium is the raw material in the production of nuclear weapons gives suppliers a national security interest in how the uranium they export is used. Since the principal uranium suppliers currently prohibit exports destined specifically for use in non-proscribed military programs, their primary concern is with the possibility that uranium sold for use in peaceful civilian nuclear reactors, or the plutonium produced from uranium sold for peaceful purposes, could be diverted to the production of nuclear weapons.

Suppliers have been particularly concerned with the danger of nuclear proliferation, whereby nuclear materials and facilities supplied for peaceful purposes would be used by states currently without nuclear weapons to develop such weapons.[1] It is widely believed that this sort of "horizontal" nuclear proliferation (to be distinguished from "vertical" nuclear proliferation, which is the accumulation of ever-increasing stockpiles of nuclear weapons by states that currently have them) would destabilize international security arrangements and increase the risks of accidental or intentional nuclear war.[2] Suppliers' nonproliferation concerns have focused on a small group of states that have the industrial and

189

technological capability to manufacture nuclear weapons and believe that perceived threats to their national security would be mitigated by the acquisition of such weapons. Lists of countries that meet these criteria typically include such candidates as Argentina, Brazil, Chile, Egypt, Greece, India (which has already tested what it called a "peaceful" nuclear explosive), Iran, Iraq, Israel, Libya, Pakistan, South Africa, South Korea, Taiwan, and Turkey.[3]

Neither these countries nor any others to which Canada exports its uranium pose a direct threat to Canada's national security. Canada's strategic interest in inhibiting nuclear proliferation stems instead from the belief that proliferation increases the risk of nuclear war. The Canadian government believes that even a limited, regional nuclear war would pose a critical security threat to *all* nations.[4] Public opinion since the 1960s has shared Ottawa's views about the dangers of nuclear proliferation. Opposition parties and antinuclear groups have been particularly vocal since the 1970s in pressing for stricter Canadian policies designed to minimize the risk of nuclear proliferation.[5]

The strategic interest of consumers in international uranium trade arises primarily out of uranium's role as an important source of energy.[6] Energy is of such fundamental importance to modern industrialized economies that the conditions of its supply evoke strategic concerns that go beyond economic concern about its costs.[7] During the 1960s and 1970s, nuclear power industries and many energy analysts promoted nuclear fission as a relatively inexpensive source of electricity to meet rapidly growing demand for energy. The strategic importance of nuclear energy was heightened by the oil embargo and price increases of 1973–4. Many West European countries and Japan sought to reduce their vulnerability to politically motivated energy supply disruptions originating in the Middle East. The expansion of nuclear power promised to contribute to the development of more diverse and secure sources of energy for these countries. Nuclear power could substitute for electricity generated by fossil fuels, thereby reducing dependence on imported oil.

Even though a lack of domestic resources has forced Japan and most West European countries[8] to depend on imports for most of the uranium required by their nuclear power programs, several characteristics of the international uranium market and of the nuclear fuel cycle initially appeared to reduce the risks associated with uranium import dependence. Uranium production capacity far exceeded commercial demand, which made supply constraints appear unlikely.[9] Most uranium production capacity is located in western industrialized countries, which were presumed to be more reliable suppliers than Third World suppliers of petroleum.

Nuclear power also has the advantage that, "in contrast to petroleum, interruptions of natural uranium supplies would not have an immediate and dramatic effect on the generation of electricity."[10] The process of transforming natural uranium to reactor fuel elements involves a number of stages and causes a considerable time lag between natural uranium production and final consumption. Consequently, even if natural uranium supplies were interrupted, there would be sufficient uranium in the supply pipeline to provide reactor fuel for at least two years.[11] Finally, the relatively long life of reactor fuel elements contributes to the delay between the interruption of uranium supplies and the onset of reactor fuel shortages.[12]

The dual strategic implications of international uranium trade have frequently come into conflict in the past two decades. Uranium's role as an essential raw material in the production of nuclear weapons has led almost all exporters to impose conditions to prevent consuming countries from diverting uranium supplied for peaceful nuclear programs to the production of nuclear weapons. These conditions have often been resisted by import-dependent uranium-consuming countries. The latter view uranium as a strategically important source of energy

TABLE 1: Canadian export earnings from uranium and related materials* 1956–84

Year	Value of exports ($000)
1956	45,776
1959	311,904
1962	166,008
1965	59,250
1970	33,981
1971	33,399
1972	70,200
1973	67,707
1974	99.873
1975	133,475
1976	253,089
1977	236,603
1978	658,139
1979	980,939
1980	856,041
1981	849,870
1982	792,614
1983	430,190
1984	874,401
1985	824,672
1986	841,430

*Includes primarily uranium ores and concentrates and uranium hexafluoride (a processed form of uranium that is subsequently enriched and used to fabricate reactor fuel elements), although radioactive isotopes for medical and industrial purposes are also included.
Sources: Statistics Canada, *Merchandise Trade: Exports, 1984,* 170, 243; *Canadian Minerals Yearbook,* various years

and therefore seek maximum security of supply and freedom from external sources of influence in their imports.[13]

The conflict between suppliers and importers is paralleled in Canada by a conflict between the economic and strategic implications of uranium exports. Canada's large uranium reserves have provided the basis for a strong export trade, making a positive contribution to this country's balance of payments (see Table 1) and to employment and regional development in Ontario and Saskatchewan. Successive governments have therefore sought to promote uranium exports. However, there has also been concern that Canadian uranium could contribute to nuclear proliferation. Consequently, there has been a continuing tension in Canadian uranium export policy between promoting exports and controlling them to prevent uranium-importing countries from acquiring nuclear weapons.[14] A similar tension is even more significant in the closely related area of nuclear reactor and technology exports,[15] although these are beyond the scope of this chapter.

Canada has been deeply involved in international debates surrounding uranium trade, mainly because of its role as one of the world's largest producers and the world's largest exporter of uranium. As Table 2 shows, Canada has been second only to the U.S. as a uranium producer in the non-Communist world throughout most of the industry's history; today its production levels far exceed those of the United States. Since utilities seek long-term assurances of nuclear fuel supply,[16] an equally important measure of Canada's status as a uranium sup-

TABLE 2: Production of *uranium in concentrates* by major non-communist producing countries (tonnes U)

Country	1960	1970	1980	1982	1984	1986
United States	13,650	9,900	16,800	10,330	5.720	5,200
Canada	9,815	3,530	7,150	8,080	11,170	11,720
South Africa	4,935	3,167	6,150	5,815	5,740	4,610
Namibia	—	—	4,040	3,725	3,690	3,300
France	1,090*	1,250	2,630	2,860	3,170	3,250
Niger	n/a	—	4,100	4,260	3,400	3,100
Gabon	n/a	400	1,030	970	1,000	900
Australia	925	254	1,560	4,555	4,390	4,150
Other	2,025 +	100	510	700	950	870
Total	32,440	18,610	43,970	41,330	39,230	37,110
Canada's % share	30.3	19.0	16.3	19.6	30.0	31.6

*Includes Gabon
+ Primarily Belgian Congo
n/a = not available
Sources: *Canadian Minerals Yearbook,* various years (Ottawa: Department of Energy, Mines and Resources); J.W. Griffith, *The Uranium Industry: Its History, Technology and Prospects* Mineral Report 12 (Ottawa: Department of Energy, Mines and Resources 1967)

TABLE 3: 1983 estimates of uranium resources in the non-communist world

Country	Reasonably assured resources (RAR) recoverable at costs* up to		Estimated additional resources (EAR) recoverable at costs* up to	
	$80/kg U	$130/kg U +	$80/kg U	$130/kg U +
		(1,000 tones U)		
Australia	314	336	369	394
Brazil	163	163	92	92
Canada	176	185	181	229
France	56	68	27	33
Namibia	119	135	30	53
Niger	160	160	53	53
South Africa	191	313	99	147
United States	131	407	30	83
Others	158	276	33	138
Total	1,468	2,043	914	1,222
Canada's % share	12.0	9.1	19.8	18.7

*Costs expressed in January 1983 U.S. dollars
+ Includes resources recoverable at costs up to $80/kg U
Source: OECD, Nuclear Energy Agency/International Atomic Energy Agency, *Uranium: Resources, Production and Demand* (Paris: OECD 1983). Changes in assigning deposits to IAEA categories as well as further exploration have led to substantial downward revisions from previous IAEA estimates for some countries, especially the United States and Canada.

plier is its share of world uranium reserves and resources. As Table 3 indicates, Canada accounts for a substantial share of the non-Communist world's known uranium reserves and resources. Furthermore, some other large uranium producers are also large uranium consumers and therefore have little if any uranium available for export. The bulk of uranium production in the United States is consumed domestically, and the U.S. is now a major importer. France also consumes most of its own uranium domestically, and controls and consumes a very large share of the uranium produced in Gabon and Niger, former French colonies. Thus, import-dependent industrialized countries have looked primarily to Canada, South Africa, Australia, and Namibia for uranium supplies.[17]

The concentration of the non-Communist world's uranium supply in a small number of western industrialized countries is mirrored by a concentration of consumption and imports among another small group of western industrialized countries. During the 1950s and 1960s, the nuclear weapons programs of the U.S. and the U.K. dominated consumption in the non-Communist world. Ninety per cent of Canada's exports from 1955 to 1963 went to the U.S., 9 per cent to the U.K., and the remaining 1 per cent to twelve other countries.[18] This pattern persisted until demand from commercial nuclear power programs in West Germany, Japan, and the U.K. began to pick up in the late 1960s, and these three countries accounted for the bulk of Canadian exports in the early 1970s.[19] Canada was unable to make any sales in the growing U.S. commercial nuclear power market during the 1960s and early 1970s because of the effective U.S. import embargo, discussed in the preceding chapter, which was eased only in 1974. The pattern of exports since 1974, shown in Table 4, highlights Canada's continuing reliance on the U.S., Japan, the U.K., and West Germany, but also points to the growth of a number of non-traditional export markets.

TABLE 4: Canadian uranium under export contracts concluded between September 1974 and December of the year listed,* in tonnes U

Country	1978	1980	1982	1984	1987
Belgium	850	938	3,030	3,030	3,325
Finland	1,770	1,769	2,000	3,510	3,512
France	1,540	1,538	3,850	9,390	9,620
Italy	1,390	1,385	1,120	1,120	1,115
Japan	16,960	19,507	22,630	22,740	25,046
South Korea	230	1,910	5,140	5,140	6,841
Spain	4,810	4,808	4,230	3,940	3,559
Sweden	670	906	3,880	5,310	8,477
Switzerland	500	154	150	150	154
United Kingdom	7,690	7,693	7,700	7,700	8,293
United States	18,460	12,032	25,570	30,360	45,188
West Germany	6,000	6,384	7,660	11,580	14,264
Total	60,870	59,024	86,960	103,970	129,394

*Includes both contracts for deliveries already made and contracts for future deliveries into the 1990s concluded during the specified period. Changes from one year to the next indicate new contracts and revisions to existing contracts.
Sources: *Canadian Minerals Yearbook*, various years

CANADIAN URANIUM IN THE COLD WAR: THE 1940S AND 1950S

Uranium mining began in earnest in Canada during the Second World War. It had been produced as a by-product of radium mining in the Northwest Territories from 1933 to 1940, but was stockpiled as there was no use for it at the time. In 1942, the U.S. and Britain, seeking a secure North American source for the

Allied atomic bomb programs, purchased the stockpile and persuaded the Canadian government to reopen the mine. In the interests of national security, the federal government took control of all aspects of the uranium industry by 1946. The Crown corporation Eldorado Mining and Refining Limited and the Atomic Energy Control Board were created as the instruments of this control.[20] During the war and in the early postwar years, all Canadian-produced uranium was turned over to tripartite agencies to be allocated among the nuclear programs of the United States, Britain, and Canada. The U.S. dominated these agencies and received the bulk of Canada's uranium output.[21]

During the early postwar years, Canada strongly supported the idea of an international regime to promote peaceful uses of nuclear energy while inhibiting the spread of nuclear weapons. In an influential memorandum to Prime Minister Mackenzie King in November 1945, Lester Pearson (then Canadian Ambassador to the United States) emphasized that all industrialized countries could manufacture atomic weapons in the near future and that the Soviet Union would probably soon do so. All countries could eventually find themselves threatened by this revolutionary new kind of weapon. The conclusions Pearson drew from this have guided Canadian nuclear export policy ever since:

> Any constructive solution of the war use of atomic energy must be international—not national. There is, in fact, no national solution. This... means that [the U.S., Britain, and Canada] should exploit the temporary advantage they now possess in order to bring this weapon under international control, so that it can never be used by anyone. This can be attempted by trading the knowledge they alone possess at present, for renunciation by all nations of the right of production or use, except, possibly, on orders from the United Nations. This in its turn means international supervision and control of the development and use of atomic energy.[22]

The stress on international controls, and on exchanging access to nuclear technology and supplies for a commitment not to develop nuclear weapons, have been central elements of Canadian nuclear export policy to the present day.

American and British leaders were thinking along similar lines, and later that same month President Truman, Prime Minister Attlee, and Prime Minister King met and agreed upon a Tripartite Declaration on Atomic Energy. This Declaration made clear the signatories' intention to use their dominance of nuclear technology to create a regime of international safeguards to prevent other countries from developing atomic weapons: "We are... prepared to share, on a reciprocal basis with others of the United Nations, detailed information concerning the practical industrial application of atomic energy just as soon as effective enforceable safeguards against its use for destructive purposes can be devised."[23]

Canadian leaders saw a regime of international nuclear co-operation and safeguards as a mechanism for resolving the conflict between the economic and strategic implications of atomic energy. Co-operation to promote the peaceful uses of atomic energy would generate international trade in nuclear materials from which Canada, as an early technological leader and the repository of substantial uranium reserves, could hope to benefit. At the same time, a system of strict international safeguards to prevent graded materials and technology from being diverted to military uses would ensure that nuclear trade did not threaten world peace and Canada's national security.

International negotiations for a nonproliferation regime began in 1946 under the auspices of the newly established United Nations Atomic Energy Commission. Differences between the United States and the Soviet Union, particularly concerning what to do about the American monopoly of nuclear weapons, dominated the discussions and ultimately proved irreconcilable. By mid-1947 the first attempt to create an international nonproliferation regime had reached a deadlock, much to the disappointment of Canadian diplomats, who had searched for a compromise acceptable to the main protagonists.[24]

The absence of such a regime did not prevent the rapid development of the Canadian uranium industry. In 1947, against the background of concern that uranium supplies were not expanding rapidly enough to meet strong military demand, the U.S. Atomic Energy Commission (USAEC) began to offer incentives to encourage uranium exploration and mining in friendly foreign countries. These incentives were made more attractive in the wake of the successful Soviet tests of atomic and thermonuclear explosives in 1949 and 1953. In 1947 the U.S. also persuaded Britain and Canada to allocate all of Canada's uranium output in the immediate future to the United States, and to allow the latter to control the flow of uranium supplies to Canadian and British nuclear programs. Canada agreed to give Washington this control over its uranium because of the urgency of U.S. military requirements for uranium in the context of the deepening Cold War.[25]

The USAEC incentives created a short-lived boom in the Canadian uranium industry. Many new mines were opened and entire towns were built out of the wilderness to service them.[26] Production grew rapidly, and in 1958 Canada was the world's largest producer of uranium. In that year and again in 1959, uranium was the most valuable metal produced in this country. It also ranked as the fourth most valuable Canadian export commodity in 1959.[27]

The Canadian nuclear industry was entirely dependent upon the United States throughout this early period. Uranium production was destined almost exclusively for U.S. military consumption, and the Canadian civilian nuclear power research program depended upon access to American information, technology, and materials. This dependent relationship was apparent in the Canada-U.S. nuclear co-operation treaty of 1955. Reflecting Cold War concerns, the preamble to the treaty stated that for the present and for the forseeable future, priority of materials and personnel must be given to defence needs.[28] At the same time, Canada agreed not to use any U.S.-supplied material for military purposes. The flow of American information and materials required by the Canadian research program was carefully restricted to exclude anything with significant military applications. With respect to safeguards, both countries agreed not to retransfer materials or technology to third parties without the consent of the original supplier. More generally, Canada agreed to continue to accept the provisions of the U.S. Atomic Energy Act of 1954 as defining the safeguards to be imposed on nuclear exports.[29]

Two characteristics of Canadian uranium export policy in this early period are particularly noteworthy. The first is the search for an international regime to encourage peaceful uses of nuclear energy within the framework of a strict system of international safeguards. An international safeguards regime promised to enable Canadian exports of uranium and nuclear reactors (in which the Canadian government was investing enormous funds and scientific talent) to flourish without compromising Canada's security interest in nonproliferation. Since there was virtually no popular opposition to nuclear exports (public perceptions of the peaceful uses of atomic energy were generally positive in the 1940s and 1950s), the search for an international nonproliferation regime was not motivated by domestic political concerns; Ottawa's efforts were geared more to ensuring that nuclear export promotion did not undermine other objectives pursued by makers of foreign policy.

Second, Canadian policy was noteworthy for the complete assurance of supply it provided to the United States and Britain, which sought Canadian uranium for their nuclear weapons programs. The economic and security implications of these uranium exports were happily in harmony; uranium exports strengthened Canada's allies in the Cold War struggle with the Soviet bloc and provided much-needed U.S. dollar export earnings.[30]

TURMOIL IN MARKETS AND POLICY: MID-1950S TO LATE 1960S

The boom in the Canadian uranium industry and the harmony in Canadian uranium export policy proved to be short-lived. By 1955 the USAEC realized that its incentives for uranium mining had been too successful. Far more uranium than was actually required was being brought into production in the United States, Canada, and other countries to which the incentives had been directed. Consequently, in that year the USAEC announced that it would not sign any new contracts for additional Canadian uranium after 31 March 1956. This announcement brought exploration in Canada to an abrupt halt. A further blow came in 1959, when the USAEC announced that it would not exercise options it had previously taken out to purchase additional supplies from Canadian producers. Since USAEC purchases accounted for 90 per cent of Canadian output, these decisions would have virtually shut down the Canadian uranium industry when the existing contracts ran out in 1963.[31] In order to cushion the blow, the Canadian government negotiated arrangements with the American and British governments to stretch out contracted purchases until 1966 and to allow contracts to be transferred from high-cost to low-cost producers.[32]

Despite these arrangements, by mid-1964 all but four mines had ceased production, and their output was a fraction of Canadian output in the late 1950s. In the absence of foreign demand for uranium, the federal government instituted costly stockpiling programs (involving expenditures of well over $100 million) to permit Canadian mines to stay in operation.[33]

The uranium market remained depressed throughout the 1960s, although the problem was thought to be temporary. Both government and industry believed that strong demand for uranium would soon come from the nascent civilian nuclear power generating industry. The stretch-out program, operating subsidies to government-owned Eldorado Nuclear (originally Eldorado Mining and Refining), and various stockpiling programs were viewed as measures "to maintain a nucleus of a uranium industry" until the commercial nuclear power market developed.[34] The best prospects for commercial markets were in the U.S., where the civilian nuclear industry was well advanced and the market promised to be large. However, U.S. uranium producers had also suffered from USAEC purchase cutbacks, and successfully pushed for regulations that prohibited American utilities from using foreign uranium in their nuclear power reactors.[35] The Canadian government made repeated representations to the American government about this import embargo during the 1960s and 1970s, but it stayed in place and dampened the prospects for Canadian producers.[36]

The virtual collapse of U.S. military demand followed by the closing of the U.S. commercial market to foreign uranium sparked a search for new markets. An opportunity arose as early as 1956, when France offered to purchase a large volume of Canadian uranium. France initially sought to purchase the uranium on an unrestricted basis for use in its nuclear weapons program. Canada insisted that any sale be accompanied by safeguards to ensure that it was used for peaceful purposes only. This Canadian demand was consistent with American preferences, and Washington pressed Canadian officials to reject the sale in the absence of safeguards.[37]

A second obstacle to the sale was the unwillingness of the United States to make uranium available to France. As noted earlier, Canada had agreed in 1947 to give the U.S. control of all of its uranium output. Since France wanted the uranium delivered in the period from 1958 to 1960, and the U.S. was reluctant to share Canadian uranium with even the British during that period, "there was no great probability that the Americans would agree to move over. . . to satisfy a country that was not even a member of the atomic 'club' and whose bomb program they hoped to discourage."[38]

Inasmuch as France needed uranium for civilian as well as military nuclear programs, it was willing to accept a peaceful-uses-only condition, but only if Canada would accept a 25 per cent reduction in price from that paid by the U.S. and Britain. French negotiators argued that they were not getting the same material as those two countries, which were of course free to use Canadian uranium for military purposes, and should therefore not have to pay the same price. Canada was willing to accept a 19-per cent reduction in price, but this was insufficient to persuade France to accept the safeguards demanded by Canada. The deal collapsed.[39]

Even if Canada and France had been able to reach a compromise on price and safeguards, however, the second obstacle would probably have been insurmountable. The United States was opposed to the sale and could have blocked it even if Ottawa had been willing to go ahead. The episode demonstrated both the conflict between the economic and strategic implications of uranium exports and the continuing dominance of the U.S. in Canadian nuclear developments.

Conflicting Canadian objectives were also apparent in the 1955 decision to transfer a research reactor to India. While reactor exports are beyond the scope of this study, the agreement under which this reactor was transferred is worthy of attention both for the light it sheds on Canadian policy and because of its importance to Canadian uranium export policy in the 1970s. Canada agreed to transfer a CANDU research reactor to India under an arrangement that "contained no safeguard, reporting or inspection procedures, only a naked promise by the Indian government. . . 'that the reactor and any products resulting from its use will be employed for peaceful purposes only.' 'Peaceful purposes' was not defined."[40] India had not committed itself never to develop nuclear weapons and publicly objected to safeguards on the grounds that they served to perpetuate the nuclear weapons monopoly of the developed countries.[41]

Presumably, the transfer of the weakly safeguarded reactor was approved because it served other Canadian diplomatic and economic objectives. It provided a concrete demonstration of Canada's commitment to assisting Third World development, as the reactor was exported under the auspices of Canada's Colombo Plan foreign aid program. Furthermore, the peaceful use of nuclear energy was one area in which Canada could claim a special expertise and therefore play a distinctive role. The provision of a CANDU reactor as aid might also give Canada an edge in the emerging international nuclear market, thereby returning a long-term commercial benefit. Finally, Canadian leaders wanted to develop close ties with India, a fellow member of the Commonwealth and one of the most influential of the underdeveloped nations. On all of these grounds, Ottawa was willing to give India the benefit of the doubt and export the reactor with minimal nonproliferation controls.[42]

Dissatisfaction with the way the negotiations with France had proceeded and concern about the agreement with India led Ottawa to formulate a more explicit policy to facilitate the expansion of exports within the confines of nonproliferation safeguards. A procedure was established for reviewing nuclear export agreements, and guidelines were prepared for nuclear co-operation agreements with states interested in acquiring Canadian nuclear technology or materials. These procedures and guidelines were followed with respect to the bilateral nuclear co-operation agreements Canada concluded with nine countries and Euratom (the atomic energy agency of the European Economic Community) between 1957 and 1965. While the details of the individual agreements varied, all included some reference to using Canadian-supplied materials for peaceful purposes only and specified that safeguards must be in place prior to the exchange of any materials to ensure that Canadian-supplied materials or technology were not diverted to military purposes. Canada was given the right to inspect facilities and receive information to assure itself that diversion did not occur.[43] The safeguards provisions were modelled on those required by Washington for American exports. Furthermore, since most overseas consumers of Canadian uranium needed to fuel light-water reactors that require enriched rather than natural uranium, most Canadian uranium destined for overseas markets "was first shipped to the United States for enrichment. In its enriched form it was legally subsumed under the American safeguard system, and Canadian safeguards responsibility over it lapsed."[44]

The conditions under which uranium and other nuclear materials and technology were exported from Canada in the 1950s and early 1960s reflected some ambivalence in Canadian policy. Recognition of the dangers of nuclear proliferation was apparent in the pledges of peaceful use and the safeguards that were demanded of consumers of Canadian nuclear materials and technology. On the other hand, most pledges of peaceful use were neither specific nor concrete, there were many gaps in the coverage of the safeguards, and mechanisms of enforcement were lacking.[45] Canada did not seriously attempt to devise strict nonproliferation controls to attach to its nuclear exports, despite concern about the problem of nuclear proliferation within the Department of External Affairs. Ottawa's tendency was to rely primarily on U.S.-led international efforts to resolve the problem rather than to use Canada's status as a supplier to inhibit proliferation on a unilateral or bilateral basis.[46]

Consistent with this policy, Canada gave strong support to the creation of the International Atomic Energy Agency (IAEA) in 1957. President Eisenhower's "Atoms for Peace" speech of late 1953 revived efforts to create an international agency to promote nuclear energy while inhibiting the spread of nuclear weapons. The IAEA came into existence in July 1957, although its safeguards systems did not become operative until the early 1960s. The "fundamental compromise at the heart" of the IAEA involved a promise by nuclear supplier states to make technology and material for peaceful applications of nuclear energy available to non-nuclear weapons states in exchange for a commitment by the latter not to use that technology and material to develop nuclear weapons.[47]

The IAEA safeguards system suffered from a number of weaknesses. Safeguards were applied only to individual facilities or transfers of material rather than to all civilian nuclear activities in the recipient countries, and supplier states were under no obligation to impose safeguards as a condition of supply. The IAEA system also accepted the concept of "peaceful" nuclear explosions.[48] These shortcomings and continuing international concern about the problem of nuclear proliferation led to the negotiation of the Non-Proliferation Treaty (NPT) in 1968, again with Canadian support. The NPT went beyond the IAEA system by proscribing peaceful nuclear explosions and by requiring what are called full-scope safeguards; that is, safeguards were to be applied to *all* stages of civilian nuclear programs in recipient countries rather than simply to specific transfers of facilities or materials.[49]

Increasing international attention to the problem of nuclear proliferation was paralleled in Canada by the emergence of a public debate about the economic and strategic implications of uranium exports. The trigger for this controversy was once again an offer by France to purchase a large volume of Canadian uranium. Just as in 1956, France initially wanted the uranium with no conditions that would prevent it from being used in nuclear weapons production. This was clearly out of the question. Ottawa shared other NATO members' objections to France's deployment of an independent nuclear *force de frappe*. Furthermore, France had not supported joint Western efforts to stem nuclear proliferation. An unsafeguarded sale to France would be in blatant contradiction to Canada's non-proliferation policy and could undermine negotiations then underway to create the NPT. The opposition parties came out strongly against making the sale unless accompanied by stringent safeguards to prevent Canadian uranium from being used in France's nuclear weapons. The U.S. joined in urging Ottawa to reject the sale.

In light of these considerations, Canada offered to make the sale only if France would accept safeguards to ensure that the uranium would not be used for military purposes. The French government resented the fact that the U.S. and Britain were free to use Canadian uranium in nuclear weapons while France would not be permitted to do so. Just as in 1956, French negotiators apparently would agree to accept the safeguards demanded by Canada only if Canada would accept a lower price than that paid by the U.S. and Britain. The price offered by France was below Canada's costs of production, and other provisions of the revised French offer would have given France an unacceptable degree of control over Canadian uranium deposits, so the deal was rejected.[50]

While American influence probably contributed to collapse of the 1956 negotiations with France, it appears that it had little to do with the collapse of the 1965 negotiations.[51] By 1965 Canadian leaders and the Canadian public had become much more concerned with the problem of nuclear proliferation than in 1956. At the same time, American leverage over Canada in nuclear affairs had declined, a result of the growing independence of the CANDU reactor program and reduced U.S. purchases of Canadian uranium. The Canada-U.S. nuclear cooperation treaty had been amended to reduce formal American influence over Canadian nuclear policy.

The collapse of the negotiations put the Pearson government in a difficult position. The decision to insist upon safeguards entailed a considerable economic loss for an industry already suffering from a lack of markets. Understandably, the uranium industry had lobbied hard to persuade the government to go through with the sale. In order to placate it, Ottawa introduced a new publicly financed stockpiling program to enable some mines to remain in production.

The decision to insist upon safeguards before concluding the sale to France also left the government open to opposition charges of hypocrisy and to diplomatic embarrassment in Canadian-French relations, as the U.S. and Britain were still free to use Canadian uranium in their nuclear weapons programs. Consequently, at the same time as the new stockpiling program was introduced, Prime Minister Lester Pearson announced that "the Government has decided that export permits will be granted . . . with respect to sales of uranium covered by contracts entered into from now on, only if the uranium is to be used for peaceful purposes." The policy applied only to new sales; continuing minor sales to the U.S. and Britain for use in their military programs would be permitted to continue until deliveries under existing contracts were completed. Pearson also noted that Britain and the U.S. had accepted the new policy in consultations prior to its adoption.[52] One can imagine that had both countries still required Canadian uranium for their nuclear weapons programs, it would have been much more difficult for Canada to adopt a consistent nuclear export policy.

Three features of this second period in the history of Canadian uranium export policy are worth highlighting. First, the collapse of military demand in the U.S. and Britain forced the Canadian industry to look further afield for sales, leading it into potential export situations in which the economic and strategic implications for Canada were less likely to be in harmony. This was clearest in the cases of the rejected French offers to purchase Canadian uranium; in both 1956 and 1965, the government was forced to accept a significant economic cost in order to uphold its nonproliferation policy. The second notable feature was the growing importance of domestic political considerations in nuclear export policymaking, in terms of pressure from the industry to promote exports and pressure from opposition parties, the media, and the public to impose restrictions to check proliferation. This was one of the very few foreign policy issues of these years to generate significant domestic political debate, a harbinger of the 1970s. Third, the Canadian government continued to promote nonproliferation primarily through participation in broadly based international initiatives such as the IAEA and NPT, rather than through unilateral action.

THE URANIUM CARTEL: 1972 TO 1975

Canada played a leading role in the international uranium cartel that operated between 1972 and 1975.[53] The depressed conditions that characterized world uranium markets in the 1960s persisted into the early 1970s. In 1971 the news that large low-cost deposits had been discovered in Australia and the decision by the USAEC to sell off a portion of its uranium stockpile to foreign users of its enrichment services threatened to depress prices even further.[54] This prospect motivated Ottawa to hold talks with a number of uranium-producing and consuming countries during 1970 and 1971 to explore the possibility of international co-operation to support the uranium market. Japan and West Germany, as importing countries, did not favour intergovernmental action, although the West Germans reportedly indicated some interest in co-operative arrangements to ensure security of supply and orderly pricing.[55] Producing countries and firms indicated interest but were not optimistic about the prospects for an arrangement that would include consumers.[56]

The Canadian government concluded from this initial round of talks that a producer-consumer arrangement was not feasible, and decided to see if other producers would be interested in a producer-only cartel.[57] Most were, and after a series of meetings in the spring of 1972, agreement was reached on a scheme to allocate world markets outside the United States among the cartel members and to fix the prices at which sales were to be made.[58] The cartel members were Canada (which was allocated the largest share of the market, 33.5 per cent), South Africa, France, Australia, and Rio Tinto Zinc.[59]

The cartel operated from 1972 to 1975. Uranium prices soared during the period from 1972 to 1977, from less than $6 to more than $43 a pound.[60] However, other factors were primarily responsible for this increase. Demand for uranium increased sharply as a large number of nuclear power plants came onstream. The oil crisis increased consumers' interest in signing long-term contracts to assure themselves of secure supplies. In mid-1973, the USAEC began to require utilities to make firm, long-term commitments for enrichment services. Because of projections of increased reliance on nuclear energy and concern about the adequacy of enrichment capacity to meet future needs, utilities rushed to place enrichment orders. They also concluded long-term supply contracts with uranium producers so that they would have sufficient uranium to deliver to the USAEC for enrichment.

Utilities had looked to rich Australian deposits to help meet future needs, but the Labour government elected in December 1972 put an indefinite hold on new mine developments pending a review of environmental, nonproliferation, and other policy issues. Concern about energy security in the wake of the oil crisis led Canada and France to restrict exports to ensure adequate supplies for domestic nuclear programs. Finally, it was revealed in 1975 that Westinghouse (a manufacturer of nuclear power reactors) had contracted to sell far more uranium than it actually owned or had contracts to buy. Because of developments that sharply increased demand for uranium at a time when supply appeared to be contracting utilities went on a panic-buying binge and forced prices sharply upwards.[61]

The cartel began to fall behind rising market prices during 1974, and in early 1975 the Canadian government withdrew the quota and minimum price directives it had used to implement the cartel arrangements.[62] Only after the cartel had ceased to function effectively in mid-1974 did prices really begin to climb. The consensus among informed observers is that changes in the supply-demand balance that I have just discussed are sufficient to explain the increases.[63]

Energy-importing countries would normally be expected to frown on supplier-only collaboration to raise the price of an important energy source, but this did not occur with respect to Canadian participation in the uranium cartel. This is especially surprising as the uranium cartel coincided with the rise of OPEC, which was widely condemned. There are a number of possible reasons for the lack of protest from uranium-importing countries. The most important consuming countries were all aware of the cartel's existence right from the start, and some had given it their tacit approval. The Canadian government kept the

American government posted on the progress of the cartel negotiations.[64] Newspaper reports indicated that the American government, far from opposing the cartel, hoped that cartel-inspired uranium price increases would improve the export prospects of U.S. uranium producers.[65] Uranerz, a German firm involved in uranium production in Canada, received "unofficial approval" from the West German government for its participation in the cartel. The British government was almost certainly kept informed through its links with Rio Tinto Zinc.[66]

Publicly available information and interviews with government officials indicate that none of the governments of the major consuming countries criticized the Canadian government for its participation in the uranium cartel. Vehement criticism of Canada's role arose in the United States after documents detailing the cartel's actions became available in 1976, but this criticism came from Congress, the courts, and certain elements of the business community.[67] The Carter administration attempted to minimize the impact of these protests, since it did not want to undermine the Canadian support for its international nonproliferation initiatives to be discussed later.[68]

The absence of consumer-government protests against Canadian participation in the uranium cartel reflected the fact that all of the cartel participants were western industrialized countries. This characteristic minimized consumer fears that suppliers would engage in OPEC-style price gouging. As it turned out, the increase in uranium prices over the cartel period was comparable to the increase in oil prices, but consumers appear to have shared the Canadian government's view that the uranium price increase was due more to market developments than to cartel efforts. Also important was the fact that uranium accounts for only a minor share of the total cost of nuclear electricity generation. Most of the cost is accounted for by the very large capital investment required for the construction of nuclear power plants. Even at the higher cartel prices, uranium accounted for only about one-twentieth of total nuclear power costs.[69] Consumers are therefore much more interested in security of uranium supply than in uranium prices. If the cartel, by raising prices, could help to stimulate uranium exploration and mining, consumers might actually benefit.[70] In any case, consuming countries do not appear to have perceived Canada as a less secure or desirable supplier because of its participation in the uranium cartel.

In contrast, Ottawa's 1974 decision to require domestic producers to set aside large reserves to meet potential Canadian demand did arouse the ire of consumer governments and cause them to perceive Canada as a less desirable supplier of uranium. Announced in the context of OPEC-inspired fears of energy shortages, the policy was intended to ensure that strong foreign demand for uranium did not deprive Canadian utilities of access to Canadian supplies.[71] The policy appeared likely to restrict foreign consumers' access to Canadian uranium, and was seen abroad as unnecessarily restrictive since additional reserves would likely be discovered in Canada (as indeed they were). Some consumers suspected that the policy was intended primarily to push uranium prices even higher.[72] The policy was soon relaxed as estimates of future Canadian needs were revised downwards and new reserves were discovered. Nevertheless, the contrast between consumer opposition to the reserve set-aside policy and consumer indifference to Canada's participation in the uranium cartel does indicate the greater importance overseas consumers attached to security of supply than to low prices.

UNILATERAL POLICY INITIATIVES: 1974 TO 1976

On 18 May 1974, India exploded a nuclear device built with plutonium produced in the nuclear research reactor supplied by Canada in the late 1950s. This explosion triggered a significant shift in Canadian nuclear export policy and led to serious strains in Canada's relations with some of its closest political allies and most important trading partners.

India's test of what it called a "peaceful" nuclear device did not come as a complete surprise to Canadian leaders. As noted earlier, the 1956 agreement under which the CIRUS reactor would be used for "peaceful purposes" only, did not define "peaceful purposes" and did not expressly prohibit nuclear explosions. During the late 1960s and early 1970s, in the context of mounting evidence of India's intention to develop a nuclear explosive, Canadian leaders attempted to persuade that country to interpret the 1956 agreement as prohibiting the development of nuclear explosives for any purpose. India refused to accept such an interpretation, making clear its determination to maintain the freedom to develop "peaceful" nuclear explosives.[73]

The Indian nuclear test occurred in the middle of a Canadian federal election campaign. The opposition parties and media critics blamed the Liberal government for allowing India to use Canadian technology and materials to build a nuclear explosive. The criticism was especially severe since the Indian explosion followed closely in the wake of widely criticized agreements to sell CANDU nuclear reactors to Argentina and South Korea.[74] In all of these cases, domestic criticism of Canadian nuclear export policy was aimed primarily at exports of nuclear reactors, not uranium, although, as we shall see, the policy changes adopted in the wake of the Indian explosion fell very heavily on exports of uranium.

The Indian explosion triggered an important shift in Canadian nonproliferation policy. Political leaders felt a need to respond to strong domestic pressure for measures to prevent Canadian technology or materials from facilitating the spread of nuclear weapons. Makers of foreign policy believed strongly in the need for measures to inhibit nuclear proliferation. They also sought to maintain international momentum in favour of safeguards and to reassert Canada's role as a leader in international efforts to create an effective nonproliferation regime. Furthermore, policymakers believed that more stringent safeguards were necessary to persuade Canadian public opinion to support continued nuclear exports after the Indian explosion. This was an important consideration, since uranium exports contributed significantly to Canadian export earnings (see Table 1), and exports were thought to be crucial to support the sophisticated manufacturing industry that Ottawa had created to produce the CANDU nuclear reactor.[75]

Canada immediately suspended all nuclear co-operation with India. A cabinet-level review of Canadian nuclear export policy was conducted and a new policy was announced in 1974. The new policy was most notable for its departure from the traditional Canadian reliance on multilateral safeguards. While Canada would continue to work for a stronger multilateral safeguards regime, the government "also concluded that as a matter of national policy, Canada would move ahead of the international norm as it then existed."[76] Canada would impose stricter conditions on its own nuclear exports than required by the IAEA or the NPT. Canada would require "binding assurance that Canadian-supplied nuclear material, equipment and technology will not be used to produce a nuclear explosives device, whether the development of such a device be stated to be for peaceful purposes or not." In order to ensure that this commitment could not be violated, the safeguards coverage of the new policy was broadened to include all nuclear facilities and equipment supplied by Canada or using Canadian technology, "all nuclear material . . . supplied by Canada, and future generations of fissile material produced from or with these materials; they will cover all nuclear materials, whatever their origin, produced or processed in facilities supplied by Canada."[77]

Cabinet decided at the same time to require a number of other safeguards conditions in addition to those stated publicly by Donald Macdonald, Minister of Energy. For reasons that are not entirely clear, these were not announced until later in 1975 and 1976.[78] Canada would require a right of prior consent to consumers' decisions regarding transfers of Canadian-supplied material and technology to third countries, reprocessing of Canadian-origin nuclear fuel, and enrichment beyond 20 per cent. Importing countries would also have to agree to fallback safeguards to be applied to reprocessing and enrichment should IAEA safeguards lapse, and to provide adequate physical protection to prevent unauthorized access to materials of Canadian origin. The most controversial element in the new safeguards was the Canadian demand for a veto (that is, "prior consent") over decisions to reprocess spent fuel produced from Canadian uranium or in CANDU reactors.[79] Canada's position was based on its view that reprocessing technologies and facilities were particularly sensitive since they could be used to produce weapons-grade material.[80]

The new safeguards conditions were also to be applied retroactively. Existing contracts would have to be renegotiated to incorporate the new safeguards, although exports would be permitted to continue while negotiations were under way.[81]

Ottawa's decision to unilaterally upgrade the nonproliferation commitments it demanded from importers of Canadian uranium depended critically upon Canada's market power as the dominant world uranium exporter. Uranium enjoyed a sellers' market in the mid-1970s, and Canada appeared to be the only seller that would have a large exportable surplus in the 1980s, when demand for uranium was projected to be strong.[82] As indicated in Table 3, known uranium reserves and resources were concentrated in a small number of countries. Two of these countries (the United States and France) consumed the bulk of their production domestically, while others (South Africa, Namibia, and a small number of black African countries) were thought to be politically unstable. France withdrew entirely from the export market in 1974 in the wake of the oil crisis and a decision to accelerate its domestic nuclear program. South Africa, where uranium is produced as a by-product of gold mining, began to cut back uranium production in 1973 as an incidental result of changing gold-mining economics. And, as noted earlier, the Australian government had halted the development of newly discovered deposits and the signing of new export contracts in December 1972.[83]

In the absence of this apparent monopoly position, Canada's attempt to upgrade safeguards would have led merely to the loss of markets. The Department of External Affairs stated publicly that it was Canada's importance as a supplier that permitted Canada to take the initiative in upgrading nonproliferation controls.[84] Consumers facing limited alternative sources of uranium supply might be persuaded to accept safeguard conditions that went well beyond those required by multilateral agreements.

Ottawa's bargaining position was also strengthened by concurrent moves in the United States to strengthen the international nonproliferation regime in the wake of India's test of a nuclear explosive. Under Presidents Ford and Carter, the U.S. initiated efforts to upgrade safeguards on existing types of material and technology transfers, and to limit the spread of enrichment and reprocessing technologies it felt carried special proliferation dangers (see below). Consistency among supplier countries' nonproliferation policies reduced the opportunities for importing countries to bargain with individual suppliers for relaxed safeguards.

As noted above, Canada's December 1974 policy required that all its nuclear co-operation agreements with foreign consumers be renegotiated to incorporate the new safeguard requirements. Agreements incorporating the new safeguards were negotiated with Argentina, South Korea, Finland, and Spain in 1975 and 1976, and with Sweden in early 1977.[85] However, Canada was unable to reach agreement with the European Economic Community, Japan, or even the United States—the largest importers of Canadian uranium—or with Switzerland. In the case of the United States, there were few substantive differences, and the primary impediment to the conclusion of a new agreement was the length of time it took to formulate a new U.S. nonproliferation policy in the wake of the Indian explosion.[86]

The obstacles to agreement with the EEC and Japan were more serious. The main problem concerned Canada's demand for a right of prior consent to consumers' decisions to reprocess spent fuel of Canadian origin. Consuming countries opposed granting a right of prior consent to Canada because it might interfere with their efforts to achieve energy security in the wake of the oil crisis. The shock of OPEC's politicization of energy supplies had made consumers extremely wary of political conditions on their energy imports, and parallels were drawn between OPEC's actions and Canada's demands for the renegotiation of existing supply contracts for political reasons.[87]

The EEC was particularly interested in using reprocessing technologies to reduce the volume of natural uranium that had to be imported, thereby improving its energy security. It was concerned that Canada might try to interfere with reprocessing efforts, although Canadian spokesmen had argued that they were not opposed in principle to reprocessing in cases in which it could be economically justified and adequately safeguarded. Europeans were also suspicious of the commercial and political implications of Canada's demands. Forestalling the development of reprocessing would maintain demand for Canadian supplies (and therefore also Canada's ability to set conditions on its uranium exports), and would inhibit European nuclear industries from exploiting their technological lead in reprocessing in the international marketplace.[88] Some Europeans linked Canada's opposition to reprocessing to its concurrent moves to increase uranium export prices, strengthening the belief that Canada's concerns were primarily commercial.[89]

Negotiations with the EEC were also impeded by the ambiguous status of France's nuclear program in Euratom and in the IAEA safeguards system. Acceptance of Canada's demands for full-scope safeguards and for the application of IAEA safeguards to all future generations of nuclear material produced from material of Canadian origin would mean that such material could not be used in French facilities, since France had not signed the NPT or otherwise accepted full-scope safeguards and had not concluded a trilateral French-Euratom-IAEA safeguards agreement. Excluding Canadian-origin material from French facilities would interfere with the EEC's nuclear program, which involved enriching and reprocessing material in France for use in other Euratom member countries.[90]

A different obstacle in Canada's negotiations with Japan concerned the so-called "double labelling" of Canadian uranium that was enriched in the United States before being re-exported to Japan. This made uranium subject to both American and Canadian safeguards, which the Japanese felt was unnecessary and might interfere with their security of energy supply. "Japan argued that Canada should accept U.S. control as fully meeting Canadian policy," but this was not acceptable to Ottawa.[91] Negotiations with Japan were also delayed by the lack of progress in Canada-EEC negotiations, since Japan was reluctant to accept conditions more stringent than those the EEC might ultimately accept.[92]

Very little progress was made in negotiations between Canada and its major uranium consumers in 1975 and 1976. European negotiators apparently argued that the EEC should be exempted from the new safeguards requirements, since France and Britain already possessed nuclear weapons and other member states were not interested in acquiring their own nuclear weapons. However, Canada was unwilling to exempt European consumers. Ottawa believed that consistency in application was necessary to maintain the credibility of the nonproliferation policy.[93] Canada also sought to avoid the appearance of discrimination against developing countries, especially the states without nuclear weapons that had signed the NPT, in favour of developed states, one of which (France) had not even signed the NPT. The appearance of discrimination by the main nuclear supplier states has impeded the development of the international nonproliferation regime, a goal pursued by makers of Canadian foreign policy. A discriminatory Canadian policy might also arouse resentment that could make it even harder to sell CANDU reactors in the Third World.

Against this background of unsuccessful negotiations, Canada announced a further extension of its nuclear export policy in December 1976. Henceforth, Canadian uranium would be exported only to those states without nuclear weapons that had ratified the NPT or otherwise accepted full-scope safeguards. Equally important, the government decided to suspend shipments of uranium to those countries that had not yet agreed to the upgraded safeguards commitments required by the new 1974 Canadian policy.[94] Accordingly, shipments of uranium to Japan, the EEC, and Switzerland were suspended on 1 January 1977. Shipments to American utilities were also restricted until an upgraded Canada-U.S. safeguards agreement could be negotiated. The total value of uranium shipments halted was approximately $300 million.[95] This would appear to confirm the government's claim that it was "prepared to accept the commercial consequences of being clearly ahead of other suppliers."[96]

The decision to embargo uranium exports to these countries was taken after considerable debate within the government. Prime Minister Trudeau and the Ministers of External Affairs; Energy, Mines and Resources; and Industry, Trade and Commerce reportedly all favoured an embargo. Opposition to an embargo focused on the concern that an embargo would damage Canada's reputation as a supplier, thereby also damaging the uranium industry's export prospects and growth. There was also concern that the imposition of an embargo could cause lasting damage in Canada's relations with the EEC and Japan.[97]

The uranium-producing companies were vehemently opposed to the embargo and, indeed, to the effort to upgrade the safeguard commitments demanded of importers of Canadian uranium. According to the Director of the Canadian Nuclear Association, the 1974 and 1976 decisions to demand that importers accept safeguards more stringent than demanded by other nuclear suppliers caused "amazement and consternation" in the Canadian nuclear industry. The industry believed that Canada would lose its reputation as a reliable supplier and, consequently, would lose sales of uranium and reactors. It also argued that the policy was self-defeating even in terms of its nonproliferation objectives, since Canada's demands would merely encourage importers to turn to suppliers who cared less about the possibility of nuclear proliferation than Canada did.[98]

Domestic political pressures encouraged the federal government to embark on the radical new nonproliferation policy despite industry opposition and the concerns of some government officials. According to the official announcement, the government adopted the new policy in response "to the demand of Canadian public opinion."[99] Opposition parties and antinuclear groups had kept up their criticism of government policies and their demands for stricter export controls ever since the Indian nuclear test. In discussions with consuming countries, Canadian officials argued that strict controls were necessary to maintain public support in Canada for nuclear exports and therefore ultimately to ensure security of supply for importers.[100] Domestic political pressures strengthened the forces within the government that were calling for stricter safeguards on grounds of diplomatic security.

Canada's strong market position as an apparent monopoly supplier of uranium made it possible to satisfy nonproliferation concerns without excessive cost to the industry. Canada was the dominant world exporter of uranium at a time when international demand was rising rapidly. The fact that the United States and Australia, the most important alternative suppliers, were also upgrading their export safeguard controls appeared to further strengthen Canada's hand.[101] Had market conditions not appeared so favourable, it is extremely unlikely that the Canadian government would have decided to act unilaterally or to impose an embargo on uranium exports to the EEC and Japan.

RESOLUTION OF BILATERAL DISPUTES: 1977 TO 1981

The United States was the first of Canada's major uranium consumers to conclude a new bilateral safeguards agreement. The timing of the settlement had
little to do with Canadian export restrictions and much to do with the pace of
the internal policymaking process within the United States. Reached in November 1977, the agreement covered an interim period pending the effectivity of a
U.S.-IAEA agreement covering U.S. civilian nuclear facilities and the approval by
Congress of a new U.S. nonproliferation policy.[102] According to a Canadian official, this agreement "fully met the 1974 [Canadian] policy requirements."[103] The
provisions of the interim agreement were incorporated into a permanent and
comprehensive revision of Canada-U.S. nuclear trade agreements in mid-1980.
Each country agreed not to use materials supplied by the other or the derivatives
of such materials in the research or production of nuclear explosives. They also
agreed to supplier vetoes over reprocessing and enrichment beyond 20 per cent.
The agreement noted the American intention to reach an agreement with the
IAEA providing for safeguards over its civilian nuclear program (such an agreement was concluded in 1981), and made arrangements for bilateral safeguards in
the interim.[104]

The agreement also recognized in principle, but qualified in practice, Canada's right of control over the retransfer of Canadian-supplied materials to third
parties and the enrichment of Canadian-supplied material on behalf of third
parties. The qualification related primarily to the problem of double labelling of
Canadian uranium destined for Japan. The U.S. was required to consult with
Canada prior to transferring material of Canadian origin to a third country, but
was not required to secure Canadian approval if the third-party recipient did not
notify the U.S. that Canada's approval was required.[105] This arrangement cleared
the way for the conclusion of a safeguards agreement with Japan, but only by
reducing Canada's ability to impose safeguards on final users of Canadian
uranium that had been enriched in the United States. This would not be a practical problem as long as the U.S. and Canada pursued similar nonproliferation
policies.[106]

The EEC and Japan were alarmed by Canada's imposition of an embargo on exports of uranium, but this did not make them noticeably more willing to give in
to Canada's demands. As time wore on, it became increasingly apparent that
Canada's market power was insufficient to persuade these consumers to accept its
most controversial demands. Consumers found alternative sources of supply to
replace embargoed Canadian uranium. Most important, the United States
resumed uranium shipments to Europe in May 1977, thereby undermining the

consensus among suppliers that had encouraged the imposition of the embargo in the first place. [107]

Ottawa was also becoming more aware of the foreign policy costs of the embargo. There was strong diplomatic pressure from the EEC and Japan to remove a measure they felt was inconsistent with Canada's status as a close ally and its desire for closer economic ties. As External Affairs Secretary Donald Jamieson noted in announcing the lifting of the embargo in December 1977, the embargo was "beginning to exact very serious penalties and impose heavy strains on our friends in the EEC who are also our allies, part of the Western alliance and members of NATO. We can scarcely regard them as being, in such a context, suspect." [108] It also became more apparent to Canadian leaders that continuing the embargo could increase the likelihood of nuclear proliferation by encouraging consumers to develop technologies such as fast-breeder reactors and reprocessing, which would reduce their dependence on imported natural uranium but which also held greater proliferation risks. [109]

Complaints from consuming countries and from Canadian uranium producers made policymakers more aware of the potential economic costs of the embargo. As Secretary Jamieson noted when announcing that the embargo would be lifted: "We cannot go on indefinitely mining uranium and keeping it in stockpiles. There is an economic side to it. It was not in any sense a dominant issue, but I have no doubt that if we had, in an unreasonable way, refused to resume shipments to the Community there would have been criticism on the other side that, because of what is essentially a narrow question of disagreement, we had in fact caused problems for our friends and difficulties at home." [110]

The revised assessment of the diplomatic and economic costs of maintaining the embargo had to be weighed against the anticipated benefits. Since consumers had already accepted most of Canada's new safeguards demands (see the review of final agreements, below), the most that could be hoped for was a veto over consumers' reprocessing decisions (instead of merely prior consultation), Japanese acceptance of dual Canadian and American safeguards on Canadian uranium enriched in the U.S. for consumption in Japan, and the application of full-scope safeguards to the French nuclear program.

The establishment of the International Nuclear Fuel Cycle Evaluation (INFCE) in mid-1977 (see below) provided the basis for a compromise between Canada and Europe. In July 1977 Prime Minister Trudeau and West German Chancellor Helmut Schmidt agreed that shipments of Canadian uranium to Europe would be resumed for the duration of the INFCE consultations on the condition that the Europeans would consult with Canada (without having to receive Canadian consent) prior to reprocessing Canadian-origin fuel, and provided that agreement was reached on other, less critical issues.[111] The existence of INFCE would give Canadian diplomats another opportunity to convince the Europeans of the dangers of reprocessing. If all else failed, Canada could return to its original demands and even reintroduce the embargo at the conclusion of INFCE.

The embargo on uranium shipments to the EEC was lifted upon the conclusion of a formal agreement in December 1977. The agreement consisted of two parts: a main agreement which included most elements of the safeguards demanded by Canada and which was a permanent agreement; and an annexed agreement on reprocessing and enrichment beyond 20 per cent, which was an interim agreement pending the outcome of the INFCE discussions. In the main agreement, the Europeans gave binding assurance that no Canadian-supplied material, equipment, or technology would be used for explosive purposes and accorded Canada the right of prior consent to the retransfer of Canadian-supplied material to third parties. Retransfer of Canadian-supplied technology would be subject to bilateral safeguards to be negotiated between Canada and each Euratom member country. The agreement stipulated that no Canadian uranium could be used in French reactors until France accepted IAEA safeguards on its civilian nuclear program (France did so in 1978). In the meantime, however, in order not to disrupt current Euratom programs, Canada also agreed to permit Canadian-supplied material to be enriched in France for subsequent use by other Euratom members.[112] This compromise ensured that Canada was not helping to fuel the French nuclear weapons program. However, the arrangement also revealed that while Canada had been able to persuade its uranium customers to accept safeguards on the material they imported from Canada, it had been unable to persuade the EEC to accept full-scope safeguards as a condition of access to Canadian uranium.

The provisions regarding reprocessing represented a careful diplomatic compromise. In the main agreement, "Canada reserved the right in principle" of prior consent to Euratom decisions to reprocess or enrich Canadian-supplied uranium beyond 20 per cent, but in a separate annex to the main document Canada "waived that right in favour of 'consultation' for the two-year duration of the interim agreement."[113] During this period, exports of Canadian uranium would be limited to that volume required to meet current EEC needs: "by preventing the accumulation of uranium stocks under the interim agreement, Canada would avoid undermining its position in the later negotiations."[114]

The interim agreement on reprocessing and enrichment was replaced by a permanent agreement negotiated in 1981, after INFCE had come to a rather inconclusive end (see below). By this time market conditions had changed sufficiently to ease the concerns of both consumers and exporters regarding reprocessing and nonproliferation. The development of excess uranium production capacity and supply by 1980-1 reduced pressure on consumers to move to reprocessing and other controversial fuel cycle technologies in order to achieve energy security. Declining interest in these technologies eased producer concerns about the proliferation risks associated with their spread. Oversupply in the market also reduced the bargaining power of producers.

By mid-1982, both the United States and Australia had in effect dropped their demands for a right of prior consent to consumers' reprocessing decisions, leaving Canada as the only major supplier still insisting on such a right.[115] In the face of this erosion of the common supplier position and Ottawa's new view that the nonproliferation threat posed by European reprocessing plans was not as serious as had previously been thought, Canada and the EEC were able to reach agreement on a permanent pact, signed in December 1981, to replace the 1977 interim agreement on reprocessing and enrichment beyond 20 per cent. The agreement gave Canada considerable assurance that its uranium would not be reprocessed in a manner that could facilitate nuclear proliferation, but did not give Canada the veto over reprocessing decisions initially demanded. The pact's vague wording left considerable room for conflicting interpretations of Canada's rights and the EEC's obligations should the current consensus on reprocessing erode. In contrast, the EEC accepted what was in effect a right of prior consent for Canada over Euratom decisions to enrich Canadian uranium beyond 20 per cent. "Because the Euratom research program had not even been started concerning the use of [highly enriched uranium] in commercial reactors, Canadian authorities refused to agree to the same type of procedures instituted for the reprocessing of spent fuel."[116]

The conclusion of agreements with the United States and the EEC cleared the way for an arrangement with Japan, and in January 1978 Japan signed an agreement that fully met Canada's safeguard conditions.[117] Japan pledged not to use any Canadian-supplied materials in nuclear explosives, and accorded Canada a right of prior consent to decisions over retransfers, enrichment beyond 20 per cent and, most notably, reprocessing. Japan's acceptance of a right so strongly resisted by the EEC no doubt reflected the fact that the 1959 Canada-Japan nuclear co-operation agreement already accorded Canada the right of prior consent to Japanese reprocessing of Canadian-supplied material.

MULTILATERAL EFFORTS: 1974 TO 1981

Canada continued to promote measures to strengthen the international non-proliferation regime even while unilaterally upgrading Canadian nuclear export safeguards beyond those required by international agreements. Unilateral and multilateral measures were closely linked in Canadian policy; stricter Canadian export controls might help to persuade other countries to support stricter multilateral controls, while "raising and coordinating the general standards demanded by other states" through multilateral diplomacy could help to prevent other suppliers from undercutting the bilateral safeguards demanded by Canada.[118]

Canada joined with the U.S. in pushing for stricter safeguards in the 1970s. In the early years of the decade, the main nuclear supplier states met under the auspices of the IAEA and the NPT to draft a set of common procedures and standards to apply to their nuclear exports. The so-called Zangger Committee publicized its conclusions in September 1974, shortly after the Indian nuclear test. The suppliers agreed to require the application of IAEA safeguards to all exports of nuclear materials and equipment identified on a common "trigger list" of items.

The Zangger Committee's results fell short of what the U.S. and Canada felt was necessary in light of India's nuclear test and pending European sales of advanced nuclear fuel cycle technology to Third World states. They continued to press for stricter common safeguards requirements in secret meetings of the main nuclear suppliers that began in late 1974. These meetings included France, which had not signed the NPT and which therefore did not participate in the Zangger Committee. The United States and Canada argued that full-scope safeguards should be made a condition of all nuclear exports, and that exports of proliferation-sensitive technology (especially reprocessing and enrichment) should be prohibited or severely restricted. Canadian and American diplomats believed that reprocessing and enrichment facilities in the Third World countries presented the extreme danger that weapons-grade material would be diverted to a nuclear weapons program, and that safeguards alone could not contain this danger. However, France and West Germany refused to make full-scope safeguards a condition for all nuclear exports, and agreed only to exercise restraint in the export of sensitive technologies. The nuclear suppliers did agree late in 1975 to expand the Zangger Committee's trigger list and to apply safeguards to exports of sensitive technologies (rather than simply materials and equipment).[119]

The 1977 embargo experience strongly suggested to Canadian leaders that they had gone as far as they could by acting unilaterally. In the words of one key official:

> The suspension of deliveries made Canada more aware of the limits on the extent to which national safeguards policies, imposed unilaterally, can be an effective instrument for advancing the cause of nonproliferation. Measures imposed unilaterally can, in certain circumstances, promote nuclear proliferation rather than impede it, by compelling consumers to turn to

sources of supply with less stringent controls and by increasing the incentive to adopt nuclear technologies which carry a higher proliferation risk.[120]

Fears of supply interruptions and of control over energy policy shifting to nuclear-exporting countries encouraged Japan and Western Europe to support uranium exploration and mining in countries (especially in the Third World) that were less concerned with imposing nonproliferation export controls. These fears also encouraged consumers to contemplate resorting to exactly those raw material-saving technologies (reprocessing, fast-breeder reactors, and high enrichment) opposed by Canada and the United States.[121]

Canadian leaders ultimately concluded that "[i]t is probably not possible to put in place a fully effective system of nonproliferation controls through national policies imposed unilaterally. . . [A]n effective regime must be based upon international agreement."[122] The primary Canadian objective since the lifting of the embargo at the end of 1977 has been to try to persuade other countries to strengthen the international nonproliferation regime, rather than to try to further upgrade Canada's own safeguards requirements.[123]

The main forum for attempts to persuade other nuclear trading countries to upgrade multilateral safeguards in the period 1978 to 1980 was INFCE. At the initiative of U.S. President Carter, the leading industrialized nations agreed in May 1977 to establish an International Nuclear Fuel Cycle Evaluation to discuss proliferation and safeguards issues associated with reprocessing and other nuclear fuel cycle options. Carter's hard line against reprocessing and other technologies seen to facilitate nuclear proliferation had led to a diplomatic impasse between the U.S. on the one hand and Western Europe and Japan on the other. The establishment of INFCE was viewed as a device to overcome the impasse and to provide a forum in which to persuade energy-importing countries that reprocessing and associated technologies were both dangerous and unnecessary.

Although INFCE was supposed to be a technical evaluation of alternative fuel cycles for dealing with the problems of nuclear energy security and nonproliferation safeguards, rather than a political negotiation, it was not able to resolve differences between uranium consumers and producers over reprocessing. The former claimed that the INFCE final report showed that reprocessing was necessary and the latter claimed that INFCE had shown it to be uneconomic and unnecessary. The INFCE report also held that the proliferation risk associated with fast-breeder reactors and reprocessing was no worse than those of the standard once-through fuel cycle using enriched natural uranium.[124] This contradicted the Canadian view that these alternative fuel cycles posed greater proliferation risks. In this respect and others, including the weight it gave to assurances of fuel supply, INFCE did not support Canada's call for a substantially more stringent non-proliferation regime. Multilateral negotiations among nuclear suppliers in the 1970s led to some strengthening of common safeguards demands, but these results fell far short of Canadian hopes, and international safeguards requirements continued to be less stringent than those Canada imposed on its own nuclear exports.

THE 1980S

Nonproliferation policy has been a less contentious issue in Canadian foreign policy in the 1980s. Canada was able to persuade uranium-importing countries to accept most of the safeguards demanded by the 1974 and 1976 policies. On the most contentious issue—Canada's demand for a right of prior consent to reprocessing of fuel of Canadian origin—the degree of conflict has been diminished by changing conditions in the uranium market. Uranium demand has been far weaker than predicted due to declining global interest in nuclear power, while supply has been plentiful due to the development of rich new deposits, most notably in Saskatchewan. Weak demand, plentiful supply, and lower prices have lessened the appeal of reprocessing and other technologies that, Ottawa believes, carry special proliferation risks. The same changes have reduced importers' concerns about security of supply, concerns that in part motivated their efforts to introduce raw material-saving technologies. While still believing that the risk of proliferation is minimized when once-through fuel cycles are used, Canada is now more willing to accept the use of reprocessing and similar technologies in countries that have made a comprehensive, credible nonproliferation commitment.[125] As a result of these changes in market conditions and government policies, Canada and countries that import its uranium now have less to be concerned about as far as each others' policies are concerned.

Diminished controversy about Canadian nuclear export policy also results from the collapse of the CANDU reactor export program. No new sales have been concluded since 1976.[126] The lack of reactor sales is important because the events that triggered changes in Canadian nuclear export policy in the mid-1970s were all related to the export of reactors: India's use of a Canadian-supplied reactor to build the nuclear explosive tested in 1974 and the controversy surrounding CANDU sales to Argentina and South Korea. Reactor exports to the Third World raise much more serious questions about proliferation than do uranium sales to advanced industrialized countries.

There have been low-key discussions between Canada and countries that import Canadian uranium, discussions to minimize the degree to which Canada's nonproliferation conditions interfere with the importers' nuclear energy programs. Regarding Canada's policy requiring a right of prior consent to retransfers of Canadian material from the original importer to third countries, Ottawa has moved towards giving advance consent for retransfers to those countries whose nuclear co-operation agreements with Canada include the 1974 and 1976 nonproliferation commitments and safeguards. Similarly, Canada has adopted a "programmatic approach" towards reprocessing and plutonium storage and use by importing countries, approving programs adopted by Euratom, Sweden, Finland, and Japan rather than requiring consent on a narrower case-by-case basis. [127] These changes in policy came largely in response to EEC pressure. [128]

Canada has continued to push for a more stringent international safeguards regime. It has urged other suppliers to make full-scope safeguards a condition for supplying any nuclear material, equipment, or technology. Canada joined with Australia in lobbying for this at the Third NPT Review Conference in 1985. The final report of the Conference did endorse full-scope safeguards as a desirable objective, but due to the opposition of several West European countries, it did not require suppliers to immediately incorporate full-scope safeguards into their nuclear export agreements. [129]

Two recent developments in related Canadian trade and security policies have implications for Canada's uranium export policy. The recently concluded Canada-U.S. Free Trade Agreement contains a number of provisions concerning uranium trade. The agreement calls on the U.S. to exempt Canada from any future application of restrictions on the enrichment of foreign uranium for use in U.S. reactors. A 1964 amendment to the Atomic Energy Act of 1954 was the legislation used to keep foreign uranium out of the U.S. commercial market from the late 1960s to the early 1980s; the exemption should provide Canadian producers with more secure access to the U.S. market. Uranium is also subject to the provisions of the agreement regarding the sharing of energy resources in times of shortage. These call on the two countries not to reduce the proportion of supply that is exported to the other country in time of shortage to below the proportion that was exported in the preceding thirty-six-month period, and not to charge a higher price for exports than for output consumed domestically. [130] While this provision has raised controversy in Canada primarily because of its implications for oil and natural gas, it could also limit Canada's freedom to impose policies that raise uranium export prices (as it did in the regulations implementing the cartel in the early 1970s) and to set aside a large portion of domestic reserves for future domestic consumption (as it did in 1974). It is extremely unlikely that Canada would seek to reintroduce such measures, given current and anticipated conditions in the international uranium market, but the agreement does appear to provide U.S. uranium consumers with greater security of supply should market conditions change radically.

At the same time, the Free Trade Agreement gives both countries complete freedom to introduce export restrictions for national security reasons, including the implementation of national nonproliferation policies.[131] The trade agreement therefore does not provide American utilities with security of supply in the admittedly unlikely event that Canada demands nonproliferation conditions unacceptable to the U.S. government.

Another recent government action that may have implications for uranium export policy is Ottawa's plan to purchase nuclear-powered submarines for the Canadian Navy. Should the purchase go ahead, Canada will have to import enriched uranium to fuel the submarines (Canada has plentiful supplies of uranium, but currently has no enrichment facilities). However, Canada's own nonproliferation policy prohibits importers (including Canada's military allies) from using Canadian uranium for *any* military purpose, including as fuel for nuclear-powered submarines. If current policies are not revised, Canada will be in the hypocritical position of demanding that foreign countries maintain higher nonproliferation controls than Canada itself is willing to maintain. The Department of External Affairs currently insists that the nuclear submarine program will not lead to a relaxation of Canada's nonproliferation policy, a position that flies in the face of common sense.[132] There is also the broader question of how consistent the acquisition of nuclear-powered weaponry is with Canada's principled opposition to the spread of nuclear weapons. This question can be answered only subjectively, and opinions differ.[133] To this observer, the willingness to acquire nuclear-powered weapons indicates that nonproliferation is no longer the overriding foreign policy objective that it was claimed to be in the 1970s.[134]

CONCLUSIONS: CANADA AS AN INSECURE SUPPLIER

Canada's demands for stricter safeguards on its uranium exports and its imposition of an export embargo to persuade consumers to accept the new safeguards caused uranium importers to perceive Canadian supply as less secure than they had thought. "[T]he shock of politically caused supply disruptions damaged European and Japanese confidence in policy-makers in Ottawa,"[135] especially since these disruptions came at a time when Canadian leaders professed to be seeking closer economic ties with Europe and Japan to counterbalance Canada's dependence on the United States.

Some consuming countries responded to the embargo by seeking alternative sources of supply. This effort probably cost Canada some exports.[136] However, the loss was limited by certain characteristics of the international uranium market.

As Table 3 indicated, there are few sizable alternative sources of supply. Furthermore, African suppliers pose greater security-of-supply risks than does Canada, while Australia's uranium export policies have been at least as turbulent as Canada's. This suggests that while Canadian uranium supply has not been very secure by the standards of most mineral markets, it has been no worse than average by the standards of the uranium market.

Market conditions in the early 1980s have also reduced the impact of Canada's nonproliferation policies on its exports of uranium. The existence of excess uranium production capacity, the emergence of active secondary markets for natural and enriched uranium, [137] and the accumulation of massive inventories in consuming countries have all reduced consumer fears. In this environment, consumers are more concerned about prices than supplier reliability, and Canada is well placed to compete on price. Large high-grade, low-cost reserves in Saskatchewan have been developed in recent years. These mines have captured a large proportion of new international uranium demand. [138]

Because of the desire to maintain access to Canadian uranium reserves in the face of uncertainty about Canadian export policy, utilities and other firms from Germany, France, Japan, Britain, and other consuming countries have become increasingly involved in exploration and mining in Canada. This involvement has been actively encouraged by the governments of importing countries. By investing in Canada, consumers hope to gain some leverage over the Canadian government in order to restrict its ability to manipulate supply to achieve economic or political objectives. [139]

The behaviour of uranium importers suggests that Canada is considered an insecure supplier of uranium. [140] This insecurity results from the lack of a dependable consensus within Canada on the issue of nuclear exports; the country has had great difficulty making collective decisions about nuclear exports and modifying those decisions in light of changing circumstances.

The absence of a consensus on nuclear exports characterizes both the federal government and Canadian public opinion. Some Canadian leaders and government officials are strongly committed to promoting exports of uranium and nuclear reactors, while others are much more concerned with preventing the spread of nuclear weapons and are willing to forego export sales in pursuit of this objective.

The lack of consensus within government is mirrored and exacerbated by a lack of consensus among the public. Canadian public opinion does not fully support nuclear exports even when accompanied by stringent safeguards. Antinuclear groups are active on the issue of exports, and the overall level of public interest is high. Nuclear export policy must therefore be very sensitive to domestic political considerations. While the Canadian nuclear industry has consistently opposed safeguards that are more restrictive than international norms, its voice has not prevailed in periods when nuclear export policy has become a prominent domestic political issue.

A strong consensus in favour of nuclear exports existed only in the late 1940s and 1950s, when the economic and security implications of such exports to Canada's closest allies were mutually reinforcing. This period also predated the rise of vocal anti-nuclear sentiment domestically. In subsequent periods, there have been frequent conflicts between economic and security considerations. These led, in 1974–7, to the adoption of policies that caused consumers to perceive Canada as a less secure supplier of uranium.

While policies implemented from 1974 to 1981 have reduced public concern about the danger that Canadian exports will contribute to nuclear proliferation, opposition to nuclear exports is far from dead. An external shock comparable to the Indian nuclear explosive test of 1974 could trigger renewed domestic opposition to nuclear exports. Given the lack of consensus within government on the issue, such a shock could lead to another period of instability in Canadian policy.

The conflict between Canada's economic interest in nuclear exports and its perceived security interest in preventing nuclear proliferation is paralleled by an international conflict between importers' and exporters' strategic interests in international nuclear trade. Overall, there has not been a strong international consensus on arrangements to ensure both security of supply and nonproliferation. Neither importers nor exporters are willing to sacrifice important strategic objectives. Countries in one group have not been in a strong position (individually or in concert) to impose their conception of proper arrangements on countries in the other group. The ever-changing attempts to resolve this conflict have been heavily influenced by market conditions. Canada attempted unilaterally to modify safeguard arrangements in the mid-1970s when it appeared to have considerable market power. Conflict with importers was intense because their concerns about energy security were very high in the period immediately following the oil crisis. Final resolution of the conflict in 1981 was facilitated by a combination of increasing supply and unexpectedly slow growth in demand. The resulting market weakness reduced Canadian fears that consumers would turn to proliferation-sensitive nuclear fuel cycles, and reduced consumers' fears about energy security. Oversupply and the emergence of alternative sources also reduced the ability of traditional suppliers to press for upgraded safeguards. The conflict between importers' and exporters' strategic concerns will likely remain muted as long as current market conditions persist and as long as there are no major shocks comparable to the oil crisis or the Indian nuclear test.

Cutting across both the issue of Canada's insecurity as a supplier and the strategic concerns of importers and exporters are issues of Canadian economic development. Canada's increased interest in export controls in the 1970s was triggered primarily by the consequences of inadequately safeguarded exports of nuclear *reactors,* not uranium. These exports (to India and Pakistan) or agreements to export (to Argentina and South Korea) were part of a conscious government strategy to establish a strong Canadian presence in a high technology industrial sector.

However, while the security concerns were triggered by exports of reactors, they were dealt with primarily through the attempted exercise of market power in the uranium sector. Exports of CANDU reactors were subject to the same controls as exports of uranium. However, the international reactor market has long been a buyer's market, with a number of governments promoting and subsidizing reactor exports. This meant that withholding access to CANDU reactors did not provide Canada with any bargaining leverage to implement upgraded nuclear safeguards. In contrast, the international uranium market in the mid-1970s was very much a seller's market. Export controls on uranium appeared to hold the promise of achieving political and security objectives without excessive economic sacrifices. [141] While these export controls contributed to Canada's ability to get consumers to agree to stricter nuclear safeguards, they did so only at a cost to Canada's reputation as a secure supplier of strategic minerals.

NOTES

1 Analysts stress that a state intent upon developing nuclear weapons can reach that objective more quickly and cheaply by means of a nuclear program designed expressly for that purpose than it could by means of an adjunct to a civilian nuclear reactor program. Nevertheless, a country wishing to secretly acquire nuclear weapons could use a civilian nuclear program to clandestinely divert plutonium to a weapons program and to acquire the technological capacity and some of the specialized facilities needed to produce nuclear weapons. Robert Boardman and James F. Keeley, "Introduction," in *Nuclear Exports and World Politics: Policy and Regime,* ed. Boardman and Keeley (London: Macmillan 1983), 4–5.

2 An academic exception to this consensus is Kenneth Waltz, "The Spread of Nuclear Weapons: More May be Better," *Adelphi Papers,* no. 171 (London: International Institute for Strategic Studies 1981). No Western governments publicly support this view, although Third World governments interested in acquiring nuclear weapons presumably believe that the acquisition would enhance their own national security.

3 Boardman and Keeley, "Introduction," 5–6, 13; Leonard S. Spector, *Nuclear Proliferation Today* (Cambridge, MA: Ballinger 1984).

4 Mark J. Moher, Director, Nuclear Division, Department of External Affairs, "Nuclear Suppliers and Nonproliferation: A Canadian Perspective," in *The Nuclear Suppliers and Nonproliferation: International Policy Choices,* ed. Rodney W. Jones et al. (Lexington, MA: Lexington Books 1985), 43. The belief in the danger of nuclear proliferation coexists with the Canadian government's belief that nuclear weapons enhance Canada's own national security, as manifested by Canadian support for NATO's and NORAD's nuclear deterrent forces. See David G. Haglund, "The Canadian SSN Program and the Nonproliferation Question," in *The U.S.-Canada Security Relationship: The Politics, Strategy, and Technology of Defense,* ed. David G. Haglund and Joel J. Sokolsky (Boulder, CO: Westview Press 1989).

5 Ottawa's efforts to reduce the likelihood of nuclear proliferation predated the rise of strong popular concern; see below.

6 Those countries that possess or seek to acquire nuclear weapons may also have a more traditional military strategic interest in uranium trade.

7 See introduction to this volume.

8 With the exception of France, which has substantial domestic resources and production.

9 Thomas L. Neff, *The International Uranium Market* (Cambridge, MA: Ballinger 1984), 42.

10 Steven J. Warnecke, *Uranium, Nonproliferation and Energy Security* (Paris: Atlantic Institute for International Affairs 1979), 10.

11 Neff, *International Uranium Market*, 5–6. This advantage exists, of course, only if the processing stages are located either in the consuming country itself or in countries that pose less of a security-of-supply risk than do the uranium producers.

12 Warnecke, *Uranium, Nonproliferation, and Energy Security*, 10.

13 The nonproliferation conditions suppliers impose on their uranium exports are by no means the only factor influencing import-dependent consumers' perceptions of supply security. Nevertheless, they have been the primary source of political conflict between exporters and importers. Canadian participation in the uranium cartel, which generated some tension in Canadian-American relations, will also be dealt with briefly below.

14 This tension is recognized by Canadian officials; see, for example, Mark. J. Moher, Director, Nuclear Division, Department of External Affairs, "The Policies of Supplier Nations," in *Nuclear Nonproliferation and Global Security*, ed. David B. Dewitt (London: Croom Helm 1987), 85.

15 This is a central theme of Ron Finch, *Exporting Danger: A History of the Canadian Nuclear Energy Export Programme* (Montreal: Black Rose Books 1986).

16 Most uranium is sold on forward contracts rather than spot markets.

17 Neff, *International Uranium Market*, 214–6.

18 J.W. Griffith, *The Uranium Industry: Its History, Technology and Prospects*, Mineral Report 12 (Ottawa: Mineral Resources Division, Department of Energy, Mines and Resources 1967), 21.

19 *Canadian Minerals Yearbook 1974*, 558.

20 See Robert Bothwell, *Eldorado: Canada's National Uranium Company* (Toronto: University of Toronto Press 1984), especially Ch. 4 and 5; Griffith, *The Uranium Industry*, 7–8; Finch, *Exporting Danger*, Ch. 1 and 102–4.

21 James Eayrs, *In Defence of Canada: Peacemaking and Deterrence* (Toronto: University of Toronto Press 1972), Ch. 5: "Controlling the Atom."

22 Cited in J.A. Munro and A.I. Inglis, "The Atomic Conference 1945 and the Pearson Memoirs," *International Journal* 29 (Winter 1973/74):96, 98.

23 "Joint Declaration on Atomic Energy," in *Canadian Foreign Policy 1945–54: Selected Speeches and Documents*, ed. R.A. Mackay (Toronto: McClelland & Stewart, 1971), 113.

24 Eayrs, *In Defence of Canada: Peacemaking and Deterrence*, 282–95.

25 Jonathan E. Helmreich, *Gathering Rare Ores: The Diplomacy of Uranium Acquisition, 1943–1954* (Princeton, NJ: Princeton University Press 1986).

26 One of these was Elliot Lake, located in soon-to-be-Prime Minister Lester Pearson's riding, adding a personal dimension to the potential conflict in Canadian policy between the economic and security implications of uranium exports. Earle Gray, *The Great Uranium Cartel* (Toronto: McClelland & Stewart 1982), 70–1.

27 Gray, *Great Uranium Cartel*, 41–53; Griffith, *Uranium Industry*, xi, 9–12.

28 "Agreement for Co-operation Concerning Civil Uses of Atomic Energy Between the Government of Canada and the Government of the United States of America," signed 15 June 1955. *Canada Treaty Series* 1955, no. 15, p. 2.

29 For example, Canadian access to enriched uranium (even when Canada was the original supplier of that uranium) was limited to an amount that the USAEC deemed not to be of military significance. *Canada Treaty Series*, 10, 14–16.

30 "Canada experienced a balance of payments crisis in 1947, as imports from the U.S. expanded much faster than exports to the U.S. after the end of the war and European consumers were unable to pay for Canadian goods in convertible currencies. Expanding exports to the U.S. was a high priority of makers of Canadian economic policy in the late 1940s and 1950s. R.D. Cuff and J.L. Granatstein, *American Dollars—Canadian Prosperity* (Toronto: Samuel-Stevens 1978).

31 The U.K. Atomic Energy Agency instituted similar cutbacks, although its purchase had never approached the scale and importance of USAEC purchases.

32 Gray, *Great Uranium Cartel*, 58–9; Griffith, *Uranium Industry*, 13; Marian Radetzki, *Uranium: A Strategic Source of Energy* (London: Croom Helm 1981), 43.

33 Griffith, *Uranium Industry*, xi; Ted Greenwood with Alvin Streeter, jr., "Uranium," in *Natural Resources in U.S.-Canadian Relations*, Volume II: *Patterns and Trends in Resource Supplies and Policies* Carl E. Beigie and Alfred O. Hero, ed. (Boulder, CO: Westview Press 1980), 346–7; Gray, *Great Uranium Cartel*, 68.

34 Radetzki, *Uranium: A Strategic Source of Energy*, 45; Griffith, *Uranium Industry*, iii, 82–3; interviews.

35 The USAEC decreed that foreign uranium enriched in its facilities (then the only enrichment facilities outside the Soviet bloc) could not be used in domestic nuclear reactors; Gray, *Great Uranium Cartel*, 80–6.

36 Statement by the Honourable Alastair Gillespie, Minister of Energy, Mines and Resources, and "A Background Paper on the Canadian Uranium Industry's Activities in International Uranium Marketing," Ottawa, 11 Sept. 1976. Hereinafter cited as Gillespie, "Statement and Background Paper."

37 As noted above, the 1955 Canada-U.S. nuclear co-operation agreement required that transfers to third parties be covered by U.S.-specified safeguards. See also Lawrence Scheinman, "Security and a Transnational System: The Case of Nuclear Energy," *International Organization* 25 (Summer 1971):637–8.

38 Bothwell, *Eldorado*, 408.

39 Bothwell, *Eldorado*, 407–9.

40 Constance Hunt, "Canadian Policy and the Export of Nuclear Energy," *University of Toronto Law Journal* 27 (Winter 1977):77.

41 Bothwell, *Eldorado*, 404.

42 Finch, *Exporting Danger*, 33, 81–2; Bothwell, *Eldorado*, 404–5; Michael Tucker, *Canadian Foreign Policy: Contemporary Issues and Themes* (Toronto: McGraw-Hill Ryerson 1980), 204.

43 Hunt, "Canadian Policy and the Export of Nuclear Energy," 78–81.

44 Robert W. Morrison and Edward F. Wonder, *Canada's Nuclear Export Policy*, Carleton International Studies 1978/III (Ottawa: Norman Paterson School of International Affairs, Carleton University, Oct. 1978), 60.

45 Hunt, "Canadian Policy and the Export of Nuclear Energy," 81.

46 Morrison and Wonder, *Canada's Nuclear Export Policy*, 61.

47 James F. Keeley, "Canadian Nuclear Export Policy and the Problems of Proliferation," *Canadian Public Policy* 6 (Autumn 1980):615.

48 Department of External Affairs, "A Background Paper on Nuclear Safeguards and Canadian Safeguards Policy" (Ottawa, 30 Jan. 1976), 12. Other weaknesses that were not addressed in the NPT are summarized in Finch, *Exporting Danger*, 193–8, 201–5.

49 Department of External Affairs, "Background Paper on Nuclear Safeguards and Canadian Safeguards Policy," 12–13.

50 Charlotte S.M. Girard, *Canada in World Affairs*, vol. 13: *1963–1965* (Toronto: Canadian Institute of International Affairs 1979), 213–24. For additional details, see P.R. Johansson and Douglas Ross, "Canadian Nuclear Export Policy and the International Nonproliferation Regime" (unpublished manuscript).

51 However, French negotiators again attributed Canada's stance to U.S. pressure; see Scheinman, "Security and a Transnational System," 638.

52 House of Commons, *Debates*, 3 June 1965, 1948–9, and 4 June 1965, 1980–1.

53 The uranium cartel is discussed in greater detail in Michael C. Webb with Mark W. Zacher, *Canada and International Mineral Markets: Dependence, Instability, and Foreign Policy* (Kingston, Ont.: Queen's University Centre for Resource Studies 1988).

54 Gray, *Great Uranium Cartel*, 95–9; Hugh C. McIntyre, *Uranium, Nuclear Power, and Canada-U.S. Energy Relations* (Montreal and Washington: Canadian-American Committee 1978), 15.

55 N.M. Ediger, Memo of meeting on 8 Dec. 1971 with Mr. Austin and Mr. McNabb of EMR, quoted in L.T. Gregg to H.E. Hoffman, "Draft: Summary of Developments in International Uranium Meetings," 17 Feb. 1971, in: United States, Hearings Before the Subcommittee on Oversight and Investigations of the Committee on Interstate and Foreign Commerce of the House of Representatives, *International Uranium Cartel*, vol. 1, 95th Cong., 1st sess. (Washington: U.S. Government

Printing Office 1977), 462 (hereinafter cited as *International Uranium Cartel*, vol. 1; the second volume of these hearings will be cited as *International Uranium Cartel*, vol. 2).

56 Interview with government official; Gray, *Great Uranium Cartel*, 102–4; Larry R. Stewart, "Canada's Role in the International Uranium Cartel," *International Organization* 35 (Autumn 1981):662.

57 Interview with government official; Gillespie, "Statement and Background Paper."

58 For remarkably detailed accounts of these meetings, see Gray, *Great Uranium Cartel*, Ch. 8; documents reprinted in *International Uranium Cartel*, vols. 1 and 2, and in United States, Hearings Before the Subcommittee on Oversight and Investigations of the Committee on Interstate and Foreign Commerce of the House of Representatives, *International Uranium Supply and Demand*, 94th cong., 2nd sess., 4 Nov. 1976. (Washington: U.S. Government Printing Office 1977) (hereinafter cited as *International Uranium Supply and Demand*).

59 See document containing text of agreement reached at Johannesburg, 29 May to 2 June 1972, in *International Uranium Supply and Demand*, 184–95.

60 Neff, *International Uranium Market*, 16. Prices given are in nominal U.S. dollars. The 1977 price in 1972 dollars was $30 per pound.

61 Neff, *International Uranium Market*, 46–50, 113–4; Radetzki, *Uranium: A Strategic Source of Energy*, 81–94, 125, 129; Nuclear Exchange Corporation, "Significant Events in the Uranium Market 1969–1976," 15 Oct. 1976, reprinted in *International Uranium Supply and Demand*, 363–74.

62 Gray, *Great Uranium Cartel*, 150–3; Greenwood, "Uranium," 347–8.

63 See Neff, *International Uranium Market*, 49, for a representative view. Radetzki, *Uranium: A Strategic Source of Energy*, Ch. 7, attributes more of the price increase to the activities of the cartel.

64 At least in the early stages; see Gray, *Great Uranium Cartel*, 105–6, 161, for details of communications between Canada and the United States.

65 *Manchester Guardian*, cited in Gray, *Great Uranium Cartel*, 163.

66 O.J.C. Runnals, "Memorandum: Meeting of Canadian Uranium Producers, May 9," Department of Energy, Mines and Resources, in *International Uranium Cartel*, vol. 1, 535, regarding Uranerz. See June H. Taylor and Michael D. Yokell, *Yellowcake: The International Uranium Cartel* (New York: Pergammon Press 1979), 72, on the close ties between RTZ and the British government.

67 Not even all uranium-consuming utilities were critical.

68 Stewart, "Canada's Role in the International Uranium Cartel," 684–7.

69 Radetzki, *Uranium: A Strategic Source of Energy*, 112.

70 See Warnecke, *Uranium, Nonproliferation, and Energy Security*, 110–11, for an argument from a European perspective that cartel prices were not excessive in light of the security-of-supply concerns.

71 O.J.C. Runnals, Department of Energy, Mines and Resources, "The Uranium Industry in Canada" (Brief submitted to the Cluff Lake Board of Inquiry, Regina, Saskatchewan, Apr. 1977), 35, 48–51.

72 Radetzki, *Uranium: A Strategic Source of Energy*, 128.

73 See exchange of letters between Prime Minister Trudeau and Prime Minister Indira Gandhi in 1971, cited in Finch, *Exporting Danger*, 83–4. See also Tucker, *Canadian Foreign Policy: Contemporary Issues and Themes*, 204–6.

74 Keeley, "Canadian Nuclear Export Policy and the Problems of Proliferation," 614–15.

75 J.S. Stanford, Director General of the Bureau of Commercial and Commodity Relations, Department of External Affairs, "Commentary on Foreign Policy and International Control," in *Canadian Nuclear Policies*, ed. G. Bruce Doern and Robert W. Morrison (Montreal: Institute for Research on Public Policy 1980), 161; Morrison and Wonder, *Canada's Nuclear Export Policy*, 63, 103–4; Finch, *Exporting Danger*, especially 98.

76 Department of External Affairs, "Background Paper on Nuclear Safeguards and Department Safeguards Policy," 17; see also Hunt, "Canadian Policy and the Export of Nuclear Energy," 83.

77 House of Commons, *Debates*, 20 Dec. 1974, 2429.

78 Finch, *Exporting Danger*, 87, suggests that the additional safeguards were not announced until it was known whether South Korea and Argentina would agree to have these conditions attached to their pending purchases of CANDU reactors; "It appears . . . that Ottawa did not want to commit itself domestically to anything that could threaten a reactor export."

79 Morrison and Wonder, *Canada's Nuclear Export Policy*, 64, 103.

80 Department of External Affairs, "Background Paper on Nuclear Safeguards and Canadian Safeguards

Policy," 21. The fact that India had derived the plutonium used in its nuclear test from the reprocessing of spent fuel appears to have contributed to the determination of Canadian leaders to impose strict safeguards on reprocessing. See Department of External Affairs, "Canada's Nuclear Non-Proliferation Policy," *Canadian Foreign Policy Texts* (May 1982), 9.

81 House of Commons, *Debates*, 20 Dec. 1974, 2428. The deadline was subsequently extended to 31 Dec. 1976.

82 McIntyre, *Uranium, Nuclear Power, and Canada-U.S. Energy Relations*, 49.

83 Nuclear Exchange Corporation, "Significant Events in the Uranium Market 1969–1976"; Neff, *International Uranium Market*, 49.

84 Department of External Affairs, "Background Paper on Nuclear Safeguards and Department Safeguards Policy," 6.

85 John J. Noble, Special Adviser, Safeguards, Commodity and Energy Policy Division, Department of External Affairs, "Canada's Continuing Search for Acceptable Nuclear Safeguards," *International Perspectives* (July/Aug. 1978), 44–5.

86 Both Presidents Ford and Carter experienced difficulty in devising an administration policy and in getting legislation approved by Congress. Carter's Nuclear Nonproliferation Act did not finally pass until March 1978. See Neff, *International Uranium Market*, 57–63, on this tortuous process. See Johannson and Ross, "Canadian Nuclear Export Policy," Ch. 5, 25–7, on Canada-U.S. negotiations.

87 Warnecke, *Uranium, Nonproliferation, and Energy Security*, 11, 18, 23–4, 79; Frank Langdon, *The Politics of Canadian-Japanese Economic Relations, 1952–1983* (Vancouver: University of British Columbia Press 1983), 106.

88 The European position is outlined in detail in Warnecke, *Uranium, Nonproliferation, and Energy Security*.

89 Representatives of West German utilities claimed that Canadian officials had told them the embargo would be lifted if consumers agreed to provisions for escalating prices in new uranium contracts. See Johannson and Ross, "Canadian Nuclear Export Policy," Ch. 5.

90 Excluding material of Canadian origin from French facilities would also conflict with the Euratom principle of non-discrimination, although France itself had violated this principle. Neff, *International Uranium Market*, 32–3, 56.

91 Noble, "Canada's Continuing Search for Acceptable Nuclear Safeguards," 45.

92 Langdon, *Politics of Canadian-Japanese Economic Relations*, 106.

93 Moher, "Nuclear Suppliers and Nonproliferation," 43–4.

94 House of Commons, *Debates*, 22 Dec. 1976, 2255, 2260.

95 Noble, "Canada's Continuing Search for Acceptable Nuclear Safeguards," 45.

96 House of Commons, *Debates*, 22 Dec. 1976, 2256.

97 Johannson and Ross, "Canadian Nuclear Export Policy."

98 W. MacOwan, "The Nuclear Industry and the NPT," in Dewitt, *Nuclear Non-Proliferation and Global Security*, 145–7.

99 House of Commons, *Debates*, 22 Dec. 1976, 2255.

100 Stanford, "Commentary on Foreign Policy and International Control," 161. Critics argued that the new safeguards policy was merely a sop to public opinion that would permit uranium and reactor exports to continue while doing little to ensure that Canadian uranium and reactor exports did not contribute to nuclear proliferation; see Finch, *Exporting Danger*, especially pp. 98–9. This argument ignores the independent commitment that most makers of foreign policy had to nonproliferation and the costs (lost uranium exports and, more significant, lost CANDU sales) attributable to the policy.

101 Morrison and Wonder, *Canada's Nuclear Export Policy*, 96.

102 Johannson and Ross, "Canadian Nuclear Export Policy," Ch. 5; Noble, "Canada's Continuing Search for Acceptable Nuclear Safeguards," 45.

103 Noble, "Canada's Continuing Search for Acceptable Nuclear Safeguards," 45.

104 Johannson and Ross, "Canadian Nuclear Export Policy," Ch. 5.

105 The same arrangement applied to material of U.S. origin in transit through Canada.

106 Johannson and Ross, "Canadian Nuclear Export Policy," 30.

107 Keeley, "Canadian Nuclear Export Policy and the Problems of Proliferation," 622.

108 House of Commons, *Debates*, 19 Dec. 1977, 1997.

109 Stanford, "Commentary on Foreign Policy and International Control," 163.

110 House of Commons, *Debates*, 19 Dec. 1977, 1998.
111 Noble, "Canada's Continuing Search for Acceptable Nuclear Safeguards," 45–6.
112 Noble, "Canada's Continuing Search for Acceptable Nuclear Safeguards," 45–6; Morrison and Wonder, *Canada's Nuclear Export Policy,* 96.
113 Quoted in Morrison and Wonder, *Canada's Nuclear Export Policy,* 96; Noble, "Canada's Continuing Search for Acceptable Nuclear Safeguards," 46.
114 Keeley, "Canadian Nuclear Export Policy and the Problems of Proliferation" 620.
115 Neff, *International Uranium Market,* 63, 65–8.
116 Johannson and Ross, "Canadian Nuclear Export Policy," 41–2.
117 The agreement took the form of a protocol amending the 1959 Canada-Japan nuclear co-operation agreement.
118 Keeley, "Canadian Nuclear Export Policy and the Problems of Proliferation," 623.
119 The 1975 agreement was not made public until 1978. See, on the Zangger Committee and the Nuclear Suppliers' Group: Spector, *Nuclear Proliferation Today,* 446–50; Moher, "The Policies of Supplier Nations," 90–3; Lawrence Scheinman, *The International Atomic Energy Agency and World Nuclear Order* (Washington: Resources for the Future 1987), 23, 190–1; and Keeley, "Canadian Nuclear Export Policy and the Problems of Proliferation," 623.
120 Stanford, "Commentary on Foreign Policy and International Control," 163.
121 Warnecke, *Uranium, Nonproliferation, and Energy Security,* 26–7.
122 Stanford, "Commentary on Foreign Policy and International Control," 163.
123 Department of External Affairs, "Canada's Nuclear Non-Proliferation Policy," 22.
124 Philip Gummett, "From NPT to INFCE: Developments in Thinking About Nuclear Non-Proliferation," *International Affairs* 57 (Autumn 1981):557–61.
125 Moher, "Nuclear Suppliers and Nonproliferation: A Canadian Perspective," 50.
126 A possible sale to Romania negotiated in the mid-1970s appears to have collapsed due to Romania's inability to pay for it; Finch, *Exporting Danger,* 141–4.
127 Moher, "Nuclear Suppliers and Nonproliferation: A Canadian Perspective," 48–50.
128 On European pressure, see *Globe and Mail,* 22 Apr. 1983, B6, and 6 May 1983, B3.
129 Moher, "The Policies of Supplier Nations," 103–4; David A.V. Fischer, "The Third NPT Review Conference, Geneva, 27 August to 21 September 1985: A Retrospective," in Dewitt, *Nuclear Nonproliferation and Global Security,* 218.
130 Department of External Affairs, *The Canada-U.S. Free Trade Agreement: Text and Explanatory Notes* (Ottawa: Minister of Supply and Services 1988), 145–46.
131 Department of External Affairs, *Canada-U.S. Free Trade Agreement,* Article 907, 147–8.
132 Haglund, "The Department SSN Program and the Nonproliferation Question," 24–5.
133 Haglund, "The Canadian SSN Program and the Nonproliferation Question," assesses a number of possible answers.
134 Others argue, from very different perspectives, that there has always been a great deal of hypocrisy in Canada's nonproliferation policy. Finch, *Exporting Danger,* argues that promoting nuclear reactor exports has always had a higher priority than nonproliferation except when domestic anti-nuclear sentiment was high. Haglund, "The Canadian SSN Program and the Nonproliferation Question," suggests that Canada's nonproliferation policy is inconsistent with its active membership in NATO and NORAD, military alliances that explicitly rely on nuclear weapons to defend North America and Western Europe.
135 Warnecke, *Uranium, Nonproliferation, and Energy Security,* 19. On the basis of interviews in Japan, Frank Langdon concluded that "a lasting impression among Japanese officials was that they could not rely upon Canadian economic cooperation." *The Politics of Canadian-Japanese Economic Relations,* 108.
136 Neff, *International Uranium Market,* 234–5, 247, on Germany and Japan. See also Warnecke, *Uranium, Nonproliferation, and Energy Security,* 96–102.
137 Utilities that signed contracts for supplies far in excess of their eventual needs have tried to sell some of the excess to other consumers; this is what is meant by the term "secondary market."
138 This has been possible because the federal government has been willing to approve export contracts at prices well below those specified in the late 1970s. On the Saskatchewan mines and their place in the market, see Neff, *International Uranium Market,* 12–15.
139 Warnecke, *Uranium, Nonproliferation, and Energy Security,* 85, 96, 99–102; Neff, *International Uranium Market,* 12–15.

140 The constant efforts of government officials to present Canada as a secure supplier—and to argue that strict nonproliferation controls are necessary to maintain the security of Canadian supply, since Canadian public opinion would oppose exports not accompanied by stringent safeguards—reveal that Ottawa recognizes the doubts that its policies have raised in the eyes of foreign uranium consumers.

141 In contrast, export controls clearly led to the loss of a number of reactor sales that the Canadian reactor industry needed in order to survive.

Part V

8

Conclusion: Current Issues in the International Politics of Strategic Minerals and Their Implications for Canada

David G. Haglund

INTRODUCTION

As shown in earlier chapters, concern for some aspect of their strategic mineral supply has been an intermittent worry of the industrialized states for much of this century. This chapter assesses the likely implications for Canada in the event of a renewed wave of uneasiness regarding strategic minerals; of particular interest will be the possibility that such worry might get translated into policies on the part of Canada's trading partners that could have an impact, positive or otherwise, on Canadian mineral production. Although Canada itself, as has been noted in both the Finlayson and Blair chapters, does have significant *import* interests that are not substantially different from those of other developed countries, it is primarily the export side of Canadian strategic mineral developments that will merit attention in this concluding chapter. On the one hand, Canadian mineral supply might come to take on a "political value added" due to the perception of Canada as a stable, reliable source of supply in a world marked by increasing instability and chaos.[1] On the other hand, in some instances Canada might be adversely affected should nervous consumers, above all the United States, begin to adopt mineral-sourcing strategies that inadvertently redound to the detriment of Canadian export interests. Among the most widely discussed possibilities in this context, of course, has been the seabed-mining question, but as we shall see, other "vulnerability-reducing" options potentially open to the U.S. and fellow OECD members could have a backlash on Canada.

CONTEMPORARY MEANING AND NATURE OF VULNERABILITY

Because of its relevance to any basic understanding of strategic minerals questions, the concept of "vulnerability" warrants a brief discussion here—a discussion that supplements my earlier treatment of the term in Chapter 1. There I denoted some of the conditions held by most minerals analysts to be associated with a finding that a commodity, or country, is in some sense "vulnerable" to supply disruption, and I only wish at this juncture to note again that it is a staple of minerals analysis to regard "dependence" as being qualitatively different from the far more serious condition we call vulnerability. To treat the two synonymously is not only fallacious; it is also counterproductive, if what one intends to do is contribute to rational policy debate.

Few would quarrel with the above conclusion. Indeed, Bruce Russett has recently summed up the major reasons for not letting a concern about import dependence boil over into a conclusion that only forcible access will provide guarantees for the continued provision of raw material supply; and in his argument (to which I shall presently return) he draws upon the much discussed distinction, developed by Robert Keohane and Joseph Nye, between "sensitivity" and "vulnerability" interdependence.[2] However laudable, not to say vital, is the objective of attaining rigour in policy analysis, it is far from easy to achieve conceptual clarity, even in regard to such highly important terms as dependence and vulnerability. Take, for example, the Keohane/Nye distinction: if the differentiation is to have any use whatsoever, it is precisely because it permits us to gauge the relative efficacy of measures designed to reduce the adverse costs imposed from without that we associate with the negative aspects of interdependence. As the authors phrase it, "in terms of the costs of dependence, sensitivity means liability to costly effects imposed from outside before policies are altered to try to change the situation. Vulnerability can be defined as an actor's liability to suffer costs imposed by external events even after policies have been altered."[3]

The problem with the terminology available to the mineral analysis community is not, as is sometimes argued, that interdependence cannot logically mean anything other than "vulnerability" interdependence, although those who make such claims (for instance, David Baldwin or Kenneth Waltz) are not without support for their arguments.[4] The problem is rather that vulnerability has commonly come to be used in a way that denudes it of the static qualities that apparently give it the meaning it is supposed to have, if, to repeat, it is to be distinguished from dependence. States, according to this view, are truly only vulnerable if they lack policy options that can mitigate the costly effects of their dependence upon other states; if they have such options, they are at worst sensitive to the imposition of short-term costs generated beyond their borders, by forces over which, for the moment, they have little control.

One logical implication of a strict interpretation of vulnerability along the lines of, say Keohane and Nye, is that it becomes almost a contradiction in terms to speak of strategies for reducing or mitigating vulnerability; for, as we have seen, the truly vulnerable are precisely those luckless states that suffer what they must at the hands of countries and forces more powerful than they. It quickly becomes clear what is wrong, for the purposes of minerals analysis, with such a construe: in attempting to render more flexible our language, so as to answer the very compelling need for concepts that will enable us, as Bruce Russett and others argue, to make the kinds of distinctions we need between one's levels of imports—in and of themselves suggestive of nothing necessarily more noteworthy than convenience—and one's inability to achieve any freedom of manoeuvre vis-à-vis international minerals markets, we run the risk of impoverishing our vocabulary. Ironically, though we take notice of those authors, such as Baldwin or Waltz, who would have us discard the notion that there could be something labeled "sensitivity interdependence,"[5] we might rather pay heed to a call for abolition of the concept "vulnerability interdependence." For insofar as raw material supply is concerned, the reality is how *little* most industrialized states really are at the mercy of minerals forces beyond their control. We are all, it seems, able to avoid the pains of genuine vulnerability, at least when it comes to our mineral imports, though this is not a universally accepted contention, as is shown below.

Why is such frequent resort made to the notion of vulnerability in attempting to describe and explain contemporary minerals postures and policies of so many Western consuming countries?[6] The short answer is that it seems to be necessary, and nothing better has suggested itself than this somewhat misleading term. This is so because such heavy use is made of that other term, "dependence," when referring to the *net import reliance* of any given country.[7] All this is more than a little reminiscent of the famous Abbott and Costello skit, "Who's on First?" What we have been engaged in is a confusing series of conceptual displacements, a linguistic Gresham's law, with perfectly good terminology being bumped aside by newer, but imperfect, usages. Consider the reasonably cogent attempt made several years ago by James Caporaso to draw a line between dependence and dependency: while the latter term was held to connote nothing so much as the "absence of actor autonomy," the former was considered to be subject to structural specification. What Caporaso's analysis showed him was that import dependence involved a combination of the following characteristics: essentiality of the good in question; concentration of its supply; and the substitution, conservation, or diversification options available to the consumer of the good.[8]

Now compare this set of conditions with that drawn up by two prominent minerals economists, Hans Landsberg and John Tilton, who take pains to differentiate sharply between import dependence and vulnerability. It may be, they argue, that the former is a necessary condition of the latter; but it is not a sufficient one. Among other factors relevant to a determination of vulnerability are: the identity of exporters; the diversification prospects of importers; domestic production possibilities; opportunities for substitution and conservation; the essentiality of the imported commodity; and the presence of stockpiles.[9] Though their index contains a few more items than Caporaso's, it is apparent that what the two economists mean when they employ the term "vulnerability" is nothing other than what the political scientist intends by the word "dependence."

As a political scientist who has a tolerable respect for the sharp edge of Ockham's razor, it might seem odd that I advocate employing the economists' category of vulnerability. I do so as a concession to practice; for the reality is that, to the majority of minerals analysts, vulnerability has become since the mid-1970s a virtually irreplaceable concept; whereas dependence has come to take on the connotation formerly associated with levels of imports (or, net import reliance). By now such copious reference has been made to the hazards of "import vulnerability," and the need for policies capable of reducing, mitigating, or even eliminating it, that it would be senseless to insist upon the synonymous usage of vulnerability and dependence, at least for the purposes of the present volume on minerals. Accordingly, I shall treat the two concepts as having a decidedly different magnitude of significance, and shall speak—cognizant that some might question the logic of such language—of policies and strategies open to states seeking to reduce their vulnerability to disruptions of their supply of strategic minerals. Most important, I shall explore the possible implications for Canadian mineral producers of the various options open to the United States and other Western consumers who are once again casting about for measures that would afford them greater security in the face of world mineral developments. Before analysing the range of potential vulnerability-reducing options available to OECD members, I want to make some comments about the contemporary nature of vulnerability.

Those who analyse contemporary questions of mineral vulnerability tend to fall into one of two camps: one group argues that to the extent industrialized (and industrializing) states have cause for concern about their future supplies of industrial commodities, it is largely due to *economic* considerations; the other group holds that while economic symptoms may indeed manifest themselves in disturbed minerals markets, the underlying cause of supply disruption in at least the short-term future will be *political* in nature. I shall address these two competing assessments in turn.

ECONOMIC DIMENSION OF VULNERABILITY

The economic interpretation of minerals vulnerability can itself take two forms. As discussed in some detail in Chapter 1, there has been fairly recently (though not during the past five or so years) uneasiness on the part of some analysts who convinced themselves that the limits to growth were not only apparent, but proximate—and this because of shortages of raw materials in an absolute, physical sense. I have already indicated what I believed to be erroneous about such a perspective, and shall not dwell on the matter here. However, there is a more plausible economic argument that does deserve some attention: it is expressed in the fear that the future supply of minerals will be jeopardized by a current lack of investment in the global mining sector.

This fear had a fairly wide currency in the OECD countries during the latter part of the previous decade, but has abated in the past few years due to the combination of recession early in the 1980s and the persistence of glut in most minerals markets until the last two years. The concern that lack of investment might at some future date imperil the West's mineral supply, though founded in part on a bleak reading of recent minerals market trends, also owes its existence to the belief that the less-developed countries (LDC's), in flexing their commodity "muscles" over the past two decades, and above all in proscribing the freedom of manoeuvre of international mineral extraction enterprises, have put themselves in the unhappy position of being unable to develop their own resources at levels sufficiently high to sustain anticipated future world demand, yet at the same time are either unwilling or unable to attract the foreign investment they need for resource development. According to this perspective, the LDC's are living off the legacy of past, and efficient, control of their mining sector by the foreign multinational corporations (MNC's). But eventually they will have to conduct their own exploration and development, and the worry is that for a variety of reasons the task will prove too much for them.[10] Thus, according to some writers, the most likely future cause of mineral supply disruption will be the presumed current lack of investment in prospecting and exploration, something that has been aggravated though not caused by an investment climate for minerals in general that has been unfavourable for much of the current decade.[11]

There is reason to dispute the above assumption concerning the ability of

LDC's to sustain output in minerals, at least if the recent record of Latin American countries is any indication. In the past decade or so mining enterprises in this part of the Third World—and not, it bears noting, only in those countries disposed to private sector efforts—show little sign of being unable to generate increased levels of production; to the extent that Latin countries will be able to pick up any slack occasioned by shifts in productive capacity away from Africa, then the region appears in a position to reassume the significance to minerals markets it possessed during the 1930s, when it was a substantial mineral province.[12] Anyone familiar with recent analyses of the supply side of "structural change" in the world mineral industry will be only too aware that the problem with Latin America is hardly one of *under*production.[13]

Caution should also be exercised in concluding that a shift in investment away from LDC's, assuming this still to be an accurate claim, must translate into a loss of investment in the world mining sector. The recent hard times aside, there seems to be little basis to the worry that huge net losses in mineral investment *were* taking place in the 1970s. What seems to have been occurring during the last decade, at least, was a relative displacement of mining investment from the LDC's to such "developed market economies" (DME's) as Canada, Australia, the Republic of South Africa, and even the United States. Between the start of the 1960s and the mid-1970s, for example, the LDC portion of overall mineral exploration investment experienced a substantial decline in relative terms, falling from 35 per cent of the total for 1961–5 to 14 per cent for 1971–5.[14] Since ore grades tend to be lower in the DME's than in the LDC's, it is alleged that the shift in mining activity necessarily implies higher-cost production in the future. This assumption can only be sustained if it can be shown that ore grade must always have a determinative bearing on extraction costs, a proposition that some mineral economists find unpersuasive. Whatever the relationship between ore grade and extraction costs, there is, as Phillip Crowson observes, "certainly no clear tendency for costs to be lower in less developed countries."[15]

Some analysts go so far as to suggest that the world has had too much exploration activity in recent years, and that there are now more ore bodies awaiting development than ever before. As the discussion of nickel in Chapter 6 demonstrates, fear of future shortage can serve as a powerful stimulus to new exploration efforts, culminating in the expansion of global productive capacity and, ultimately, depressed prices.[16] We have seen in Chapter 1 that the argument that world resources cannot sustain future mineral demand is itself not sustainable; neither, apparently, is the argument that insufficient investment today must redound to the detriment of consuming countries, if for no other reason than that it is not clear there is insufficient investment.[17] It may well turn out that the current optimism about long-term mineral supply will seem as ill-considered a decade from now as the prevalent pessimism of the early 1970s appears today.[18] We cannot know. What we can state, however, is that those who ponder the OECD members' vulnerability to mineral supply disruption resort much more to political than to economic explanations.

POLITICAL DIMENSION OF VULNERABILITY

The starkest, and to some, most appealing aspect of political vulnerability of world minerals markets takes the form of the "resource-war" hypothesis—an argument that achieved some popularity at the start of the 1980s, but that has been flagging of late. In its heyday, the resource war was widely seen to consist of a two-pronged, and dual motive, Soviet effort to interfere with the West's supply of essential minerals. Prong one was the oil supply of the Persian Gulf; prong two the hard rock minerals of southern Africa, a region it became fashionable to regard as the "Persian Gulf" of nonfuel minerals. The motives were as clear as the methods. The first was the crippling of Western military potential, and thus military prowess, by withholding those minerals most needed by OECD economies. This was argued to be a credible avenue to world supremacy for the Soviets, one that would avoid the perils of a direct military confrontation with the West (although why acts of blatant economic warfare should have been held to be relatively risk-free was never adequately explained by the resource war theorists).

The second motive—and this was an argument pursued by many who read geopolitical significance into recent short-term shifts in patterns of Soviet mineral trade—was linked to an assumption that raw material depletion stalked even the mightily endowed Soviet Union, and that faced with scarce supplies of industrial minerals and equally scarce amounts of foreign exchange, the Soviets would simply have to rely on military force to secure access to resources.[19] Though most often invoked to account for Soviet policy in the Persian Gulf, and secondarily in southern Africa, the resource war could and did serve as a handy device for plumbing the materialist depths of other aspects of Soviet foreign policy, such as the invasion of Afghanistan.[20]

Although scarcely credible today, statements such as the following had a surface plausibility at the start of this decade: "The United States and its Free World allies are in an undeclared and, so far, bloodless 'resource war' with the Soviet Union—and are in grave danger of losing that war."[21] The situation, being parlous, called for quick action, and among the necessary corrective measures were an arms build-up (especially expansion of the U.S. Navy, so vitally needed to guard far-flung "sea lines of communications," or SLOC's as they came to be called); the abandonment of détente, the sooner the better; and the construction of a newer and closer relationship with the Republic of South Africa, heralded by many resources warriors as constituting nothing less than the bulwark of the material base of Western civilization. "If South Africa is lost to the West," warned one proponent of the resource war, "the next step aimed at achieving the Soviet goal of global domination could be a disruption of oil supplies to the West, attempts at Marxist takeovers in Chile, Peru, and Brazil, and the promotion of labour unrest through Communist-dominated labour unions in Australia."[22]

Seldom has the right assimilated more thoroughly the teachings of left-wing foreign policy analysts than during the height of the resource war. What Lenin had instructed an earlier generation of students of foreign policy behaviour, and what more recent "radical revisionist" analysts such as Harry Magdoff and Michael Tanzer have reiterated—namely that capitalist economies were impelled toward imperialism and globalism in some important measure became of their need to secure access to raw materials—was now being trumpeted, *mutatis mutandis,* by conservative exponents of the resource war.[23] Lose access to vital industrial minerals, they cautioned, and the West will lose economic and ultimately military power vis-à-vis the Soviet Union, just as certainly as if it had been bested in military struggle.

Ordinarily, one would not be terribly surprised to encounter diminishing audiences for economic determinism of the sort displayed by the resource war theorists. After all, Marxian and other radical revisionists have not had an easy time gaining widespread acceptance in U.S. foreign policy circles. But while the policy relevance of radical revisionism might remain minimal today, what *is* surprising when one contemplates the fate of the resource war perspective is that it foundered in seas decidedly calmer, from an ideological point of view, than those in which radical theoretical vessels have come to ruin. How is one to account for this?

In some measure, the recent tribulations of the resource war theorists have been curiously related to the above-mentioned ideological congeniality. One of the most important, if maddening, questions confronted by those who try to understand and explain foreign policy is the relative power of "ideology" versus "interests" as motivating forces in statecraft.[24] I will not attempt to resolve the conundrum here, for it strikes me as the sort of puzzle that will generate confusion for some time to come, but I do introduce it to make a point: that the opponents of détente seized upon the presumed (and presumably justifiable) need to defend material interests as a primary explanation for and focus of their extreme disquiet with détente. Although no doubt some true believers among the resource war school probably did ground their opposition to détente entirely or largely in terms of an assessment of American material interests, it is difficult to escape the conclusion that for many resource warriors of the late 1970s the spectre of raw material conflict was a heaven-sent way of demonstrating the folly of what they took to be a misguided, immoral, and ideologically unsound policy toward the USSR.

The linkage to an ideological aversion to détente and a heightened concern for American mineral supply was initially made in the mid-1970s, following the decade's first oil shock.[25] It was not long before disturbing parallels were being drawn between U.S. setbacks in the Persian Gulf and Soviet/Cuban gains in southern Africa; and after Congress rebuffed the Ford administration's attempt to arrange military assistance for the FNLA and UNITA, on the basis of there being no "vital" U.S. interests at stake in Angola, anti-détente advocacy quickly became embedded in an interest-based calculation of risk and gain. With the Vietnam experience so recent, it is hardly surprising that this should have been the case.

Another factor that has contributed to the reduced plausibility of the resource war hypothesis is the relaxation of concern in the West about mineral supply—a relaxation that has in the past few months, however, itself begun to dissolve. During the latter 1970s and throughout the 1980s, many analysts in the West were making dire forecasts about future access to strategic minerals, oil in particular, but certain nonfuel minerals as well. For crude oil, the Iranian revolution seemed to portend such a grim energy future for import-dependent Western countries that well-respected energy experts such as Walter J. Levy could and did foresee "a series of future emergencies centering around world oil [that] will set back world progress for many, many years. And the world, as we know it now, will probably not be able to maintain its cohesion, nor be able to provide for the continued economic progress of its people against the onslaught of future oil shocks—with all that this might imply for the political stability of the West, its free institutions, and its internal and external security."[26]

Given the apparent sharpening of a nonfuel mineral "crisis" at roughly the same time as the world oil situation was threatening to turn critical again, it seemed only logical to assume that nonfuel strategic minerals shared attributes that in the early 1970s had been associated primarily with oil: essentiality, as well as grave uncertainty as to future supply and price. For nonfuel minerals, an event that was the near equivalent of the Iranian revolution took place in the summer of 1978—the Katangan rebel attacks near Kolwezi.[27] This event disrupted copper and cobalt production in Zaïre for two months and set off a panic in cobalt markets, which resulted in a greater than 700 per cent increase in the spot market price for cobalt, from U.S. $6.75 a pound to $50 a pound.[28] Principally as a result of the Kolwezi (or "Shaba II") incident, analysts in the United States and other dependent Western countries began to reach hasty conclusions that their countries' dependence on nonfuel minerals was as important—and troubling—as their dependence on imported oil. Indeed, in the United States some claimed that dependence in nonfuel minerals was an even graver problem than dependence in oil; the United States, it was held, might conceivably regain self-sufficiency in oil, but "in many cases there are no substitutes for the [nonfuel] minerals imported from foreign sources, countries which are often unstable at best, hostile at worst."[29]

Those who equated nonfuel-mineral dependence with oil dependence failed to pay proper heed to the tremendous differences in magnitude between the former and the latter. In the case of the United States during the cobalt panic, net imports of nonfuel minerals amounted to not quite $3 billion, as compared with net energy (mostly oil) imports of nearly $75 billion. Internationally, aggregate exports of metallic ores, concentrates, and scrap accounted for slightly more than 1 per cent of total world exports, contrasted with a 20 per cent share for fuel exports.[30] In Chapter 1, I noted that for minerals to be strategic they must be essential to economic well-being: by this gauge it is clear that, in value terms, oil is vastly more essential than all the nonfuel minerals put together. Given the diminution of anxiety about oil supply of the past few years, it is hardly surprising that there should have been a concomitant lessening—until the upsurge in violence in South Africa—of concern about oil's "analogue," the nonfuel minerals. One positive aspect of the recession of the early 1980s, at least from the standpoint of the consuming countries, was that it relieved pressure (and worry) in respect of their access to minerals; not since the Depression of the 1930s had most minerals been so abundant and, in real terms, so cheap.

Some additional considerations must be adduced to explain the recent lack of receptivity encountered by the resource war advocacy. The first relates to the changing perception of LDC commodity power. It is apparent, from the coign of vantage of the late 1980s, that nervous analysts such as C. Fred Bergsten greatly overestimated the influence effect of "poor power" during the early part of the 1970s.[31] Though it might be thought that such alarmist prognosticators were in the distinct minority, the opposite appears closer to the truth: where a vigorous OPEC once inspired tremulous visions of future developments in world mineral markets, the wave of the future seems to be the hapless International Tin Agreement.[32] The world, by the mid-1980s (less so today), had become a buyers' market with a vengeance, and this altered marketing context did not provide fertile soil for the resource war advocacy.

Further contributing to the woes of the resource warriors has been the rather successful effort made by numerous Sovietologists to debunk their alarmist scenario of a Soviet economic offensive. It may well be that in the Alice-in-Wonderland domain that is the precinct of Kremlinologists, ordinary canons of empirical scholarship should never be invoked; nevertheless, until it can be demonstrated persuasively why we should abandon a critical insistence upon at least some confirming evidence of theses, we are perhaps well advised to observe what Robert Legvold told a U.S. Congressional subcommittee eight years ago: "simply no evidence exists suggesting that Soviet leaders think in terms of strangling the West by denying it strategic nonfuel minerals in peacetime."[33] Although not in itself proof of anything, such a statement does reflect the position of the academy and seems to be consistent with the mineral policy community in Western Europe, where the resource war never was taken very seriously—not even in NATO headquarters, where one might have expected at least a glimmer of interest in such an hypothesis.[34]

But if it cannot be shown that the Soviet Union ever embarked upon a conscious effort to deny Western industrial societies access to raw materials, it should not be concluded that it has had no interest in world mineral markets. The Soviet Union has been and remains a leading mineral producer, one that derives a substantial proportion of its foreign exchange from mineral exports.[35] Though one of the most self-sufficient countries, it is also a significant importer of certain minerals, notably barite, bauxite and alumina, bismuth, cobalt, fluorspar, tin, and tungsten.[36] To some observers, the Soviets are entering a "transitional period" in which they move from a position of self-sufficiency to one of increasing import dependence, the implication being that they will be providing stiffer competition to Western countries for scarce raw materials. Not surprisingly, this possibility has been heralded as an imminent probability by resource war analysts, who hoped to demonstrate that the Soviets would seek abroad what they could no longer produce at home.[37] Those who prefer an alternative explanation for recent surges in Soviet imports argue that price differentials and not depletion have been responsible for Soviet purchases in world markets, where commodities often can be had for less than the cost of domestic production.

Whatever the reasoning behind Soviet mineral import policy, overall Soviet mineral planning continues to envision maximum feasible self-sufficiency, and the USSR remains one of the few countries capable of having and realizing such a policy objective. But whether or not they will "need" foreign minerals more in the future than they have in the past, the Soviets can be expected to try to avail themselves of opportunities to further their economic and political interests wherever possible, including the sensitive southern African region, the focus of so much minerals anxiety since the late 1970s. It is conceivable, maybe likely, that Soviet foreign policy interests of a non-mineral nature will have an impact on mineral developments in southern Africa and elsewhere, but this hardly constitutes a basis for assuming that the USSR has launched a resource war: to infer from Soviet activity in Africa the existence of a resource-denial strategy is to commit the fallacy of mistaking correlation and consequence for motivation and cause.

This brings me to the final point worth making in connection with the demise of the resource war thesis, and also leads into an assessment of the most likely contemporary cause of supply disruption. I refer, of course, to the current situation in South Africa. Outside of the Republic of South Africa itself, the resource war hypothesis in its fullest bloom never got anywhere the reception that it got in some circles in the United States, where it was disseminated by important foreign policy lobbies such as the Committee on the Present Danger and other conservative groups.[38] It was even a theme in the 1980 campaign speeches of presidential candidate Ronald Reagan, as well as others associated with the Republican campaign. One such person was Alexander Haig, jr., who dramatically announced to a House subcommittee in September 1980 that "the era of the 'resource war' has arrived."[39]

During this earlier period, it was common for resource warriors to speak of *southern* Africa as the problematical region, one that in many ways was similar to the Persian Gulf, in the sense of being both mineral-rich and politically volatile; it was what geopoliticians would refer to as a classic "gray area" in international politics.[40] During the cobalt scare of the late 1970s, it was Zaïre that occasioned the most discomfort among minerals analysts; but the discomfort was mitigated somewhat, for the resource warriors at least, by the solace of knowing that the root "cause" of the West's cobalt difficulties ultimately was the source of all that was wrong with the world, namely the Soviet Union (abetted by its Cuban ally). Today, in the case of South Africa, we lack the certitude of having a nefarious and clearly identifiable foe at hand, and this has worked to the detriment of the resource war advocacy.

It has worked to its detriment precisely because the moral dimension of the current struggle to dismantle the apartheid regime must make any government—including and especially those headed by George Bush and Margaret Thatcher—draw back from what, just a few years ago, was a logical implication of the resource war argument. A half-dozen or so years ago, it was not uncommon to encounter pleas for the preservation of the southern African status quo that were predicated upon frank considerations of material interest: certainly there were many in the Republic of South Africa who focused upon the presumed need of the Western countries for South African minerals as sufficient reason to believe that the West, loathe though it might apartheid, would simply be incapable of doing anything about it. Either support us and our institutions, ran the familiar argument, or bear the material consequences that would attend the destruction of that system, of which you in the West, whether you like it or not, have been the principal beneficiaries.[41]

The resource war has not been able to withstand the change in its theatre of operation, for what the shift from the broader southern African context (with its ominous spectres of Soviet/Cuban imperialism) to the narrower South African one has done has been to expose the moral dilemma that confronts states with an interest in protecting their material interests. The odious nature of the current South African regime renders it simply impossible for even its least hostile Western critics to give so much as the appearance of buttressing the status quo for the sake of mere material interests. Instead of finding its mineral customers rallying, however grudgingly, behind it in its struggle for survival, Pretoria witnesses its trading partners—sometimes noisily, sometimes not—exploring alternative sources of supply for those raw materials whose production and reserves South Africa dominates. Thus, when President P.W. Botha publicly reminds Western states how vitally dependent they are, for example, on the Republic's chromite, the effect of the reminder is almost the opposite of that intended. Rather than cow them, such not-so-veiled threats to withhold supply impel Botha's Western critics to continue doing what the more astute among them have in any event been undertaking for some years, namely attempting to reduce their vulnerability to disruption in mineral supply coming from South Africa.

To return to a distinction introduced at the start of this chapter, it seems that those resource warriors who imagined that the West must be led into backing South Africa on the basis of mineral considerations committed the analytical error of confusing dependence—even near-total dependence—with vulnerability. There is no reason to dispute the obvious fact that South Africa today accounts for an impressive share of world production of certain vital industrial minerals; furthermore, it similarly possesses a significant proportion of global reserves of these same commodities. Taking just the most "problematical" of the strategic nonfuel minerals, it can be seen that South Africa in 1986 produced roughly the following percentage shares of world output of: *chromite,* 34; *manganese,* 17; *platinum group metals* (PGM), 46; and *vanadium,* 53. Not only is South Africa a leading producer of each of these minerals, it also has the following percentage share of world reserves of: *chromite,* 84; *manganese,* 74; PGM, 89; and *vanadium,* 47.[42]

Where the resource war advocacy made its most serious mistake was in substituting an impassioned call for securing access, with all that such a dramatic policy might entail, for a more sober contemplation of the means available to Western states to reduce their collective and individual vulnerability. I shall presently review some of these means, with a special emphasis on their potential implications for Canadian export interests; but before ending this section on the contemporary aspect of vulnerability, I wish to emphasize that Western states do have a legitimate worry about supply disruption in at least a limited range of strategic minerals, economic arguments based on postulations of glut to the contrary notwithstanding. It is not given to any of us to say what the future holds for South Africa. Nevertheless, one can advance some reasoned speculation on the likely causes of mineral supply disruption associated with the current political turmoil there. In dismissing the resource war thesis as a credible explanation, I do not wish to imply that there is no potential supply problem that might, with proper policy measures, be remedied, if only in part. On the contrary, it strikes me that a prudent calculation of supply disruption prospects would rate as eminently possible, if not imminently probable, for any of a number of scenarios. Some, for example, concentrate on the effect that sanctions (or counter-sanctions), if rigorously applied, might have on mineral supply.[43] Others, however, foresee disruptions occurring not as a result of such deliberate policy choices as sanctions, but rather as an unintended consequence of heightened socio-political chaos—chaos that would have the same effect on South African nonfuel-mineral production as turbulence in Iran had on that country's oil production and exports several years ago.

Political risk assessors, in their more candid moments, will confess that theirs is an exceedingly aleatory business. It is true, as one text explains, that "comparison of policies' economic benefits and costs is a critical element in policymaking." However, this same book goes on to note that invariably, "measurement of these costs rests heavily on a subjective appraisal of risk and on judgments as to how heavily one should weigh possible effects."[44] Henrik Ibsen expressed part of the risk assessor's dilemma when in *Hedda Gabler* he had one character, Tesman, observe that "we know nothing of the future." To this another character, Lovborg, replied: "No, but there is a thing or two to be said about it all the same."[45]

The "science" of political risk assessment, it is commonly conceded, has little predictive power. One cannot reasonably demand or realistically expect precise statements about the unknowable—namely, the prospects for future supply interruptions in the supply of strategic minerals currently being produced in South Africa. This does not amount to an abandonment of any and all attempts to forecast probable developments affecting international minerals markets; it is simply to acknowledge the reality that all such attempts run the risk of verging upon "vulgar" empiricism. Econometric forecasting, which can give the superficial appearance of predictive prowess, can say nothing at all about the economic consequences of difficult-to-foresee political factors. The most that one can expect from political forecasting is that it proceed on the basis of reasoned, or reasonable, conjecture.

In the matter of the resource war, I argued that the conjecture was neither reasoned very well, nor very reasonable. The same charge should not be levelled against assessments of risks associated with the current unrest in South Africa, and, for that matter, other parts of the southern African region. There is, in both the Republic and the region, enough evidence of recent political turmoil to presage further instability. If South Africa possessed few or no minerals, then the raw material implications of its political upheaval would be nugatory. But South Africa is not Northern Ireland or Lebanon, and until the West is able to mitigate its vulnerability to supply disruptions associated with South Africa, then it will come as a surprise to no one that analysis of contemporary issues in strategic minerals will largely take the form of thinking about the future of South Africa.

South Africa represents far from the first episode of politically induced strategic mineral concern in the West; it is unlikely to be the last. In the geopolitics of minerals, the only thing that seems constant is the axiom, "Gray areas come, and gray areas go." But South Africa does constitute the "crisis" of the moment, to the extent that there is one. Let us, then, examine the potential implications for Canadian export interests in nonfuel minerals, in the increasingly likely event that Western consuming states continue their attempt to reduce their vulnerability with respect to South African minerals.

REDUCTION OF VULNERABILITY AND ITS IMPLICATIONS
FOR CANADIAN EXPORT INTERESTS

As the section on oil in Chapter 6 demonstrates, there are several options open to consuming countries seeking to mitigate their vulnerability to disruptions in the supply of their imported strategic minerals. The five categories cited in that earlier chapter encapsulate the range of options available to importers in the contemporary period of concern over minerals sourced from South or southern Africa: (1) stockpiling; (2) import diversification; (3) increased domestic production; (4) substitution; and (5) conservation. In the pages below, I probe the degree to which this range of choice could present both challenges and opportunities to Canadian mineral production and exports.

As a major mineral exporter—and the world's leading exporter of nonfuel minerals—Canada stands to be affected by vulnerability-reducing strategies adopted by Western consuming states. More than 10 per cent of the Canadian GNP is accounted for by mineral production (including fuels), which in 1985 totalled $45 billion. Of this amount, some two-thirds was sold abroad, reflecting the country's high propensity to export. In 1985, more than 25 per cent of Canadian merchandise trade exports consisted of crude and fabricated nonfuel minerals. The United States takes the lion's share of Canada's mineral exports, and was the market for 73 per cent in 1985. That same year, Japan absorbed 8 per cent, the EEC (excluding Britain) 5 per cent, and Britain 3 per cent of Canadian mineral exports.[46]

In a world where politically induced disruption worries seem to be on the increase, Canada would appear to rank as a most reliable source of supply. The problems associated with mineral development in much of the world seem to be pleasantly absent from Canada: in particular, there is no impending political upheaval to curtail mineral production and exportation, and foreign investors, despite some infrequent grumbling, really are offered as hospitable an environment in which to carry on development as they are likely to find anywhere else. Nor is the changed political climate merely a function of the priorities of the Progressive Conservative government that came to power in September 1984; as David Yudelman noted in Chapter 3, Canadian mineral policy has undergone a minor revolution in the past decade, in recognition—albeit somewhat belated recogition—of shifting international realities in the domain of minerals.

But old memories have a way of lingering; and what is striking is that, though the assumption of Canadian reliability as a source of supply contains much more truth than myth, there remains a group of mineral analysts who are somewhat dubious of the wisdom of becoming more dependent upon Canadian mineral supply. This has been, of course, particularly so in the case of uranium, for reasons Michael Webb indicated in the previous chapter. But other instances of Canadian "unreliability" continue to surface from time to time, thus casting some doubt upon presumptions that Canadian-sourced minerals must, by dint of their country of origin, have the kind of "political value added" referred to earlier in this chapter.

For example, some British commodities experts have expressed scepticism about Canadian dependability, either because of perceived labour militancy or because they retain an outdated belief that Canadian governments—at both the provincial and federal levels—continue to regard the mining industry as a natural adversary.[47] One such expert reminded me that the only genuine minerals "crisis" Britain has experienced in the entire post-Second World War years occurred in 1969: the disruption of Canadian nickel exports resulting from a long strike.[48] Similar reference is made in a recent widely publicized U.S. Congressional report on vulnerability, where the claim is made that "of the few significant interruptions in U.S. materials supply in the past 30-odd years . . . the most disruptive was probably the loss of nickel from Canada during the 4-month nickel strike in 1969."[49]

Nor was nickel the sole commodity to be identified in this context. Japan sought and achieved a greater diversification of its molybdenum supply as a result of labour unrest at Canadian molybdenum mines in 1979, which retarded production.[50] Sometimes it has been Canadian foreign policy aims, and not labour militancy, that have stimulated anxiety on the part of Canada's customers. We have already detailed the effect that uranium-export policies have had on several European states and Japan.[51] In some extreme instances, there were even those (especially in the United States) who by the end of the 1970s came to look upon Canada as an ideologically suspect country, with all that this could entail for those states dependent upon Canadian mineral supply. According to this narrowly held perspective, "the developing minerals and energy situation in Canada is such that the reliability of traditionally friendly Canada as a long-term source of strategic minerals for America must be questioned."[52] To those who adopted this view, Canadian participation in the uranium cartel, and a mooted (by none other than Prime Minister Trudeau himself) formation of a nickel cartel in 1977, provided disturbing evidence of an ominous trend.[53]

Despite the undeniable evidence that not all would or do regard Canada as a quintessentially reliable source of supply, most minerals analysts do consider Canadian supply to be, if not perfect, nearly as "safe" as domestic supply, which itself can be and often is subject to labour-related disruptions. With respect to the geopolitics of minerals, Canada remains what it has been for some decades: a valued producer and supplier of a range of nonfuel minerals. Thus, to determine whether Canadian export interests can expect to derive benefit from the contemporary vogue of uneasiness over minerals availability requires us to ask whether Canada can realistically step up its output of those minerals whose supply many hold to be increasingly problematic. As we have seen, it is primarily those minerals whose productive capacity and reserves are concentrated in South (and, to a lesser degree, southern) Africa that have lately been occasioning the most concern in nonfuel minerals markets. These may or may not be the most "strategic" minerals, but they do tend to elicit the most attention from import-dependent states: chromium, manganese, the platinum group metals (PGM), vanadium, and—though this is less and less a source of consternation—cobalt.

Not all consuming countries have identical lists of minerals they worry about. The United States, for example, regards vanadium as a strategic mineral, but has had no great concern about it, since the country has until the recent woes of both the U.S. steel and uranium-mining sectors been nearly two-thirds self-sufficient.[54] In addition to those found in the "core group" of problematic commodities, some other minerals are variously cited by consuming countries as being worthy of attention. The Economic Directorate of NATO has isolated the core group as well as the following, in its research on the collective vulnerability of the Alliance: asbestos (blue), titanium, columbium/niobium, tantalum, tin, tungsten, and antimony.[55] In its own study of group vulnerability, the European Community has listed the above (minus asbestos, tin, and tungsten) but added phosphate rock, molybdenum, and nickel.[56] At the start of the 1980s France considered itself to have either a "very great" or "great" vulnerability in respect of silver, PGM, industrial diamonds, phosphate, zirconium, titanium, cobalt, vanadium, antimony, copper, manganese, molybdenum, and tungsten.[57]

Britain remains what it has been for some time, import-dependent on a broad range of minerals, but curiously has not been as nervous about its near total reliance in some minerals upon South Africa as some think it should be, though it did undertake a modest stockpiling effort a few years ago in cobalt, chromium, manganese, and vanadium.[58] On the other hand, part of the Thatcher government's resistance to the imposition of economic sanctions is probably related to the country's substantial dependence upon South African chromium, PGM, and manganese; for although it only conducts 1.2 per cent of its total foreign trade with South Africa, Britain does get nearly 90 per cent of its chromium, 60 per cent of its PGM, and 55 per cent of its manganese from the Republic.[59]

For its part, West Germany had contemplated stockpiling in the wake of the nonfuel minerals scare of the late 1970s, but abandoned this effort in November 1980. The German stockpile was intended to contain chromium, manganese, cobalt, vanadium, and blue asbestos (crocidilite)—although in the case of the last commodity, it was more than a little curious that blue asbestos was being targeted, in one part of the FRG bureaucracy, for banning (on health grounds) at the very same time that another branch of the government was considering stockpiling it.[60] Germany, like Britain, has a fairly high degree of dependence upon South Africa in some of the problematic minerals. Its dependence in manganese is about 70 per cent, and in chromium nearly 50 per cent; but in PGM German dependence on South Africa appears to be much lower than is the case for Britain, although one is ill advised to generalize too much from import statistics, for while Germany does purchase substantial amounts of PGM from the Soviet Union, it also gets a good deal of platinum and palladium *metal* from countries such as Britain and Switzerland, which themselves are large importers of South African PGM.[61]

Japan began to stockpile minerals in the 1970s, more to stabilize commodity prices than because of security-of-supply considerations.[62] But in April 1983 a complicated stockpiling plan was approved by the Japanese government, designed to provide a short-term (sixty-day) supply buffer for several minerals needed by Japanese industry. The plan calls for the creation of three stockpiles, one operated by the government, one by the private sector, and the third jointly operated by government and business—all of which would be under the general supervision of the Ministry of International Trade and Industry (MITI). Included among the minerals stockpiled are cobalt, chromium, manganese, molybdenum, nickel, tungsten, and vanadium.[63]

As the above partial survey of problematic minerals reveals, once one departs from the "core group" of strategic minerals, there is a lack of consensus on the importance of the remaining minerals. As I argued in Chapter 1, this lack of consensus constitutes one of the best arguments for a broad construction of the term "strategic minerals." Canada, by virtue of its being the world's largest exporter of nonfuel minerals, becomes according to a broad interpretation the world's pre-eminent supplier of strategic minerals. But how helpful is such a designation in practice, given the current uneasiness about mineral supply engendered by events in South Africa? It would seem not to be very helpful, for the good reason that Canada does not particularly stand out as a supplier of the "core group" of minerals. Indeed, Canada is 100 per cent dependent upon imports for three of the five core-group minerals (vanadium, manganese, and chromium)—although for some time there has been talk of Canada undertaking minor production in vanadium.[64] The country's dependent position has led some analysts to suggest that Ottawa might be advised to create a strategic stockpile of its own, an idea that to date has not met with much enthusiasm in either government or industry.[65]

Canada is, however, a non-negligible producer of two of the five minerals in the core group: cobalt and PGM. It is one of the half-dozen largest cobalt producers in the world, and though not in the same category as Zaïre, which accounts for more than half of global production, it still furnishes around 6 per cent of world supply.[66] Canada ranks third in world production of PGM, and is responsible for some 6 per cent of world mine output in this group.[67] But both cobalt and PGM are by-products of copper and nickel production in Canada, as indeed they are in the USSR and many other producing countries—though there has been a recent surge of exploration activity in Canada intended to identify deposits that could be worked for their platinum content alone.[68] Barring any major discoveries, it seems unlikely that Canada could dramatically increase its production of either PGM or cobalt in response to supply disruptions in southern Africa, unless of course the marketing prospects for nickel and copper (especially the former) were such as to permit economic expansion of output. Until the last year or so, this did not appear probable, given the sluggish markets that each of these commodities had been experiencing since the start of the decade.

In theory it could be argued that a total cut-off of southern African PGM and cobalt supply might cause such dramatic price spikes in either mineral as to make their production profitable as primary products in their own right, with nickel and copper becoming co-products. But if such price spikes were to occur, there would no doubt be both a severe contraction in consumption *and* an increase in production from other countries' currently marginal or subeconomic deposits. The result would then be either a global production share for Canada that is not appreciably different from the present share, or a larger relative share for Canada of a declining global output. In either event, it is difficult to see how Canada could expand greatly its production of PGM or cobalt unless nickel and copper were the engines of such expansion.

Interestingly, there is probably some potential for Canada to enter production of two of the other core-group minerals: chromium and manganese. Currently mining neither chromium nor manganese (though it did exploit some domestic chromium deposits in the Eastern Townships of Quebec as recently as 1949), Canada has deposits of both—resources that, according to some, might sustain economic production if prices were to rise "significantly."[69] Production prospects are probably greater for chromite than for manganese, and one of the more interesting recent developments with respect to strategic minerals in Canada has been the studies done to determine whether the Bird River Sill, in Manitoba, might sustain production. The Manitoba deposits, located in the Bird River and Euclid Lake areas, are owned by Dynamic Mining Exploration, Ltd., which is not expected to make a decision on whether to go into production for some time.[70] Canada's potentially exploitable chromite deposits are not limited to Manitoba; other provinces that have deposits are Quebec, Newfoundland, and Ontario.[71]

Canada has never produced manganese, but it does have some potentially exploitable deposits in Newfoundland, Nova Scotia, New Brunswick, British Columbia, and Quebec. The problem with Canadian manganese is exemplified by Quebec's deposits; these are so far below the minimum cut-off point for economic production that it is unlikely they will be developed in the near future. For example, though the province has deposits grading from 12 to 20 per cent manganese, ore grades currently being exploited by major world producers are in the 38 to 55 per cent range.[72] Though it is technically feasible to upgrade the ores in the 12 to 20 per cent range to 30 or 35 per cent manganese content, it is costly.

This last comment indicates that any future Canadian production of either chromite or manganese depends on either technological (or price) developments that will render economic those deposits that are currently subeconomic, or some form of government subsidization. It is this last consideration in particular that is worth pondering, given the current mood of uneasiness being expressed about the continued reliability of southern African supply. Can Canada benefit from the current malaise of import-dependent Western states? In particular, given its outsize share of Canadian mineral exports, coupled with its historic attentiveness to the security implications of mineral dependence, is there any reason to suppose that the United States might do as it has done in the past, namely subsidize the development of productive capacity in Canada?[73]

To the extent the United States has had a coherent strategic mineral policy at all (a point some will debate), it has consisted in maximum reliance upon the principle of least-cost acquisition, preferably from friendly stable countries if the least-cost producers are not domestic, *plus* reliance upon the strategic stockpile and such other government initiatives as the Defense Production Act of 1950 (DPA). In the past, each of these components of policy have had implications for Canadian mineral production levels, and these implications have been usually (though not always) positive, in the sense that they have created jobs, generated tax revenues, and earned foreign exchange. In a broader strategic sense, these policies have been instrumental in the development of a "defence industrial base" in minerals that has contributed to the economic and military strength of the NATO alliance.

The high volume of mineral trade between Canada and the United States is well known, and need not require any further elaboration here, though as I observed in Chapter 6, one can overstate the degree of U.S. mineral dependence upon Canada. Less well known are the two policy initiatives that have been developed to try to assure what the workings of interdependence might not be capable of guaranteeing: continued supply of minerals during periods of national emergency or war. The Korean War served as the precipitating factor for both, although stockpiling legislation was on the American books for a few years prior to that war. The DPA was employed by Washington to stimulate, through a variety of mechanisms, both domestic and foreign productive capacity of certain strategic minerals, among the most important of which was nickel. Hundreds of millions of dollars in U.S. government subsidies went in the 1950s to assist Canadian nickel companies—primarily Falconbridge and Sherritt Gordon—in developing capacity.[74]

The Stockpiling Act of 1946 required, as did so much of postwar U.S. security initiatives in other areas, the shock of the Korean War to enter into fairly active use as a policy measure designed to cope with minerals vulnerability. President Eisenhower was particularly concerned that raw material constraints might seriously hamper American mobilization efforts, and he was never loath to express these concerns in public. As one historian has noted, "Press conference questions on the point regularly elicited presidential lectures on the critical importance of foreign manganese, cobalt, tin, and tungsten, in terms both worthy of and gratifying to future New Left critics of American capitalism."[75] As was the case with the DPA, so it was that with the U.S. stockpiling effort came opportunities for both the expansion of Canadian productive capacity and Canadian exports in minerals; for notwithstanding the existence of the Buy American Act, strategic stockpiling purchases during the 1950s were largely of foreign (often Canadian) materials. For example, only four of the sixty-four stockpiled materials came entirely from domestic U.S. sources, and only an additional six had domestic content exceeding 50 per cent.[76] Moreover, for the entire period from the early 1950s to the early 1970s, after which time U.S. nonfuel mineral stockpiling declined dramatically from its peak level of activity, Canada remained one of the relatively few (a dozen or so) leading sources of foreign material destined for the government holdings.[77]

How likely will it be that either, or both, of these U.S. policy levers might again be employed in such a manner as to generate increased sales for Canadian mineral producers? Judging from recent and current trends, not very likely at all, and this for a few reasons. To begin with, there is much uncertainty over whether, in the current mood of fiscal restraint in Washington, the vaunted National Defense Stockpile itself may continue to exist as anything other than a shadow of its current self. For the past few years, a battle of sorts has been going on between the administration and some important members of Congress on the future shape of the stockpile: the administration would like to scale the holdings down from the 1986 inventory of $10.1 billion (against a declared goal of $16.1 billion) to less than $700 million, and bases its case for constriction on a study undertaken by the National Security Council between late 1983 and mid-1985.[78] It is impossible to determine which side will emerge from the battle victorious, although it would be unwise to underestimate the ability of Congress to stymie the administration's "modernization" efforts—efforts that appear, to some on Capitol Hill, as attempts to raid the stockpile, and mortgage national security, for the purposes of deficit reduction.[79] One veteran stockpile watcher explained to me that "although there is a lot of talk about streamlining the stockpile, you must remember that there is a big difference between planning and reality. Congress is reality."[80]

One thing seems clear, amid all the uncertainty surrounding the stockpile: Canada stands to be affected negatively should the "modernization" ever take place, while should the status quo continue, there may be at best only occasional, relatively minor, purchases of Canadian minerals for the stockpile in coming years. Unlike the earlier years of stockpiling, since the 1980s there have not been many purchases of Canadian minerals by the U.S. government—in fact, only fairly small amounts of nickel, cobalt, and tantalum have been sourced from Canada.[81] But should the president's proposal ever be enacted, significant quantities of minerals that Canada happens to produce could end up being placed on the market, a prospect that cannot inspire much rejoicing at Inco, Falconbridge, Cominco, and other Canadian companies. Not all of the redundant materials would be dumped on the market at once, but for the fiscal year 1987, it might be interesting to note that the administration had proposed, without success, to dispose of some $250 million worth of materials, among which were the following minerals of significance to Canada: *lead* ($15.2 million), *nickel* ($16 million), *cobalt* ($9.6 million), *PGM* ($20.8 million), *silver* ($43.6 million), *tungsten* ($6.3 million), and *zinc* ($31.8 million). Over the next three years, the White House proposes to sell off $2.5 billion in "surplus" materials from the stockpile.[82] The White House may propose, but it will be Congress that disposes in this matter.

One encounters, from time to time, arguments that Western countries should, individually or collectively, involve themselves much more intensively in stockpiling, to the extent of creating what have been termed "economic" or "interruption" stockpiles, at least in a limited range of the most problematical minerals.[83] But as shown in the earlier discussion of stockpiling, this option has nowhere been pursued as energetically as in the United States, and lately it appears that even the grand master of stockpiling is losing its appetite for the practice. Although it can be and is persuasively argued that the best time to stockpile is precisely when markets are flat and prices are low, the fiscal reality facing most industrialized countries makes it extremely difficult to justify expensive stockbuilding at a time when stocks seem scarcely needed—let alone justifiable.

Are there other policy options that might achieve for dependent consuming countries some measure of vulnerability reduction? As I indicated at the outset of this concluding section, several non-stockpile options exist, among the most important of which is import diversification. Given the previous discussion of the imputed "political value added" often held to be associated with mineral exports from reasonably safe sources of supply, one would think that Canada had a natural advantage waiting to be exploited. The reality, however, is different, in large measure for reasons already given and relating to Canada's relatively slight prospects for expanding productive capacity in the set of minerals implicated in contemporary discussions of vulnerability. Still, somewhat the same kind of argument could have been made during the Korean War, and of course we have seen that with American subsidization programs, productive capacity was enormously expanded, not only for Canadian (and Cuban) nickel, but also for U.S. tungsten deposits.[84] Given that Canada does have deposits of manganese and chromium, to say nothing of its existing reserves of cobalt and PGM, is there any reason to assume that the U.S. would again employ the DPA to expand Canadian productive capacity—or create some where none now exists? It does not appear that the DPA will figure in any short-term minerals planning in the United States, except perhaps on a trivial scale. Though the Act itself continues to exist and get extended every few years, it has been fairly dormant for nearly two decades. The problem is in some measure a financial one. One senior official with the Bureau of Mines explained to me that although the United States would "love" to see chromium being produced in Canada and in the United States itself, its love does not translate into the extension of subsidies the way it did in an earlier era. This official illustrated his argument: "In the Korean War, I had my hands on $8 billion in contract money; today the Department of Defense has $10 million [i.e., in DPA funding], the stockpile gets another $185 million [from the special National Defense Stockpile Transaction Fund]. In 1949 I arranged $1.3 billion for the stockpile."[85] The love affair, he concluded wistfully, would remain on a platonic level.

It should not be thought, however, that the United States government has no international programs under way that, at least in part, are motivated by a desire to render American mineral supply less uncertain. There is one initiative that likely will bode no immediate (or even longer term) good for Canadian export interests, because it holds forth the possibility that the United States might become even less of a customer for Canadian minerals than it now is. I refer to the Trade and Development Program (TDP), operated by the U.S. International Development Cooperation Agency. The program has three interrelated goals: the promotion of American prosperity, through the medium of assisting U.S. companies willing to invest in LDC mineral projects; the promotion of American security by reducing U.S. vulnerability to supply disruption in chromium, cobalt, manganese, and PGM; and the promotion of development in certain Third World countries.

The TDP has been involved in promoting mining ventures in certain Latin American countries, including Brazil. In many ways, Brazil stands to gain from the supply worries of the 1980s in the same sense that Canada did in the 1950s. This is especially the case with manganese, in which Brazil now ranks third among world producers, trailing only the Soviet Union and South Africa.[86] The TDP admittedly has had little to do with the development of Brazil's manganese industry; but it has been involved recently in sponsoring meetings in Washington that bring Brazilian mineral interests together with potential American investors. Nearly all who have studied Brazilian mineral prospects seem to be impressed with the potential of the country to develop into a major actor in international markets, and not just for the raw materials but also for the more processed stages of fabrication, such as ferro-alloys, in which Brazil is now thought to rank third in world production, behind South Africa and Norway. It is expected that Brazil should benefit from further attempts of consuming countries to diversify away from reliance upon South African supply in ores and ferro-alloys: already, the Swedish steelmaker, SSAB, has announced that political considerations have impelled it to cease purchasing South African manganese ore, which is to be replaced by ore from Brazil.[87]

There are a couple of implications for Canada in Brazilian mineral developments. First, and perhaps most obvious, is the dampening effect that the availability of Brazil as an alternative source of supply to South Africa must have on the likelihood of subeconomic Canadian manganese deposits ever being brought into production. But a less obvious implication is that Brazil produces some minerals in which it is a direct competitor with current Canadian production: iron ore, niobium (columbium), titanium, and zinc stand out in this regard.[88] There is the possibility that Brazil and other LDC producers, with the benefit of TDP intermediation, might displace some Canadian mineral exports in the U.S. market, even if such intermediation is intended for purposes completely divorced from this. For example, the TDP has been involved in a project that is designed to stimulate cobalt production in Peru, from the tailings of a magnetite mine operated by Hierro-Peru, the state-owned iron-mining operation. A TDP study done in 1982 proposed that the cobalt from this source—which could amount to some 15 to 20 per cent of U.S. yearly consumption—be shipped to refineries in the United States, with the stipulation that in the event of a national emergency, Washington would have first claim on it.[89] Noted one recent U.S. governmental study: "This cobalt source might provide one of the quickest new supplies, given any disruption in the normal market, because the [Peruvian] iron mining operation and most of the infrastructure required are already in place. Deepwater port loading facilities are available nearby."[90]

It may turn out that any diversification of U.S. supply to such new sources could redound to the detriment of Canada, and not only in cobalt. There certainly exists a similar possibility in the case of niobium (columbium in the U.S.) Currently, one Quebec operation, Niobec, supplies about 15 per cent of global output.[91] But Brazil is showing itself to be a greater and greater force in production of this commodity, which is used in steelmaking and in the production of superalloys for the aerospace industry, and in 1985 it accounted for some 83 per cent of world production of this mineral.[92] As one official with the TDP observed, noting that Canada is the only other significant producer of niobium, "they can easily throttle whatever you have in Canada anytime they want. . . . They could totally obliterate anyone. Their Araxa columbium mine is probably the best mine I have ever seen."[93]

The point of the above discussion is not to raise the menace of Latin mineral "warfare"; it is merely to indicate that the United States, in somewhat the same fashion as the European Community, has developed policies and programs that are directed in part toward mineral producers in the developing countries, and that involve some form of bilateral or multilateral assistance that is obviously denied Canadian mineral producers. As is well known, the EC has had for some time a set of measures in place, usually in the context of the Lomé conventions, that are intended to assist Third World mineral producers and at the same time partly redress, through diversification, the vulnerability of various European countries.[94]

It is apparent that many countries have taken the position that import diversification is a worthy foreign policy aim, but as the above discussion illustrates, none have developed policies specifically aimed at increasing purchases of Canadian minerals. Are there any other vulnerability-reducing options that might affect Canadian export interests? The domestic production avenue is not one along which many import-dependent countries can travel, for the good reason that mineral production tends to correlate quite highly with geographical expanse, thus limiting the autarkic solution to all but the largest countries. Still, the domestic production option merits some consideration, given the size of the United States, as well as its importance to Canadian mineral exporters. It is evident that American deposits of a variety of minerals could be brought into production, and that the United States could reduce its import dependence, if subsidies were more freely available to stimulate such production (as they were in the 1950s), *or* if price rises were to elevate some U.S. deposits from the subeconomic into the economic category.

As noted above, the United States does have, in the DPA, the legislative means to funnel subsidies of various kinds to American producers; moreover, as was argued in Chapter 6, American producers and their Congressional supporters have availed themselves of national security argumentation to press their demands for protection against lower-cost foreign sources of uranium, and other commodities. Both cobalt and chromium were produced in recent decades in the United States, with DPA subsidization assisting in the process; indeed, as recently as 1958 the United States was close to being self-sufficient in cobalt.[95] There are deposits of chromite in several states, and it seems well within the realm of possibility, should Washington deem it worth the effort and expense, that the United States could reduce significantly its current near total dependence in chromium, and eliminate altogether its dependence in cobalt.[96]

In manganese, U.S. possibilities for sustaining significant production are much smaller; and barring the advent of what once filled the Canadian mineral producers with some dread, namely deep seabed mining, it is most unlikely that the United States could ever go very far in the direction of self-sufficiency in this commodity.[97] Of more immediate potential relevance to Canadian export interests is the recent announcement of the Chevron Corporation, along with the Manville Corporation and LAC Minerals Ltd., to move to the second phase of the Stillwater, Montana, PGM project—which is described as the "only potential primary source of platinum and palladium outside of the Soviet Union and South

Africa."[98] The mine began production in April 1987, slightly ahead of schedule, and is projected to reach a maximum annual production level by the early 1990s of some 20,000 tr. oz. of platinum and 80,000 tr. oz. of palladium, approximately 5 per cent of current U.S. demand for the two metals.[99]

Assuming U.S. consumption of PGM remains at or near the current level, it seems that the Stillwater complex will yield only a slight remedy to the problem of American vulnerability in these metals. But there remain two more vulnerability-reducing choices to discuss, *substitution* and *conservation,* before one can reach any conclusions. Each option poses potential challenges to Canadian export interests. Perhaps the most profound potential threat to Canadian interests inheres in the possibility that substitution technologies will ultimately—abetted by contemporary security concerns—displace a share of the current demand for some of Canada's minerals. Copper is often cited in this regard, and with much reason; this metal has had a fairly long history of being substituted for, in many instances by aluminum, and more recently by fibre optics.[100]

But copper, though it does have its "strategic" applications, is hardly among the problematical minerals of the day;[101] and much more worrisome from the Canadian perspective is the possibility that advanced materials such as ceramics might eventually replace metals, particularly nickel, in many applications.[102] To be sure, it is not the availability of nickel that (ordinarily) worries consumers; the supply of this metal is nothing if not diverse, with forty-four producers spread out over twenty-six countries. But there is a sense in which nickel might get caught up in consumers' efforts to reduce vulnerability in some of the more problematical minerals. For instance, high-nickel alloys contain cobalt and chromium. What will happen to nickel markets should substitution technologies develop alternatives for these alloys? One Canadian nickel expert, reflecting on this, stated: "Ceramics is the material I fear. There will be a battle of technologies in the next ten years, between metals and non-metals."[103]

Finally, *conservation* (including recycling) can serve as a buffer against supply disruption. Probably the most impressive conservation gains can be reaped in PGM recovery, in the event from the numerous automobile scrap-yards in many industrialized states. For more than a decade, the catalytic converter has been the single largest user of PGM in countries such as the United States, where it accounts for more than 30 per cent of all platinum, palladium, and rhodium consumption. A recent U.S. study has aptly referred to the country's automotive fleet as a large "above-the-ground mine" of PGM.[104] Another potential frontier for conservation efforts can be located in the superalloy industry, the largest single user of cobalt. Ever since the great cobalt scare of the late 1970s, industry has been attempting to incorporate techniques that will allow it to minimize wastage. In 1980, for instance, nearly 55 per cent of primary metal consumption was lost through downgrading or waste in the production of superalloy parts. With the further development of conserving techniques, it is expected that this sector's appetite for cobalt and such other strategic metals as chromium, nickel, and tantalum can be dampened.[105]

CONCLUSION

It has been argued that, based on a reading of recent and current trends, Canadian export interests can expect to extract few tangible benefits from whatever uneasiness currently is being experienced by Western import-dependent countries. At least this appears to be the proper conclusion, if one focuses on those minerals that are today held to be most problematical. However, although Canada's ability to capitalize on Western vulnerability concerns might appear to be limited at present, one should not conclude that actual supply disruptions of southern or South African minerals would only affect those few commodities that have been the focus of attention in the past few months. In the case of South Africa, it is not unreasonable to suggest that whatever might disrupt the production and/or export of chromium, manganese, vanadium, and PGM would also likely disrupt the production and/or export of titanium, iron ore, nickel, copper, lead and zinc, silver, tin, thermal coal, and uranium.

Canada is a major producer of all these minerals, with the exception of tin. Thus it would be difficult to imagine how Canada's production and export of nonfuel minerals outside the core group of strategic minerals would not be affected by massive internal upheaval in South Africa or, indeed, by any sharp departure from current production and export patterns on the part of a future South African government, whether or not that government was an outcome of massive internal upheaval. Although it is still too early to tell whether Western sanctions against South Africa will proceed very far, there is some reason to speculate that an American ban on uranium imports from the Republic could have had something to do with the easing of protectionist pressure on Canadian uranium in the U.S. market—pressure I described and analysed in Chapter 6. Indeed, one New Mexico legislator, Democratic Congressman Bill Richardson, had been conspicuous in trying to marry two of his major concerns: support for sanctions and support for the state's hard-pressed uranium producers. Given that South Africa provided some 28 per cent of U.S. uranium imports at the end of 1985, it is conceivable that the "import-relief" accorded by the U.S. sanctions program might have contributed somewhat to a diminution in protectionist agitation against Canadian uranium.

Finally, there is at least some reason to ponder whether the "geopolitics" of minerals might yet have the stimulative effect on Canadian production levels that was present in an earlier era, notwithstanding the thrust of most of this chapter, which has been directed at showing why Canada likely cannot derive much material benefit from the current turmoil in South Africa. Indeed, simply to put the matter in such a way might seem distasteful, and suggestive of not a little *Schadenfreude*. Deriving gain from others' losses takes on negative, sometimes sinister, connotations in the cold light of specificity; but bathed in the fuzzier tones of abstraction, it is a prospect that can inspire some hope among those who produce and market minerals in this country. The simple reality is that Canadian mineral production *has* in the past been stimulated as a result of hardship, upheaval, even war—unfortunate occurrences that have blighted international politics with regularity in this century. Thus it is worth noting that some attention has been given of late, by policymakers and policy analysts alike, to the possibility of Canadian producers of minerals and other industrial items becoming beneficiaries of a growing attentiveness in the United States to the concept of the "defence industrial base." It would require another volume devoted just to this concept to do justice to the argument, but in brief it can be stated that there has been an increase in concern, over the past half-dozen years, with the possibility that the erosion of America's industrial base might ultimately impose severe constraints from the standpoint of security, both upon the United States and its allies.

Partly, this concern has been a function of the ongoing reassessment in the strategic studies community of the possibility of non-nuclear global conflict involving the superpowers and their allies; in effect, of a Third World War not being so different from its two predecessors after all. Developments in weapons technologies, coupled with the possibility that meaningful nuclear disarmament initiatives can be developed, have led some analysts to ponder what, just a decade ago, would have seemed the height of ludicrousness. Observes one such analyst, "it is important to recognize that strategic non-nuclear war is again a proper subject for debate after some thirty years of inattention."[106] An obvious implication of such a debate is that the material basis of state power—what in an earlier age was called "war potential" and later "military potential"—now becomes an item of importance to those either planning to fight a war or planning to *deter* one.

But there is another, perhaps more valid source of disquiet over the defence industrial base—a disquiet born not out of a reassessment of strategic assumptions, but rather one occasioned by a genuine perplexity over the degree to which a country (in the event, the U.S.) can continue to shed productive capacity in a variety of industrial sectors and still remain militarily strong and politically influential.[107] What has become apparent in the domain of minerals over the past decade and a half, namely that interdependence can and often does have troublesome security implications, is now beginning to make itself visible in other sectors of the U.S. economy. Indeed, it is the shedding of productive capacity in some of the "downstream" activities (e.g., metal manufacturing and fabrication, as opposed to extraction) that is leading to a reconsideration of the merits of relying on least-cost sources of supply for minerals. For some time, the sorry state of the American ferro-alloys sectors has occasioned worry among the U.S. security community; after all, it was argued, how can one reduce vulnerability to mineral supply disruption through diversification of sources of raw material if one no longer had any "downstream" capability?[108] Recently, the American machine tools industry has been given protection under the seldom-used national security trade measure mentioned in Chapter 6: Section 232 of the Trade Expansion Act of 1962.[109] It is not possible to predict whether this will be a harbinger for other embattled industries in the United States, but one would be rash to discount the possibility, particularly in light of the continuing (if declining) trade deficits—which are likely to result in an impetus toward protectionism in the United States.

There is, then, the possibility that *security* considerations will figure more explicitly in future American trade policy; and it is this prospect that some Canadian minerals analysts—and a few policymakers—have argued might yet bode well for Canadian export interests, should some way be found of convincing Americans to pay more attention to the North American (i.e., including Canadian) defence industrial base, and purchase far fewer minerals from distant, and presumably less reliable, sources.[110] But stressing the security argument can have its perils, as has been seen with the case of uranium. One cannot do other than speculate on the efficacy of Canada's using security arguments to enhance or ensure access to the American market for minerals and other products, whether in the absence of a bilateral free trade arrangement or in the eventuality one gets concluded. What can be said, indeed what this volume's previous chapters require to be said, is that there will continue to be a substantial geopolitical content to any discussion of Canadian resource trade with the United States, and other countries.

NOTES

1 The concept of "political value added" received some currency during the oil crises of the 1970s, and in particular in the context of American prospects for diversifying their source of supply away from unstable Middle Eastern countries and toward relatively safer producers in Latin America, such as Mexico. See Richard R. Fagen, "Mexican Petroleum and U.S. National Security," *International Security* 4 (Summer 1979):39–53; Richard B. Mancke, *Mexican Oil and Natural Gas: Political,*

Conclusion

Strategic, and Economic Implications (New York: Praeger 1979); and David Ronfeldt, Richard Hehring, and Arturo Gándara, *Mexico's Petroleum and U.S. Policy: Implications for the 1980s,* Executive Summary for the U.S. Department of Energy (Santa Monica, CA: Rand Corporation, June 1980).

2 Bruce Russett, "Dimensions of Resource Dependence: Some Elements of Rigor in Concept and Policy Analysis," *International Organization* 38 (Summer 1984):481–99.

3 Robert O. Keohane and Joseph S. Nye, *Power and Interdependence: World Politics in Transition* (Boston: Little, Brown 1977), 12–13.

4 David A. Baldwin, "Interdependence and Power: A Conceptual Analysis," *International Organization* 34 (Autumn 1980):471–506; Kenneth Waltz, "The Myth of National Interdependence," in *Globalism versus Realism: International Relations' Third Debate,* ed. Ray Maghroori and Bennett Ramberg (Boulder, CO: Westview Press 1982), 81–96.

5 See, for instance, Baldwin, "Interdependence and Power," 492: "In sum, there is a distinction between drug users and drug addicts, between drinkers and alcoholics, between being sensitive to others and being dependent on them, between influence in general and dependence as a special type of influence. It is a distinction that has been recognized and understood by scholars and laymen alike for centuries. It is a distinction that the concept of 'sensitivity interdependence' blurs, but which is captured with precision and parsimony by the Hirshcman-Waltz concept of dependence [i.e., as 'vulnerability interdependence']."

6 As, to take a recent widely read example, was done by the U.S. Congress, Office of Technology Assessment, *Strategic Materials: Technologies to Reduce U.S. Import Vulnerability* (Washington, May 1985).

7 For an instance of a (rare) usage of the concept "net import reliance" instead of the more emotive "dependence," see U.S. Bureau of Mines, *Mineral Commodity Summaries, 1987* (Washington: Department of the Interior 1987).

8 James A. Caporaso, "Dependence, Dependency, and Power in the Global System: A Structural and Behavioral Analysis," *International Organization* 32 (Winter 1978):21–2. Cf. Kal Holsti's similar stipulations concerning the vulnerability of exporters, in "A New International Politics?: Diplomacy in Complex Interdependence," *International Organization* 32 (Spring 1978):516.

9 Hans H. Landsberg and John E. Tilton, with Ruth B. Haas, "Nonfuel Minerals," in *Current Issues in Natural Resources Policy,* ed. Paul R. Portney (Washington: Resources for the Future 1982), 91–5.

10 U.S. General Accounting Office, *Report to the Secretary of the Interior: Federal Encouragement of Mining Investment in Developing Countries for Strategic and Critical Minerals Has Been Only Marginally Effective* (Washington, September 1982), 3. The LDC share of global nonfuel-mineral production is described and analysed in Martin O.C. Kursten, "The Role of Metallic Mineral Resources for Countries of the Third World," *Natural Resources Forum* 7, 1 (1983):71–9.

11 Thomas Atkinson, "Future Strategic Mineral Supplies for the EEC," *Mining Engineer* (April 1979):728.

12 The geopolitical significance of Latin mineral wealth during the run-up to the Second World War is discussed in David G. Haglund, " 'Gray Areas' and Raw Materials: Latin American Resources and International Politics in the Pre-World War II Years," *Inter-American Economic Affairs* 36 (Winter 1982):23–51.

13 This is especially the case in copper, but is becoming more evident in nickel as well. See Energy, Mines and Resources Canada, *Canada's Nonferrous Metals Industry: Nickel and Copper* (Ottawa: Minister of Supply and Services 1984).

14 Energy, Mines and Resources Canada, *Mineral Policy: A Discussion Paper* (Ottawa: Minister of Supply and Services, December 1981), 146. But cf. Roderick G. Eggert "Base and Precious Metals Exploration by Major Corporations," mimeo (undated) for an analysis of trends through the 1970s.

15 Phillip Crowson, "Trend and Patterns of International Investment in Non-Fuel Minerals," in *Probleme der Rohstoffsicherung* (Bonn: Friedrich Elbert Stiftung 1981), 25–6.

16 T.P. Mohide, C.L. Warden, and J.D. Mason, *Towards a Nickel Policy for the Province of Ontario,* Mineral Policy Background paper no. 4, Dec. 1977 (Toronto: Ontario Ministry of Natural Resources, Division of Mines 1977), 12–13.

17 Phillip Crowson, "Investment and Future Mineral Production," *Resources Policy* 8 (March 1982):7–9. Also see idem, "A Perspective on World Wide Exploration for Minerals," mimeo, Feb. 1984.

18 Contrasting viewpoints are advanced in Marian Radetzki's self-described "optimistic" paper, *Will the Long-Run Global Supply in Industrial Minerals Be Adequate?: A Case Study of Iron, Aluminium and Copper,* Reprint Series no. 132 (Stockholm: University of Stockholm, Institute for International Eco-

nomic Studies 1980); and the more pessimistic article by N.A. Butt and Thomas Atkinson, "Shortfalls in Minerals Investments," *Resources Policy* 8 (1982):261–76.

19 See especially *The Resource War in 3-D: Dependency, Diplomacy, Defense,* ed. James Arnold Miller, Daniel Fine, and R. Daniel McMichael (Pittsburgh: World Affairs Council of Pittsburgh 1980); and National Strategy Information Center, *The Resource War and the U.S. Business Community: The Case for a Council on Economics and National Security* (Washington: Council on Economics and National Security 1980).

20 See John F. Shroder, jr., "The U.S.S.R. and Afghanistan Mineral Resources," in *International Minerals: A National Perspective,* ed. Allen F. Agnew (Boulder, CO: Westview Press 1983), 115–53.

21 Warren P. Baker, "Next: A Resource War?" *Seapower* 23 (October 1980):55.

22 W.C.J. van Rensburg, "Political Change in South Africa and the Importance of the Republic of South Africa as a Raw Material Supplier," in *Probleme der Rohstoffsicherung,* 99.

23 The radical revisionist case is argued in Harry Magdoff, *The Age of Imperialism: The Economics of U.S. Foreign Policy* (New York: Monthly Review Press 1969); and Michael Tanzer, *The Race for Resources: Continuing Struggles over Minerals and Fuels* (New York: Monthly Review Press 1980). An interesting discussion of certain theoretical affinities between left- and right-wing analyses is Ole R. Holsti, "The Study of International Politics Makes Strange Bedfellows: Theories of the Radical Right and the Radical Left," *American Political Science Review* 66 (Mar. 1974):217–42.

24 The greater relative importance of interests is stressed by Werner Levi, "Ideology, Interests, and Foreign Policy," *International Studies Quarterly* 14 (March 1970):1–31. But for a different assessment, cf. Stephen D. Krasner, *Defending the National Interest: Raw Materials Investments and U.S. Foreign Policy* (Princeton, NJ: Princeton University Press 1978).

25 See, for example, Edward Friedland, Paul Seabury, and Aaron Wildavsky, *The Great Détente Disaster: Oil and the Decline of American Foreign Policy* (New York: Basic Books 1975).

26 Walter J. Levy, "Oil and the Decline of the West," *Foreign Affairs* 58 (Summer 1980):1015.

27 See Barry M. Blechman, *National Security and Strategic Minerals: An Analysis of the U.S. Dependence on Foreign Sources of Cobalt,* Westview Special Studies in National Security and Defense Policy (Boulder, CO: Westview Press 1985).

28 John Orme, "Ore Wars: The Problem of U.S. Dependence on Foreign Minerals," *Fletcher Forum* 6 (Summer 1982):408.

29 U.S. Congress, House Committee on Interior and Insular Affairs, Subcommittee on Mines and Mining, *Sub-Sahara Africa: Its Role in Critical Mineral Needs of the Western World,* 96th Cong., 2d sess. (Washington: U.S. Government Printing Office 1980), vii.

30 Hans H. Landsberg, *Minerals in the Eighties: Issues and Policies* (Oak Ridge, TN: Oak Ridge National Laboratory, Program Planning and Analysis 1982), 20–1.

31 See two articles written by Bergsten: "The Threat from the Third World," *Foreign Policy* 11 (Summer 1973):102–24; and "The Threat Is Real," *Foreign Policy* 14 (Spring 1974):84–90.

32 An interesting discussion of recent changes in international commodity markets is Mark W. Zacher, "Trade Gaps, Analytical Gaps: Regime Analysis and International Commodity Trade Regulation," *International Organization* 41 (Spring 1987):173–202. On the recent travails of tin, see W. Keith Buck, "Commodity Agreements versus Study Groups: The Lessons of Tin," *CRS Perspectives* 25 (Sept. 1986):1–3.

33 U.S. Congress, House Committee on Foreign Affairs, Subcommittee on Africa, *The Possibility of a Resource War in Southern Africa,* 97th Cong., 1st sess. (Washington: U.S. Government Printing Office 1981), 67.

34 I base this remark on conversations I had with minerals analysts in various Western European capitals, and at OECD, EEC, and NATO headquarters in March and April 1983.

35 Energy, Mines and Resources Canada, *Comecon's Mineral Development Potential and Its Implications for Canada,* prepared by Nickolas M. Switucha, Mineral Bulletin MR183 (Ottawa: Minister of Supply and Services 1979), 95.

36 Richard M. Levine, "The Mineral Industry of the U.S.S.R.," in U.S. Bureau of Mines, *Minerals Yearbook 1984,* vol. 3: *Area Reports: International* (Washington: Department of the Interior 1986), 829–64. Also see James S. Grichar, Richard M. Levine, and Lotfollah Nahai, *The Nonfuel mineral Outlook for the U.S.S.R. through 1990* (Washington: Bureau of Mines 1981), 9.

37 See, for this view, Daniel I. Fine, "Mineral Resource Dependency Crisis: Soviet Union and United States," in *The Resource War in 3-D,* 37–56.

Conclusion

38 Alan C. Brownfeld, "The Growing United States' Dependency on Imported Strategic Minerals," *Atlantic Community Quarterly* 20 (Spring 1982):65.

39 Michael Shafer, "Mineral Myths," *Foreign Policy* 47 (Summer 1982):154.

40 Ruth W. Arad et al., *Sharing Global Resources* (New York: McGraw-Hill 1979), 75.

41 See, for an example of this argument, Dirk C. Neethling, "The Geopolitics of Mineral Supply: Access to and Availability of the Mineral Resources of Southern Africa," in *Southern African Metals and Minerals in a World Context Conference*, ed. Trevor Tarring and Wynford Davies (Worcester Park, Eng.: Metal Bulletin Congresses 1981), D1-D11. A useful compendium of the geopolitical importance of South African minerals to the industrialized West is L.E. Andor, comp., *South Africa's Chrome, Manganese, Platinum, and Vanadium: Foreign Views on the Mineral Dependency Issue, 1970–1984*, Bibliographical Series no. 13 (Braamfontein: South African Institute of International Affairs 1985).

42 U.S. General Accounting Office, *South Africa: Summary Report on Trade, Lending, Investment, and Strategic Minerals* (Washington, Sept. 1988), 41.

43 See James M. Markham, "The Debate on Sanctions Gets More Intense," *New York Times*, 14 September 1986, E2; and "Sanctions on South Africa: Double-Edged," *Economist*, 16 August 1986, 42–3. Also see U.S. Bureau of Mines, *Estimated Direct Economic Impacts of a U.S. Import Embargo on Strategic and Critical Minerals Produced in South Africa* (Washington: Department of the Interior 1988).

44 Michael W. Klass, James C. Burrows, and Steven D. Beggs, *International Minerals Cartels and Embargoes: Policy Implications for the United States* (New York: Praeger 1980), 29.

45 Cited in Joseph V. Micallef, "Political Risk Assessment," *Columbia Journal of World Business* 16 (1981):47.

46 Energy, Mines and Resources Canada, *Canadian Minerals Yearbook 1985: Review and Outlook* (Ottawa: Minister of Supply and Services 1986), 1.1–1.12.

47 Philip Crowson, *Non-Fuel Minerals and Foreign Policy* (London: Royal Institute of International Affairs 1977), 6–7.

48 Interview, London, 12 April 1983.

49 U.S. Congress, OTA, *Strategic Materials*, 48.

50 Canada, Department of External Affairs, *Canada's Export Development Plans for Japan* (Ottawa: DEA 1982), 166–7.

51 In addition to the Webb chapter, also see Ted Greenwood and Alvin Streeter, jr., "Uranium," in *Natural Resources in U.S.-Canadian Relations*, vol. 2: *Patterns and Trends in Resource Supplies and Policies*, ed. Carl E. Beigie and Alfred O. Hero, jr. (Boulder, CO: Westview Press 1980), 356–7.

52 James Miller, quoted in the *Globe and Mail*, 19 Oct. 1981. Miller, an advocate of the resource war thesis discussed above, edits a Washington newsletter, *Alarm*, which focuses on resource politics.

53 On the Trudeauvian nickel "cartel," see Michael C. Webb and Mark W. Zacher, "Canada and International Regulation of Primary Commodity Markets: The Case of Minerals," in *Canada and International Trade*, vol. 1: *Major Issues of Canadian Trade Policy*, ed. John M. Curtis and David G. Haglund (Montreal: Institute for Research on Public Policy 1985), 337–8.

54 The principal use of vanadium is as an alloying element in steel; it is not infrequently found as a byproduct or coproduct of uranium (and other metals). Peter H. Kuck, "Vanadium," in U.S. Bureau of Mines, *Minerals Yearbook 1984*, vol. 1: *Metals and Minerals* (Washington: Department of the Interior 1985), 941–55; idem, "Vanadium," U.S. Bureau of Mines Preprint from Bulletin 675 (Washington: Department of the Interior 1985).

55 Interview, NATO Headquarters, Brussels, 29 March 1983.

56 United Kingdom, House of Lords, Select Committee on the European Communities, *Strategic Minerals*, sessions 1981–2, 20th Report (London: Her Majesty's Stationery Office 1982), xxii–iii.

57 Phillip Crowson, "The National Mineral Policies of Germany, France and Japan," *Mining Magazine* 142 (June 1980):547.

58 Interview, London, 31 Mar. 1983.

59 "The Debate on Sanctions Gets More Intense," *New York Times*, 14 September 1986, E2; Tatiana Karpinsky, "The Mineral Industry of the United Kingdom," in U.S. Bureau of Mines, *Minerals Yearbook 1984*, 3:883–4.

60 Interview, Bonn, 25 March 1983.

61 Federal Republic of Germany, Bundesanstalt fuer Geowissenschaften und Rohstoffe, *Jahresbericht zur*

Rohstoffsituation, 1981/82 (Hanover, February 1983), 5; George A. Rabchevsky, "The Mineral Industry of the Federal Republic of Germany," in U.S. Bureau of Mines, *Minerals Yearbook 1984* 3:329–31.

62 John Hataye, "Japanese Begin to Allot Funds for Non-ferrous Stockpiling Program," *American Metal Market,* 13 February 1976.

63 John C. Wu, "The Mineral Industry of Japan," in U.S. Bureau of Mines, *Minerals Yearbook 1984* 3:465–6.

64 "Plant Planned for Rare Metals," *Globe and Mail,* 13 Apr. 1985, B12.

65 Canadian import dependence in chromium and manganese is discussed in Jock Finlayson, "Canada and Strategic Minerals," *International Perspectives* (September/October 1982):18–21. Good analyses of Canadian import dependence, and its potential implications, are found in Energy, Mines and Resources Canada, *Vanadium: An Imported Mineral Commodity,* Mineral Bulletin MR 188 (Ottawa: Minister of Supply and Services 1981); and idem, *Chromium: An Imported mineral Commodity,* Mineral Bulletin MR196 (Ottawa: Minister of Supply and Services 1983).

66 U.S. Bureau of Mines, *Mineral Commodity Summaries, 1986,* 39.

67 U.S. Bureau of Mines, *Mineral Commodity Summaries, 1986,* 119. The platinum group comprises platinum, palladium, iridium, osmium, rhodium, and ruthenium.

68 Energy, Mines and Resources Canada, *Canadian Minerals Yearbook 1985,* 21.1, 47.1; "Costly Search for Platinum Paying Off for Equinox," *Financial Post,* 27 Sept. 1986, p. 28.

69 Energy, Mines and Resources Canada, *Chromium,* 12; *Mineral Policy: A Discussion Paper,* 34.

70 Interview, EMR, Ottawa, 18 Feb. 1985; D.M. Watson, "Chromite Reserves of the Bird River Sill" (Winnipeg: Manitoba Energy and Mines 1985).

71 R.C. Annis, D.A. Cranstone, and M. Vallee, *A Survey of Known Mineral Deposits in Canada that Are Not Being Mined,* Mineral Bulletin MR181 (Ottawa: Energy, Mines and Resources Canada 1978), 57, 69–70, 90, A1–A4, A6–A7, A9, A28, A30, A38. Also see R. Marcotte, *Gîtes et indices de chromite au Québec* (Québec: Ministère de l'Energie et des Ressources 1980).

72 Interview, Ministère de l'Energie et des Ressources, Québec, 3 June 1985; Thomas S. Jones, "Manganese," U.S. Bureau of Mines Preprint from Bulletin 675 (Washington: Department of the Interior 1985), 3.

73 For U.S. concern over the security aspects of dependence in minerals, see Alfred E. Eckes, jr., *The United States and the Global Struggle for Minerals* (Austin: University of Texas Press 1979).

74 John E. Cameron, "Nickel," in Beigie and Hero, *Natural Resources in U.S.-Canadian Relations* 2:69.

75 John Lewis Gaddis, *Strategies of Containment: A Critical Appraisal of Postwar American National Security Policy* (New York: Oxford University Press 1982), 132. On the broader link between Korea and the enlargement of U.S. security interests, see Walter Lafeber, *America, Russia, and the Cold War, 1945–1980,* 4th ed. (New York: John Wiley 1980), 101–27.

76 Glenn H. Snyder, *Stockpiling Strategic Materials: Politics and National Defense* (San Francisco: Chandler 1966), 80.

77 Alfred R. Greenwood, "The Reagan Administration Proposes Dramatic Changes to National Defense Stockpile Goals," 86–578 ENR (Washington: Library of Congress, Congressional Research Service, Feb. 1986), 57.

78 U.S. General Accounting Office, *National Defense Stockpile: Adequacy of National Security Council Study for Setting Stockpile Goals,* GAO/NSIAD-86-177BR (Washington, Aug. 1986).

79 Interview, Washington, 25 June 1985.

80 Interview, Washington, 19 June 1985. The two most influential defenders of an ample stockpile are James A. McClure, recently Chairman of the Senate's Committee on Energy and Natural Resources; and Charles E. Bennett, Chairman of the House Committee on Armed Services' Subcommittee on Seapower and Strategic and Critical Materials.

81 Interview, Washington, 17 June 1985; U.S. Federal Emergency Management Agency, *Stockpile Report to the Congress, April–September 1985* (Washington, Dec. 1985), 20.

82 Alfred R. Greenwood, "National Defense Stockpile Policy: The Congressional Debate," 86–863 ENR (Washington: Library of Congress, Congressional Research Service, Aug. 1986), Appendices A and B.

83 Arguments to this effect include: Raymond F. Mikesell, "Economic Stockpiles for Dealing with Vulnerability to Disruption of Foreign Supplies of Minerals," *Materials and Society* 9, 1 (1985):59–128; Hanns W. Maull, *Raw Materials, Energy and Western Security,* Studies in Interna-

tional Security:22 (London: Macmillan, International Institute for Strategic Studies 1984), 339–49, 385–8; and idem, "French and European Community Policies for Securing the Supply of Primary Commodities," in *Probleme der Rohstoffsicherung*, 193–8.

84 Percy W. Bidwell, *Raw Materials: A Study of American Policy* (New York: Council on Foreign Relations, Harper & Bros. 1958), 160; U.S. Congress, OTA, *Strategic Materials*, 113.

85 Interview, Washington, 18 June 1985.

86 U.S. Bureau of Mines, *Mineral Commodity Summaries, 1986*, 99.

87 "Ferro-Alloys Sector Surging Ahead," *Latin America Commodities Report*, 4 Sept. 1986, 2.

88 H. Robert Ensminger, "The Mineral Industry of Brazil," in U.S. Bureau of Mines, *Minerals Yearbook 1984* 3:131–45.

89 U.S. International Development Cooperation Agency, Trade and Development Program, *The Marcona Iron Mine: A Potential New Source of Cobalt in Peru* (Washington, November 1982).

90 U.S. Congress, OTA, *Strategic Materials*, 166.

91 Harold R. Newman, "The Mineral Industry of Canada," in U.S. Bureau of Mines, *Minerals Yearbook 1983* 3:166.

92 U.S. Bureau of Mines, *Mineral Commodity Summaries 1986*, 41.

93 Interview, Washington, 27 June 1985.

94 House of Lords, *Strategic Minerals*, vii–ix.

95 U.S. Congress, OTA, *Strategic Minerals*, 167–8.

96 For a discussion of the mineral potential of just one state, Alaska, see James C. Barker et al., *Critical and Strategic Minerals in Alaska: Cobalt, the Platinum-Group Metals, and Chromite*, Bureau of Mines Information Circular 8869 (Washington: Department of the Interior 1981).

97 Canada's worry was not that the United States would become a producer of manganese; it was that the U.S. would, in exploiting the "manganese nodules" of the seabed, also develop into a significant producer of nickel, one of the leading metallic constituents of the nodules. See W.E. Cundiff, *Nodule Shock?: Seabed Mining and the Future of the Canadian Nickel Industry*, Occasional Paper no. 1 (Montreal: Institute for Research on Public Policy 1978). Current prospects for deep seabed mining are discussed in Elisabeth Mann Borgese, "Law of the Sea: Crossroads Again," *International Perspectives* (July/August 1986), 12–14; and Nicholas Wetzel, Joseph L. Ritchey, and Scott A. Stebbins, "A Strategic Mineral Assessment of an Onshore Analog of a Mid-Oceanic Polymetallic Sulfide Deposit," in U.S. Bureau of Mines, *Minerals and Materials: A Bimonthly Survey* (June/July 1987), 6–13. Also see, for a discussion of possible exploitation of cobalt-rich crusts lying within the U.S. exclusive economic zone, F.T. Manheim, "Marine Cobalt Resources," *Science* 232 (2 May 1986):600–8.

98 Information contained in a letter to the author from R.K. Doran, Chevron Resources Co., 29 Sept. 1986.

99 *Minerals and Materials*, Apr./May 1987, 24–5.

100 Energy, Mines and Resources Canada, *Canada's Nonferrous Metals Industry*, 3. On post-Second World War substitution pressures, especially from aluminum, see Theodore H. Moran, *Multinational Corporations and the Politics of Dependence: Copper in Chile* (Princeton, NJ: Princeton University Press 1974), 45–9.

101 The strategic aspect of copper is stressed in Louis J. Sousa, *The U.S. Copper Industry: Problems, Issues, and Outlook*, Mineral Issues: An Analytical Series (Washington: Department of the Interior, Bureau of Mines, Oct. 1981), 3.

102 The prospect of ceramics and composites ultimately replacing some strategic minerals is discussed in W. Wendell Fletcher and Kirsten U. Oldenburg, "Strategic Materials: How Technology Can Reduce U.S. Import Vulnerability," *Issues in Science and Technology* 2 (Summer 1986):83–4. Also see Joel P. Clark and Frank R. Field, "How Critical Are Critical Materials?," *Technology Review* 88 (August/September 1985):38–47. For nickel itself, see Johannes P. Schade, "Current and Future Uses of Nickel: Defending Existing Markets and Searching for New Ones," *Minerals and Materials* (Apr./May 1986), 6–9.

103 Interview, Toronto, 24 May 1985.

104 U.S. Congress, OTA, *Strategic Materials*, 239.

105 U.S. Congress, OTA, *Strategic Materials*, 219.

106 Carl H. Builder, "The Prospects and Implications of Non-Nuclear Means for Strategic Conflict," *Adelphi Papers* 200 (London: International Institute for Strategic Studies 1985), 31.

107 Paul Seabury, "Industrial Policy and National Defense," *Journal of Contemporary Studies* 6 (Spring

1983):5–15. Also see U.S. Congress, House Committee on Armed Services, *The Ailing Defense Industrial Base: Unready for Crisis,* 96th Cong., 2nd sess. (Washington: U.S. Government Printing Office 1980).

108 To address this concern, the Reagan administration decided to ensure a continuation of some domestic productive capacity in this sector by extending a contract to Macalloy Corp. for the purposes of providing this ferrochromium producer work, in this case upgrading chromite from the National Defense Stockpile, *Minerals and Materials* (Feb./Mar. 1987), 23–4.

109 "Reagan to Seek Cutbacks on Machine-Tool Imports," *Washington Post,* 21 May 1986, G1.

110 See the address by Paul Lafleur, until recently a Counsellor (Commercial) at the Canadian Embassy in Washington, delivered to the National Defense Executive Reserve, in Phoenix, Arizona on 23 Sept. 1984. Entitled "Strategic Materials in the Context of U.S.-Canada Trade," Lafleur's talk was published in *Alarm* 93 (October 1984). The concept of the defence industrial base is analysed in John Treddenick, 'The Economic Significance of the Canadian Defence Industrial Base," in *Canada's Defence Industrial Base: The Political Economy of Preparedness and Procurement,* ed. David G. Haglund (Kingston, Ont.: Ronald P. Frye 1988), 15–48.

Index